Labour Law Reforms in Eastern and Western Europe

P.I.E. Peter Lang
Bruxelles · Bern · Berlin · Frankfurt am Main · New York · Oxford · Wien

Tomas Davulis (ed.)

Labour Law Reforms in Eastern and Western Europe

Cultures juridiques et politiques
Vol. 12

Cover picture: Map of countries in Europe and the surrounding region, by San Jose (map), Hayden120 (retouch), via Wikimedia Commons.

With financial support of Faculty of Law Vilnius University and Lithuanian Society for Labour Law and Social Security.

The book was subject to a double blind refereeing process.

Éditions scientifiques internationales
Brussels, 2017
1 avenue Maurice, B-1050 Brussels, Belgium
brussels@peterlang.com; www.peterlang.com

Printed in Germany

ISSN 2235-1078
ISBN 978-2-8076-0416-2
ePDF 978-2-8076-0417-9
ePub 978-2-8076-0418-6
Mobi 978-2-8076-0419-3
DOI 10.3726/b11454
D/2017/5678/51

Library of Congress Cataloging-in-Publication Data

Names: Davulis, Tomas, editor. Title: Labour law reforms in Eastern and Western Europe / edited by Tomas Davulis. Description: Frankfurt : Peter Lang, 2017. | Series: Cultures juridiques et politiques ; Vol. 12 | Includes bibliographical references and index. Identifiers: LCCN 2017022326 (print) | LCCN 2017017277 (ebook) | ISBN 9782807604179 (ePDF) | ISBN 9782807604186 (ePUB) | ISBN 9782807604193 (emobi) | ISBN 9782807604162 (alk. paper) Subjects: LCSH: Labor laws and legislation--Europe, Eastern. | Labor laws and legislation--Europe, Western. | Law reform--Europe, Eastern. | Law reform--Europe, Western. Classification: LCC KJC2855 (print) | LCC KJC2855 .L33 2017 (ebook) | DDC 344.401--dc23 LC record available at https://lccn.loc.gov/2017022326

Bibliographic information published by "Die Deutsche Nationalbibliothek".

"Die Deutsche Nationalbibliothek" lists this publication in the "Deutsche National-bibliografie"; detailed bibliographic data is available on the Internet at <http://dnb.d-nb.de>.

Table of Contents

Introduction

Labour Law Reforms in Eastern and Western Europe

Tomas Davulis

Unlike other branches of law, labour law lacks the legacy of centuries-long tradition. Even if the main objectives of the labour law do not alter, changes in detailed legal regulation and case law within a short span of time may be impressive. Most fundamental transformations are triggered by structural changes in the economy, but they could also emanate from pressure to reshape the balance between capital and labour in response to temporary economic difficulties or in reaction to ongoing changes in technological and organizational patterns of work.

The dynamism of legal regulation of employment is worthy of the close attention of academics, social partners and those involved in drafting and applying social legislation. The increased competition of national labour markets which goes along with fierce international economic emulation intensifies the debate about trends and developments. Consequently, it may result in either significant or in less ambitious changes of the domestic legislative framework of employment and industrial relations.

This selection of articles traces recent developments in labour law and in related areas like social security in European countries. Some of the developments may truly be labelled as 'reforms' but the majority are examples of a gradual evolution, which is necessary in order to overcome errors or shortcomings or to provide the necessary adaptation to technological, social or economical reality.

Part one is devoted to general trends in recent amendments of labour law at national level. First of all, *Tamàs Gyulavári* presents a broad overview of the reforms in Eastern Europe in his identification of three stages of labour law. The first reforms were needed to adjust the former Soviet Labour Codes to the needs of a market economy, either by several amendments to the original Labour Code (e.g. in Poland and Czech Republic), or by passing a new Labour Code (e.g. in Hungary in 1992).

The second cluster of reforms served to implement EU labour law before EU accession. The third, most recent reforms are closely connected to the changing world of work, the financial crisis and also the political will to increase the employment rate. When dealing with the latter, the author critically assesses the increased enthusiasm in Eastern European countries about the need to promote various forms of atypical employment. He also draws attention to the phenomenon of self-employment and predicts that the danger of bogus self-employment will be among major concerns which have to be addressed at national level.

The most recent example of overall national labour law reform is presented by *Tomas Davulis*. He explains in detail the background to the re-codification of labour law in Lithuania and analyses both the changes needed to modernize the legal attitude towards the employment relationship and the measures to balance the desired flexibility for business with new forms of employee protection. In his the new legislation shall modernize the employment relationship in a much broader perspective – to revive the spirit of cooperation between the parties both at individual and collective level, to increase the judicial protection of employees, to allow for wider acceptance of technologies, investment in human capital and respect of the employee's personality and his/her family commitments.

On the other hand, *Polonca Končar* refuses to use the word 'reform' when addressing legislative changes which are not of an in-depth nature. Instead she reminds us of the innate dynamism of the labour law to adapt to political, economic and social development. From this perspective she assesses recent developments in the field of the labour market and labour law – changes aimed at both reduction of employee protection (e.g. lowering costs of dismissals) and providing new forms of protection (disincentives for fixed-term employment, limitation of temporary work, broadening the scope of protection for the self-employed).

Detailed analysis of individual and collective labour law reforms in Germany is provided by *Manfred Weiss*. He suggests that German labour law is moving not in the direction of deregulation but to a re-regulation, stabilizing the already existing protective schemes. Recent amendments strengthened the institutions of collective bargaining and co-determination, whereas the reforms on minimum wage, fixed-term contracts, part-time work and temporary work agreements have provided new shapes for individual employment law. The author concludes, that the labour law reforms in Germany are not an expression of a well-planned strategy but are rather reactions to upcoming needs on the labour market. However, the legislator rarely initiates changes but shapes legislative proposals on the basis of intensive dialogue with the social partners.

Niklas Bruun's paper presents the efforts to reform labour laws in Finland within the framework of a so-called package of competitiveness which aims at reducing labour costs by way of sectoral collective agreements. The involvement of social partners in the reformist agenda seems to be a true test for of the Finish labour law system in which the collective bargaining, which was initially designed for sharing benefits, was used instead to manage deduction of protection and cuts in remuneration.

The second set of contributions (**Part Two**) deals with issues of industrial relations, which in Eastern Europe tend to be known as 'collective labour law'. First of all, *Paul Marginson* and *Christian Welz* reveal tendencies in collective wage-setting mechanisms across Europe since the onset of the economic crisis of 2008. The pressure on national collective bargaining systems to be more 'marketized', in other words to be more responsive to economic and competitive circumstances, resulted in increased decentralization of bargaining. Due to crucial differences in their institutional arrangements the countries have taken different paths to create more room for company-level arrangements in the multi-employer bargaining systems. Authors believe that a single prescription or an enforced solution would not be efficient and could also weaken the established mechanisms of collective wage-setting.

In her contribution *Daiva Petrylaite* explores the changing role of social dialogue in the contemporary world of labour. She reflects on the importance of the social partners in the public decision-making process in the European Union and explains the differences and difficulties in the functioning of social dialogue in Central and Eastern Europe. This is a region where social dialogue is less developed and governments were allowed to take unilateral decisions during the economic crisis thus neglecting the idea and the principles of social dialogue.

Some countries experience more targeted reforms in the area of industrial relations. The implementation of information and consultation *acquis* is one of the topical issues in EU candidate countries. *Otmar Seul* investigates the legislative changes and practices in Albanian labour law related to the creation of a participative system at enterprise level. The new form of employee representation was intended to improve the environment for more democratic decision-making in companies but the new rights of information and consultation are still alien.

The Lithuanian model of social partnership has been presented by *Rytis Krasauskas*. After discussing the general features of the current legislative framework of social partners, he concludes that there is a considerable gap between the text of the law and the actual situation. It is not only unbalanced legal constructs that contribute to the stagnation of social dialogue and the absence of collective agreements, but economic, political and even psychological factors are also responsible.

Part Three is devoted to the various aspects of employment law to what is sometimes referred as individual labour law.

First of all, *Wilfried Rauws* and *Evelien Timbermont* present the series of measures which were introduced in Belgium with the main purpose to combat unemployment and provide for more flexibility. Some of those reforms were of a permanent nature while others were manifested as temporary. In the future new changes in the areas of working time and the reintegration of disabled employees are to be expected. Another perspective on Belgian labour market reforms was shown by *Marc De Vos* who analyses the change in dismissal protection from both a general perspective and from the perspective of national labour law. He argues that even some successes on the pathway to flexicurity do not alter the deficiencies of the fragmented reforms. The author advocates for a comprehensive reform of dismissal law towards re-employment law which also involves a change of paradigm in the philosophy of dismissal protection and active involvement of all stakeholders.

The legislators' responses to economic difficulties frequently result in changes to the dismissal protection of employees. *Cristina Aguilar Gonzálvez* analysis the changes in economic, technical, organizational or production-related reasons as justifications for dismissal of workers after the 2012 labour law reform in Spain. The new case law may recognize a greater freedom of choice for companies but it is important to ensure the requirement of a causal relationship between the company's economic situation and excessively large workforce, when applying also the test of proportionality.

By exploring recent changes in Poland with relations to fixed-term contracts, *Andrzej Marian Świątkowski* identifies the tendency of convergence of the two opposite sides of fixed-term employment – stability and flexibility. The author explains in detail the Polish legislator's intention to align fixed-term contracts with contracts for an indefinite term while, at the same time, creating room for conclusion of fixed-term contracts for work of a permanent nature.

New forms of work constitute significant challenges for many European states. New types of engagement of workforce such as on-demand work, posting of workers, work of self-employed persons are analysed by *Robert Rebhahn* from the Austrian perspective. He rightly argues that the European Union struggles to address the new problematic forms of work with the new legislative instruments. A broader socio-political debate is needed on what role the labour law and social security law of the European Union should play under the new economic paradigm – should it aim at stabilizing the differences in conditions that exist between different regions and countries or help to equalize these conditions. *Gaabriel Tavits* adds to the discussion with his question of whether flexibility is still important in the European Union? He supports the more active role of the European legislator arguing that the new forms of employment should be subject to the current occupational health and safety requirements. Similar thoughts may provoke an analysis of how dramatically technological advancements change the patterns of work. In some countries the legal adjustment of employee protection remains in the domain of the case law whereas in some other countries we may witness pro-active engagement of social partners and legislators to address this topical issue. The contribution of *Lourdes Mella Mendez* is devoted to the new individual right of an employee – the right to disconnect.

New ways on how to approach the phenomenon of flexicurity were presented by *György Kiss.* After providing an in-depth theoretical analysis into substantial attributes of the employment relationship, namely the legal subordination of the employee and long-term nature of this relationship, the author suggests new ways of interpretation which would serve both flexibility as well as protection of the employee's legal status. The theory of the contract of employment as a relational contract integrates the elements of commercial contract into labour law and this could have great potential for new developments of individual labour law.

The interplay of labour law and civil law instruments may be of importance in times of desired dynamism of labour law. In many countries labour law functions by way of implementation of restrictions of individual freedom of the contract and autonomy of the parties. The deficits of strict and rigid national legislation on individual employment contracts may sometimes be corrected by the judiciary. Using the examples of the application of the 2002 Lithuanian Labour Code in courts *Tomas Bagdanskis* provides us with evidence of the reformist role of judges making law in circumstances when legislators fail to adapt necessary changes in the new context of the socio-economical environment. Another civil law instrument – non-competition agreements and their way into the employment contracts was discussed by *Beata Martišienė* who supports the idea that a timely balanced legislative approach is more desirable than judge-made rules when dealing with these new phenomenon for the better protection of employees.

Labour law reforms may be employed not only to introduce the measures necessary to boost employment, flexibility and adaptivity. *Eglė Tamošiūnaitė* provides an analysis of how the Lithuanian legislator advanced the implementation of the transfer of undertaking directive. *Arnas Paliukėnas* presents his insights on the new possibilities to arbitrate individual employment disputes. *Gintautas Bužinskas* presents a comparative analysis of the individual grievances procedure in the three Baltic states (Estonia, Latvia, Lithuania), providing examples of the similarities of the pre-trial procedure in those countries.

Part Four of this collection is devoted to the accompanying branches of social security and labour market policies. The majority of changes in this area were inspired by implementation of the principles of flexicurity or provoked by the need to compensate the reductions in employee protection. The greater coverage of the new forms of employment, increased benefits and new family-related accommodations are among popular issues in the reformist debates. *Silvia Spattini* presents the latest changes in Italy's social security system which was reorganized with the objective of greater equity through the rationalization and universalization of benefits. The Polish legal novelties towards combating unemployment among older people are presented by *Tatiana Wrocławska*. The reformist changes with regard to greater articulation of childcare leave in Latvia are highlighted in the contribution of *Kristine Dupate*. An overview of the legal framework of unemployment benefits in Russia is presented by *Olga Chesalina* and in Lithuania by *Audrius Bitinas*. They reveal the fundamental problems of the Eastern European unemployment benefits system – the low level of benefits and low coverage. Against this background, implementation of flexicurity policies which aim at balancing flexibility with state support for the unemployed seem to be rather problematic. It may succeed only if reforms of the unemployment benefits system were included in the complex reform of social insurance, labour relations, social assistance and employment.

This selection of articles cannot cover all the aspects of the current state of recent reformist efforts on the labour markets. Instead, by picturing separate developments in different European countries, it intends to assist in identifying regional similarities. Furthermore, it provides opportunities for exchange of ideas, experiences and practices for shaping labour law both at European and national level.

Part one

General Trends

Labour Law Reforms in the Eastern European Member States

Towards a New Structure of Work Relationships?

Tamás GYULAVÁRI*

Abstract

The post-socialist countries of Central and Eastern Europe are still the least developed EU Member States. These countries have very similar labour law traditions, labour market conditions and economic development. However, there are also remarkable subregional differences (e.g. Baltic States, Balkans and Visegrád group[1]), and their economic growth has been quite divergent since EU accession. At the same time their labour law reforms have served identical aims. These labour legislations had to meet two fundamental demands in the last 20 years, firstly the change from a socialist planned to a market economy (1990s), and secondly the implementation of EU labour law as a legal condition of EU accession (2000s). The most recent Eastern European labour law reforms are connected to the changing world of work, the financial crisis and the related objective to increase employment. The paper focuses on the evolving new structure of work relationships, respectively its impact on these national labour laws and labour markets. Two potential sources of employment flexibility are analysed in this regard: atypical employment contracts and the various forms of (genuine, false) self-employment. Atypical employment contracts do not play an important role in this region, despite the detailed regulation of atypical employment enforced by labour law harmonization. Typical, full-time and indefinite-term employment contracts are still the dominant employment relationships. The need of employers for flexibility (meaning cheaper workforce) is met by other sources, especially false self-employment, which has rapidly expanded in spite of various legal and administrative measures. Thus, increasing numbers of workers are leaving typical employment, but the parties opt rather for non-employment forms of work instead of finding flexibility in an atypical employment contract. Therefore, the

---

* Tamás Gyulavári is Professor of Labour Law and Head of the Labour Law Department at Pázmány Péter Catholic University of Budapest. He is the author and co-author of several books and articles on European and Hungarian labour law in Hungarian and in English. Prof. Gyulavári is also the Labour Law Adviser of the Hungarian Supreme Court. The author is grateful to Zoltán Bankó and Gábor Kártyás for their comments on earlier drafts of this paper.

1 The Visegrad Group (also known as the 'Visegrad Four' or simply 'V4') mean the four countries of the Central European region: the Czech Republic, Hungary, Poland and Slovakia.

paper analyses the aims and conditions of recent labour law reforms and their impact on the legal framework of legal relationships aimed at work.

Keywords: Labour Code, atypical work, fixed-term contracts, false self-employment, economically dependent work

Introduction

The 11 Eastern European states joined the EU in three waves in 2004, 2007 and 2013. The analysis of labour law reforms in this group of countries seems to be a relevant topic, since they show remarkable common characteristics. Similarities within this group of Member States include the legacy of socialist law and economy, the existence of a Soviet type of Labour Code, akin to economic development and labour market conditions. All of these national labour laws have constantly changed in order to, first, establish decent employment conditions for a market economy, and later to implement all EU law requirements in this field. Recent reforms have faced the new challenges of the low employment rate and its increase by flexibilization of labour law. However, this is also a challenging topic, since there are a number of national and sub-regional peculiarities (e.g. compare Bulgaria with the Czech Republic or Estonia).

The large topic of labour law reforms would exceed the potential of this paper, hence it highlights solely the development of legal relationships aimed at work. First, labour law reforms in general will be described. This introductory part is followed by the picture of atypical employment relationships, respectively the evolution of self-employment, false self-employment and the potential regulation of a third type of labour law definition (economically dependent work). The aim is to understand and predict changes in the legal employment framework in the region.

1. Labour law reforms in the Member States of Central and Eastern Europe

The post-socialist countries of Central and Eastern Europe joined the European Union in three waves between 2004 and 2013[2]. In spite of their fast overall economic growth, these are still the poorest EU Member States, representing only 45–84% of the EU average (Bulgaria

[2] The following EU Member States will be examined: the Czech Republic, Estonia, Hungary, Latvia, Lithuania, Poland, Slovakia and Slovenia joined the EU in 2004, Bulgaria and Romania in 2007, finally Croatia in 2013.

with 45 and the Czech Republic with 84% in 2015)[3]. However, there are noteworthy differences between the economic development and GDP growth of certain subgroups of countries in the region. The table below shows, that the poorer countries in the group (such as Poland or Romania) have shown faster improvement than the former 'champions' (Slovenia or Czech Republic). Consequently, the most dominant trend is economic equalization in the region.

GDP per capita in selected eastern European Member States between 2000 and 2015 (compared to national 100% in 2000)

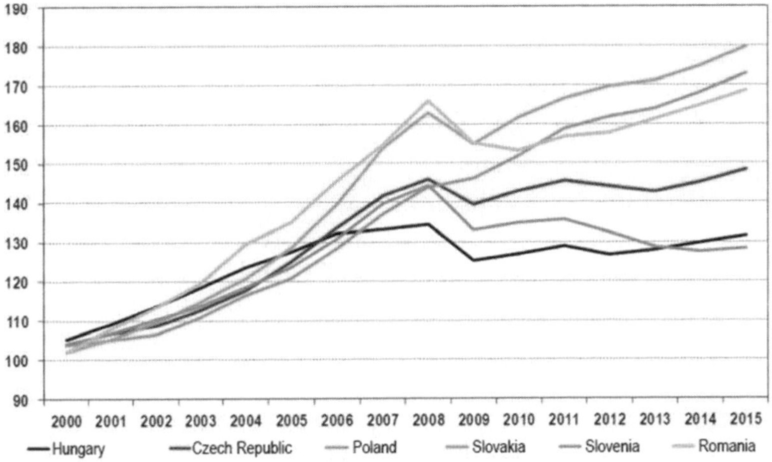

Source: http://budapestbeacon.com/economics/gki-issues-economic-outlook-for-hungary-in-2015/15695

Concerning employment policy, the low level of employment has always been and still is the most crucial problem of these labour markets. After the Southern European EU Members, the Eastern European countries have the lowest level of employment in the whole EU, and the Czech Republic is the exhilarating exception. In Hungary, the employment level seems to be around the medium level; however, this relatively good employment level is reached by including around 250,000 public workers and all Hungarians working abroad in the employment rate.

[3] Eurostat News release, 16 June 2015. Retrieved May 5, 2016 from http://ec.europa.eu/eurostat/documents/2995521/6885941/2-16062015-BP-EN.pdf.

Employment rate, age group 15–64, 2014 (%)

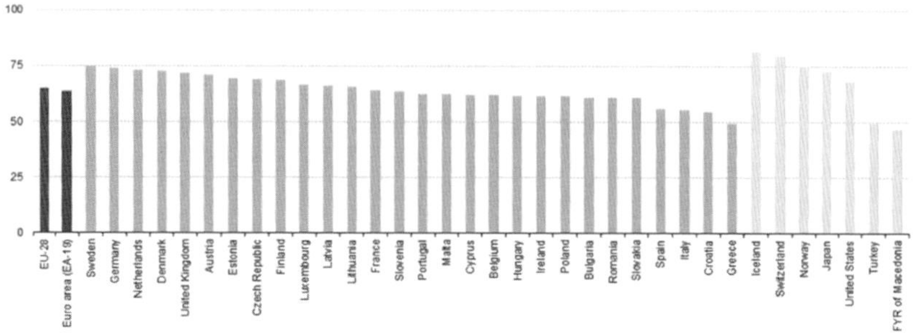

Source: Eurostat (online data code: Ifsi_emp_a)

Consequently, the growth of employment seems to be the primary aim of employment policy and labour legislation in all these countries. Certainly, there are other secondary objectives in several countries, such as handling the global crisis and resolving demographic problems in Poland (Skupień, Łaga and Pisarczyk, 2016), as well as renewing the legal text fragmented by too many amendments in Hungary (Gyulavári and Kártyás, 2016). At the same time, the creation of jobs by flexibilization (deregulation) of national labour law looks like the regional trend, as is best demonstrated by the Hungarian labour law reform in 2012 (Gyulavári and Kártyás, 2016)[4].

However, employment protection is relatively weak in most of these Eastern European Member States, particularly in comparison with more developed OECD countries (see table below). If a low level of employment was attained by a rather flexible labour law regulation, then it is a questionable strategy to create more jobs by more flexibility. It is not the aim of this paper to deeply analyse the debate on flexibilization of national labour laws in Europe, however, this issue had to be mentioned here due to its role in developments concerning the structure of employment forms.

---

4 See also the developments in Lithuania (Petrylaitė, 2015), Romania (Placintescu, 2015) and Slovakia (Harvan and Machlica, 2011).

Employment protection is relatively high in the euro area
Index scale from 0 (least restrictive) to 6 (most restrictive)

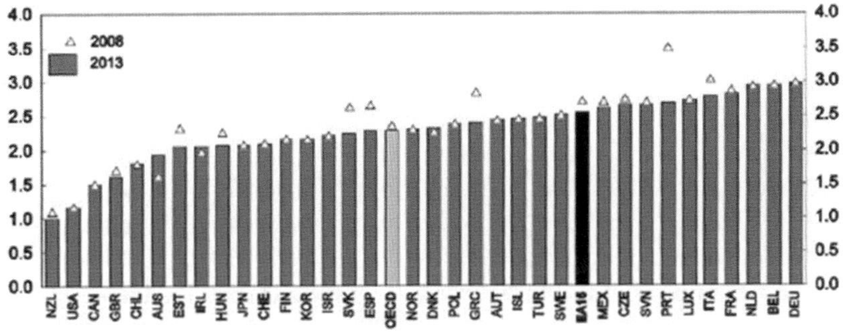

Source: Eurostat (online data code: Ifsi_emp_a)

In these post-socialist countries the Soviet tradition of a separate Labour Code, containing most of the rules on employment protection, is still flourishing. In my view, it is a beneficial legal heritage, since it makes labour legislation easier to apply, and at the same time more comprehensive. Thus, employment relationships are regulated by a Labour Code in all of these countries following the 'Soviet model'. For that reason, employment law is, after 26 years in the market economy, still based almost exclusively on the regulation of the employment contract, with the exception of civil law contracts regulated by the Civil Code.

Thus, labour law reforms have been achieved either by several amendments of the Labour Code, or by the passing of a new codex. The former socialist Labour Code is still in force in three of these countries: the Czech Republic (1965)[5], Poland (1974)[6] and Bulgaria (1986)[7]. Certainly, these 'old' Labour Codes have been amended many times, so they hardly resemble the original, socialist texts. In the other eight Member States, the former socialist codexes have been replaced by new Labour Codes.

The first wave of these new codexes was passed before the first round of EU accessions in 2004. In the Baltic States the former Soviet Labour

5 Act No. 65/1965. Retrieved May 5, 2016 from http://www.ilo.org/ifpdial/information-resources/national-labour-law-profiles/WCMS_158893/lang--en/index.htm.

6 Labour Code of 26 June 1974. Retrieved May 5, 2016 from http://www.ilo.org/dyn/natlex/natlex4.detail?p_lang=en&p_isn=45181&p_country=POL&p_classification=01.02.

7 No. 26 and No. 27, 1986, Retrieved May 5, 2016 from http://www.ilo.org/dyn/eplex/termmain.showCountry?p_lang=en&p_country_id=180.

Code of 1972 was followed by a new law in Latvia[8] and Lithuania[9] in 2002, later in Estonia (2008)[10]. New Labour Codes were passed before EU accession also in Slovakia (2001)[11], Slovenia (2002)[12] and Romania (2003)[13]. Harmonization of the labour law directives had proven to be a good opportunity to rewrite the Labour Codes in these countries.

Hungary[14] and Croatia[15] are the exceptions to the above trend, as the new Labour Codes were passed in these two neighbouring countries as a response to the financial crisis (in Hungary in 2012 and in Croatia in 2014). Thus, these are the best recent examples of comprehensive labour reform in the region. Evidently, there have been some other proposals for new Labour Codes, for example the failed draft in Poland in 2006[16] and the just debated draft in Lithuania in 2016[17]. Simultaneously, there have almost been as many amendments to the existing Labour Codes in the other countries as well in the last few years. On the whole, a new wave of labour law reforms has been initiated in a number of countries, which is generated by the political will to handle the new social and economic tensions, but above all to create more jobs. These reforms will

8 Retrieved May 5, 2016 from http://www.ilo.org/ifpdial/information-resources/national-labour-law-profiles/WCMS_158912/lang--en/index.htm.

9 Law No. IX-926. Retrieved May 5, 2016 from http://www.ilo.org/ifpdial/information-resources/national-labour-law-profiles/WCMS_158913/lang--en/index.htm.

10 Law of 17 December 2008 on Employment Contracts. Retrieved May 5, 2016 from http://www.ilo.org/dyn/natlex/natlex4.detail?p_lang=en&p_isn=81840&p_country=EST&p_count=295&p_classification=01&p_classcount=71.

11 No. 311/2001. Retrieved May 5, 2016 from http://www.ilo.org/dyn/natlex/natlex4.listResults?p_lang=en&p_country=SVK&p_count=382&p_classification=01&p_classcount=52.

12 The Employment Relationship Act [ERA], 2002, No 42/02. Retrieved May 5, 2016 from http://www.ilo.org/dyn/eplex/termmain.showCountry?p_lang=en&p_country_id=17.

13 Law No 53/2003. Retrieved May 5, 2016 from http://www.ilo.org/dyn/eplex/termmain.showCountry?p_lang=en&p_country_id=14.

14 Retrieved May 5, 2016 from http://www.ilo.org/dyn/travail/docs/2557/Labour%20Code.pdf.

15 Law of 18 July 2014 (Text No. 1872). Retrieved May 5, 2016 from http://www.ilo.org/dyn/natlex/natlex4.detail?p_lang=en&p_isn=99294&p_country=HRV&p_classification=01.02.

16 Retrieved May 5, 2016 from http://www.mpips.gov.pl/prawo-pracy/projekty-kodeksow-pracy/.

17 Retrieved May 5, 2016 from http://www.labourlawnetwork.eu/national%3Cbr%3Elabour_law/national_legislation/legislative_developments/prm/109/v__detail/id__6570/category__21/index.html.

be analysed below exclusively in respect of the employment forms and the legal structure of legal relationships aimed at work.

2. Promotion of atypical employment: is it really what we need?

A typical employment relationship, in other words full time employment with an indefinite term[18], has always been and still is the dominant legal form of work in the Eastern European countries (see table below). The former socialist Labour Codes have traditionally regulated fixed-term and part-time employment relationships as rarely used forms of employment (European Communities, 2009). The detailed regulation of several atypical forms of employment, especially temporary agency work and telework, is a new phenomenon, and the effect of EU law harmonization in the new Member States.

Percentage of employees with indefinite labour contracts in the EU27, and in six other European countries and Turkey (percentage of all employees) (2010)

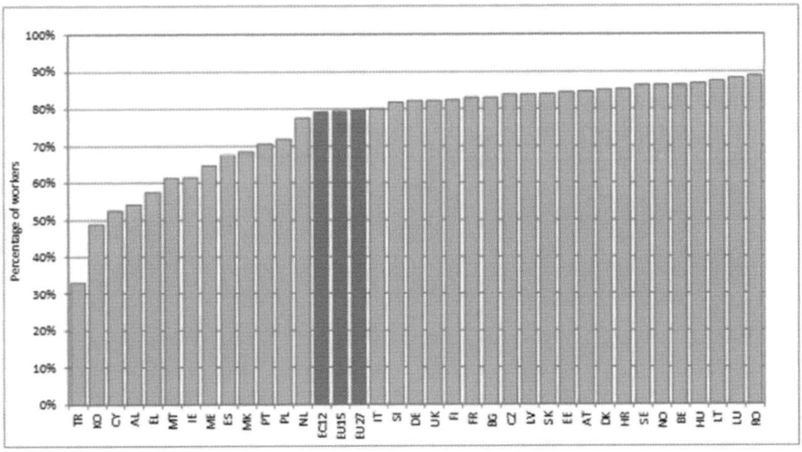

Source: https://oshwiki.eu/wiki/File:Figure1.PNG

---

18 Further attributes of the classic employment model are the relationship with only one employer, working at the employer's premises, with the employer's materials. Formerly the rigid organization of working time was also an inherent feature of the classical employment model, however, it has become a major source of flexibility within the regulation of employment relationships.

Thus, EU law had a fundamental, positive effect on the regulation of atypical employment contracts. The detailed regulation of atypical forms of employment is one of the tangible effects of labour law harmonization, since EU law enforced these new Member States to regulate in detail fixed-term, part-time and temporary agency work, moreover, the regulation of telework is optional. Thus, the detailed provisions on these forms of employment are primarily the results of implementing the labour law directives, but also useful for the wider implementation of other EU law measures, such as the Equality Directives.

At the same time, there are several atypical forms of employment, such as on-call work, job sharing or employment by multiple employers, which are not regulated at all by EU law, thus, its regulation is the exclusive power of national legislation. These very atypical forms are rarely regulated in these countries (e.g. the new Hungarian Labour Code)[19].

Atypical forms of employment cannot be considered a widely used practice in the case of Central Eastern European countries (Lipták, 2011, p. 12), which fact is at least partly explained by the lack of tradition in this regard. The traditional model is almost intact in the Baltic States and still dominant in the Czech Republic, Slovakia and Hungary. In the Baltic States, non-standard types of work are not widespread, so they are among the least atypical labour markets in the EU (European Parliament, 2007). However, all of these countries are characterized by a much lower level of atypical employment contracts than most of the Western European Member States. The low coverage of part-time employment is a good example of this phenomenon, which has never really spread in the region, mostly due to the low pay it entails. Similar data show the low level of temporary agency work in Eastern Europe compared to other Member States (see table below).

---

19 http://www.eurofound.europa.eu/observatories/eurwork/comparative-information/flexible-forms-of-work-very-atypical-contractual-arrangements.

Part-time employed (% of total employment)

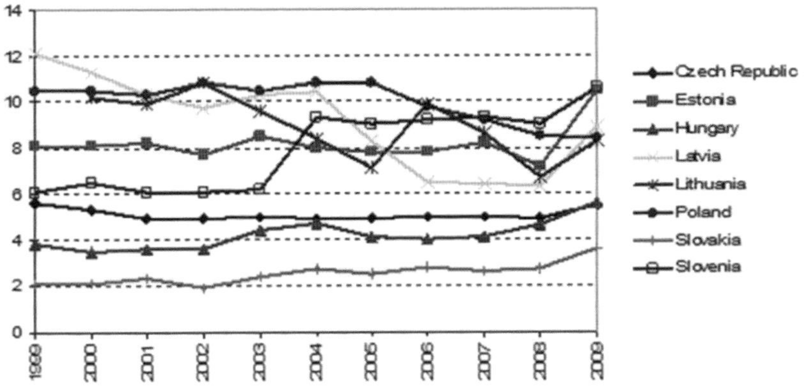

Source: Lipták, 2011, p. 6.

Percentage of temporary employment agency employees in the EU27, and in six other European countries and Turkey (percentage of all employees) (2010)

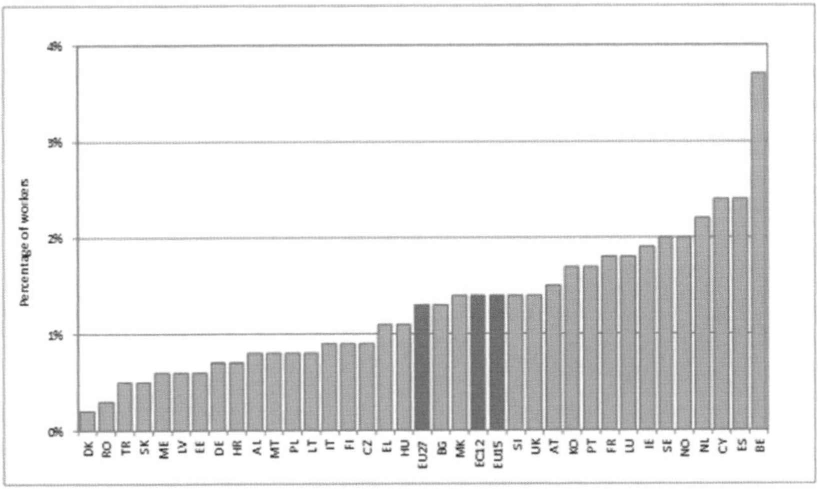

Source: https://oshwiki.eu/wiki/Temporary_Workers

Correspondingly, there is a low percentage of fixed-term employment contracts in almost all Eastern European Member States. As in the case of part-time contracts, the implementation of EU directives has not had a perceptible effect on the number of such employees. The two exceptions are Poland and Slovenia, where the rate of those employed with fixed-term contracts has increased significantly since 2000. An interesting question is why the highest value in the EU is found in Poland (Lipták, 2011, p. 8–9).

Most probably, the cost of termination is the key issue in this respect. The Polish legislation is very liberal as regards the termination of fixed-term contracts before their expiration date. In the case of fixed-term contracts of more than six months and that have a clause about the possibility of early termination by notice, a fixed-term contract may be terminated at any time, with two weeks notice, regardless of its duration. The employer is neither obliged to present a reason for dismissal in writing, nor to consult the trade union representing the worker prior to dismissal. These obligations are imposed on the employer in case of termination of an indefinite-term contract and in case of termination of an employment contract without notice (Unterschütz, 2015, p. 25). Thus, fixed-term contracts are treated as a means to achieve flexibilization of the employment relationship (Skupień, Łaga and Pisarczyk, 2016, p. 8). In contrast, the Hungarian termination of fixed-term contracts is more expensive, since the employer must pay the period remaining from the fixed term (up to twelve months)[20]. It seems, that the higher cost of termination discourages employers from using false fixed-term contracts.

Fixed-term labour contracts in the CEE countries (% of total employment)

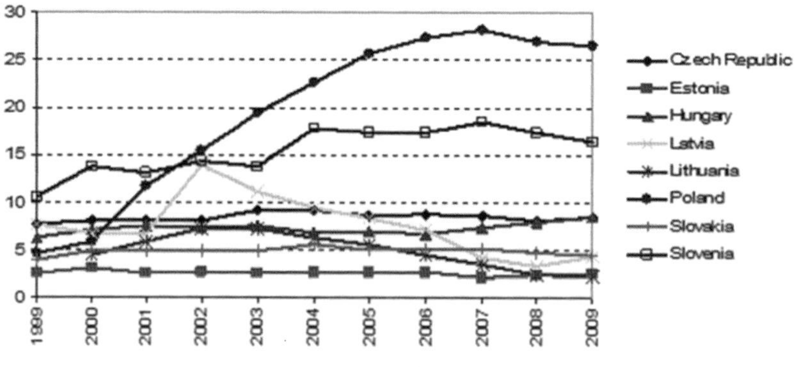

Source: Lipták, 2011, p. 8.

[20] Termination by notice is possible in very limited cases.

Proportion of employees with a contract of limited duration, age group 15–64, 2014 (% of total employees)

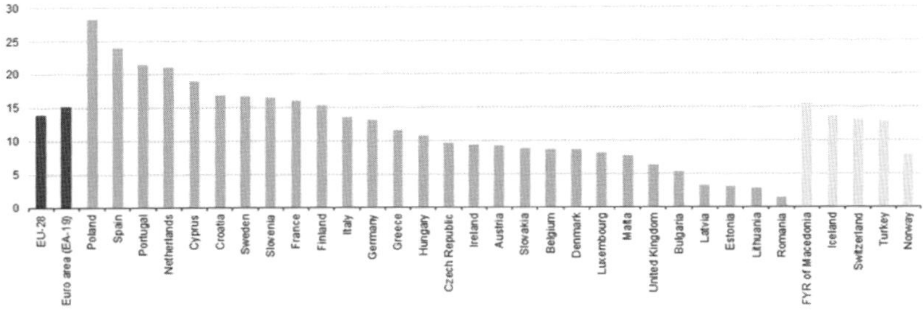

Source: Eurostat (online data code: Ifsa_etpga)

As is evident form the tables above, atypical employment contracts have never been and are still not important forms of employment in Central and Eastern Europe. Typical, full-time and indefinite-term employment contracts still dominate in these labour markets. Apparently, the need of employers for flexibility is met by other sources, such as a lower level of employment protection, flexible working time rules, undeclared work, false self-employment etc. It is quite obvious, that the implementation of EU directives on atypical work has not promoted these flexible forms of employment. Polish fixed-term contracts are the only exceptions, however, their story is rather a bad example to learn from, than a best practice. In my view, atypical contracts will not play a much more important role in the future either in this region. Thus, it is worthwhile looking at self-employment as a potential source of flexibility in terms of regulation and social burdens.

3. Fight against bogus self-employment

The definition and employment protection of self-employed workers is still not regulated by EU law. Unlike the EU law concept of subordinate employment ('worker'), self-employment has not been defined in detail by EU law or even the CJEU[21]. The binary legal framework (employment and self-employment) was necessitated by the laws on the fundamental EU right of establishment, since the free movement of workers must be

[21] See exceptions: C-268/99 *Jany* and others [2001] ECR I-8615, paragraph 70; 300/84 *Van Roosmalen* [1986] ECR 3097, paragraphs 17, 20, 22.

provided for workers and the right of establishment to self-employed persons[22]. In this respect, those workers who are not employees are considered as self-employed in EU law (Van Peijpe, 2012, p. 42).

Consequently, the general definition of self-employment is usually missing from the labour laws of the Western-European Member States as well, though there are some exceptions[23]. Accordingly, the Eastern European Member States have never had the legal category of self-employment in their legal systems[24]. Since this legal term (self-employed) was necessary to define the scope of certain EU laws[25], these national laws considered all legal relationships aimed at employment as self-employment in the course of legal harmonization, which were not established by an employment contract and thereby not falling under the scope of the Labour Code.

In Eastern European legal systems self-employment usually covers so-called civil law (service) contracts aimed at employment[26], and rarely some other, less popular types of contracts (e.g. casual work in Hungary)[27]. Typically civil law contracts of private entrepreneurs and the personal contribution of members of small (one-man) companies fall within this category and are generally perceived as the dominant

---

[22] See the personal scope of national laws: Countouris N., Freedland M. *The Personal Scope of the EU Sex Equality Directives. European Network of Legal Experts in the Field of Gender Equality*, European Union, 2012. At the same time several national social security laws contain this definition for the sole purpose of these acts.

[23] See for example Däubler, 2011, p. 132.

[24] For more detailed analysis of this chapter see: Gyulavári T. Trap of the Past: Why Economically Dependent Work is not Regulated in the Member States of Eastern Europe. *European Labour Law Journal,* Vol. 3-4, 2014, pp. 267–278; Gyulavári T. A bridge too far? The Hungarian regulation of economically dependent work. *Hungarian Labour Law E-Journal,* No. 1, 2014, pp. 1-22; Gyulavári T., Kártyás G. *The Hungarian Flexicurity Pathway – New Labour Code after Twenty Years in the Market Economy. Budapest: Pázmány,* 2015.

[25] For example the directive on equal treatment of self-employed persons and the regulation on the right to establishment.

[26] According to the Polish understanding of self-employment: 'offering services (work) to one (or several) entities by natural persons that run, on their own behalf and responsibility, economic activity as entrepreneurs who do not employ other persons or use other persons' services on basis of civil contracts' (Turowiec, 2007, p. 5).

[27] In 2010, the Hungarian government introduced the Simplified Employment Act to amend the former regulation on seasonal and casual employment. Retrieved May 5, 2016 from http://www.eurofound.europa.eu/observatories/emcc/case-studies/tackling-undeclared-work-in-europe/simplified-employment-act-hungary.

form of self-employment[28]. In labour law scholarship self-employment is interpreted as covering civil law contracts of independent contractors including economically dependent workers (see this category later).

False self-employment[29], namely working under a civil law contract instead of an employment contract to cut labour costs, has become very popular in these countries since 1990. Self-employment as well as false self-employment has increased significantly in Romania[30] and in Poland, where it has been playing an important role in the labour market[31]. Since the early 1990s the number of persons running their own individual economic activity has been very high in Poland. It has also remained relatively unchanged with small fluctuations between 27–30% of the total workforce (Turowiec, 2007, p. 6).

Since there is no reliable data on false self-employment in these countries, we have to base our conclusions on statistics regarding self-employment. The statistics below show that the rate of self-employed workers is very high in Poland, Czech Republic and Slovakia by comparison to the rest of Europe. It should be noted in this respect that self-employed persons usually do not have employees (except in Hungary). Despite the lack of official statistics on bogus self-employment, we argue, that it is a widely existing phenomenon; this statement is supported by prolific case law on disguised employment contracts, the experience of labour inspections, as well as researches on labour law and employment policy.

---

28 For example Polish law does not provide a definition for self-employment. Providing services within the framework of conducted business activity, for one contractor or a narrow group of contracting parties is most often understood as self-employment. The direct basis for the provision of such services is one of civil law contracts concluded with the contracting party (The evolution of labour law (2009), *op. cit.*, 403).

29 'Cases where classification as self-employed is uncertain and cases of false self-employment are two different situations which need to be treated differently in law. The first concerns the interpretation (or updating) of the defining criteria of employment and self-employment, whilst the second concerns the question of how to apply the law in force' (Perulli, 2002, p. 15).

30 In 2011, Romanian national trade union confederation BNS published a report on the informal economy and its impact on the labour market. It shows that informal employment represents 31.4% of total employment in Romania. Retrieved May 5, 2016 from http://www.eurofound.europa.eu/ewco/2012/02/RO1202019I.htm. Informal employment includes several forms of work, such as undeclared work and false self-employment.

31 European Parliament: *The impact of new forms of labour on industrial relations and the evolution of labour law in the European Union*. Study, 2007. Retrieved May 5, 2016 from http://www.europarl.europa.eu/meetdocs/2009_2014/organes/empl/empl_20090902_1500.htm.

Self-employment rates, Europe-24 countries, Q2 2014

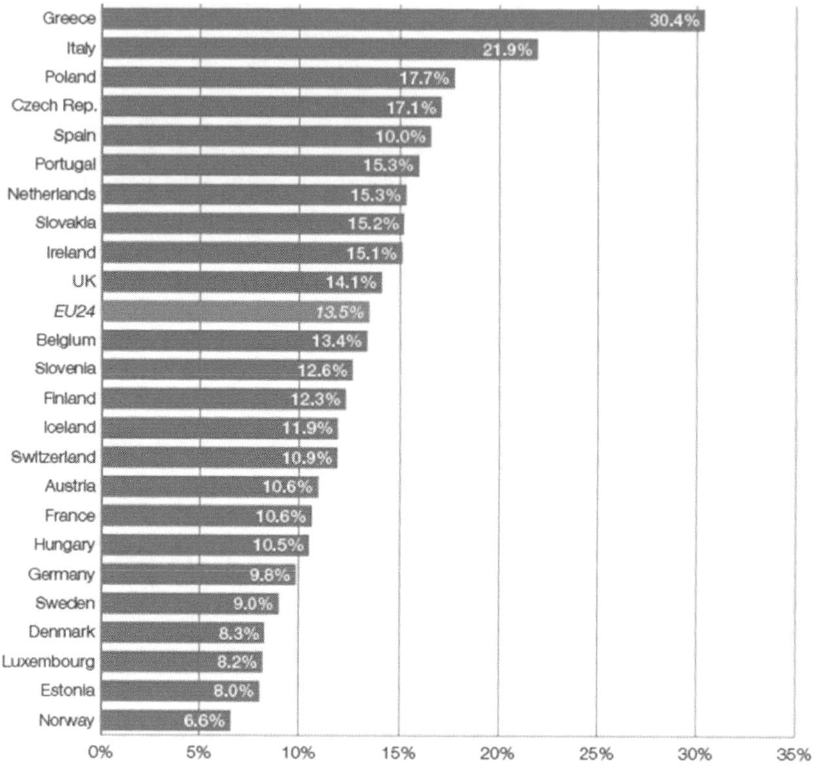

Source: Hatfield I. (2015). Self-employment in Europe. Retrieved May 5, 2016 from http://ippr.org/read/self-employment-in-europe#self-employment__self-employed-employers.

Percentage of self-employed workers with employees in Europe-24 countries, 2013

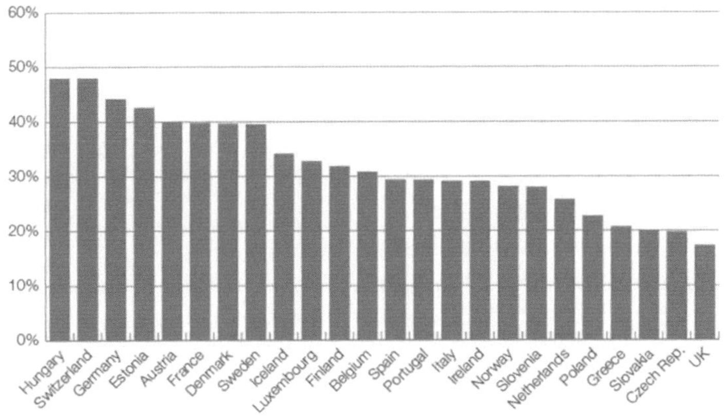

Source: Izzy Hatfield (2015). Self-employment in Europe. http://ippr.org/read/self-employment-in-europe#self-employment__self-employed-employers.

The popularity of false civil law contracts is based on two main motives – legal and financial. The legal, although indirectly financial reason is certainly putting aside the rather costly employment protection incorporated by the Labour Code and all other labour related acts[32] and applying the Civil Code instead, since the latter does not contain any provision on employment protection. The second, purely financial reason seems to have a major influence on employers' decisions. The lower social security and tax payments seem to be far more important in this cost-cutting triangular game between the state, employers and employees, because tax and social burdens have a less avoidable and more crucial effect on overall costs of employment than application of labour law. Therefore, the lower employment cost is the real motive of employers and the exploitation of civil law instead of labour law is the consequence of false self-employment. This case is similar to the expansion of fixed-term contracts in Poland (see above).

Unfortunately, national legislations have often weakened labour law through the lower taxation of a civil law work contract instead of a costly employment contract[33]. This misguided financial policy

[32] Certainly, there are some exceptions, such as equal treatment, health and safety provisions, which have to be applied to all legal forms of any economic activity.

[33] For example in Poland the tax regulations are advantageous for the self-employed (*Poland: Self-employed Workers*. EIRO. Retrieved May 5, 2016 from http://www.eurofound.europa.eu/comparative/tn0801018s/pl0801019q.htm).

has weakened labour law protection of employees, as it incentivizes false self-employment through cheaper civil law contracts[34]. This policy is based on the assumption, that new jobs may be created by decreasing the tax burden of private entrepreneurs. However, the cost of employment contracts cannot usually be similarly diminished, since it would result in considerable losses in the central budget. This policy comes up against the ILO Recommendation No. 198 of 2006 on the employment relationship, which urges to remove incentives to disguise an employment relationship.

The aforementioned expansion of bogus self-employment was reflected by provisions prohibiting disguised employment in several Member States (e.g. Slovakia, Czech Republic, Hungary[35], Poland[36]) around the time of EU accession[37]. According to the amended Polish Labour Code, it is not permitted to replace an employment contract by a civil contract if the work is performed under the conditions of an employment contract (Unterschütz, 2013, p. 6).

The national prohibitions on false self-employment are usually based on the basic labour law definitions, since statutory definitions of the employment relationship or the employment contract are in effect in many of these countries (e.g. Czech Republic[38], Estonia[39], Hungary[40],

---

[34] Hungary is a good example for this financial policy, where taxation law and social security law slowly but efficiently suffocates labour law, as many of the employees of small and medium sized enterprises exchanges their employment rights for taxation advantages. In certain cases the Hungarian tax burden of employment is many times more than in case of certain self-employment taxation methods.

[35] Article 75/A of the Hungarian Labour Code came into force in 2003 on the prohibiton of false self-employment and such a contract is considered as an indefinite employment contract.

[36] Article 22 §1(2) of the Polish Labour Code, added in 2002.

[37] These countries joined the EU on 1 May 2004.

[38] Czech Labour Act (No. 262/2006 Coll.), Article 2(4): 'Dependent work means exclusively personal performance of work by an employee for his employer within the relationship of the employer's superiority and his employee's subordination, according to the employer's instructions (orders), or according to the instructions given in the employer's name, for a wage, salary or other remuneration paid for work done within the working hours (or otherwise determined or agreed time) at the employer's workplace (or at some other agreed place), at the employer's costs and liability (responsibility).'

[39] Article 1 of the Estonian Employment Contract Act.

[40] Article 42 of Act 1 of 2012 on the Labour Code: (1) An employment relationship is deemed established by entering into an employment contract. (2) Under an employment contract: a) the employee is required to work as instructed by the employer; b) the

Lithuania[41], Poland[42], Romania[43], Slovenia[44], Slovakia[45]). However, these definitions are too vague and far from exhaustive, hence many statutory provisions do not go beyond simply stating that personal work is to be carried out by the person who works for the contractual partner. Therefore, these definitions are usually not very useful in court practice.

In most countries, certain criteria are used to determine whether or not a contract is a contract of employment. Some countries do not provide a statutory definition of an employment relationship or a contract of employment (e.g. Bulgaria and Latvia). Instead of definitions of the employment relationship or the employment contract, only the statutory definition of an 'employee' can be found in Latvia[46], where an employee is a natural person, who performs work under the supervision of an employer on the basis of an employment contract against remuneration (European Network, 2009, pp. 2–4).

The mere prohibition of false self-employment is surely not enough to stop this negative trend. Therefore, the prohibition of disguised employment is supported by strengthened labour inspection, increased labour fines and labour court practice qualifying legal relationships aimed at work in several

employer is required to provide work for the employee and to pay wages (Retrieved May 5, 2016 from http://www.ilo.org/dyn/travail/docs/2557/Labour%20Code.pdf).

41 Article 93 of the Lithuanian Labour Code.

42 Article 22 §1 of the Polish Labour Code stipulates that 'by the establishment of an employment relationship the employee shall oblige himself/herself to perform specific work for the benefit of an and under his supervision in place and time appointed by an employer and the employer obliges himself to employ employee for remuneration.' (Unterschütz, 2013, p. 5).

43 Article 10 of the Romanian Labour Code.

44 Slovenian Employment Relationships Act (Ur.I.RS, No. 42/2002, 193/2007): 'Article 4 (1) An employment relationship is a relationship between the worker and the employer, whereby the worker is voluntarily included in the employer's organised working process, in which he in return for remuneration continuously carries out work in person according to the instructions and under the control of the employer. (2) Each of the contracting parties in an employment relationship shall exercise the agreed and prescribed rights and obligations.'

45 Slovak Act No. 348/2007 Coll., Article 1(2). 'Dependent work, which is performed in a relationship where the employer is the superior and the employee is subordinate, is defined solely as work performed personally as an employee for an employer, according to the employer's instructions, in the employer's name, for a wage or commission, during working time, at the expense of the employer, using the employer's tools and with the employer's liability, and also consisting mainly of certain repeated activities'.

46 Article 3 of the Latvian Labour Code.

countries. Administrative bodies, e.g. labour inspectorates (Bulgaria, the Czech Republic, Hungary, Latvia, Lithuania, Romania and Slovakia, Slovenia), tax and social security authorities (Hungary, Latvia, Lithuania), or other authorities (Estonia[47]) are competent to investigate the true nature of an employment relationship.

Civil or labour courts usually evaluate civil law contracts, if the nature of the legal relationship and thereby the applicable law is disputed, especially in cases of termination of employment or liability of the employer for damages in case of work accidents, as the civil law provisions are much more favourable for employers (e.g. Bulgaria, the Czech Republic, Estonia, Hungary, Latvia, Poland) (European Network, 2009, pp. 60–6). In our opinion precisely regulated, well-financed and trained labour inspection may be an effective way of fighting bogus self-employment.

4. Regulation of economically dependent work: one of the ways out?

The regulation of economically dependent work is a relatively new phenomenon and it is present only in a couple of Western European Member States. At the same time, this legal issue has rapidly become one of the most popular topics of labour law literature worldwide[48]. Eastern European Member States are still lagging behind in this respect, both regarding employment regulation and labour law literature. The reason behind the lack of developments in relation to the definitional system of the Eastern European Member States' Labour Codes is the wilful adherence to the traditional binary system consisting of employment contracts and civil law contracts[49]. Therefore, none of these Member States has elaborated provisions on economically dependent work.

---

[47] Individual employment disputes commissions (European Network, 2009, p. 64).

[48] See for example Araki T., Blanpain R. & Ouchi S. (eds.) *Labour Law in Motion – Diversification of the Labour Force & Terms and Conditions of Employment.* The Hague: Kluwer Law International, 2005; Pennings F. & Bosse C. (eds.) *The Protection of Working Relations.* The Netherlands: Kluwer Law International, 2011; Casale G. (2011). The employment relationship. A General Introduction. In Casale G.: *The employment relationship. A Comparative Overview.* Geneva: Hart Publishing, 2011.

[49] In English law the traditional binary system differentiates two distinct contractual forms: contract of service (employee) and contract for service (independent contractor).

As a consequence of the long tradition of this system, labour lawyers are still thinking in the binary division of working relationships, not even considering the possibility of regulating the third type of legal relationship. For example, even the extremely flexible forms of employment (e.g. casual work for one day without a contract) is regulated as an atypical employment contract in Hungary[50]. This is the main reason why new contractual forms have not really been regulated outside the Labour Code, as third type of work contracts.

This binary perception of the employment structure is further strengthened by the common post-socialist legal tradition of these legal systems having a Labour Code applying to all employment relationships and a Civil Code regulating all other commercial relationships aimed at employment. Evidently, there are exceptions to the abovementioned trends, however, these minor changes have not broken the traditional division of regulation by the Labour Code and the Civil Code. The regulation of economically dependent work and the expansion of the scope of labour law is still missing, although economically dependent work is present in these Members States. However, two remarkably different proposals, in Poland and Hungary, have been encountered on the regulation of the third type of working relationships.

In Poland, the draft of a new Labour Code in 2006[51] aimed at including work carried out other than on the basis of an employment contract into labour law[52]. An agreement establishing a legal relationship between the employer and a person who is not an employee is not regarded as an employment agreement. The main difference between an employee and a non-employee with such an agreement is that the latter may obtain help from family members if they live in the same household. It is a legal fiction of personal work despite the possibility of work carried out by a limited circle of third parties. The necessary condition for a person to be considered as a 'non-employee with an agreement' is that he/she carries out continuous and repeatable actions for the employer or others in return for remuneration of more than half of the minimum wage. These non-employees would be protected by the provisions of the draft Labour

---

[50] See the Hungarian Act 75 of 2010 on simplified employment.

[51] Retrieved May 5, 2016 from http://www.mpips.gov.pl/prawo-pracy/projekty-kodeksow-pracy/.

[52] The draft Labour Code was submitted by the Codification Commission to the Minister of Labour and Social Policy, but it has not been passed by the Parliament (Swiątkowski, 2011, p. 110).

Code on collective agreements, fair remuneration and conditions of work with a special attention to health and safety regulations (Świątkowski, 2011, pp. 122–123).

In Hungary, the first proposal of the 2012 Labour Code[53] suggested to extend the application of the rules of the Labour Code on minimum wage, holidays, notice of termination of employment, severance pay and the liability for damages to other forms of work. A 'person similar to an employee' works under any kind of contract, and whereby a) the individual undertakes to perform any work personally, for remuneration, on a regular basis for another person, and b) beyond performing this contract it cannot be expected from this person to do any other work for remuneration on a regular basis[54]. As to this last condition, the proposal excluded the application of these rules if the income from the contract in question exceeded 500% of the national minimum wage[55]. This legal concept could have been a remarkable development, but it was deleted from the Draft due to the refusal by the social partners (Kiss, 2013, p. 13).

Conclusion

Certainly, labour law is characterized by constant political, social and economic changes. However, there have been three major waves of labour law reforms in Central and Eastern European countries since the political changes in 1990. The first reforms adjusted the former Soviet Labour Codes to the needs of a market economy, either by several amendments to the original Labour Code (e.g. in Poland and Czech Republic), or by passing a new Labour Code (e.g. in Hungary in 1992[56]). The second

---

53 See the Hungarian text of the First Draft of the Labour Code. Retrieved May 5, 2016 from http://www.pazmanymunkajog.com/images/files/docs/2011/MT_2011_juliusi_Tervezet.pdf.

54 There is no specific statistical data on the number of economically dependent workers in Hungary. In 2006, 466,000 self-employed persons acted as sole traders or were members of work partnerships, amounting to 11.9% of the total working population. Moreover, the issue of economically dependent workers may affect another 1.12 million employees – constituting 29% of the working population – who are employed in businesses with fewer than four employees (*Economically dependent workers in Hungary*. Retrieved May 5, 2016 from http://www.eurofound.europa.eu/eiro/2007/04/articles/hu0704019i.htm).

55 Article 3 of the first proposal of the new Hungarian Labour Code.

56 Act 22 of 1992 on the Labour Code.

cluster of reforms served the implementation of EU labour law before EU accession. The third, most recent reforms are closely connected to the changing world of work, the financial crisis and also the political will to increase the employment rate.

Out of the complex developments and challenges of labour law reforms, the paper focused merely on the evolving structure of work relationships and its impact on labour legislation and labour market. Two potential sources of flexibility have been analysed: atypical employment contracts and various forms of self-employment. Evidently, atypical employment contracts do not have a tradition in this region. Despite the detailed regulation enforced by EU law harmonization, typical, full-time and indefinite-term employment contracts still dominate in these labour markets.

Apparently, the need of employers for flexibility is met by other sources, especially false self-employment. Bogus self-employment has rapidly expanded in spite of legal and administrative measures. Thus, an increasing number of workers are leaving typical employment, but they opt for non-employment forms of work instead of finding flexibility in an atypical employment contract. The escape from an employment relationship to cheaper, but not protected work relationships is a great challenge for labour legislation for at least the next decade. This complex issue cannot be settled merely by flexibilization of employment relationships.

Bibliography

Araki T., Blanpain R. & Ouchi S. (eds.) (2005). *Labour Law in Motion—Diversification of the Labour Force & Terms and Conditions of Employment.* The Hague: Kluwer Law International.

Casale G. (2011). The employment relationship. A General Introduction. In: Casale G. *The employment relationship. A Comparative Overview.* Hart Publishing.

Däubler W. (2011). Protection of Working Relationships in Germany. In: Frans Pennings & Claire Bosse (eds). *The Protection of Working Relations.* Kluwer Law International, pp. 127–42.

EIRO (2007). *Economically dependent workers in Hungary.* Retrieved May 5, 2016 from http://www.eurofound.europa.eu/eiro/2007/04/articles/hu0704019i.htm.

European Communities (2009). *The evolution of labour law in the EU-12 (1995–2005)*, Vol. 3. Retrieved May 5, 2016 from http://ec.europa.eu/social/main.jsp?catId=738&langId=en&pubId=94&type=2&furtherPubs=yes.

European Network (2009). European Network of Legal Experts in the field of Labour Law. *Characteristics of the Employment Relationship. Thematic Report.* Retrieved May 5, 2016 from www.labourlawnetwork.eu.

European Parliament (2007): *The impact of new forms of labour on industrial relations and the evolution of labour law in the European Union.* Retrieved May 5, 2016 from http://www.europarl.europa.eu/meetdocs/2009_2014/organes/empl/empl_20090902_1500.htm.

Gyulavári T. (2014a). 'Trap of the Past: Why Economically Dependent Work is not Regulated in the Member States of Eastern Europe'. *European Labour Law Journal,* 2014, pp. 267–278.

Gyulavári T. (2014b). A bridge too far? The Hungarian regulation of economically dependent work. *Hungarian Labour Law E-Journal,* 2014, pp. 1–22.

Gyulavári T. & Kártyás G. (2015). *The Hungarian Flexicurity Pathway—New Labour Code after Twenty Years in the Market Economy.* Budapest: Pázmány Press.

Harvan P. & Machlica G. (2011). *Slovakia has the tenth most flexible Labour Code in the OECD since September.* Financial Policy Institute, Ministry of Finance SR, Policy Brief 2011/23. Retrieved May 5, 2016 from www.finance.gov.sk/ifp.

Hatfield I. (2015). Self-employment in Europe. Retrieved May 5, 2016 from http://ippr.org/read/self-employment-in-europe#self-employment__self-employed-employers.

Kiss Gy. (2013). 'A munkavállalóhoz hasonló jogállású személy problematikája az Európai Unióban és e jogállás szabályozásának hiánya a Munka Törvénykönyvében'. *Jogtudományi Közlöny,* 68 (1).

Lipták K. (2011). 'Is atypical typical? – Atypical employment in Central Eastern European countries.' *Employment and Economy in Central and Eastern Europe,* No. 1/2011. Retrieved May 5, 2016 from http://www.emecon.eu/fileadmin/articles/1_2011/emecon%201_2011%20Liptak.pdf.

Petrylaitė D. (2015). *Modernisation of the Lithuanian Labour Law.* @ADAPT_bulletin, 25 February 2015. Retrieved May 5, 2016 from www.adaptinternational.it.

Perulli A. (2002). *Economically dependent/quasi-subordinate (parasubordinate) employment: legal, social and economic aspects.* European Commission. Retrieved May 5, 2016 from http://ec.europa.eu/social/main.jsp?catId=709&langId=en&intPageId=217.

Placintescu A. (2015). *More flexibility in labour relations following the recent amendments of the Romanian labour legislation.* Retrieved May 5, 2016 from http://www.musat.ro/wp-content/uploads/2015/04/Romanian-Labour-Legislation-Terralex-Article-August-2011.pdf.

Skupień D., Łaga M. & Pisarczyk L. (2016). 'Polish labour law: the impact of the economic crisis and demographic problems'. *Hungarian Labour Law E-Journal,* Vol. 3 (1), pp. 1–21. Retrieved May 5, 2016 from http://hllj.hu/letolt/2016_1_a/A_01_Skupien_Laga_Pysarczyk_hllj_2016_1.pdf.

Świątkowski A. M. (2011). The Protection of Working relationships in Poland. In: Pennings F. & Bosse C. (eds.): *The Protection of Working Relations.* The Netherlands: Kluwer Law International.

Turowiec A. (2007). *Case Study: self-employment in Poland. The impact of new forms of labour on industrial relations and the evolution of labour law in the European Union.* Manuscript.

Unterschütz J. (2013). *Fixed-term contracts in Poland: protection or flexibility.* Manuscript.

Unterschütz J. (2015). 'Fixed-term contracts in Poland: protection or flexibility.' *Hungarian Labour Law E-Journal,* 2015, Vol. 2 (1), pp. 23–39. Retrieved May 5, 2016 from http://hllj.hu/letolt/2015_1_a/03.pdf.

Van Peijpe T. (2012). EU limits for the personal scope of employment law. *European Labour Law Journal,* 2012. Vol. 3 (1), pp. 35–53.

The Dynamics of Slovenian Labour Law

Between the Reforms and Permanent Evolution

Polonca Končar*

Abstract

Slovenia, like other European countries has experienced pressure from EU institutions to flexibilize its labour market in order to improve labour law flexibility and reduce employment protection. In the context of labour law developments after the declaration of the independence of Slovenia in 1990, this paper focuses on Slovenian labour law reforms and adjustments. It gives a more detailed review of recent changes concerning temporary employment agencies and other labour market issues regulated by the Labour Market Regulation Act. Moreover, attempts to flexibilize labour law and broaden the employment protection to independent workers in the new Employment Relationships Act are assessed.

Key words: flexibilization, labour law reform, temporary employment, fixed-term contract, independent workers, economically dependent person.

Introductory remarks

In relation to the title of the contribution my starting point has to be explained. We continually encounter complaints about the inefficiency and rigidity or inflexibility of the national labour law systems, which allegedly constitute a major obstacle to economic development. The requirements to reform labour law/labour market are constantly directed to us either from the institutions in Brussels or from the OECD. The latter usually link the requirements to the reduction of the EPL index. The question, what do we understand by the term 'reform' seems to me to be very

* Professor Emeritus at the university of Ljubljana, Faculty of Law. Prof. Končar has taught Labour Law, International Labour Law and EC Employment Law. She is former President of the European Committee of Social Rights, Strasbourg. Prof. Končar was a member of the Executive Committee of the International Society for Labour and Social Security Law (Vice-President of the Society, 2003–2006). She was national expert in the Free Movement of Workers Network and is a member of the Scientific Committee and national expert in the European Labour Law Network.

important. The term has a number of different senses. For example, it can mean amendments of what is defective, corrections of abuses and errors or changes in law, intended to improve, supplement or change the regulation. It can also have a more comprehensive meaning in comparison to such terms as amendment, changes, improvement etc. for example. It may relate to changes to the foundations of a legal discipline or to the majority of institutes that represent the core characteristics of, for example, the labour law. There is no doubt that labour law, like other legal fields, does not exist and evolve in a vacuum. Technological and technical advancements, innovations in work organization, increased competitiveness in the context of globalization of the economy, the financial and economic crisis are circumstances in relation to which the need for a fundamental reform of labour law are emphasized in our countries. But do we have always in mind a complete, fundamental labour law reform or would a mere adaptation and/or minor changes suffice instead? Personally, I prefer to use the term 'reform' only when in-depth changes are addressed. Otherwise, it is more suitable, in my view, to use terms with which we denote the ability of the labour law, proved many times in the past, to adapt to political, economic and social development and thus prove its dynamism[1]. The dynamism can be illustrated on the basis of various characteristics, one of which is also flexibility. Different content has been attributed to the term 'flexibility'. In the 1980s the term has been very often equated with the so-called deregulation in the sense that collective bargaining is largely replaced by individual negotiations between the employer and the employee. It also entailed the introduction of non-standard employment contracts, and the reduction of the protection functions of labour law. Nowadays, other meanings are attributed to the concept of 'flexibility'. In Europe, the concept of flexicurity became established.

This paper gives examples of the in-depth reforms of Slovenian labour law. They will be followed by an overview of recent developments in the field of labour law and labour market regulation.

1. Labour law reform in Slovenia

The first step of the labour law reform took place in the former Yugoslavia and Slovenia as an integral part of it in 1989/1990. The new labour law legislation reflected the process of economic and political

[1] French scholars, for example, used to refer to the dynamism of labour law as one of its characteristics. See Camerlynck G. H., Lyon–Caen G. *Droit du Travail*, Précis Dalloz, Librarie Dalloz, 1973, pp. 17–25; Javillier J.-C. *Manuel de Droit du travail*, L. G. D. J., 1998, pp. 19143.

reforms and the transition to the market economy, democratization and pluralism of political and other relations. It was characterized by some general provisions indicating the replacement of so-called associative employment relationships[2], known in the previous system of self-management, with the contractual employment relationships (relationships based on the employment contract), and the introduction of the collective bargaining system[3]. The process of in-depth adaptation/reform of the labour law to the labour market rules intensified in the period after the declaration of the independence of Slovenia in the 1990s. The following new acts from that period, which represented the labour law reform (reform in the strict sense) in Slovenia can be mentioned:

By the Workers Participation in Management Act from 1993 (ZSDU)[4] the self-management of workers was replaced with the participation of workers in management. Due to the introduction of trade unions' pluralism the Representativeness of Trade Unions Act (ZRSin) was laid down the same year[5]. The grey economy had already been recognized as a big problem at that time and the Prevention of Undeclared Work and Employment (ZPDZC) was enacted in 2000[6]. In the field of individual employment relationships the following important novelties of a reform nature were brought about by the Employment Relationships Act from 2002 (ERA)[7]: the statutory definition of the employment relationship, which contains basic elements of the employment relationship; the prohibition of work on the basis of a civil law contract where there are elements of employment relationship present; the presumption of the existence of employment relationship if the elements of the employment relationship exist; introductions of the primacy of facts in

---

2 They were not viewed as relationships between two parties, but as relationships between workers working with the resources in social ownership and, on the basis of the right to self-management under the law, deciding themselves on their rights stemming from work.

3 See Končar P. On Dual system of Workers' Representation in Slovenia. In Blanpain R., Lyutov N. (eds.) *Workers' Representation in Central and Eastern Europe, Challenges and Opportunities for the Works Councils' System. Bulletin of Comparative Labour Relations*, Wolters Kluwer, 2014, p. 213.

4 *Ur.l.* RS (Official Gazette of the RS, No. 42/93, 56/01, 26/07, 42/07 (ZSDU – UPB1) (official consolidated text).

5 *Ur. l.* RS (Official Gazette of the RS, No. 13/93).

6 *Ur.l.* RS (Official Gazette of the RS, No. 36/00, 118/06, 12/07- UPB1 (official consolidated text), 29/10, 57/12, 21/13- ZUTD-A, 32/14-ZPDZC-1, 47/15-ZZSDT.

7 *Ur.l.* RS (Official Gazette of the RS, No. 42/02, 79/06, 46/07).

relation to the existence of employment relationship; explicit prohibition of discrimination; completion of the provisions on non-standard employment contracts (fixed-term, part-time and home work) provided for by the law also before 2002, with the new provisions on the temporary agency work, public works and employment contracts with managers[8]; the new provisions on the transfer of undertakings; the new regulation on the termination of employment contract (ordinary, extraordinary termination, notice periods, severance payment, termination on the basis of a judicial decision etc.). Amendments to the ERA from 2006 and 2007 did mostly contain adjustments to EC law and some improvements of a terminological nature. The new labour law system was only rounded up in 2006 by the enactment of the Collective Agreements Act (ZKolP)[9].

In relation to the labour market, the Labour Market Regulation Act from 2010 (ZUTD)[10] has to be mentioned. To a great extent, it can be viewed as an act of a reform nature. The Act has replaced the former Employment and Unemployment Insurance Act. It has given greater emphasis to active employment policy measures, public works included. A new chapter on posting workers to work in a user undertaking has been included in the Act.

2. Recent developments in the field of labour market and labour law

One can start with the following general observation: As we did in the 1980s, we still witness constant pressure, from the employers' side and from some international institutions, to lower the level of labour law protection. Growing unemployment and the required flexibilization of the labour market result in new forms of employment and work. The growing segmentation of the labour market has become a serious problem. People are working more and more outside the scope of employment protection legislation and many of them, especially those in so-called disguised employment relationships, would in fact need labour law protection. Many are calling attention to the fact that the human rights' perspective of our labour law system should not be overlooked and they require a legal system that would assure everybody a decent job. They are

8 Employment contracts in all these cases are dealt with within a chapter titled 'Specific features of employment contracts'.

9 *Ur.l.* RS (Official Gazette of the RS, No. 43/06, 45/08).

10 *Ur.l.* RS (Official Gazette of the RS, No. 80/10).

not always successful in their opposition to the constantly present neo-liberal requirements of the flexibilization of the labour market and labour law, particularly strong during the recent economic and financial crisis. I shall now focus on answers given by the labour market and labour law legislation to the dilemmas raised by the above-mentioned phenomena.

3. Labour market legislation

The Labour Market Regulation Act (ZUTD) from 2010, was amended three times in 2013. ZUTD-A[11] provided the right of pensioners to perform a temporary or casual work based on a temporary or casual work contract. By ZUTD-B[12] provisions on public works have been supplemented. The possibility for the long-term unemployed who are receiving unemployment benefit, to be included in public works, has been provided for. ZUTD-C[13] has focused on three different issues. The possibility that social partners perform services on the labour market on the basis of the given concession has been laid down. The Act has fixed a lower pecuniary share in the case when the foundation for the improvement of employment possibilities is founded by the social partners, parties to branch collective agreement. The majority of the novelties of the amended Act related to temporary employment agencies. The objectives of the amendments were to reduce abuses arising from performing their activity and to promote the foundation of companies specialized in placing workers at user undertakings. It was underlined that placement of workers in user undertakings should represent the principal activity of temporary employment agencies. The practice according to which temporary employment agencies may perform different forms of employment brokerage, should be abolished. A new definition of 'activity'[14] has been set forth. The conditions under which the agency may actively perform the activity and its duties have been completed/sharpened. The Act has introduced a new permit for activity performance which is determined as a prerequisite for entry in the register and/or records (for agencies with a registered office in another EU Member

[11] *Ur.l.* RS (Official Gazette of the RS, No. 21/13).

[12] *Ur.l.* RS (Official Gazette of the RS, No. 63/13).

[13] *Ur.l.* RS (Official Gazette of the RS, No. 100/13).

[14] The definition was adopted in order to delimit the activity of the temporary employment agency from performing services on the basis of civil law contracts (contract for work or for services).

State). A new system of reviewing the activity of temporary employment agencies has also been introduced.

4. The new Employment Relationships Act (ERA-1)

The ERA-1[15] represents an attempt to tackle labour market segmentation by increasing labour market flexibility (also by reducing EPL).

On one hand the legislator took into consideration recommendations addressed to Slovenia by the EU (to adjust EPL as regards open-ended contracts in order to reduce labour market segmentation, to tackle the parallel labour market caused by student work), and by the OECD (to ease EPL for open-ended employment contracts, to tackle student work). On the other hand the practice/employers required that the new Act would ease the termination of the employment contract in the sense of abolishing redundant procedural requirements and would reduce the labour costs by, for example, shorter notice periods and the abolition/reduction of severance payments. Experts in the field, in principle, did not object to the concept of flexicurity. As the issue of the termination of the employment contract was one of the core issues addressed in public discussions on how greater flexicurity could be reached, experts insisted that the possible new regulations should not contradict the obligations of the state deriving from binding international treaties and EC law. They advocated solutions that would overcome the shortcomings and ambiguities which have surfaced in the more than eight years of the application of ERA and would mean the search for a balance between flexibility and security.

ERA-1 has laid down many provisions of a procedural nature intended to simplify the procedure of termination of the employment contract (reduction of administrative barriers). The provisions on shorter notice periods and lower severance pay should contribute to the reduction of the costs of open-ended contracts and to the reduction of labour market segmentation due to the decrease of the EPL Index.

High labour market segmentation is one of the great problems of Slovenian society. Different forms of work, known already in the past (student work, undeclared work, high proportion of older unemployed persons, bogus self-employment) or emerging so-called new forms of work, lead to great labour market segmentation. The high proportion of fixed-term employment contracts is particularly recognized as an acute

15 *Ur.l.* RS (Official Gazette of the RS, No. 21/13).

problem. By ERA-1 an attempt was made to partly reduce labour market segmentation by financial disincentives to reduce the use of fixed-term contracts. The point of departure of the legislator was not only to reduce the costs of open-ended employment contracts but to increase at the same time the costs of fixed-term contracts. For this reason, severance pay for fixed-term workers has been introduced, unless a fixed-term contract is transformed into an open-ended contract. Furthermore, the provisions exempt employers from paying contributions against unemployment during the first two years of permanent employment and they are obliged to pay a higher amount in the case of fixed-term employment.

In addition to changes related to the termination procedures of employment contracts, ERA-1 contains quite a number of provisions to increase internal[16] and external[17] flexibility.

It is not possible to go into all the details of the new regulation of employment relationships and labour market issues. Nevertheless it is worth pointing out, that temporary employment and the operation of temporary employment agencies has received great public attention in the last few years. They are covered not only by the Labour Market Regulation Act, as already mentioned above, but also by ERA–1 which was completed in order to align legislation with Directive 2008/104/EC. Regrettably, all the ambiguities in the regulation of temporary agency work have not been abolished. It is worth noting the introduction of the quota system regarding the number of workers that may be assigned to a user undertaking. It has been laid down, that 'the number of workers assigned to a user undertaking may not exceed 25% of the number of workers employed by the user undertaking, except if otherwise provided by a branch collective agreement. This limitation does not include workers who are employed for an indefinite duration with the employer providing work.' (Par 3 of Article 59) The said limitation shall not apply

---

16 Measures to enhance internal flexibility:

– in specific circumstances possibility to order performance of other suitable work by the employer,

– the employer is no longer obliged to offer employment under different conditions when terminating the employment contract due to business reasons or incapacity,

– introduction of temporary waiting for work with 80% wage compensation,

– more options for a 'different' regulation in collective agreements etc.

17 Measures for increasing external flexibility:

– inclusion of workers in active employment policy measures during notice period,

– possibility of temporary and occasional work for retired persons etc.

to a user undertaking that is a smaller employer. From the viewpoint of the Directive, the provision might be questionable, but it was adopted in order to prevent the situation where user undertakings perform their activities exclusively by employing temporary agency workers.

5. Cases of Broadening the Employment Protection to Independent workers

Traditionally, the labour law has been associated with the dependent employment relationship. It can be based on standard or non-standard employment contracts. In this way the notion of the term 'employment' became homogeneous. Additionally, the term applies today also to the work of independent workers, i.e. persons who work for another person outside an employment relationship on the basis of civil or commercial contracts. From the legal point of view the use of the same term in different contexts seems to be much too imprecise and problematic. In individual situations it is difficult to distinguish the actual legal situation of persons for whom the term 'employment' is used and to establish to whom labour law applies. The number of people working outside the scope of labour law protection is growing. This leads us to a discussion about the future of labour law. Should it be dissolved or on the contrary should its scope be widened so that an adequate level of employment protection is guaranteed to different forms of work?

The developments of labour law in Slovenia up to now show that to a large extent the protection of dependent workers has been dealt with from the human rights perspective. In the financial and economic crisis and after the adoption of austerity measures, the postulate of 'decent work' in particular has been placed to the forefront. Due to such an approach it is easy to understand that many consider it necessary to extend the validity *ratione personae* of the labour law to persons engaged in various forms of work outside an employment relationship[18]. In accordance with the mentioned approach, examples of so-called widened employment protection can be found in the current Slovenian labour law system. They shall be briefly presented below.

---

[18] Kresal B. Mutating or dissolving labour Law? The fundamental right to dignity of working people questioned (once again). In: Rigaux M., Buelens J., Latinne A. (eds.) *From Labour Law to Social Competition Law?* Intersentia, 2014, p. 157.

5.1 Health and Safety at Work

First of all, the Occupational Health and Safety at Work Act (ZVZD-1) has to be mentioned. It recognizes the *right to health and safety at work* not only to workers performing work under the employment contract but also to persons performing work on any other legal basis or performing work for training purposes[19].

5.2 Limited employment protection to specific categories of workers

Labour legislation and legislation in the field of labour market regulation recognize limited employment protection to:

- volunteer trainees;
- children under 15 years of age and students (when performing work in accordance with the law);
- economically dependent self-employed persons; and
- pensioners who perform temporary or occasional work.

The status of the listed categories of workers will be briefly presented below.

5.2.1 Trainees

Traineeship is an institute introduced in the legal system that applied on the territory of today's Slovenia between the two world wars. At the beginning, training in the form of traineeship was limited to public servants. After the Second World War, it became a compulsory form of training for all workers who entered the employment relationship after finishing their schooling, even in the enterprise sector. It contained a strong employment aspect. Compared with traineeship elsewhere, trainees in Slovenia completed their traineeships for independent work within the employment relationship. Under certain conditions, the legislation of 1990 permitted voluntary traineeship. According to Article 124 of ERA-1 voluntary traineeship is allowed on condition that it is provided for by a special act[20]. The voluntary traineeship can be completed on the basis of a special contract on voluntary traineeship

---

19 *Ur.l.* RS (Official Gazette of the RS, No. 43/2011), Article 3.

20 The provision indicates that voluntary traineeship may only be introduced in the public sector.

which is not an employment contract. Nevertheless, the provisions of ERA-1 on the duration of traineeship and the implementation of the traineeship programme, the limitation of working time, breaks and rest periods, reimbursement of work-related expenses, liability for damages and safety and health at work apply to voluntary trainees.

5.2.2 Children under the age of fifteen and students

As for the exceptionally allowed work of children under the age of 15 and the work of secondary school and university students it has been laid down that the provisions of ERA-1 on discrimination, equal treatment with regard to sex, working time, breaks and rest periods, special protection of workers under the age of 18, and liability for damages shall apply. Notwithstanding these provisions, ERA-1 guarantees children under the age of 15 special protection regarding the right to limited working time[21].

5.2.3 Economically dependent persons

In the period of new forms of organization of work and business relationships (for example, 'outsourcing') the category of self-employed persons is gaining significance. As regards *self-employed persons* their share in the labour force in Slovenia is on the rise. On the one hand, some of the active employment policy measures stimulate individuals to become self-employed, and on the other hand, this is a result of often illegal practices of employers forcing workers to obtain the status of an independent entrepreneur and afterwards performing the same work for their former employers which they performed when they were in an employment relationship[22]. Very often, we are dealing with a false self-employment, which can be remedied by ERA-1 with the statutory presumption of the existence of an employment relationship[23].

---

21 ERA-1, Article 212.

22 On the disguised forms of employment see: Senčur Peček, D., Neuporaba in spremenjnena uporaba institutov delovnega prava [Non-application and changed application of labour law institutes], *Podjetje in delo*, No. 6-7, 2015, pp. 191–207.

23 The statutory presumption on the existence of the employment relationship is stipulated by Article 18 of the ERA-1. The Act defines the employment relationship. The definition includes so-called basic elements of the employment relationship (inclusion in the organized working process, paid-off work, work in person, continuous work, work according to the instructions and supervision). In the event of a dispute on the existence of an employment relationship between the worker and the employer, it shall be presumed that an employment relationship exists if elements of the employment relationship exist.

The cases of disguised employment, which encompass disguising the true legal nature of a particular contractual relationship, should be distinguished from the issue of economically dependent self-employed persons. Since 2013, in Slovenia this group has enjoyed limited legal protection. ERA-1 defines the economically dependent person as 'a self-employed person who on the basis of a civil law contract performs work in person, independently and for remuneration for a longer period of time in circumstances of economic dependency and does not employ workers'[24]. Economic dependency means that a person obtains at least 80% of his or her annual income from the same contracting party. It is up to the economically dependent person whether he or she will claim eligibility to limited labour law protection and whether to that end he or she will at the end of a calendar or financial year provide his or her contracting party with the information upon which an eventual existence of economic dependency could be established. If economic dependency is established, 'provisions of ERA-1 regarding the prohibition of discrimination, minimum notice periods, prohibition of the termination of a contract in cases of unfounded grounds for termination, assurance of payment for contractually agreed work appropriate for the type, scope and quality of the undertaken work, taking into consideration the collective agreements binding the contracting party, and the enforcement of liability for damages should be applied'.

Notwithstanding the legislator's good intentions to improve the precarious status of the growing number of economically dependent persons, there is doubt as to its efficacy in practice[25]. The regulation was adopted without any prior analysis and it is relatively general, thus raising many dilemmas.

5.2.4 Temporary or casual work of pensioners

Pensioners are the last category of persons for whom the current legislation recognizes limited labour law protection. The amendments to the Labour Market Regulation Act (ZUTD-A, 2013) recognized under certain circumstances and limitations (e.g. duration limitation or limitation related to the annual income) the right of pensioners to perform temporary or casual work based on a temporary or casual work contract. Such work is

[24] ERA-1, Article 213.

[25] Tičar L. Delovnopravno varstvo ekonomsko odvisnih oseb – novost ZDR-1 [Labour Protection of Economically Dependent Persons – New Regulations in the ERA-1], Delavci in delodajalci, No. 2-3, 2013, pp. 151–67.

regarded as a special civil law contractual relationship. Resumed activation should give the pensioner the opportunity of some extra income and thus improve his or her financial situation. So, formally, pensioners do not perform work within an employment relationship, however, they do have certain rights characteristic of the employment relationship. Some provisions of ERA-1 are applicable for them, namely those prohibiting sexual and other harassment and workplace mobbing (maltreatment), gender equality, working time, breaks, rest periods and liability. They enjoy the right to health and safety in the workplace, as well. Selection of the rights covered by the protection may be subjects of critical discussion. Besides, one must also be aware of the fact that temporary and casual work outside the employment relationship may be performed by anyone, including pensioners. Lastly, the regulation of temporary or casual work of pensioners may be criticized because the 'temporariness' and 'casualness' are defined in relation to the status of the person carrying out such work and not in relation to the nature or the content of the work itself[26]. Many expressed their doubts as to whether it was necessary and/or appropriate to enact the possibility of this so-called new form of work. Doubts were justified in practice as pensioners rarely choose this form of work.

Conclusion

Under the term of 'reform' I understand in-depth changes of legal norms, which can contribute to the improvement, supplement or change of the national legal system. For example, we can speak about labour law reform in Slovenia when the legislation was changed and adapted to the labour market rules. The broadening of employment protection to independent workers carrying out work within certain new forms of work is in principle also of a reform nature. More often we witness labour law adjustments either to minor economic or social changes or to new solutions which are necessary in order to overcome the shortcoming, ambiguities or errors and have surfaced in the application of the legal norms in force. History shows us that labour law is a legal field which has many times demonstrated its ability to adapt to the economic and social development.

---

[26] Strban G. Prenova zavarovanja za brezposelnost in ukrepov aktivne politike zaposlovanja [The renovation of unemployment insurance and the active employment policy measures], Pravna praksa, No. 35, 2013, pp. 17-18.

Main Features of Lithuanian Labour Law Reform 2016

Tomas DAVULIS*

Abstract

This article presents and analyses the main characteristics of the new Lithuanian Labour Code. The reforms of the Lithuanian labour market have been initiated to meet the challenges of fierce international competition, to find a new balance between the flexibility desired by business and the required social protection of workers and to bring the law into the line with contemporary changes at work. However, re-codification is not only about changes in the areas of working time, dismissal protection, fixed-term employment or other forms of atypical work. The Labour Code of 2016 ought to modernize the employment relationship in a much broader perspective – to revive the spirit of cooperation both at individual and collective level, to increase the judicial protection of employees, to allow for wider acceptance of technologies, investment in human capital and respect of the employee's personality and his/her family commitments. Changes in the collective representation system are also necessary to revitalize collective bargaining and increase industrial democracy in the workplace.

Keywords: labour market reform, re-codification, Labour Code, industrial relations, individual employment contract

Introduction

Reforms of labour market regulations in times of economic growth and good economic situation are not usual in Europe, where historically major legislative changes were initiated in response to economical and financial difficulties. Balancing the protective labour legislation at the national level is often perceived here as a possible responsive measure to increase the competitiveness of companies and economies. The current

* Tomas Davulis is a Full Professor of Labour Law at Vilnius University Faculty of Law, Lithuania. His main areas of research include international and European Union labour law, non-discrimination law and industrial relations. In 2014-2015 he was presiding over the working group entrusted with preparation of the draft legislation on the new 'social-model' of Lithuania, which also includes the new version of the Labour Code.

proposals which seek a new consensus on balancing the protection of workers with flexibility for employers can hardly be underpinned by well-known traditional arguments on 'austerity' or 'inter-state competition.' However, their context and the rationale behind them may well be explained by national developments and the domestic political agenda. It may also suggest, that a 'crisis-free' environment might provide for a more sober and ideology-neutral ground when modernizing domestic labour legislation in order to keep the labour market prepared for future global and local challenges.

The paper intends to explore the aims and main characteristics of the re-codification of Lithuanian labour law, which started in 2014 and which aimed to be finished in 2017. The first part of the paper presents the origins of the reform and its underlying principles. The second part is devoted to an analysis of the legal provisions of the new Labour Code. First, the author tries to map the structural changes that have a more general or horizontal effect over employment relationships. Later, he outlines the major novelties which have been introduced in the areas of dismissal protection, working time, forms of atypical work, reconciliation of work and family, and vocational training. Particular attention is devoted to changes in the collective representation system which aim to reshape the structure of collective bargaining and the competences of information and consultation.

1. Proposal for re-codification of Lithuanian labour law – just another reform?

Lithuania's transition to democracy with a free market economy started in 1990, but the labour law was only fully re-codified in 2002[1]. The very late adoption of the 2002 Labour Code, (most of the draft text had already been prepared in 1992–1994, but had come to a standstill in the Parliament[2]) had a significant impact on the further development of labour law. The reformist agenda of 1992 was not essentially revised in

1 For details see Davulis T. The Fifth Anniversary of the New Lithuanian Labour Code: Time for Change? In: Blanpain R. (ed.) *The Modernization of Labour Law and Industrial Relations in a Comparative Perspective. Bulletin of Comparative Labour Relations,* Kluwer Law International, 2009, pp. 356–358.

2 Tiazkijus V. Darbo teisės reforma Lietuvoje [The Reform of Labour Law in Lithuania]. In: Davulis T., Petrylaite D. (eds.) *Šiuolaikinės darbo teisės ir socialinės apsaugos teisės problemos* [Problems of Contemporary Labour Law and Law of Social Security], Vilnius, 2009, p. 59.

the preparation of the 2002 Labour Code therefore it lacked ambitions to change the general paradigm of the regulation of employment – it remained rigid and strict with little regard to the economic, social and technological changes that society had undergone in the previous decade.

The structural deficit of the labour legislation lay in the fact that from the onset of the reform labour law regulations were not perceived as an instrument of labour market policy. The debate emphasized the need to restrict the role of the state in the functioning free market and to adapt legislation to the emergence of private employers[3] rather than to foster the creation of new jobs, contribute to the reduction of unemployment, generate youth employment and reduce incentives to work illegally or receive undeclared income. These goals were simply not acknowledged at that time. Moreover, the effectiveness of labour legislation was undermined at the level of enforcement – the formally strong and strict socially protecting legislation was not practically observed at the workplace level[4]. This has had far-reaching implications in the case law – if the legislator lacks the wisdom or political will to introduce necessary legislative changes in order to bring the legislation in line with contemporary changes in the existing work culture, the courts sometimes take the initiative to revise the outdated provisions[5] or to fill the existing gap[6].

---

3 Nekrošius I. Lietuvos Respublikos darbo kodekso rengimo ir įgyvendinimo problemos [The Problems of Preparation and Implementation of the Labour Code of the Republic of Lithuania]. In: *Darbo teisė suvienytoje Europoje* [Labour Law in United Europe], Vilnius, 2004, p. 154.

4 The statement can be underpinned by the simple fact that during the peak of the economic crisis the majority of employment contracts were not terminated on the initiative of the employer (by giving 2 months' notice and with severance payments from 1 to 6 monthly wages) but by the resignation of the employee or mutual agreement, i.e. with employee's refusal to invoke statutory dismissal protection and statutory guaranteed severance payments. See Mačiulaitis V. *Darbo santykių nutraukimas darbdavio iniciatyva nesant darbuotojo kaltės lankstumo ir saugumo aspektu* [Dismissal at the Initiative of Employer in the Context of Flexibility and Security], MRU, 2013, p. 189.

5 Article 141 (3) 2002 Labour Code requires the employer to pay the employee his/her average pay as a sanction for delay in final financial settlement on the day of dismissal. The duration for calculating pay as sanction is not limited by law but the Supreme Court (Ruling of 28 October 2010 of the Supreme Court in Case No. 3K-3-365/2010) mitigated the unrestricted effect of the provision by making the amount of sanction subject to the proportionality test.

6 Attempts to introduce non-competition agreements in the 2002 Labour Code failed in 2003. Shortly after that, the Supreme Court recognized them as an allowed arrangement between the parties of the Contract of employment because the law does not prohibit parties from entering into 'civil law regulated agreements' (Ruling of 22

The Lithuanian practice of having overregulation or exaggerated regulation of the employment relationship has lead to the emergence of a somewhat three-tier system. At the level of legislation (1 tier) we can observe the remaining Soviet tradition that inspired strong individual protection of employees. At the enterprise level (2 tier) employees were left to face the overall impotence of this protection because of the weak collective representation structures and weak administrative or judicial control over the implementation of labour legislation by the employers. The progressing case law (3 tier) contributed to what we can consider the 'third dimension' of the labour law. In individual litigation cases the outcomes started to be unpredictable: when applying the Labour Code, the court may take a loose civil law approach or, on the contrary, enforce the labour law rules formally with a great degree of severity.

The disparities between these three levels of labour legislation reduced the legal certainty and the effectiveness of social protection. Despite all the strictness of the legislation on paper, individual employees found themselves unprotected when wronged by employers. On the other side, individual employers were complaining about the lack of legal certainty, exaggerated social protection and administrative burden and bureaucracy related to the enforcement of labour legislation. The evolution of collective labour law came to a deadlock – even numerous legislative experiments and attempts to boost collective bargaining did not led to the emergence of new agreements and strengthening of collective representation. Finally, with the advancing new technologies, the young generation of employees and new emerging businesses considered the labour legislation superfluous, too clumsy and bureaucratic to be governed by and were seeking civil law solutions instead of employment contracts.

The changes in labour law were advocated in a wide range of questions – from the integration of the new case law into the existing labour law provisions to essential amendments to the collective bargaining system. Lack of flexibility in working time, complexity of recruitment and high redundancy costs were criticized not only by foreign investors and national employers, but (although more reservedly) also by the European Union institutions[7]. The need to adapt Lithuanian labour law to the

October 2007 of the Lithuanian Supreme Court in Case No. 3K-3-415/2007). The permission of those contracts by case law, however, did not solve problems related to the scope and contents of those agreements.

7 Council recommendation on Lithuania's 2014 national reform programme (COM(2014) 416 final), states: 'Review the appropriateness of labour legislation, in

essential changes in the working life and to increase the social protection of employees against new threats of modern economic developments was advocated by academics[8]. Revision of the domestic rules was also desirable from the prospective of EU law – the majority of Directives were implemented even before accession and the practice had shown their deficits and shortcomings.

Overall revision of labour legislation does not seem unreasonable. One should also bear in mind that due to mass protests the conservative Lithuanian Government did not succeed in introducing essential anti-crisis measures in the labour law in 2008-2009[9]. The newly formulated need to re-codify the labour law also emanated from political acknowledgement of the existence of the strong link between labour market regulation and competitiveness of domestic businesses and attractiveness to foreign investment. The labour market reforms in countries such as Estonia, Hungary, Slovakia served, at least at the political level, as examples of possible trends.

In 2014 (in the middle of its term of office) the Social Democrat-led Lithuanian government did not opt for a 'step-by-step' gradual improvement of labour market regulation by way of negotiations on an ad hoc basis – the approach taken by the government since the unsuccessful attempts at reform attempts in 2009[10] – but for a more ambitious integrated approach – overall reform of labour market regulation, including also such areas as state social security and state insurance as well as state support for the unemployed. The idea of combining all three branches of social law does not seem alien to the general idea of 'flexicurity' – to protect employees through more advanced labour market policies and unemployment benefits instead of strict protection of jobs. When combined with social protection, the re-codification

---

particular with regard to the framework for labour contracts and for working-time arrangements, in consultation with social partners.' The recommendations of previous years are worded similarly.

8 Davulis T. Lietuvos darbo teisės modernizavimo perspektyvos [The Perspectives of Modernization of Lithuanian Labour Law]. *Jurisprudencija*, No. 8 (110), 2008, pp. 27–33.

9 Davulis T. Die Entwicklung des litauischen Arbeitsrechts 2009-2010. *Europäische Zeitschrift für Arbeitsrecht*, No. 3, 2011, pp. 427–35.

10 See Davulis T. Lietuvos Respublikos darbo kodekso pakeitimai 2009-2010 metais – besikeičianti darbo teisėkūros paradigma? [Amendments to Lithuanian Labour Code in 2009-2010 – Changing Paradigm of Social Legislation?] In: *Labour market of 21st century: looking for flexibility and security*, TIC, 2011, p. 241.

may gain more credibility, especially when reform of social insurance sought to increase the scope and level of benefits. The comprehensive re-codification of the Labour Code should bring more legal certainty and transparency to the labour market, make legal regulation more balanced and thus foster creation of new and 'better' jobs, offered by new emerging businesses and foreign investors.

Against that background, the Ministry of Social Security and Labour entrusted a consortium of three leading universities to develop research-based legislation in the areas of labour law, state social insurance and state support of the unemployed. The project was called 'social model'[11] and more than 40 legal acts were proposed. A new version of the Labour Code was considered to be crucially important.

The draft labour legislation was prepared by a group of labour law academics and professionals therefore the impact of ideologies and the influence of social partners was in fact rather minimal. The Government quickly approved the draft Code and submitted it to the Tripartite Council – the national level tripartite body of social dialogue, which found consensus on approx 80% of the text of the Code[12]. The political decision on the rest of the text had to be taken by the Parliament.

The general elections were scheduled for October 2016 and the political agenda has had a significant impact on the adoption of the new Labour code. Despite the fact that the working group intended to propose a balanced compromise, in the public eye the new legislation was labelled as 'extremely liberal', 'slavery' and 'anti-social'. Despite the Government's determination to push the reform legislation through as quickly as possible, individual members of parliament submitted more than 600 individual proposals. Most of the proposals were aimed at

---

11 The project started in February 2014 and the legislation proposals were submitted in February 2015. The research materials, proposals and documentation of the project are available (in Lithuanian mostly) under www.socmodelis.lt.

12 At the very beginning, the Tripartite Council, under the presidency of trade unions, refused to discuss the draft labour legislation asserting that the time schedule proposed by the Government was too tight. The Government then submitted the bill directly to the Parliament without receiving the opinion of the Tripartite Council (June 2015). This decision created an unprecedented wave of public indignation, but the legislative process was not locked – the discussions at the Tripartite Council continued in parallel (from March till September 2015) with work in the Parliamentary Committee of Social Affairs and Labour. The compromises agreed at the Tripartite Council were then inserted (March 2016) in the draft bill signed by the leaders of the political parties forming the governing coalition. However, this has not prevented members of parliament from submitting hundreds of other proposals.

bringing back the provisions of the 2002 Labour Code. Trying to achieve a balance in these proposals took more than six months before the Labour Code was adopted on 24 June 2016.

Despite the fact that many agreements were reached at different stages of negotiations on the Code, in public there was overall a very negative opinion on the text of the Labour Code. Even the President, who previously supported the reforms, vetoed the new legislation on the grounds that it 'lacked social sensitivity'. However, the veto was rejected on 14 September and the Labour Code is projected to come into force on 1 January 2017.

As rightly pointed out by political observers, the rejection of the veto and the adoption of the 'liberal' Labour Code was one of the decisive factors for the loss of the ruling social democrat party in the general elections in October 2017. Not surprisingly, the new Parliamentary majority led by the Peasant and Greens union declared the revision of the Labour Code among their first priorities. In December 2016 the entry into force of the new Labour Code was postponed to 1 July 2017 in the hope that the social partners in the Tripartite Council will be able to improve the adopted legislation. However, there is very limited room for possible changes and it is realistic to expect that the new legislation will come into force on 1 July 2017 with only very minimal changes.

2. 2016 Labour Code: new horizontal provisions having horizontal effect

The Lithuanian labour law reform of 2002 could be defined as a structural reform – important transformations had to be adopted to implement labour market principles and international and EU labour standards. The legislator had to decide, for example, about the scope of application of the labour law (wide application to all forms of dependent work or only to employment relationship *stricto sensu* only), the definition and hierarchy of the sources of labour law, the main principles of interpretation and application of labour law rules. The governing principles of a number of institutes to be regulated by the Labour Code had to be revised. Special attention also had to be paid to the core of the national industrial relation system – the model of collective representation of employees.

In contrast, the re-codification of 2016 can hardly be described as a fundamental reform. From the very outset, work on the new legislation began with rectifying the general problems of the labour legislation in force. The working group on the preparation of the new Labour Code (hereinafter – Working Group) has identified seven problematic areas where improvement or change of existing legal regulation was deemed to be crucial:

1) lack of flexibility and security in regulation of individual contracts of employment;
2) stagnation of social dialogue and the absence of collective bargaining agreements;
3) insufficient attention at statutory level to the reconciliation of family and work;
4) ignorance of the necessity of lifelong learning and vocational training;
5) unnecessary administrative burden and bureaucracy when implementing labour law;
6) lack of efficiency in the implementation of the principle of non-discrimination;
7) disregard for the need to differentiate between big and small or medium enterprises[13].

These deficits were not only deficiencies of the existing labour law (we will deal with them in the subsequent chapter). Changes needed to be adopted to modernize the employee–employer relationship in a broader context. The new 2016 Labour Code has learned the novelties which ought to have a general effect. These 'horizontal' provisions are related to an enhanced differentiation of employment relationships (by employer size, type of employment, income of employee) as well as to wider acceptance of technological advances, increased cooperation of the parties and role of procedure-oriented provisions, increased possibilities to access to justice in case of infringements of labour rights.

---

13 Compare these objectives with the declared aims of the Hungarian re-codification of 2012: a) flexibilization of labour law; b) minimum harmonization of EU law; c) approximation of labour law to civil (private) law; d) increasing the regulatory role of contractual source of labour law e) adjustment of the regulation to the needs of small- and medium sized enterprices. See Gyulavari T., Kartyas G. *The Hungarian Flexicurity Pathway – New Labour Code after Twenty Years in the Market Economy.* Pazmany, 2015, pp. 19-20.

2.1 Greater differentiation of labour law rules

Differentiation of employment relationships on various objective and subjective grounds is deemed to be one of the key elements of labour legislation[14]. However, the 2002 Labour Code undermined the practical importance of this principle by setting uniform rules for the vast majority of dependant work relations – there was no differentiation in the duties of the employer irrespective of the size or status of the employer. Only a few types of employment relationship had their own special regulations (fixed-term employment; since 2008 – also temporary workers, domestic workers etc.). A few provisions restricted the discretion of a public employer to grant public employees more generous benefits than the minimum standards provided by the law. In all other aspects the duties and obligations of an employer were stipulated in the same manner and to the same extend for big factories employing hundreds of employees and small entrepreneurs or natural persons employing a few people[15].

The new 2016 Labour Code places greater emphasis on the size of the company. For example, companies employing more than 50 or more than 20 employees start to be subject to more extensive rules on information, consultation and participation. On the other side, small employers (employers with fewer than 10 employees) enjoy reduced administrative burden and greater discretion by applying certain provisions related to annual leave of the employee, duties of notification, dismissal protection (Article 110 of the 2016 Labour Code).

The idea of differentiating employment conditions has been reinforced with the introduction of new types of employment contracts. In addition

---

[14] Nekrosius I. (ed.) Lietuvos Respublikos Darbo kodekso komentaras. I dalis. Bendrosios nuostatos. Kolektyviniai darbo santykiai [Commentary to the Labour Code of the Republic of Lithuania. Part I. General Provisions. Collective Labour Relations]. Justitia, 2003, pp. 34-36; Nekrosius I. (*et al.*) Darbo teisė (Labour Law]. TIC, 2008, pp. 28–29. The principle social legislation (Article 2 of the 2002 Labour Code) allowed to create the legal basis for different sets of provisions (usually called 'guarantees' and 'compensations') for creating special treatment or granting special exceptions for different groups of employees (pregnant women, minors, disabled persons, persons having children or in pre-pensionable age). With the entry into the European Union the majority of those provisions had to be revised on the simple ground that they are not necessarily in line with the dynamic interpretation of the principle of non-discrimination in the European Union.

[15] See also Article 153 (2) b of the Treaty on the Functioning of the European Union which requires that EU directives in the field of labour law shall avoid imposing administrative, financial and legal constraints on the creation and development of small and medium-sized undertakings.

to the already well-known types of employment contracts (indefinite-term, fixed-term, temporary employment contract), the 2016 Labour Code establishes a whole new set of employment contracts – work training contract, two types of new apprenticeship contract, a contract for unforeseen volume of work ('minimum 8 hours')[16], portfolio work contract, job-sharing or employee-sharing contract. The special rules on conclusion, performance and termination of these contracts may increase the chances that participants in the labour market will opt for a legal, suitable and transparent solution when shaping their relationship.

It is interesting to note, that in 2014 there was a proposal from the Ministry of Economy to define a statutory 'good employer', i.e. an employer who has not been sanctioned for disregard of labour law regulations and that ensures a certain level of employee income. It was suggested that those employers might enjoy greater freedom in the conclusion of fixed-term contracts, flexibility of working time etc. At that time this initiative was not successful, but the new 2016 Labour Code introduces the revolutionary deviation *in peius* from the principle of minimum protection provided by law. Pursuant to Article 33 (4) of 2016 Labour Code, the parties to the employment contract with a fixed monthly salary of not less than 2 average (national) monthly gross wage rates are allowed to depart from the mandatory rules established in the Labour Code or other labour law norm. The application of this provision is restricted by two conditions: 1) the agreement may not alter the statutory regulation of maximum working time and the minimum rest period, the conclusion and expiry of an employment contract, the minimum wage, health and safety at work, and non-discrimination, and 2) a balance between the interests of the employer and the employees is achieved by the parties.

The practical implementation of the cited provision promises to be highly problematic not only because it challenges the founding principle that the parties' autonomy shall be restricted on the ground of power asymmetry of the employment relationship. The scope and the content of those agreements remain unclear therefore the parties to individual labour disputes will play a crucial role in recognizing those agreements. The wide discretion of those institutions to define the 'balance of interests' and to decide upon the nature of agreement will trigger countless disputes before the major rules will be settled by case law.

---

[16] The contract for unforeseen volume of work was however abolished by the Parliament just two months after the adoption of the Code.

2.2 Recognition of technological advances in digital era

The relationship between technological development and work organization has a major impact on employment law. Technological progress and the accompanying economic transformations strongly influence the development of both positive law and case law. The dynamism in technological development makes it questionable whether it is possible for the legislator to react in time with the adoption of preventive or protection measures. However, we shall perhaps agree that the framework rules may help employers and employees and their representatives to find a balance between colliding interests. These frameworks may, for example, address the right of employees' representatives to participate in the adoption of internal rules governing the related issues within the enterprise.

To this end the 2016 Labour Code tries to enhance the participation rights of works councils by requiring that information and consultation procedures shall be conducted before establishing internal local rules on a) the procedure for introducing new technological processes; b) the introduction of employee surveillance by means of information, audio and video detection technology; c) the introduction of measures which may prejudice the privacy of employees; d) the introduction of measures which may prejudice the protection of employees' personal data; e) policy of storage of personal data and its implementing measures (Article 206 (1) of 2016 Labour Code).

At the level of individual employment relationship, technological advancement is acknowledged by the important new provision on 'communication' between the parties. Traditionally, the hand-signed document was of principal importance when establishing the existence of the relevant fact or will of the party to the contract. For example, in case of misbehaviour of an employee, the procedural rules required the employer to request the employee to provide a written explanation about the breach of duties after which a disciplinary punishment (again in writing) could be issued. The prominence attached to the signed written documents has penetrated all aspects of working life and increased unnecessary administrative costs. The new general 'communication' clause allows acceptance of data that has been transmitted by commonly used means of information technologies (by email, mobile equipment, etc.), provided that it is possible to identify the information content, its supplier, the fact and time of its submission as well as ensuring that there is reasonable accommodation to preserve the information (Article 25 (2) of 2016 Labour Code). Email, intranet, and mobile communications will be recognized equally as exchange of written documents. In cases where a party to an employment contract raises reasonable doubts regarding these two conditions, the obligation to prove that they exist lies with the employer.

2.3 Increased co-operation of the parties to the contract

The difficulties in complying with the duties imposed by labour legislation can be partially explained by the rigidity of compulsory provisions. This is true especially in cases where working life has changed significantly but the legal provisions are not taking those changes into account. The greater discretion of the parties to shape their relationship by way of mutual agreement seems to be an appropriate instrument especially for the introduction of more flexibility in the workplace. To this end the Labour Code 2016 expressly provides models of possible agreements on part-time or distance work, individually agreed working time regimes, non-competition arrangements or an employer's financial contributions toward the qualifications of an employee. In addition, the new Labour Code reinforces the obligations of the employer to give serious consideration to an employee's proposal to amend their working conditions. For example, the legislation grants any employee the right to request part-time work or to work at home or in job-sharing (and the right to change any contractual obligation or working condition Articles 40 (4), 52, 93, 46 of the 2016 Labour Code. A refusal to satisfy an employee's written request to change the essential or the contractually agreed additional condition of the employment contract shall be reasoned and submitted in writing not later than within five working days of the employee's request. This 'soft' provision makes it easier for the parties to engage in a dialogue with the purpose of being flexible in adapting the contract to their needs.

2.4 Access to justice in case of infringements of labour rights

The system of defence of labour rights has remained shaped by the Soviet tradition for a very long time. Before filing a complaint with the court of civil jurisdiction the law obliged the parties to settle the dispute in bipartite commissions of the enterprise. The Individual Labour Dispute Commission composed of representatives of the employer and elected employee representatives at the level of the workplace proved to be very ineffective. In 2015 the Commissions were reformed to include the State Labour Inspector and two representatives of the regional and branch level organizations of trade unions and employers' organizations. The State Labour Inspectorate was made responsible for the technical and organizational support to the Commission.

The accessibility of the Commission, increased number of cases and quality of investigations are among the positive effects of the reform of individual labour grievances. The 2016 Labour Code continues to improve the legal enforcement of labour rights by making the Commission responsible for the investigation of all labour disputes – cases of dismissal as well as collective labour-law related cases fall within the competence of the Individual Labour Disputes Commissions. The parties may disagree with the decision of the Commission and refer the case to a court of general jurisdiction, but the simplicity of the procedure and the prohibition to award lawyers' fees in case of the loss of a case (Article 217 (3) of the 2016 Labour Code) make access to justice for employees more accessible.

In addition, the rights of employees' representatives were strengthened in the way that Individual Labour Disputes Commission is entitled to impose a fine on the employer in case of breach of the collective type obligation. The amount of the fine shall be proportionate to the gravity of the violation and deter the employer from breaching the law in the future (Article 217 (2) of the 2016 Labour Code).

3. Different areas of Labour Law affected by the novelties of 2016 Labour Code

The re-codification has affected all aspects of labour law. Significant changes were introduced in concluding employment contracts, rest periods and annual leave, employee's liability (for example, Soviet era phenomena such as special 'disciplinary' liability and special 'material' liability of the worker were abolished). Several groups of provisions which may reflect the general features of the new legislation deserve special attention.

3.1 Flexibility and security–changes in dismissal protection and working time

The idea of 'flexicurity' has been widely debated in Eastern European countries where it was accepted more enthusiastically than in the traditional systems of Western Europe. The ideology of 'flexicurity' is suitable for attempts at liberalizing the employment relationship – the negative effects of recalibrating the existing (sometimes rigid rules) may be compensated by the increased level of social protection and social assistance as well as with effective labour market policies. As Roger Blanpain, one of the fathers of European labour law, correctly pointed out, 'flexicurity'[17] is one of those magic words we can agree upon. However, the practical reconciliation of flexibility and security is rather problematic since we deal with vague notions of 'increased level of protection' or 'effective policies' in different branches of law.

The national rules on dismissal protection are among the primary targets of the recalibration measures which are triggered at the national level by the increased need for flexibility and international competition of labour law regimes. The 2016 Labour Code brings certain innovations as far as grounds for the expiry of an employment contract[18], protection of individual groups of employees, formalization of dismissal procedures, and severance payments for employees. The major changes though relate to the costs of dismissal. The notice period has been shortened to one month (if the employment has lasted for less than one year – two weeks)[19] whereas before it varied from a minimum 2 to 4 months. A dismissed employee shall be paid severance pay in the amount of two average monthly wages, and where the employment has lasted for less than one year – severance pay of half the average monthly wage. The 2002 Labour Code provides for more generous payments of from one to six monthly

[17] Blanpain R. Flexicurity in A Global Economy. In: *Labour Market in 21st Century: Looking for Flexibility and Security*. TIC, 2011, p. 19.

[18] 2016 Labour Code adds a new ground for dismissal of an employee on the basis of an employee's underperformance. Pursuant to Article 57 (5) of the Labour Code the results of the employee's work may constitute a reason to terminate an employment contract if the employee does not reach the results which were set in a mutually agreed plan for improvement of the results comprising a period of at least two months.

[19] These notice periods shall be doubled with regard to employees who would reach pensionable age in less than 5 years and tripled with regard to employees who are raising a child (adopted child) up to 14 years or a disabled child up to 8 years; disabled employees and employees who would reach pensionable age in less than 2 years are also included.

wages depending on seniority, but the 2016 Labour Code divides this payment duty between the employer and the special public fund, which has been specifically established to provide a severance payment of from one to three monthly wages to long-time employees.

Furthermore, the employers have been given additional flexibility to dismiss workers even if there is no fault on the part of the employee – if the law does not provide a formal ground for dismissal, but dismissal is necessary, the employer may part from the employee by paying a severance payment of six monthly wages (Article 59 of the 2016 Labour Code). Applying this provision in practice seems to be very problematic because of the difficulties involved in establishing a genuine legitimate ground other than the ground already provided by the existing legal provisions. Perhaps the real objective of this provision is to assist parties in their negotiations on financial compensation – the six monthly wages compensation will serve as a direction for the parties in case of termination of a contract by mutual agreement.

The changes in dismissal protection had to be accompanied by compensatory measures in the area of active labour market policies and financial support for the unemployed. These changes were, however, rather symbolic[20].

As far as the working time is concerned, it should be borne in mind that Lithuania has inherited a detailed and stringent regulation of work and rest time from the Soviet era, which was, in principle, designed for large enterprises. For example, the Labour Code of 2002 did not allow a maximum working time of longer than 48 hours per week, including overtime; overtime was allowed only in very special cases and only 4 hours over two days or 120 hours over a year; it also made it more difficult to change the standard 8 hours per day and 5 working days per week, apply longer reference periods only for uninterrupted production, etc. In this way, the duration of working time and spreading it over a day or a week was regulated in a detailed manner. The European Union directives which were mostly aimed at regulating rest periods were rewritten into the Labour Code without any revisions of the earlier legal rules. Hence,

---

20 The new version of the Law on Social Insurance against Unemployment eased the conditions for qualifying for unemployment benefit (the necessary record of insurance has been decreased to 12 months in a period of 24 instead of the current 18 months in 36 months). The unemployment benefit was increased slightly to 50% of insured income for the first 2 months, 40% for the next 2 months and to 30% for the last two months.

a 'jungle' of double regulation was created where it is difficult to respond to labour demand variations.

In 2016 Labour Code, the concept of rate of working time is introduced; this is distinct from the concept of work time regime. The rate of a working time of 40 hours per week is applied, whereas the work time regime allows flexible distribution of the rate of working time in a working day (shift), week, month or other recording period which may not exceed three consecutive months. The 2016 Labour Code introduces general requirements for the maximum working time and requirements for the minimum period of rest which comprise the requirements for the working time under Directive 2003/88. For example, it is provided that the average working time for each seven-day period, including overtime, but excluding the time of additional work, must not exceed 48 hours, and working time during a working day (shift), including overtime and work under the agreement on additional work, may not exceed 12 hours, excluding a lunch break. These requirements are of a mandatory nature and may not be derogated from by any agreement. The working time of employees working at night is newly regulated in accordance with the requirements of the above-mentioned European directive. The employer may assign an employee to do overtime work not exceeding one hour during the working day (shift) only with the consent of the employee. During a period of 7 consecutive calendar days, an employee may not work more than 8 hours of overtime, unless the employee expresses his/her consent in writing to work up to 12 hours of overtime during a week. When working overtime, the requirements for the maximum working time and minimum rest period may not be violated. As for recording working time, it is agreed to abandon the formal recording of the working time of each employee; instead, it is required to record working time only where there are deviations from the work time regime: overtime worked during public holidays and working time during rest days if it has not been provided for in the work schedule.

3.2 Social dialogue—collective representation, collective bargaining, information and consultation

The system of social dialogue and collective bargaining does not seem to be functioning well in Lithuania. Only 9% of the work force is covered by trade unions and collective bargaining is in general underdeveloped. The Tripartite Council at the cross-industry level has some political importance (e.g. it is involved in setting the minimum wage), but regional or industry-level collective bargaining is almost not-existent. The interaction between employers and employees' representatives is predominately organised at the enterprise level. However, even there the number of agreements is very low because the coverage varies from 5 to 10% of all employees. The rare examples of existing collective agreements are mostly declaratory or have little impact on the actual working conditions of employees. The need for strengthening of incentives for collective bargaining is crucial.

Workshop-level trade unions are non-existent in more than 95% of all enterprises. This therefore means that a great number of employees are left with no collective institutional representation. The 2002 Labour Code allowed the creation the new structures of collective representation in the companies with no trade union presence – works council shall be elected on the initiative of 1/10 of employees and have the rights of collective bargaining, information and consultation. However, the works councils did not become a wide spread phenomenon because of the lack of adequate tradition and mentality[21]. The strengthening of their independent position may help through information and consultation promote industrial democracy at the workplace.

In the 2002 Labour Code the right to collective bargaining and the right to strike at the level of enterprise is based on the principle of single and universal representation of all employees[22]. Various historical reasons lie behind this solution, but following that concept, the legislator requires the employees' representative (trade union or the works council) to have the support of the majority of the employees (including non-members) when concluding a collective agreement or calling a strike at the enterprise level. In this regard, there could be situations where the (minority) trade union would not be allowed to enter into agreement with an employer or would be deprived of the right to take industrial action, if the (majority) trade union or (in the case of an elected works council – works council) had the stronger support of all employees within

21 One should bear in mind that a similar form of employee involvement existed in the Soviet Labour Code which allowed trade union committees (later also a general meeting of employees) enjoy significant rights in supervising the management of an enterprise.

22 Although the local trade unions in an enterprise retained the role of the primary channel of representation of employees, where they did not exist, it became possible to choose among two alternatives – to authorize the branch level trade union to represent the employees of the given enterprise or to elect a works council (Article 19 of the 2002 Labour Code).

the enterprise. Such a situation would not be in line with the established principle of the freedom of collective bargaining which shall be enjoyed by each association.

The 2016 Labour Code tries to redesign the existing system of industrial relations in Lithuania. It suggests introducing a dual channel of employee representation instead of the existing single channel where one body (trade union or works council) enjoys all the rights of collective representation of employees at the company level. Based on the example of Western European countries, the dual model would allow the existence of two autonomous bodies (trade union or works council) with different competences. The trade union would be responsible for collective bargaining while the works council would take over the information and consultation procedures. Following this approach, the law prescribes the obligation to elect works councils in any company or enterprise that has an average of 20 or more employees. The functional duality also means that the works council is henceforth prohibited from engaging in collective bargaining (an exclusive right reserved for trade unions) and consequently the right to strike.

The fundamental rights to collective bargaining and industrial action will be strengthened by way of plurality of trade unions and their enhanced freedom to take action. Firstly, a trade union will have the right to make decisions by itself about the conclusion of a collective agreement, and the support of a general meeting (conference) would no longer be necessary. Secondly, the application of a collective agreement is strictly related to the membership of the organization which concluded it: the collective agreement applies only to the members of the trade unions and employers' organizations that concluded it. This concept justifies the idea that only a direct representative of employees (a trade union) may agree on employee working conditions *in favorem* or, in the framework provided by the law, *in peius*. It is stipulated that a collective agreement applies generally to the employees–members of the trade union that conclude it, however, the other party, the employer, has the right to apply the conditions *in favorem* also to other employees, if the agreement provides so. The possibility to combine *in favorem* and *in peius* principles is established by stating that the norms of collective agreements at a higher level may contain derogations from the conditions laid down in the Code, naturally, with exceptions (e.g. maximum work time and minimum rest time), provided such collective agreements balance the interests of both the employee and the employer. Works councils would enjoy all the rights of involvement in employer's decision making through information and consultation and so-called participation[23].

3.3 New paradigm for the implementation of the principle of non-discrimination

Lithuanian anti-discrimination law is largely shaped by the requirements of European directives. The constitutional principle of equality (Article 29 of the Constitution) is developed in the Act of Equal Opportunities for Men and Women of 1 March 1998 and the Act of Equal Opportunities of 18 November 2003. The principle of equal treatment of all employees on number of grounds[24] were listed among the principles of labour law also in Article 2 of 2002 Labour Code. The Code also contained only limited provisions on equal pay for men and women. The basic rules on the non-discrimination of employees were still consolidated in the above-mentioned special equality legislation, but not in the Labour Code. This could explain why the State Labour Inspectorate and even social partners showed little interest in the enforcement mechanisms – there were no collective agreements nor litigation related to discrimination.

The 2016 Labour Code tries to create more solid ground for practical implementation of the principle. First of all, it aims at easing the access to judicial remedies by stipulating in detail the actions prohibited by an employer and the subjective rights for employees. The description of forms of discrimination, allowed exceptions, clearly defined scope of application intends to inform and to facilitate the bringing of individual or collective claims against the discriminatory practices. The idea is to underline that discrimination cases are not solely an area and responsibility

23 The Law on State and Municipal Enterprises was amended accordingly to introduce the right of works council to appoint 1/5 of the members of the management board. This is a first attempt to provide employees' representatives with participation rights on statutory lev.

24 Lithuanian anti-discrimination law covers equally not only the prohibition of discrimination on grounds provided by the European Union directives 2006/54 (gender), 2000/43 (race and ethnic origin) and 2000/78 (age, disability, religion and belief, sexual orientation) but also nationality, language, origin and social status. The 2002 Labour Code extends the list of prohibited grounds extensively by adding 'all the circumstances unrelated to the employee professional qualities'. However, there is no comprehensive and reliable evidences on how the long list of prohibited grounds influences the practical implementation of the principle – discrimination related cases are very rare.

of the Equal Opportunities Ombudsperson but shall be dealt with at all levels of labour rights protection. The trade unions and the State Labour Inspectorate shall also be more involved in investigations and promotion of equal opportunities. The Individual Labour Disputes Commissions and the courts have to deal with infringed rights of employees, including violated equality rights.

The set of rules however, consolidate proactive measures for the implementation of the principle of equal treatment. First of all, the law requires companies with more than 50 employees to adopt a specific internal document – a policy of equal opportunities (Article 26 of the 2016 Labour Code). The Code is silent on the content and the status of this internal document but it is believed that the adoption of this document (in information and consultation procedures) will not be formal, but will trigger at least discussions on what has to be done to promote equal opportunities at the workplace. Secondly, the Code also requires companies with more than 20 employees to provide anonymised data on the average wages of employees according to gender and profession groups, except those in managerial positions, to works councils and trade unions (Article 23 (2) of the 2016 Labour Code). This information will indicate problematic differences in pay for men and women and which has potentially to be dealt by the social partners. Thirdly, the law also requires companies with more than 50 employees to adopt a remuneration scheme and to make it accessible for employees. The system of remuneration for work shall specify categories of employees according to position and qualification, and the remuneration for each of them, the grounds and procedure for granting additional payment (bonuses and additional pay), the procedure of wage indexing (Article 140 (3) of the 2016 Labour Code).

The new approach to equality and non-discrimination will bring more transparency and subsequently more justice into the Lithuanian wage system which is today defined as very flexible[25].

[25] Pursuant to global statistical data, Lithuania ranks 11th in the world in terms of flexibility in wage determination whereas the labour regulations are among world's most restrictive (place 116 in hiring and firing practices, place 106 in redundancy costs, place 76 in cooperation of labour-employer. Retrieved September 24, 2016 from http://reports.weforum.org/global-competitiveness-index/country-profiles/#economy=LTUwage).

3.4 Reconciliation of work and private life

The balance between work and private life will become a major issue in the years ahead. We will not only be focusing on limiting interventions in private life such as in 'the right to disconnect' (in France, for example, in force since 1 January 2017) in order to disengage employees from the workplace and to make full use of their rest period. Distance work where a employee temporarily provides services away from home creates another set of issues that have to be dealt with in relation to reconciliation. These issues have not been dealt with by the Lithuanian legislator; most of the principles will be created by case law. However, there is one area that stands out in particular, politically and legally – family-oriented working arrangements.

Traditionally, Lithuanian legislation has been heavily loaded with different types of family oriented guarantees. However, already the word 'guarantees' indicates that the legislator is focusing only on the provision of benefits (for example, in the form of paid time off[26]) and restrictions[27] or enhanced social protection measures[28] rather than to the adaptation of work or working patterns to the needs of employees with children. The perfunctory approach to these needs can be demonstrated by the example of how the entitlement of parents to work part time is enforced. Since the part-time regime should generally be agreed by the parties, the legislator imposes on employers the obligation to grant part-time work to some groups of employees (e.g. pregnant woman, parents raising a child until it reaches three years of age or single parents raising a child until the age of 14 years etc. When allowing an employee to request part-time work, the 2002 Labour Code contains no provision on an employer's obligation to consider the reverse request

[26] For example, employees who have two children under the age of 12 are entitled to a so-called 'mama-day' – one paid day off per month. In the case of three children employees are entitled to two 'mama-days'. Of course, these days can also be taken by papas. Both parents may take these days off simultaneously.

[27] For example, an employer is prohibited from dismissing an employee who has a child under three years of age if there is no fault on the side of the employee. An employee with a child under the age of 14 is also entitled to longer notification periods in case of redundancy (4 months instead of 2). They also have priority over other employees for their position.

[28] For example, employees are entitled to parental leave for a maximum period of 3 years. During that period they receive social allowance equal to 100% of their income for the first year or 70% for the first year and 40% for the second year. However, part-time parental leave arrangements are not known in Lithuania.

of an employee, i.e. to return to full-time work after childcare related part-time work. It should also be noted that the 2002 Labour Code does not regulate for an employee's right to request a temporary reduction in working time, to change the working time model, to share their job with another employee (job sharing), to work remotely at home, to choose when to take annual leave etc.

One of the objectives stated for amending the labour code for was to improve the balance between work and family responsibilities. Therefore, the Labour Code entails a set of provisions which aim to provide more flexibility for employees with children rather than guarantee the provision of certain benefits. First of all, the Labour Code consolidates the general principle of the obligation of an employer to respect an employee's family commitments (Article 28 of the 2016 Labour Code). The principle does not serve as a formal declaration. It supposes to oblige an employer to take measures to help the employee fulfil his or her family commitments, except for cases when it is impossible due to specific features of the work or the employer's activities. The employer must consider and give a reasonable response to an employee's requests. The employee's conduct and his actions at work shall be assessed by the employer with the view to practically and effectively implementing the principle of work-life balance. Furthermore, the 2016 Labour Code sets forth that at the employee's request and with the employer's consent, during the working day (shift), an employee may be granted unpaid time off for their personal needs. The parties may agree to move the working time to another working day (shift) without violating the requirements for the maximum working time and the minimum rest period.

The 2016 Labour Code gives better opportunities for specific groups of employees to work on a part-time basis, as well as using teleworking as a form of work organization. An important novelty is the introduction of the possibility to return to work on a full-time basis after working part-time with two weeks' notice. In addition, distance work shall be allowed if requested by a pregnant employee, an employee who has recently given birth, a breast-feeding employee, an employee with a child under three years of age, a single parent with a child under 14 years entail excessive costs due to production necessity or peculiarities of the organization of work, he/she must accept an employee's request to opt for distance work for at least one fifth of their working time. An additional opportunity is connected with the job-sharing scheme: an employee with a child (or adopted child) under seven years of age can opt for this new form of employment contract (where two employees share the same job) as a temporary replacement for an existing employment contract.

These working time arrangements shall be granted on condition that they are possible in light of the organization's circumstances. The practical application of this exception will have to be observed in the near future in the case law of the Individual Labour Disputes Commissions and courts.

3.5 Investment in employee qualifications

Working practices are changing rapidly. Advances in automatization, artificial intelligence, use of information technologies, changes in the whole structure of the modern economy transform how employees work and what type of work will be needed tomorrow or the day after tomorrow. Technological, demographical and social factors are disrupting the existing working pattern of 'one life-one job' and the increasing phenomenon of the 'multi-career' life will require new skills and adaptability. Lifelong learning and the ability to absorb new skills and new opportunities will become vital elements for individual success, quality of employment and sustainability of the labour market.

To leave this issue to self-regulation or the private initiatives of the parties to a contract of employment is not the smartest option in a post-Socialist labour market, where the quality of self-regulation and attention to long-term aims is not well perceived. The more active involvement of the legislator where labour law measures are combined with other incentives (Social security, taxation etc.) is needed.

The new 2016 Labour Code makes some improvements here by providing detailed regulation on compensation for an employer's investment in the qualifications of employees as well as by giving employees the opportunity to request time off or paid time off for the purpose of vocational learning. For example, the parties to the employment contract may make a special arrangement that should an employee leave an enterprise he will reimburse the employer the cost of his training (Article 37 (1) of the 2016 Labour Code)[29]. The incentive to invest in an employee's qualification is promoted with the new provision that if an employer invests in the employee's studies for a bachelor's or

[29] Only the expenses which are related to the provision of knowledge or skills to employees, which exceed the minimum requirements for the work activities, may be compensated. The expenses may be compensated only if they are incurred during the last two years before expiry of the contract.

master's degree and (or) a professional qualification, the parties may agree that the contract can only be terminated at the employee's initiative only after compensation of the employer's expenses[30]. This obligation of the employee remains for the same number of years as his studies were financed by the employer.

If an employee wishes to study at his/her own initiative, Lithuanian labour law already allowed them to request leave for educational purposes. However, the leave was unpaid unless a special arrangement has been reached with the employer. Article 135 of the new Code entitles an employee to five working days per year to participate in non-formal adult education programmes. Such leave shall be granted provided the employer receives at least 20 working days' notice and this leave may be accumulated for no longer than three years. Employees who have worked with the same employer for more than five years shall receive at least half their average wage for 10 days educational leave per working year, if participation in these non-formal adult education programmes is related to improvement of the employee's qualifications.

Conclusions

The rapid evolution of positive law[31] is one of the special features of modern labour law. However, as A.Sobczyk rightly points out, such rapid development is not added value but rather a sign of its weakness. This is one of the reasons why the codification of labour law is still a fairly rare phenomenon and where the codes are introduced – it happened decades later[32]. The Lithuanian 2016 re-codification is a perfect example of such belated legislative activity. The lack of political will to gradually introduce the necessary changes contributed to the significant accumulation of problems which then made it possible to explore the option of a complex solution – the adoption of the new Labour Code alongside amendments to state social insurance legislation. The 2016 Labour Code not only approximates the labour law to current practice and increases the legal certainty but also tries to balance the desired flexibility for business and

---

30 Such obligation of the employee is valid for the same number of years that were financed by the employer.

31 Szubert W, cited by Sobczyk A. Flexibility – Market Expectations and Labour Law Doctrine. In *Labour Market in 21st Century: Looking for Flexibility and Security*. TIC, 2011, p. 67.

32 *Ibid.*, p. 68.

with new forms of protection for employees. Re-codification brings not only changes in working time, dismissal protection and other forms of atypical work. The new Code ought to modernize the employment relationship in a much broader perspective – to revive the spirit of cooperation both at individual and collective level, to increase the judicial protection of employees, to allow for wider acceptance of technologies, investment in human capital and respect for the employee's personal life and his/her family commitments.

Labour Law Reforms in Germany

Manfred WEISS*

Abstract

This paper analyses both individual and collective labour law reforms in Germany. Changes in the regulation of collective bargaining are presented by the amendment on the declaration of general binding collective agreements, the Act on Collective Bargaining Unity, as well as by the introduction of the statutory minimum wage, which has had a strong influence on German collective bargaining. Also, special attention is paid to reforms on the works councils system. In the field of individual labour law, the author considers older reforms on fixed-term contracts and part-time work and their influence on current employment relations. Moreover, the paper focuses on the amendments to temporary work agreements and on the bill proposed to avoid fake independent work.

Key words: labour law reforms, collective bargaining, minimum wage, works council, fix-term contracts, part-time work, temporary work, independent workers.

Introduction

German labour law is particularly characterized by a high degree of stability of the institutional system of collective labour law. The development in this legal area is rather aimed at incremental changes than paradigm shifts. The basic principles of the institutions of collective labour law prove fairly resistant to social change. This applies to the system of collective bargaining as well as to the system of worker' participation, be it the works council system or the system of workers' representation in supervisory boards of big companies.

---

* Manfred Weiss is Professor Emeritus of labour law and civil law at Goethe University of Frankfurt am Main, Germany. He is the author and co-author of many books on individual as well as collective labour law and has published numerous articles on German, European and comparative labour law. Manfred Weiss was a permanent consultant to the International Labour Organization as well as the European Commission. He also served as President of the International Labour and Employment Relations Association (ILERA).

Individual labour law is, of course, closely interrelated with this framework. Stability of collective labour law, therefore, also guarantees to a certain extent stability of individual labour law, even if individual labour law is, to a much greater extent, subject to labour law reform.

Legal change is not only a reaction to domestic developments, but is also significantly influenced by the global interconnectedness of the economy and the striving for European integration. The effects of European requirements on German labour law are of particular interest in this context.

In Germany, modifications in labour law are not only effected by the intervention of the legislator, but quite often also by judge-made law, with the Federal Labour Court (FLC) playing a particular role[1]. Due to its function, this court is often referred to as 'quasi legislator'. However, in this short contribution, the FLC's judgements will only be covered in as far as they led to legislative reforms. The focus almost exclusively will be on legislative interventions since the turn of the century. Instead of describing in detail every change of the law, only the main innovations will be looked at.

Germany does not have a comprehensive labour code, labour law is spread in a multitude of specific topics. Attempts to integrate at least the individual labour law in one code have failed so far. And there is no likelihood that this will change.

According to its importance for the labour law system as a whole the description begins with collective labour law, and then turns to individual law in order to conclude with an attempt at an overall assessment.

1. Collective Labour Law

1.1 Law on Collective Bargaining

1.1.1 The Attempt to stop the Erosion of Sector Agreements

The normal pattern in German collective bargaining are agreements for a whole sector, be it for Germany as a whole or at least for a region[2]. However, in Germany only members of the contracting trade union

---

1 For the basic features of this system see Weiss M. Labour Dispute Settlement by Labour Courts in Germany. *Industrial Law Journal (Johannesburg)*, 1994, pp. 1 et seq.

2 For a detailed description of the system of collective bargaining see Weiss M., Schmidt M. *Labour Law and Industrial Relations in Germany*, Kluwer Law International, 2008, pp. 180 et seq.

employed by a member of the contracting employers' association are covered by the collective agreements. This was not a problem as long as the rate of membership in trade unions and employers' associations was high. In the last decades this rate fell more and more on both sides. The rate of membership in trade unions fell constantly and has only in the last few years reached a stable low point. On the employers' side not only did many – especially medium-sized employers – leave the employers' associations to eschew a binding commitment to collective agreements but also an intermediate form has been established that leads to the same result under the collective bargaining law i.e. membership without a binding commitment to collective agreements. Based on membership without a binding commitment to collective agreements, the companies indeed want to take advantage of the associations' services but get rid of their obligations from collective agreements on employment conditions. After controversial debates the FLC approved the possibility of this type of membership[3].

In practice, employers and non-unionized employees often refer in the individual employment contracts to the collective agreements for the sector, thereby extending the coverage. However, there is first no guarantee that this de facto coverage happens and secondly it is much easier to change the conditions of an individual employment contract than those of a collective agreement.

The law provides a possibility to extend the coverage of collective agreements to non-organized employers and non-unionized employees by way of a declaration of general binding. At first sight, this declaration of general application of collective agreements may appear to be an adequate instrument to stop the decreasing importance of the industry-wide collective agreement. However, the legislator imposed high hurdles for the use of this instrument[4]. General application of collective agreements could be requested only if a minimum of 50% of employees falling within the scope of the collective agreement work for employers with a binding commitment to collective agreements. In addition, a general application of collective agreements can only be enacted by the responsible Federal Ministry and only in the event of prior agreement of a committee of three representatives each from the employers and employees umbrella organizations, and if it is in the general public interest.

---

3 FLC of 18 July 2006, *AP No. 19 to § 2 Collective Agreements Act, Collective Bargaining Competence.*

4 For details see Weiss M., Schmidt M., *op. cit.*, pp. 190 et seq.

By an amendment to the Collective Agreements Act the legislator in 2014 has facilitated the declaration of general binding by removing the requirement of 50% and by defining the general public interest in a way that makes it easier to pass such a declaration. Now the general public interest is to be assumed if the collective agreement has gained main relevance in the sector for which it is made or if the declaration of general binding is necessary to prevent wrong economic consequences. Thereby, the legislator has significantly reduced the discretion of power of the Federal Ministry. Whether this amendment makes a big difference in actual practice, still remains to be seen.

1.1.2 Statutory Minimum Wage as Support for Collective Bargaining

Up to recently Germany did not have a statutory minimum wage. This can be mainly explained by the fact that in the Nazi-Period collective bargaining was destroyed and wage policy exclusively executed by the government. As a reaction to this development, the trade unions and employers' associations after World War II agreed to never again let the state do the job, but made wage policy an exclusive matter for collective bargaining. This historical experience also explains that even the trade unions until recently were against a statutory minimum wage. Their attitude only changed when they saw that due to the already explained erosion of collective bargaining in quite a few sectors decent wages could no longer be guaranteed.

By a law passed in 2014, Germany got a statutory minimum wage of EUR 8.50 per hour, from 1 January 2015. However, until 2017 this minimum wage does not put aside existing collective agreements in which a lower minimum wage is fixed. This still is the case for some branches.

The law established a Minimum Wage Commission which is supposed to propose the appropriate amount of the minimum wage in order to adapt it to new conditions. The commission consists of three members from the trade unions, three from the employers' associations and a chairperson. The ordinary members are appointed by the Federal Government on respective proposals by the Confederation of Trade Unions and the Confederation of Employers' Associations. The term of office for all members is five years. The proposals are made by majority vote. They have to take account of the results of the bargaining round in the respective year.

In addition to the ordinary members of the commission, the Federal Government appoints two persons from the academic world, one proposed by the Confederation of Trade Unions and one by the Confederation of Employers' Associations. These academics have to be independent, neither employed by trade unions nor by employers' associations. They only have an advisory function and are not entitled to vote.

The commission does not meet in public. It has access to external expert knowledge. The commission's proposal fixes the amount of the statutory minimum wage. It is up to the Federal Government whether it wants to turn the commission's proposal into a binding Decree. Referring to the amount, the proposal is binding. The first proposal is to be made until 10 June 2017 in order to become effective on 1 January 2018.

The statutory minimum wage applies to employees and – at least in principle – to persons in internship. However, there are some exceptions, for example for juveniles up to 18 years of age, for persons in the regulated system of vocational training and for newly hired long-term unemployed persons (at least one year unemployment) for the first six months of their employment.

The introduction of the statutory minimum wage is to be welcomed as an important asset in Germany's system of labour law. In spite of pessimistic warnings mainly by economists that it would lead to job losses, it has turned out to not negatively affect the labour market. The big problem still is that the self-employed are not covered by this minimum wage. Since the demarcation line between employment and self-employment cannot be drawn easily, the danger of undercutting this minimum level remains.

1.1.3 Collective Bargaining and Trade Union Pluralism

The Collective Agreements Act does not answer essential questions of collective bargaining law. If, for instance, there are several collective agreements covering the same subject, that means there are competing collective agreements, the act does not tell which collective agreement shall apply. The judiciary resolves this conflict in accordance with the principle of specialty and favours the collective agreement that is more suitable and appropriate for the company[5]. Following this logic the company agreement replaces the industry-wide collective agreement.

[5] FLC of 26 January 1994, *AP No. 22 on Section 4 Collective Agreements Act, Competing Collective Agreements.*

However, the judiciary went even further. Since collective bargaining coverage only applies to the relationship of the members of the contracting trade union with the members of the contracting employer association or the contracting individual employer, it would be generally possible that different collective agreements concluded with different trade unions apply to different employments in the company. However, the judiciary had rejected collective bargaining plurality and postulated, primarily for practical reasons, the principle of collective bargaining unity. An employer was to be bound by only one collective bargaining agreement[6]. Subsequently, thanks to the combination of the principles of specialty and collective bargaining unity, the company agreement replaced the sector collective agreement even if it had been concluded with another trade union. A co-existence of collective agreements in one and the same business was not tolerated.

This much criticised principle of collective bargaining unity did not provide a convincing solution for the case of several competing company agreements concluded with different trade unions. In this case, the principle of specialty as a criterion for the precedence of collective bargaining failed.

In 2010, the Federal Labour Court[7] performed a spectacular U-turn abolishing the principle of collective bargaining unity in favour of collective bargaining plurality. Neither side was amused by this: the employers saw themselves exposed to the potential danger of continuous collective bargaining and strikes, while the trade unions organized within the Federation of German Trade Unions (DGB) felt threatened by the implied upgrading of the specialised unions representing individual occupational groups. This led to a unified approach of the Confederation of German Employers' Associations (BDA) and the Federation of German Trade Unions (DGB), who produced a jointly developed draft law which was not only to lay down the return to the principle of collective bargaining unity, but also to replace the principle of specialty by the principle of majority. Hence, the trade union, which had more members in the company, was to prevail. Thus, the radius of action of competing trade unions would be significantly limited and their possibilities to go on strike largely eliminated. In spite of irritations between the DGB trade unions, the DGB continued to support the project. The political parties forming the present Government agreed in

6 FLC of 20 March 1991, *BAGE* 67, pp. 330 et seq.

7 FLC of 7 July 2010, *Neue Zeitschrift für Arbeitsrecht*, 2010, pp. 1068 et seq.

the so-called coalition treaty to pass a law according to the indicated lines. This law was passed in summer 2015. However, it is attacked by the trade unions representing specific professional groups. They argue that this law violates the constitutionally guaranteed freedom of association. The case is presently pending at the Federal Constitutional Court (FCC). The outcome of the lawsuit cannot be predicted.

1.2 The Works Council System

Workers' participation by works councils has a long tradition in Germany[8]. It is considered by many to be the backbone of German industrial relations, regulated by the Works Constitution Act. This law was amended in 2001 aimed at also encouraging the law's breakthrough in small and medium-sized enterprises, adapting the traditional structure of the works council system to the change in company and business reality, improving the effectiveness of the works council activities and extending its rights. Here only the essential changes are to be sketched[9].

Although the law provides that a works council may be elected in establishments with five employees upwards most small and medium-sized companies have no works council. The reasons for this are manifold. They range from a lack of information to the fear of competitive disadvantages employers convey to their staff because, unlike major companies, the necessary know-how must be acquired from external providers which might lead to unforeseeable cost increases. In order to remedy the deficiency, the amendment significantly simplified the electoral procedure for businesses with up to 50 employees and at the same time allowed to extend this simplified procedure to businesses with up to 100 employees by concluding an agreement between the electoral board and the employer. It was foreseeable that this amendment would have only moderate success, the electoral procedure not being the major reason for the low coverage rate.

The different provisions for white- and blue-collar workers were eliminated by the amendment, thereby implementing an overdue correction. At the same time, the composition of the works council was

8 For a detailed description of the system see Weiss M., Schmidt M., *op. cit.*, pp. 222 et seq.

9 For further details see Weiss M. Modernizing the German Works Council System: A Recent Assessment *The International Journal of Comparative Labour Law and Industrial Relations*, 2002, pp. 151 et seq.

changed so that the gender that accounts for a minority of staff must be at least represented proportionally whenever the council consists of three members or more. In addition, the amendment concludes that tele-workers are considered employees in the sense of the law and temporary agency workers may also participate in works council elections if they have worked for the business for more than three months.

The system of works councils is earmarked for conventional businesses and companies with a clear hierarchy which are increasingly less common in reality. It is therefore of special importance that the amendment has provided a regulation allowing to adapt the structure of the works constitution to the change. The collective bargaining parties are now endowed with manifold regulatory powers. In multi-branch companies, uniform works councils can be established or multiple branches grouped together if this helps to represent the interests of the employees more efficiently. In companies and groups with product or project-specific business branches, branch-specific works councils can be set up for the same reason. For better representation of the interests of the employees, alternative or additional structures can also be established at all levels. Without going into further detail, it becomes evident that collective agreements allow to take account of the needs of an increasingly complex reality. Nevertheless, the complexity of the rules often seems to overstrain the actors.

With a view to increasing the effectiveness of the activities of the works council, the amendment brings several changes. For example, it is made clear that information and communications technology are part of the equipment of the works council to be made available by the employer. The possibility to exempt a works council member from normal work duties in establishments with 300 employees was lowered to establishments with 200 employees and also the popular partial releases of works council members were implemented. The works council's right to draw on competent employees as experts was expressly stated if required for proper performance of tasks. The fact that in the context of operational or organizational changes a works council may, without further conditions, draw on an expert of its choice in establishments of more than 300 employees is of significant importance in practice. Prior to the amendment, works councils were not allowed to delegate tasks to committees, except in businesses with more than 300 employees. This number has been reduced to 100.

A key part of the amendment is the extension of the works council's rights. The focus in this context is on a new regulation which assigns the works council a major role in safeguarding and promoting employment. The works council cannot only make suggestions (e.g. with regard to flexibility in working time, the promotion of part-time work and progressive retirement, new forms of work organization, operating procedures and sequences, qualification of employees, outsourcing or contracting out work to other companies as well as production and investment programmes), but the employer is also obliged to discuss these suggestions with the works council. Rejection of the suggestions shall be justified, in establishments with more than 100 employees even in writing. Although this is not yet a right of co-determination, the employer must embark upon the suggestions submitted by the works council. Since he relies on a good relationship with the works council with regard to the co-determination in quite a few other matters, a prudent employer is well advised to avoid a reckless rejection of such suggestions.

The amendment furnished the works council with an additional right of co-determination with regard to the provision and execution of vocational training for employees who lack the necessary qualifications for their functions because their work has changed or will change as a result of measures implemented or planned by the employer. The catalogue of rights of co-determination already listed in the law was further complemented in reference to principles for execution of teamwork. This was to adapt the rights of the works council to a modern work organization where teamwork plays an increasingly important role.

To conclude, it can be said that the amendment with its numerous corrections has only incrementally adapted the works constitution to new facts but not changed the basics.

2. Individual Labour Law

2.1 Fixed-Term Contracts

The deregulation of fixed-term contracts started already in 1985. Until then fixed-term contracts only where allowed if there was a specific justification. In order to fight unemployment by an Act of 1985 fixed-term contracts were allowed without any precondition for newly hired employees for a maximum period of two years. Since the legislator was not sure what consequences this new law might have, its life-span was limited to five years. Even if the factual impact remained to be controversial, it was renewed twice, each time for another five years. Finally, in 2001 a permanent Act further confirmed the deregulation of fixed term contracts. Unconditional fixed-term contracts are not only allowed for newly hired persons for up to two years but can be split in three portions. For newly founded companies the possibility of unconditional fixed-term contracts is extended to a maximum of four years. The conclusion of such a fixed-term contract, however, is invalid if an employment relationship with the same employer, be it of limited or of unlimited duration, has ever existed before. According to the Act 2001 this means that it is completely irrelevant how much time has passed since the first employment relationship. However, the FLC has modified this rule, forbidding such fixed-term contracts only if the former employment was within the last three years before hiring.

For any fixed-term contract beyond the maximum limit explained above a specific justification is required, as it was before 1985 for all fixed-term contracts. There is, however, an exception for elderly employees. If they are at least 52 years old and, directly before being hired, were unemployed for at least four months, a fixed-term contract up to a maximum period of five years – be it in one row or split in several parts – can be concluded. A former more extended version of this exception was considered by the Court of Justice of the EU (CJEU) to be invalid[10].

2.2 Part-time work

2.2.1 The right to part-time work

Part-time work is regulated in the same Act of 2001 as fixed-term contracts. The most important innovation in this Act is the employee's right to reduce the agreed working time, the so-called right to part-time work[11]. The right to part-time work was introduced to promote job creation and to contribute to equal employment opportunities for men and women. The right to part-time work applies if only two conditions are fulfilled: an employee must have been continuously employed for

---

[10] For a comment on this judgment see Schiek D. The ECJ Decision in Mangold: A further twist on effects of directives and constitutional relevance of Community equality legislation. *Industrial Law Journal*, 2006, pp. 329 et seq.

[11] For details see Schmidt M. The Right to Part-Time Work under German Law: Progress in or a Boomerang for Equal Employment Opportunities? *Industrial Law Journal*, 2001, pp. 335-351.

more than six months by an employer employing more than fifteen employees. Small employers are released from the organizational and administrative burdens resulting from the right to part-time work. The right to part-time work is applicable to employees of any category, be it full-time, part-time, temporary, or fixed-term employees. The right to part-time work also applies to employees in managerial positions.

The employee has to request the reduction of his or her agreed working time and to specify the volume of the reduction at least three months in advance. Reasons for the employee's request do not have to be given. The three-month period shall give the employer sufficient time to provide for organizational arrangements. Voluntary agreements to reduce the working time can, of course, still be concluded at any time. The law furthermore stipulates that the employee shall, together with the request to reduce the working time, inform his or her employer of the requested distribution of the reduced working time, i.e. from when to when the employee would like to work. The employer is obliged to discuss the requested reduction of working time with the employee, explicitly with the aim of reaching an agreement. Employee and employer shall furthermore reach an agreement about the distribution of the working time. This demonstrates the legislator's hope that the parties to the employment contract will usually voluntarily agree to reduce the working time. If such an agreement is reached, the employment contract changes accordingly. If no agreement can be achieved, the employer nevertheless has to grant the requested reduction of working time and to determine the distribution of working time in accordance with the employee's wishes, provided that there are no conflicting 'operational reasons'. The Act explicitly states that operational reasons may in particular be found if the reduction of the working time interferes considerably with the organization, the course of work or the safety in the establishment, or if the reduction of working time causes disproportional costs. According to the case law of the FLC,[12] the existence of 'operational reasons' has to be tested in three steps:

1. First of all the organizational concept, developed and executed by the employer, and underlying the regulation of working time regarded as operationally necessary has to be identified;
2. Then it has to be verified whether the regulation of working time resulting from the organizational concept in fact conflicts with the reduction of working time desired by the employer;

---

12 Fundamentally FLC of 18 February 2003, *AP No. 2 § 8 Act on Part-Time and Fixed Term Contracts*.

3. Finally, it has to be examined whether the conflicting operational reasons are so grave that the implementation of the employee's desire to change the working time would considerably interfere with the mentioned conditions.

In spite of the rather complicated technicalities, the right to part-time work normally does not create problems. Unfortunately, there is only a right to reduce the agreed working time. There is not yet a respective right to go back afterwards to full time. Only if there is a vacancy does the part-timer have to be given preference if he or she so wishes. The present government, however, has indicated the willingness to soon establish such a right of part-timers to return to full time.

2.2.2 Marginal Part-Timers

The 2001 Act also applies to marginal part-time employees who are excluded from the statutory systems of social security. This category is very problematic. The exclusion from the system of social security contains an incentive for employers and employees. Employers pay less contributions to the social security system and for employees – at least in a rather dangerous short-term perspective – gross wage means net wage.

If the monthly remuneration for any employment is less than EUR 450, the job is a so-called 'mini job'. Persons employed in a 'mini job' are excluded from the statutory systems of social security, irrespective of the number of weekly working hours worked. The employer has to pay only a low rate of social security contributions for any 'mini jobber' plus low flat-rate taxes of 2%. The employee performing a 'mini job' is neither obliged to pay statutory social security contributions nor taxes on the income resulting from the 'mini job'. Nor is he or she entitled to benefits from the statutory systems of social security. He or she can, however, opt to pay voluntarily which in actual practice never happens.

This regulation has led to a dramatic increase in 'mini-jobs'. For a large majority of them it was the only source of income which meant that they needed social assistance in addition to make a living. Thereby, the unemployment rate was significantly decreased. But nevertheless this pattern particularly by the trade unions is considered to be a scandal. The claim to re-integrate the 'mini jobbers' into the social security system and treat them in the same way as all other employees, although supported by many groups, has not yet been successful. However, recently the number of 'mini jobs' has been reduced significantly due to the statutory minimum wage. It transpired that 'mini jobbers' in most cases did not even earn the hourly minimum wage and have now become less attractive for employers. Due to the booming labour market in Germany this fortunately has not led to an increase in unemployment but to a significant increase of jobs covered by social security.

2.3 Temporary Agency Work

In Germany temporary agency employment is structured as follows: the temporary employee has a normal contractual relationship with an employer (hirer-out), usually a so-called temporary employment agency[13]. The hirer-out assumes any of the usual employer's duties. Different from a normal employment relationship, both parties agree that the employee will be regularly hired out to a third party (user), where he or she is to perform work. The period for which a temporary employee can be hired-out to a user (originally three months) has been extended constantly. It was not allowed to hire the temporary employee only for the time to be hired out to a user (prohibition of synchronization). Temporary agency work was forbidden in the construction industries.

There are contractual relationships between hirer-out and user on the one hand, and between hirer-out and temporary employee on the other hand, but there is no contractual relation between temporary employee and the user for whom the employee is working. Hence, the temporary employee receives his wages from the hirer-out. Nevertheless certain duties as regards work performance are incumbent on the temporary employee towards the user; the user also has some rights and duties towards the temporary employee. The law aims at an effective control of the operation of temporary work and, at the same time, at a minimum protection of the temporary employees as to employment conditions and social security. The temporary agency needs a licence which only can be granted under certain restrictive conditions.

The original legal framework of 1972 was modified by quite a few amendments. The most significant change happened by an amendment of December 2002, in force since 1 January 2003. The driving force behind this amendment was the idea to develop a tool to decrease the amount of unemployment by facilitating temporary agency agreement and at the same time improve the conditions for temporary employees.

---

[13] For a detailed description of the system see Weiss M., Schmidt M., *op. cit.*, pp. 64 et seq.

The amendment abolished the prohibition of synchronization and the maximum amount of time to be spent in the user's enterprise. Thereby, the hiring-out enterprises' chances to obtain a licence and to act in a more flexible way have increased significantly. The amendment has not totally abolished the prohibition of temporary work in the construction industries but significantly facilitated it. In addition the use of temporary work employees between enterprises of the construction industries has been further facilitated, in particular in view of enterprises of the construction industries seated in other Member States of the EU and hiring-out temporary work employees to German enterprises in the construction industries. In addition, the hiring-out enterprises as well as the user-enterprises have been liberated of some administrative duties.

The trade-off for this far-reaching deregulation was the equal treatment of temporary work employees as comprehensively and as early as possible. According to the respective section of the statute, the temporary work employee is entitled 'for the time of his or her stay in the user enterprise to the same essential working conditions, including remuneration, of comparable employees in the user's enterprise'. Remuneration is to be understood in its broadest sense, including fringe benefits etc.

The principle of equal treatment did not apply for the first six weeks 'if the temporary work employee was previously unemployed and is paid by the hiring-out enterprise a net remuneration of at least the amount he or she received from the unemployment insurance'. This, however, does not apply if at any time in the past there has been an employment relationship between this temporary work employee and the same hiring-out enterprise. Much more important was the second exception: the equal treatment principle does not apply if a collective agreement allows for a different treatment. This shifted the responsibility for the final pattern which will be relevant in actual practice to the social partners, to the trade unions and the employers' associations and/or the individual employers. There was no restriction to the scope of deviation from the principle of equal treatment by collective agreement. As indicated collective agreements in Germany only apply to those employees who are unionized and are employed by an employer who either is member of the concluding employers' association or party of the collective agreement. All others are not bound. However, according to the amendment employers and temporary work employees who are not bound by such a collective agreement are entitled to extend its content by so-called reference clauses in the individual employment contract.

If the hiring-out agency is not fulfilling its duties in reference to the essential working conditions, the temporary work employee is entitled to claim these conditions from the user. In addition to the written information already to be given, the hiring-out enterprise has to provide written documentation also on 'the kind and amount of remuneration and other working conditions for periods in which the temporary work employee is not working in a user enterprise'. The user is obliged to include in the written contract with the hiring-out enterprise information on the essential working conditions, including remuneration, of comparable employees in the user's enterprise. Finally the temporary work employee is entitled to claim this very same information from the user.

Due to this amendment of the law the focus was on collective bargaining. After the amendment collective agreements with trade unions belonging to the DGB were concluded fixing the amount of remuneration at around 80% of the equal treatment level. The trade unions did not negotiate as a separate group but jointly as a bargaining team. However, these collective agreements were undercut by collective agreements concluded with a marginal trade union movement, the Christian Trade Union (CTU), fixing the level below 60%. Since the unionization rate in this sector is rather low, the reference clauses in individual employment contracts became important. And in most cases reference was made there to the collective agreements concluded with the CTU. However, in Germany trade unions do have to meet specific requirements to be allowed to conclude a collective agreement. Most important in this context is the requirement of sufficient power to exert pressure on the employers' side. The necessity of sufficient power is based on the assumption that proper functioning of the autonomous system of collective bargaining would be undermined if powerless trade unions were allowed to participate in collective bargaining. Today a trade union is considered to possess the necessary power if it is taken seriously by the employers' side[14]. When this requirement is met, is difficult to decide. According to the Federal Labour Court (FLC) all circumstances of the respective case have to be taken into account[15]. The number of members is an important indicator. However, as the FLC emphasizes, a small number of members may be sufficient if the ability to exert sufficient pressure on the employers' side results from the fact that the trade union's members are specialists who work in key positions and, in

---

14 For details on these requirements see Weiss M., Schmidt M., *op.cit.*, pp. 183 et seq.

15 FLC of 14 December 2004, *AP No. 1 § 2 TVG Collective Bargaining Competence.*

case of industrial action, cannot or can only be replaced with difficulty at short notice. The uncertainty of this criterion shows the wide range of the FLC's leeway in allowing or preventing a trade union to participate in collective bargaining.

By a judgment of the FLC of 2010[16] it was denied that the Christian trade unions have sufficient power to be an actor in collective bargaining. This led to the effect that all these collective agreements are null and void which implies that the temporary agencies have to repay the workers also for the past difference between the wages fixed therein and equal pay. And they also have to repay social security contributions for this difference to the social security authority.

The sketchy overview of the situation as it was since 2003 should be sufficient to show that already before the transposition of the EU Directive on Temporary Agency Employment the concept of the German law on temporary agency work was very much in line with the Directive. Nevertheless, a few innovations have been introduced by the transposing amendment which are rather important.

The already mentioned prohibition of temporary agency work in the construction industry has remained. It is very doubtful whether this restriction can be justified under the EU Directive.

One of the big problems in Germany lay in the fact that to an ever bigger extent temporary agency workers receive an assignment for an indefinite time, thereby substituting employees in the user company. This was strongly opposed by the trade unions. Now in line with the Directive, German law now specifies that the temporary agency worker only can be assigned to a user company 'temporarily'. Thereby, it has become clear that a timely unlimited substitution for employees of the user company is no longer possible. Nevertheless this notion has become the by-far most discussed topic[17]. The interpretation of 'temporarily' has become difficult since the legislator has not put a maximum limit into the law. There is only consensus that the assignment has to be for a limited time. In November 2015 the Federal Government presented a bill, already amended in February 2016, to further specify the law according to which the maximum time to be hired-out in a user company would be 18 months. If between two engagements of the same temporary

---

[16] FLC of 14 December 2010, *Arbeit und Recht,* 2011, pp. 41 et seq.

[17] See for example Zimmer R. Vorübergehender' Einsatz von Leiharbeitnehmerinnen. *Arbeit und Recht*, 2012, pp. 422 et seq.

employee with the same user there is not a gap of at least six months, the former period is to be fully added in the counting of the 18 months. The period can be extended by a collective agreement or by a work agreement between the works council and employer if it is permitted by a collective agreement. If the maximum period is exceeded an indefinite employment relationship between the temporary employee and the user company is presumed if within a month the temporary employee does not declare that he or she is not interested in such a relationship. The proposal is highly controversial since it focuses on the individual engagement, thereby allowing continuous rotation with other temporary workers.

The equal treatment pattern already existing before in German law has been kept. But the exception for the first six weeks if the temporary work employee was previously unemployed has been abolished. In line with the Directive the derogation by collective agreement is possible, as before. However there is now a minimum level to be respected.

The possibility to derogate from the principle of equal treatment by collective agreement, however, is excluded for the case mentioned in the beginning of this contribution. If an employee's employment relationship in a company is terminated and the same employee is hired out to this same company by a temporary work agency within less than six months, there is no possibility to derogate the principle of equal treatment by collective agreement. The same applies if the employee's employment relationship is terminated and the same employee is hired out to a company which is part of a group with the original company where the employee was employed. In such a case equal treatment applies for the whole time of the assignment, even if there is a derogating collective agreement. Thereby a strategy whereby companies simply exchange the status of employees to save costs is prevented.

As mentioned above unionization of temporary agency workers always has been and still is marginal. Therefore, the still existing possibility of extending the derogation to non-unionized temporary workers by reference clauses in individual employment contracts is the decisive instrument. It is however, doubtful whether this possibility of extension by an instrument of individual labour law is in line with the spirit of the Directive[18]. If the CJEU were to consider it to be a violation

18 For a discussion of this problem see Waas B. A Quid pro Quo in Temporary Agency Work: Abolishing Restrictions and Establishing Equal Treatment – Lessons to be learned from European and German Labour Law? *Comparative Labor Law & Policy Journal*, 2012, pp. 47 et seq. (59 et seq.).

of the Directive, the possibility of derogation from the principle of equal treatment would have almost no practical effect in Germany.

According to the mentioned bill for an amendment the possibility to derogate from the principle of equal treatment by collective agreement only applies up to nine months of the engagement of the temporary employee. The period can be extended to 15 months under very specific conditions.

On the whole one can say that the position of the temporary agency workers has been improved compared to the situation after 2003.

2.4 Independent Workers under Civil Law

Due to the stricter regulation of temporary agency work employers prefer to an increasing extent to contract with independent workers. They are governed by civil law and not by labour law. And they are not integrated into the social security system. The problem, however, is that there is a suspicion that many of the independent workers in fact are employees and that the recourse to these fake independent workers is nothing else but an intolerable abuse of legal categories. Therefore, the trade unions are fighting against this fake independent work, trying to bring these persons under the umbrella of labour law and social security law. This claim has now been taken up by the Federal Government in the already mentioned bill of law.

The bill defines the employment contract as a relationship in which the employee who provides services is integrated in an organization of somebody else and has to obey orders. If the wording of the contract and the factual performance contradict each other, the factual performance is relevant for the legal categorization. Thereby, the result of the case law of the FLC would be taken up by the legislator. However, the original version of the bill went further and listed indications according to which a person is supposed to be integrated in an organization of somebody else and has to obey orders. This has to be assessed by a comprehensive view of such indications which, of course, would give the courts enormous power of discretion. According to this list a presumption for an employment relationship would be indicated if the person (a) is not free in shaping his or her working time or his or her work or in determining the location of work performance; (b) performs the work mainly in the premises of the organization; (c) regularly uses someone else's equipment for performing the work; (d) performs the work in cooperation with other persons recruited by somebody else; (e) exclusively or mainly works for the organization; (f) does not have an organization of his or her own to perform the work; (g) performs work which is not meant to reach a specific result; (h) does not guarantee the result of his or her work. This met with strong resistance from the employers. Therefore, the revised version of the bill abandoned this list of indicators and states that an overall view of all circumstances decides whether there is an employment relationship. This very vague formula would shift the responsibility to the courts as is already the case today.

It is much too early to predict whether the bill will soon become law and what this law will look like. It may well be that it will significantly change during the deliberations in the Federal Parliament.

Conclusion

This short 'tour d'horizon' through the essential recent reforms of German labour law does not cover comprehensively all the minor changes, the most important of which happened in dismissal law. The Act on Protection against unfair Dismissals formerly only excluded small establishments of up to five employees. This figure has been extended to 10 employees which worsens job security for a huge number of employees. Of course, discriminatory dismissals and dismissals in the context of transfer of undertakings, each regulated by EU law, are not affected by this exclusion. And there is generally a certain although lower degree of job security also for the employees in the excluded establishments which has been developed by the labour courts. Another area of reform not explicitly treated in this paper is the area of parental leave where significant improvements have been made in different steps[19].

Taking everything together it becomes evident that labour law reform in Germany so far not only means deregulation but to a great extent reregulation, stabilising the already existing protective scheme. In particular the institutions of collective labour law have remained relatively stable and have even been strengthened by recent amendments of the law. A very important stabilizing factor is the recent introduction of a comprehensive statutory minimum wage.

---

19 For details see Weiss M. Work-Life Balance: The German Experience. In: Mella Méndez L., Serrani L. (eds.) *Work-Life Balance and the Economic Crisis.* Cambridge, 2015, pp. 59 et seq.

Even if – as stated in the introduction – the institutions of collective labour law are surprisingly stable, a legally unresolved fundamental issue remains – the fact that no works councils exist in many small and medium-sized businesses despite the amendment of the Works Constitution Act of 2001. However, whether and how this deficiency can be removed by state intervention is questionable. A high degree of regulatory resourcefulness would be needed here. At any rate, a quick solution is not to be expected. The metalworkers trade union has just started a campaign to integrate at least all establishments of a minimum of 50 employees into the works council system. Thereby, the still existing segmentation of the labour market between big business and small and medium-sized businesses may at least be decreased.

The problem of labour law reforms in Germany is the fact that they are not an expression of a consistent, well-planned strategy but more or less the outcome of reactions to upcoming needs on the labour market. On the other hand, it has to be stressed that the legislator very seldom acts just on its own initiative, but shapes reforms on the basis of an ongoing informal but intensive dialogue with the social partners. In particular, as the attempts to codify the individual labour law into a comprehensive code have shown, a reform against the opposition of both sides of industry, employers' associations as well as trade unions, would be unthinkable.

The Battle about Labour Law Reforms and the Long and Winding Road towards the Competitiveness Pact in Finland (2015-2016)

Niklas Bruun*

Abstract

This paper presents the efforts to reform the labour laws in Finland during the governance of the new conservative national government that took power in spring 2015. The first year of this government has been marked by efforts to introduce changes in labour law in order to increase employment, reduce labour costs and increase flexibility on the Finnish labour market. The strategy of the government was to threaten the trade unions with harsh reforms in order to put pressure on the trade unions to agree with the employers' organizations on a so-called Competitiveness Pact. This Pact was finally concluded in June 2016, but the proposed legislative measures and the criticism they received for being incompatible with international labour standards (ILO-Conventions, EU-law and the European Social Charter) is of general interest and is presented in this article.

Key words: Competitiveness pact, labour law reforms, flexibility, international labour standards, free collective bargaining

Introduction

Finland got a new government in spring 2015 after the parliamentary elections. The government that was formed is a three party coalition government consisting of the Centre Party (*Keskusta*), the Conservatives (*Kokoomus*) and the True Finns (*Perussuomalaiset*). The government is often described as the SSS-government due to the initial letter in the

* Niklas Bruun LL.D., Finland, is professor of Law at the Hanken School of Economics in Helsinki. He is the Director 2009-2016 of the research programme Regulating Markets and Labour (ReMarkLab), Stockholm University where he holds a position as Guest Professor. He is an expert in labour law including equality law and intellectual property law and has published several books and articles in these fields. He has been entrusted with many missions regarding the preparation of legislation in both Sweden and Finland. He has been a member of the Freedom of Association Committee ILO and a member of the CEDAW Committee (UN) 2009-2016.

names of the party leaders of the parties involved (Juha Sipilä, prime minister, Alexander Stubb, minister of finance and Timo Soini, foreign minister). The government became the SOS-government when Petteri Orpo became party leader of the Conservatives in June 2016 after having defeated Alexander Stubb in the leadership election. He then took over as the minister of finance. All the political left wing parties (the social democrats and the socialists) as well as the environmental green party are in political opposition.

In its programme for government and as its declared main targets the government emphasized that it wants to restore the lost international competitiveness of the Finnish economy which is performing poorly due to the collapse of the NOKIA conglomerate and the difficulties in exports to Russia due to problems in the Russian economy as well as to the EU trade sanctions. The government wanted to make a 5% cost reduction in labour market or wage costs for Finnish companies and it declared that if the labour market parties are not able to reach consensus on how to introduce such a cost reduction the government will propose such changes in the labour legislation that these savings will be achieved. The prime minister asked the labour market parties (trade unions and employer organizations) to start negotiations on a national labour market package in order to achieve the savings and gave a short time limit for the negotiations. When the negotiations did not deliver results, the government presented first in August 2015 a general outline for reforms, and then later in autumn 2015, its own legislative package for labour law reform in the form of draft proposals for new legislation[1].

According to these proposals the Government intended to shorten annual leave, eliminate two bank holidays, make the first day of sick leave unpaid and cut extra pay for working overtime and on Sundays. In particular, the government announced that it would introduce new legislation that sets the maximum limits of what can be agreed collectively by collective agreements in certain cases.

The trade unions disapproved strongly of the proposals and argued that the government was interfering dangerously in the right of labour market organizations to make their own agreements. The three Finnish trade union confederations organized a large joint demonstration against

---

[1] The final draft legislative proposal was presented on 11 November 2015 and sent on a broad hearing. Some law professors were included in the list of those whose views the government wished to get. The author was included among these and his views were submitted 15 December 2015.

the government plans on Friday 18 September 2015 in Helsinki. During this day employees left work and went out to demonstrate against the proposed legislation. The demonstration brought 30,000 people to Helsinki in spite of heavy rain. The main message was to defend the unions' rights with regard to free collective bargaining and protest against austerity measures planned by the Government.

Furthermore and in parallel with this package the government announced that it intended to promote local negotiations and local agreements in order to increase flexibility on the labour market. These measures were prepared by a special investigator who was mandated to prepare legal reforms in this regard[2].

In the following article, I will present the proposals made and the debate around these measures which are very radical not only in a Nordic, but even in a European perspective. In June 2016 it became clear that the proposed legislation would not be introduced, but withdrawn and the harsh legal reforms were partly seen as having the intention to put pressure on the trade unions to agree voluntarily on reduction of existing benefits. The negotiation on collective agreements implementing some general guidelines from the central social partners was ongoing during the spring. The Competitiveness Pact was finally signed on the evening of 14 June 2016. Most of the Finnish unions endorsed the Pact and when it was signed it covered 86.5% of Finnish wage and salary earners.

This Competitiveness Pact has been the main issue in Finnish politics for more almost a year. The government was determined to cut costs for employers and forced trade unions to accept a deal that makes everyone work 24 hours more a year for the existing rates of pay. However, the Finnish debate concerning legislative reforms raised some fundamental questions regarding the limits of the power of the legislator and I think it is of general interest to reflect on these issues in a seminar discussing labour law reform. It is also clear that the reform plans reflected an opinion strongly represented in the government that wanted to use legal means in order to limit the power of trade unions and the Finnish labour market system, and as an alternative strengthen the role of the political system and players in this regard.

---

2 See further below.

1. The main content of the labour law package

The government justified its legislative plans by stating that in order to secure the citizens' constitutional social and cultural rights, as well as the right to work (the expressed legal grounds of the bill), the state must improve the competitiveness of the open sector of the economy. The government argued that only in this way could domestic economic growth be provided. In order to achieve this goal the government argued that it was necessary to boost the competitiveness of the export sector by cutting (lowering) certain terms and conditions of employment. The draft law proposal notes Denmark, Estonia, Germany, Norway, and Sweden as 'central competing countries' which reflects the idea of gaining competitive advantage notably within the-EU/EEA countries.

The government draft bill included regulation in order to establish maximum norms for collective bargaining and agreements on each of the issues below, so that for a period of three years the collective agreements (CBAs) could not validly include more favourable terms and conditions than those in the bill. In a nutshell the government aimed at:

- Transforming the Epiphany and Ascension Day (both public holidays based on law) into unpaid days-off without shortening the annual working time; i.e. this would mean prolonging the working time and abolishing the 100% bonus if people have to work on those days[3].
- Imposing, firstly, a waiting day, i.e. an unpaid day, in the sickness leave pay regime; secondly, from the second sick leave day to the eighth day the maximum pay would be 80% of normal pay; at present in most CBAs there is no waiting day and, on the other hand, the full pay applies.
- Cutting the holiday allowance, a 50% bonus in CBAs and payable on top of the proper (normal) salary of annual holiday, by 30% which means a maximum allowance of 35%.
- Cutting the length of paid annual leave and setting a new maximum of six weeks; after a service of 15 years, public servants now normally get annual leave of 38 working days, i.e. seven weeks and three days.

---

[3] Later the Government decided to reverse its plan to reduce Sunday and overtime pay, replacing those measures with a 30% cut in holiday pay instead. Holiday pay is the 50% bonus that is paid to almost all Finnish wage and salary earners for their annual vacation: for a six weeks holiday you get nine weeks salary.

2. Criticism and evaluation

2.1 Introduction

The government proposals received a lot of criticism especially from the trade union movement, but also from labour lawyers and constitutional lawyers. Since the breaking through of the collective bargaining system in Finland after World War II the labour law regulation has always introduced minimum standards which can be approved by means of collective agreements. Now the legislator was introducing maximum standards which would have made the prevailing standards existing in many agreements null and void (at least for the future agreements). These measures were questionable also from the point of view of international standards and conventions which were ratified by Finland.

2.2 Epiphany and Ascension Day

Under Article 2(2) of the European Social Charter (ESC), which Finland has ratified, the State Parties undertake to provide for public holidays with pay[4]. This provision has been regularly interpreted so that the State Parties can decide freely upon their public holidays. However, if they are based on law, those days must be paid. Further, work can be done on those days when justified due to specific circumstances, but in those cases a bonus of 100% on top of normal wage must be paid, as is the law in Finland at present. In its Conclusions of 2014, the European Committee of Social Rights addressed – because of a bonus lower than 100% – an admonition to Greece, the Netherlands, Portugal and Slovakia.

First, it was noted regarding the Epiphany and Ascension Day that Article 2 ESC deals with the right to just conditions of work. Article 2(1) lays down the principle of shortening the working time whereas the bill would prolong it. However, the prolongation would not be absolute because the employers only 'must try to arrange' compensatory work on another day. If this is not done, the arrangement would mean a pure and simple wage-cut. On the other hand, for workers – not working on Epiphany or Ascension Day – with an hourly wage the bill would abolish a specific compensation wage (of eight hours) which is at present common in sectoral CBAs.

---

4 See about the interpretation of this clause by the European Committee for Social Rights: *http://www.coe.int/t/dghl/monitoring/socialcharter/Conclusions/ConclusionsIndex_en.asp.*

The conclusion is that the working time regime of Epiphany and Ascension Day in the bill would contradict Article 2 of the European Social Charter both as prolonging working time and as preventing either normal pay (or the specific compensation in CBAs for workers with hourly pay) or the 100% bonus.

The Finnish Trade Union Confederations also raised the question of whether EU law might be of relevance and contain some restrictions on the national Finnish legislator[5]. Regarding the question of whether the planned working time arrangements for Epiphany and Ascension Day fall within the scope of EU law they argued that one has to take into account, next to the Working Time Directive, the European Social Charter (ESC). Article 151 TFEU refers to it expressly. The Revised European Social Charter of 1996 (ratified e.g. by Finland) includes – for issues relevant now – provisions identical to those of the ESC.

The organizations argued that these aspects must be taken into account in interpreting Article 151 TFEU.

The trade unions also argued that the draft bill's regulation concerning Epiphany and Ascension Day would also mean regulating working time in the sense of the Working Time Directive (WTD). Firstly, it would prolong the yearly working time. Secondly, even if the wording of the WTD refers to remuneration only for the paid annual leave, one can well find that a statute imposing certain days off to be left completely without pay and subject to a corresponding prolongation of working time would mean regulating working time and acting via the WTD within the scope of EU law. This interpretation is grounded by reading the WTD in the light of Article 151 TFEU – with its reference to the ESC – that includes the principle of improved working conditions and free social dialogue, and also in so doing taking into account the contents of the European Social Charter as described above.

Furthermore, the Trade Union Confederations put forward the following argumentation:

'As to pay, the judgment e.g. in Comisiones obreras (C-266/14, para 48) doesn't refute this position whereas it stated – in French (and in many other versions) – how the WTD doesn't apply in principle ('generally'

[5] See The Central Organization of Finnish Trade Unions SAK, Akava – Confederation of Unions for Professional and Managerial Staff in Finland and The Finnish Confederation of Professionals STTK joint statement of 13 January 2016. Finnish Government's Draft Bill on Maximum Norms Concerning Collective Agreements – A Critical Analysis.

in the English version) to remuneration. Accordingly, Article 153(5) TFEU doesn't pre-empt that position. This provision, which is to be interpreted strictly and not calling into question the objectives – like improved working conditions and social dialogue – of Article 151 TFEU (Del Cerro Alonso, C-307/05, para 39, Impact, C-268/06, para 122), means essentially that fixing the level of pay falls within the contractual freedom of the social partners at a national level and within the relevant competence of Member States (Del Cerro Alonso, para 40, Impact, para 123). Further, the Court elaborated in Impact (para 124) that Article 153(5) TFEU as an 'exception must therefore be interpreted as covering measures – such as the equivalence of all or some of the constituent parts of pay and/or the level of pay in the Member States, or the setting of a minimum guaranteed Community wage – which amount to direct interference by Community law in the determination of pay within the Community'.

So, directives adopted on the basis of Article 137 EC (153 TFEU) can have an indirect effect on pay. With these grounds one can conclude that – via the WTD, read in the light of Article 151 TFEU and its reference to the ESC – the bill's pay regime, also linked to Epiphany and Ascension Day, falls within the scope of EU law and leads to the application of Article 28 CFREU.'

2.3 Sick-time pay

Regarding sick pay leave it was discussed whether the proposed regulation that contained one obligatory waiting day of sickness without any compensation and a mandatory restriction on the payment for the next seven days of sick leave to 80% of the wages. The regulation would also contain a three-year regulation during which any clauses in collective agreements prescribing more favourable terms and conditions for the employees would be null and void.

This proposal meant a clear intervention in the freedom of the social partners to conclude collective agreements. Freely negotiated collective agreements are one of the main objects of freedom of association[6]. Therefore, the issue was raised whether this proposed regulation was compatible with the ILO Conventions on Freedom of Association,

---

[6] See Freedom of Association. The ILO Digest of decisions and principles of the Freedom of Association Committee of the Governing Body of the ILO, para 882 (Fifth revised edition), Geneva, 2006.

especially Conventions No. 87, 98 and 154. It seems evident that the proposal does not promote collective bargaining in the spirit of Conventions No. 98 and 154, but in the practice of the supervisory bodies in the ILO interventions in, and restrictions on, free collective bargaining have under certain conditions been accepted. The most important preconditions for any restrictions on free collective bargaining have been that:

- the intervention should not be made in already existing agreements, but only apply to agreements which will be made in the future;
- the economic consequences of the measures taken should be clear and undisputed;
- the measures undertaken should be discussed by tripartite mechanisms before any decisions are made on legislative instruments;
- the legislative measures should be introduced for a certain limited period as exceptional undertakings;
- the measures taken should be clearly defined (certain benefits, sectors).

In my own expert opinion, which I drafted at the request of the Finnish Ministry of Labour, I argued that the reduction of sickness benefits under collective agreements would pass the criteria adopted in the ILO practice, but, for instance, the Finnish trade unions had a different view. I did not find any other obstacles for the introduction of such legislation in Finland.

2.4 Annual Leave

The planned cut of the paid annual leaves longer than six weeks to six weeks affects mostly women working in the public sectors. About 80% of the 437,000 employees in the municipal sectors are women. According to the bill, the cut would cover 354,000 employees, out of which 52,000 work in state administration, 263,000 in the municipal sector and 9,000 for the church. For the most part these employees are low-paid who anyway have – according to the relevant CBAs – after 15 years' service nowadays the right to an annual leave of seven weeks and three days (i.e. thirty-eight working days). On top of the normal salary for the leave, they get a holiday allowance of 72% of the normal monthly salary.

Finland reported in 2012 to the committee supervising the UN's gender equality convention (CEDAW) and explained how the wage gap between genders grows according to age and is at its biggest to those who are 60 years. At that stage, the average wage of women is – according to the report – 75.3% of that of men. The same degrading development concerns all the sectors but is strongest in the public sector, the report stated further.

In the light of the statistics, it is obvious that cutting the length of the annual leave concerns especially women with a long career in the public sector. Even the draft bill recognized this without however analysing its legal implications further. There is however a strong argument that the proposed cut – anchored by the respective maximum statutes regarding CBAs – would constitute indirect discrimination of women. It cannot be objectively justified by a vague aim to secure the social care and cultural (education) rights, as well as employment since it is difficult to understand why the measures are only targeting this specific group of predominately women in the public sector. The Finnish Constitutional Act contains an explicit obligation to promote pay equality between women and men and the proposed legislation is problematic from the point of view of the Finnish Constitution as well, as it arguably might constitute a violation of the European Union Gender Equality Directive 2006/54 and Article 21 CFREU.

This very controversial legal package was put on hold when the Social partners supported by the government achieved an alternative package to improve competitiveness in early spring 2016[7]. Here an agreement was reached on reduced employer social security costs which will be transferred to the employees. Furthermore, there will be no wage increases during the coming two years and finally there will be a prolongation of working time which will be negotiated by sectoral bargaining. Also the payment of so-called holiday allowances will be reduced by 30% during the years 2017–2019 in the public sector. Therefore, it seems that the controversial legislative proposals which got a rather bad public reputation as 'Coercive or Forced Acts' will not be on the agenda any more, at least not during the present government.

7 See the Result of Negotiations on an Agreement on Competitiveness of February 29, 2016.

3. Local agreements

A separate reform package which is promoted by the new Finnish government has increased flexibility in the form of so-called local agreements on its agenda[8].

The main criticism towards the present Finnish extension system has been that it actually discriminates against SMEs. With the increased decentralization of the collective agreements, there are an increased numbers of clauses in collective agreements which make it possible to deviate from minimum standards in the agreement by the local parties. This possibility is only in some of the cases also applicable for employers who apply the agreement as generally applicable due to the Finnish legislation[9] prescribing that collective agreements are mandatory for non-unionized employers *erga omnes* if the collective agreement is generally applied in the specific sector.

Under the Employment Contracts Act, the general applicability of collective agreements presupposes that the agreement is nationwide and

---

8 Finland, a Land of Solutions. Prime Minister Juha Sipilä's government, May, 29, 2015. The programme stated the following regarding promotion of local agreements and removal of barriers to employment (p. 16):

'The Government will encourage social partners to adopt local agreement practices in workplaces and will ensure through legislative projects that conditions for local agreement are strengthened. The Government will implement reforms aimed at increasing the SMEs willingness to employ in particular, in order to create new jobs.

– The objective is that companies will be able more widely than at present to agree locally on improving competitiveness, strengthening employment, terms of employment such as pay, working hours, conditions for terminating employment, use of a working time bank, reduction of sick leave, and issues affecting wellbeing at work. The Government will initiate necessary reforms of working hours legislation and other labour legislation to support promotion of local agreement, ensure an equal position for employers in exceptional circumstances, and strengthen the position of personnel in companies' decision-making. The Government will appoint a rapporteur to prepare a proposal on developing local agreement by 15 October 2015.

– In keeping with promoting local agreement, the Government will implement reforms to lower the threshold to employment, increase companies' willingness to grow and improve the capacity of workers to adapt to changes. The government will lengthen the probationary period, allow fixed-term employment relationships of less than a year without separate justification, ease the obligation to re-employ a worker in the event of redundancy, and develop change security.

– The impacts of sick leave and sickness risk of employees on employers will be reduced by including in annual leave of five weeks or longer a six-day personal contribution period for sickness during annual leave.'

9 The Finnish Employment Contracts Act 2001, Section 2:7.

can be deemed as representative in the field in question. In considering the said criteria several factors are taken into account, the point of departure being that about one-half of the employees in the field concerned are covered by the agreement already by virtue of the Collective Agreements Act. If the criteria are fulfilled and the agreement is declared as generally applicable, its terms shall be followed as minimum conditions by all employers in the field, regardless of their membership in an employers' association. Only employers bound by another collective agreement, concluded with a nationwide trade union, are exempted from this duty.

The trade unions usually justify the limited possibilities for non-unionized employers to benefit from flexibility clauses with the argument that there is no real balance in local negotiations in small companies since often there are not competent shop stewards on the employee's side and that the outcome of local negotiations might in practice be dictated by the employers.

The first report on local bargaining was published on 15 October 2015. It was made by the government's special investigator Mr Hietala who is a government civil servant – he proposed on the one hand different measures for increased participation for employees and also increased board-level participation in small companies[10].

The government did appoint a special group to come up with a concrete legislative reform for how to develop local negotiations. The mandate for this group was however changed since there were some clear conclusions also regarding local bargaining in the 'Competitiveness Agreement'.

Here are some legislative measures clearly defined in order to reform the system:

1. Non-organized employers will be put in an equal position with unionized ones when it comes to making local agreements, to the procedural requirements regarding such agreements and regarding who is entitled to make such an agreement.
2. All disputes regarding local agreements that are based on generally applicable collective agreements will be heard by the Finnish Labour Court.
3. Furthermore, some possibility for so-called crisis agreements will be introduced. Under certain conditions a local agreement can prescribe standards below the minimum in a sectoral agreement

10 TEM 62/2015.

(mainly in order to avoid lay-offs). There will be special legislation regarding employees' right to maintain unemployment benefits and wage guarantees on the previous level in such a situation.

Several open questions still remain to be solved. Traditionally single employers are not parties to a dispute in the Labour Court. Since non-organized employers cannot be represented by the employers confederation this will result in some changes in the procedures within the Labour Court.

Another question is how to define the equal position to make local agreements for non-organized employers. Within the collective bargaining system, only shop stewards have the competence to make local agreements and some organizations representing small and medium-size companies are demanding that other mechanisms for local bargaining should be introduced.

4. Other legislative measures

In parallel to the preparations of the Competitiveness Pact some amendments to individual labour law were prepared by the government. A government proposal was given to the Parliament on 15 June 2016[11]. According to the proposed new rules, the allowed trial period during which dismissals protection does not apply would be extended from four to six months, restrictions for entering into fixed-term employment contracts would not apply to long-term unemployed and the period during which an employer must give priority to rehire a dismissed employee will shorten from nine months to four months. These reforms are negotiated outside the Competitiveness Pact.

Conclusions

The Competiveness Pact was finally signed in June 2016 and the cuts were mainly implemented through means of sectoral collective bargaining in accordance with the guidelines set out on 29 February 2016. The process clearly shows how difficult it is for a collective bargaining system designed for sharing benefits to instead manage cuts.

---

11 See Government's Proposal HE 105/2016, submitted to Parliament on June 15, 2016.

In the end it seems that the Finnish tripartite collective bargaining system stood the test and was able to handle the difficult economic situation which presently prevails in Finland, although the process was extremely difficult and relations, especially between the government and the trade unions did not show any fundamental elements of trust. Both the labour market organizations and the government finally invested a lot of prestige in the package of competitiveness which would reduce labour costs considerably in Finland. This successful implementation of the package is also in the end a sign of strength of the Finnish labour market system. A failure would have put both the government and the labour market organizations in a difficult position and it would even have been possible that the only way out of such a crisis would have been new parliamentary elections.

Part Two

Industrial Relations

European Wage-Setting Mechanisms under Pressure

Negotiated and Unilateral Change and the EU's Economic Governance Regime

Paul Marginson*, Christian Welz**

Abstract

Since the onset of the crisis in 2008, collective wage-setting mechanisms across the EU have faced pressure to become more 'marketized'. Surveying developments across EU Member States, this article finds profound changes in wage-setting mechanisms in some countries, alongside less far-reaching ones in some others and little, if any change, in yet others. Pressure for further marketization has particularly focused on multi-employer bargaining arrangements, which constitute a fundamental feature of wage setting in western Europe. In particular, state supports underpinning such arrangements in the six countries subject to international financial assistance have been curtailed or removed. More profound changes are shown to have been driven by government imposition rather than negotiation between employers and unions. European and international institutions have

* Paul Marginson is Professor Emeritus of Industrial Relations at the University of Warwick, and was Director of the Industrial Relations Research Unit at Warwick from 2002 until 2012. He has published extensively on European industrial relations including his co-authored book *European Integration and Industrial Relations: Multi-level governance in the making?* He is an associate editor of the *Industrial and Labor Relations Review.*

** Christian Welz is senior researcher, lecturer and programme manager in the fields of industrial relations (IR), EU labour law, and social policy at Eurofound. As senior programme manager (IR) Christian coordinates a cluster of projects and develops expertise and quality of research in the field of IR. He is in charge of the European IR Dictionary and a number of IR governance projects (European Social Dialogue, European Semester, key dimensions of industrial relations, capacity to negotiate/ mandate of the EU level social partners, quality of IR, the impact of the crisis on IR, Transnational Company Agreements, etc.). Christian studied law and political sciences at the Universities of Bonn, Freiburg, Aix-en-Provence and Strasbourg and holds a PhD from the University of Nijmegen. Prior to joining Eurofound, he was Deputy Director of a French-German training institute for civil servants, managed the EU unit of the Chamber of Commerce and Industry in Augsburg and was professor of EU law at the Universities of Applied Sciences in Kehl and Offenburg.

exercised considerable influence, through requirements from the 'troika' but also through the EU's new regime of economic governance. For the Member States subject to international financial assistance, an alternative to current EU policy prescriptions is to promote mechanisms facilitating company-level negotiations within, and to reinstate state supports for multi-employer bargaining frameworks.[1]

Key words: wage-setting mechanisms, collective wage bargaining, minimum wage.

Introduction

Since the onset of the crisis in 2008, collective wage-setting mechanisms across the EU have come under pressure from employers and the public authorities to become ever more responsive to firms' economic and competitive circumstances, or more 'marketized' (Crouch, 2014). The result has been profound changes in some countries, alongside less far-reaching ones in some others and little, if any change, in yet others. Pressure for further marketization has particularly focused on multi-employer bargaining arrangements, a fundamental feature of wage setting in continental western and Nordic Europe whose coverage extends to a large majority of the workforce. Under the single-employer bargaining regimes which prevail in the UK, Ireland (since 2009) and much of Central and Eastern Europe, and whose coverage is limited to a minority of the workforce (thereby leaving the majority subject to unilateral employer decisions), wage setting was already comparatively more 'marketized' prior to the crisis.

The recent changes have been initiated by a range of actors, including employers and trade unions through collective bargaining, national governments through concertation with the social partners and by imposition, and, externally, the European and international institutions through recommendations and mandatory requirement. At one end of the spectrum have been changes to wage-setting mechanisms negotiated between employers and trade unions, such as the further decentralization involving aspects of wage setting in some northern European countries in the early phase of the crisis (Glassner *et al.*, 2011; Ibsen *et al.*, 2011). At the opposite end is the insistence of the 'troika' of European and international institutions (the European Commission, European Central

---

1 This contribution is an abridged version of the article Marginson P. and Welz C., 2015. European Wage-Setting Mechanisms under Pressure: Negotiated and Unilateral Change and the EU's Economic Governance Regime. *Transfer: European Review of Labour and Research*, No. 21(4), pp. 429–450.

Bank (ECB) and International Monetary Fund (IMF)) on major changes to wage-setting mechanisms under the Memoranda of Understanding (MoUs) governing the financial assistance packages made available to Greece, Ireland, Portugal, Romania (IMF only), Spain (concerning its banking sector) and, most recently, Cyprus (Schulten and Müller, 2013; Marginson, 2015). Lying somewhere in between are the country specific recommendations (CSRs) issued by the Commission as part of the EU's new European Semester macroeconomic planning regime, which identify aspects of wage setting deemed in need of reform (Dufresne and Pernot, 2013; Schulten and Müller, 2013).

The article draws on the findings of a comparative study compiled for Eurofound based on the responses from its EurWORK network of national correspondents in the EU's 28 Member States plus Norway to a structured questionnaire, issued in the final quarter of 2013, asking about any changes in wage-setting mechanisms since 2008. The findings demonstrate that wage-setting mechanisms have indeed become further marketized but also reveal an extension of state regulation of some aspects of wage setting, notably minimum wages, at the expense of employers and trade union involvement. Further findings indicate that the result of enforced marketization of wage setting under the MoUs imposed by the troika has been a sharp decline in the number of workers covered by collective wage bargaining.

The article first addresses, conceptually and empirically, change and stability in wage-setting mechanisms in the period prior to the onset of the crisis in 2008, including growing decentralization of the level(s) of collective wage bargaining, state supports to collective wage bargaining, and minimum wage setting. Secondly, the data and methods are summarized. Thirdly, findings on changes in wage-setting mechanisms are presented. This is followed, fourthly, by an examination of the institutional sources of change in terms of the internal and external actors involved. The fifth section discusses the findings and concludes.

1. Change and stability in wage-setting mechanisms over the decades before the crisis

The recent changes to collective wage-setting mechanisms come after a lengthy period marked by an overall trend towards decentralization, consistent with a logic of marketization, but characterized by relative stability in other key features. The trend towards decentralization initially resulted from growing trade union strength and assertiveness within the workplace during the 1960s, but from the 1980s onwards has responded to employer pressure for greater scope for firm-level negotiation over (an element of) wages given increasing internationalization of, and uncertainty in, markets (Katz, 1993; Marginson and Sisson, 2004). Decentralization has been a largely negotiated development, albeit the focus of periodic conflicts between employers and trade unions in several countries. Stability in other key features includes the supports provided by the state for collective bargaining. These date back to earlier periods of economic and political turbulence and were either institutional settlements reached between employers, trade unions and the state in the face of significant industrial unrest, as in much of western Europe, or state decisions following political transformation, as in the former West Germany and in Central and Eastern Europe (Crouch, 1993; Sisson, 1987; Kohl and Platzer, 2004). In a period of renewed economic and political turbulence these state supports become more open to change.

The varying extent of recent changes and their differing nature as between countries poses two questions. First, what accounts for differences in the extent of change? Secondly, what accounts for differences in the nature of change, negotiated or imposed and incremental or radical? In analysing employer and trade union responses to the steep economic downturn which marked the first phase of the economic crisis, Glassner and Keune (2010) proposed that the incidence and outcome, distributive or integrative, of negotiated or concerted employer and trade union responses was shaped by four sets of influences: economic situation at different levels (economy-wide, sector, company); public policy; industrial relations institutions; and employer and trade union strategies. Evidence confirms the salience of the first three factors and is suggestive of the relevance of the fourth (Glassner *et al.*, 2011).

Applying and modifying Glassner and Keune's framework to the first question, variants of the same four influences are expected to inform the extent of changes to wage-setting mechanisms since 2008. Economic situation refers to the depth of the initial economic downturn and subsequently whether adverse economic conditions persist, with more extensive changes expected the worse the initial downturn and the more persistent subsequent economic adversity. Changes in public policy reflect political opportunity and include actions by the (national) state and also intervention by the troika of international institutions. On the latter, a European Commission (2012) report identified a catalogue of desirable structural reforms to wage-setting arrangements reflecting the political opportunity associated with the conditions attached to financial rescue packages: more extensive change can be expected where there is intervention from the troika. Domestic political change may also lead to shifts in pre-existing public policy supports for collective wage setting. Concerning institutions, the ways in and extent to which collective bargaining arrangements had already been decentralized will shape capacity to adjust wage setting to sharply changed economic conditions post-2008. This is anticipated to be comparatively greater where decentralization entails effective mechanisms articulating bargaining at the sector and company levels (Glassner *et al.*, 2011). Employer and trade union strategies condition their mutual preparedness and capability to secure negotiated changes to wage-setting mechanisms.

Turning to the second question, that is, what accounts for differences in the extent of change, variants of the four influences identified by Glassner and Keune (2010) are also relevant. The relationship between economic situation and the nature of change is not straightforward. In the face of adverse economic circumstances, changes to wage setting may be negotiated between employers and trade unions or imposed by the state. However, if the extent of adversity forces governments to have recourse to external financial assistance from the international institutions then imposed change becomes more likely because of the associated conditions (Schulten and Müller, 2013). Such change is more likely to be radical than incremental. Radical and imposed change is also likely to be associated with changes in (national) public policy away from the political settlement which underpinned the state supports for wage setting which prevailed over the decades prior to 2008. In contrast, continuation of previous public policy is likely to be associated with incremental change (or none at all). Institutional arrangements for collective bargaining with the capacity to adjust the balance between the sector and company levels in wage setting are expected to be associated with negotiated change. Where such capacity is weak or absent, change is more likely to be imposed. As with the extent of change, the strategies of employers and trade unions are anticipated to shape their mutual preparedness and capability to realize negotiated change.

The predominant trend since the 1980s towards more decentralized wage bargaining arrangements has involved shifts from the cross-sector to sector levels, where central agreements were in place, and towards opening up greater space for negotiation over wages at company level.

Traxler (1995) differentiates between two forms of decentralization: 'organized' under which scope for company negotiations is created within the framework of sector (or cross-sector) agreements; and 'disorganized' under which sector frameworks are abolished and wage negotiations move entirely to company level, or are replaced by unilateral management regulation. Wage setting is more marketized under disorganized than organized, decentralization. Organized decentralization has characterized western continental and Nordic Europe, with greater scope for negotiations over at least an element of wage setting being introduced in various ways (Marginson, 2015). The UK is the exception, where the disorganized variant prevailed. In Central and Eastern Europe, the bargaining arrangements established in most countries resembled the single-employer arrangements now found in the UK. Multi-employer bargaining involving sector and/or cross-sector arrangements was established in Romania, Slovakia (to some extent), and Slovenia (Meardi, 2012). The overall trend towards decentralization was tempered in some countries and at particular junctures by renewed initiatives to conclude over-arching central agreements, such as the social pacts which featured in several countries in the run up to Economic and Monetary Union (Hancké and Rhodes, 2005).

As wage-setting mechanisms became more decentralized, growing attention was paid to the issue of coordination across different bargaining units. With centralized agreements, such as those found across the Nordic countries until the 1980s (and which continue in Norway and, less consistently, Finland), horizontal coordination across different sectors is ensured. Under sector- and company-level bargaining arrangements, other mechanisms have to be called upon. Traxler *et al.* (2001) identified differing modes of horizontal coordination including: coordination by the peak-level confederations of employers and trade unions, as in the Netherlands and Spain; pattern-setting by a key economic sector, often metalworking on account of its exposure to international competition and organized strength, as in Austria, Germany, and Sweden (since the mid-1990s); and state-led coordination, as in France where government decisions on the level of the statutory minimum wage act as a signal for wage negotiators.

Multi-employer bargaining arrangements have been buttressed by supportive legal provisions enacted by the state (Traxler, 1998). These state supports include: the favourability principle, which stipulates that collective agreements can only improve on legally determined standards, and that lower levels of bargaining, such as the company, can only conclude agreements which improve on the provisions contained in those concluded in higher (sector or cross-sector) agreements; procedures legally to extend the coverage of collective wage agreements to firms, and therefore the workers employed in them, not belonging to the employers' organization (in the sector and/or territory) concluding an agreement; legal provisions governing which actors are empowered to conclude collective agreements, which generally specify trade unions (in several countries subject to meeting representativeness criteria) as the sole bargaining agent for workers; and, in some countries, measures providing for agreements to continue in force beyond their expiry until a new agreement is concluded. The main exception in terms of these state supports are the Nordic countries, where equivalence has come through a combination of the provisions of basic agreements and, in the case of extension, high levels of union density and employer organization membership.

These state supports exhibited considerable stability over the period prior to 2008 and, with the exception of continuation of agreements beyond expiry, were widely adopted prior to EU accession amongst the Central and Eastern European new Member States (even although sector-level bargaining was the exception rather than the rule in many). In the case of the favourability principal, the main exception was France, where the 2004 Fillon law inverted the principle to give precedence to standards set in the company over those contained in sector agreements. The favourability principle remains in force, however, for minimum wages and job classifications which were exempted from the law's provisions (Marginson, 2015). Concerning extension mechanisms, there has also been little recent change in the procedures involved amongst the 22 Member States which have these (Kerckhofs, 2011). Slovakia is an exception, where since 2004 changes to the legislation governing extension, variously weakening its effect and then reinstating the previous position, have followed changes in government. The main instance of change in legal provisions governing trade unions' prerogative to conclude agreements is France, where an experimental mandating procedure introduced in 1996 to promote the negotiation of agreements in companies with no union representatives was generalized in 2000 to promote the negotiated implementation of the 35 hour week (Jobert, 2002). Amongst the countries concerned, there are no indications of changes in the period before 2008 to provisions governing the continuation of agreements beyond expiry.

Two further aspects of collective wage setting (often) have general applicability across the workforce: minimum wage-setting arrangements and indexation mechanisms. In 2008, 21 of the countries of the EU's (current) 28 Member States set a universal, statutory minimum wage, whilst Cyprus fixed statutory minimum wages for specific occupations and Germany gave binding force to collectively negotiated minima in a few sectors. In the countries with no statutory minimum, Austria, Denmark, Finland, Germany (most sectors), Italy, Sweden and also Norway (included in the empirical analysis below), minimum wage rates are generally set by collective agreements (Keune, 2011). In most countries with statutory minima, employers and trade unions have some involvement in the process. Amongst western European countries this most commonly entails consultation, although in Belgium and Greece the social partners traditionally negotiated the minimum wage within the framework of the cross-sector agreement, whilst in France the state acted unilaterally. Amongst most Central and Eastern European countries, minimum wages are subject to tripartite agreement or at least an attempt at such (Schulten *et al.*, 2006). Since the late 1990s, statutory minimum wage arrangements have been introduced in further countries, in the face of growing gaps in collective bargaining coverage, including Ireland, the UK and Germany (from the start of 2015). Again, employers and trade unions are formally involved in the process which determines its level, either through negotiation (Ireland and Germany) or a tripartite commission (the UK).

Indexation mechanisms, linking wages to a measure of the cost of living, have featured in a small number of countries including, by 2008, Belgium, Cyprus, Luxembourg, Malta, and Spain. In the first four countries, the mechanisms involved are statutory in nature although subject to oversight by tripartite bodies. In Spain, the pay guidelines concluded in periodic cross-sector agreements incorporated (up until 2009) official inflation forecasts. Most collective agreements included wage revision clauses which subsequently adjusted wages for any deviation between forecast and actual inflation, thereby acting as a functional equivalent of indexation. The most recent change to this picture was the abolition of Italy's 'scala mobile' in 1992, replaced by a reference cost of living measure for sector-level wage negotiations.

2. Data and methods

The questionnaire circulated to EurWORK national correspondents in the EU's 28 Member States plus Norway in the autumn of 2013 asked about any changes which had occurred since 2008 to four main dimensions of wage setting:

- main level(s) of bargaining, and whether in the direction of decentralization or recentralization;
- linkages between levels under multi-tier bargaining (involving the cross-sector and/or sector and or/company levels), including hierarchical ordering between levels, opening and opt-out clauses, and extending bargaining competence to non-trade union based representatives;
- reach and continuity of collective bargaining, including provisions governing, and the use of, extension mechanisms and continuation of agreements following expiry;
- minimum wage-setting and indexation mechanisms.
- In addition, respondents were asked to report on changes in the volume of wage bargaining since 2008 as indicated by the number of agreements concluded.

Of the four main dimensions, two are applicable to wage setting under both multi- and single-employer bargaining regimes: main bargaining level(s); and minimum wage-setting and indexation mechanisms. Two, however, mainly concern multi-employer regimes: linkages between levels; and reach and continuity of bargaining. It is therefore useful to identify whether countries are primarily characterized by multi- or single-bargaining arrangements for wage setting. The Appendix Table shows that, for 2008, of the 29 countries covered by the study, multi-employer arrangements were prevalent in 18, whilst single-employer ones were prevalent in eight and three had mixed regimes with multi- and single-employer bargaining each covering a part of the private sector. It also shows that, as a result of significant change, two countries (Ireland and Romania) had shifted from multi- to single-employer regimes by 2012.

Where changes to wage-setting mechanisms had occurred, the questionnaire went on to ask about which different institutional actors had been involved in shaping the different types of change. The actors concerned included the social partners at cross-sector and sector levels; national governments; and European and international institutions (the Commission, ECB and IMF). In the case of the European and international institutions, further questioning asked about requirements for changes to wage setting included in the MoUs governing financial assistance packages to the six countries concerned and about CSRs on wage setting and wage policy issued under the EU's new macroeconomic governance regime.

Responses were cross-checked for internal consistency and with other sources, including Clauwaert and Schömann (2012) and Schulten and Müller (2013).

3. Main changes in wage-setting mechanisms

3.1 Main level(s) of bargaining

Table 1 shows that in 12 countries there has been some change in the main bargaining level(s) at which wages are determined since 2008, including several where the change involved has been considerable. The other 17 countries reported no changes in level. Of the 12 countries concerned, the dominant tendency was decentralization, from the cross-sector towards the sector or company levels and/or from the sector towards the company level. This accounted for changes in 10 countries: Austria, Bulgaria, Cyprus, France, Greece, Ireland, Italy, Romania, Slovenia, Spain. In two countries, Belgium and Finland, changes were in the opposite direction and involved centralization. Relatively few changes in horizontal coordination (not shown) were reported: those that were entailed weakened coordination. Abolition of the central agreements in Ireland and Romania was followed by a protocol concluded between employers and trade unions to orientate firm-level wage negotiation in the former, but by no coordination initiative in the latter. In Hungary, regular joint employer – trade union recommendations on wage increases ceased with the abolition of the national tripartite body. Overall, the prevalence of decentralization since the onset of the crisis continues, and has accelerated, the predominant tendency in the evolution of wage-setting mechanisms observed since the late 1980s.

Table 1. Changes in main level(s) of bargaining since 2008.

Increased centralization	Increased decentralization
BE: Government-imposed outcomes to 2011 and 2013 cross-sector wage bargaining roundst with no wage margin for further negotiation at sector level.	AT: Single metalworking agreement replaced by agreements covering each of six sub-sectors (2012).
FI: Cross-sector wage agreements abandoned in 2007, but returned to in 2011 and 2013.	BG: Acceleration of trend for sector agreements to be replaced by company ones.
	CY: Acceleration of trend for sector agreements to be replaced by company ones.
	EL: Legislative changes prioritizing the company level and permitting negotiations with unspecified employee representatives in smaller companies prompted an upsurge in company agreements at the expense of sector ones.
	ES: Legislative change prioritizing the company level, together with social partner encouragement, increased the weight of the company level in wage setting.
	FR: 2000 legislation requires companies with trade union representation to engage in annual pay negotiations.
	IE: Breakdown of national wage agreement following employer and government withdrawal (2009).
	IT: 2011 cross-sector agreement weakened sector-level mandate over wage negotiations in favour of the company level.
	RO: Cross-sector agreement abolished under 2011 legislation, which also had the effect of paralyzing negotiating activity in newly defined sectors. Wage negotiations now mainly at company level.
	SI: Social partners failed to agree on a renewal of the 'fall back' cross-sector agreement, which applied in the absence of a sector one (2009).

Source: Eurofound, 2014.

3.2 Linkages between levels under multi-tier bargaining

The procedures governing the vertical ordering between different levels of bargaining, usually based on the favourability principle, have undergone change in three countries (Greece, Spain and Portugal). Changes in, or the introduction of, opening clauses relating to wages (which permit variation in implementation) occurred in seven countries (Austria, Finland, Germany, Italy, Norway, Portugal and Sweden). In Austria, Germany and the Nordic countries such clauses were temporary, or one-off, responses to the early phase of the crisis. Opt-out clauses introducing the possibility of derogation from wage standards specified in sector or cross-sector agreements featured in eight countries (Bulgaria, Cyprus, France, Greece, Ireland, Italy, Slovenia and Spain). Bargaining competence has been extended to non-union representatives in four countries, with an important difference between France and Portugal where this is with union consent and Greece and Romania where it is not. Table 2 provides summary information on the changes involved.

Table 2. Changes in linkages between levels since 2008.

Ordering between levels	Opening and opt-out clauses	Extending bargaining competence to non-union representatives
	Opening clauses	
EL: 2011 legislation specifying that company agreements have priority over sector ones, although not over the cross-sector agreement, and can entail lower standards.	AT: One-off opening clause allowed in electronics providing the option not to implement the sector wage award in full (2009).	EL: 2011 legislation allowing negotiations with unspecified employee representatives in smaller companies (<50 employees).
EL: 2011 legislation specifying that company agreements have priority over sector and provincial ones, and can entail lower standards.	DE: One-off opening clauses allowing variation in implementation of wage increases in chemicals and metalworking (2009, 2010).	FR: 2008 law allowing negotiations with works committees in smaller companies (<200 employees) where no union presence.

Ordering between levels	Opening and opt-out clauses	Extending bargaining competence to non-union representatives
PT: 2012 Labour Code specifies that company agreements have priority over sector and provincial ones, and can entail lower standards.	FI: One-off opening clauses allowing variation in implementation of wage increases in several sectors (2010).	PT: 2009 legislation conferring bargaining competence on works councils in larger companies (500+ employees) with trade union consent.
	IT: 2012 cross-sector agreement promoting devolution clauses in sector agreements, aimed at widening the company-level agenda.	RO: 2011 legislation permitting negotiation with unspecified employee representatives where no 'representative' trade union present.
	NO: One-off opening clause in most private sector agreements providing the option not to implement the sector wage increase (2009).	
	PT: 2012 Labour Code enables elements of the sector bargaining agenda to be delegated to company level.	
	SE: 2010 short-time working agreement in manufacturing, facilitating local negotiation over shortened working time to maintain employment.	
	Opt-out clauses	
	BG: Increase in the number of sector agreements with opt-out clauses.	
	CY: Increase in the number of sector agreements with opt-out clauses.	
	EL: 2010 legislation introduced possibility for companies in economic hardship to opt-out of sector agreements.	

Ordering between levels	Opening and opt-out clauses	Extending bargaining competence to non-union representatives
	ES: 2010 legislation introduced possibility for companies in economic hardship to opt-out of sector or provincial agreements. 2012 cross-sector agreement encouraged inclusion of opt-out clauses in sector and provincial agreements.	
	FR: 2013 cross-sector agreement, translated into law, introduces opt-out clause for companies in economic hardship conditional on no redundancies commitment.	
	IE: Opt-out clauses on grounds of economic hardship introduced in sectors governed by binding wage-setting mechanisms.	
	IT: 2011 cross-sector agreement introduced opt-out clause from sector wage standards on grounds of economic hardship.	
	SI: Increase in the number of sector agreements with opt-out clauses.	

Source: Eurofound, 2014.

3.3 Reach and continuity of bargaining

Changes to extension procedures have taken place in five countries (Greece, Ireland, Slovakia, Portugal and Romania), whilst there have been changes in their use in two countries (Bulgaria, Germany). In addition, although there is no legal procedure for extension in Italy judicial decisions have underpinned de facto extension of wage provisions in sector agreements. Changes to clauses providing for the continuation of agreements beyond expiry have featured in four countries (Croatia, Greece, Spain and Portugal). Summary information on the changes is given in Table 3.

Table 3. Changes in the reach and continuity of collective agreements since 2008.

Extension mechanism changed	Use of existing extension mechanisms changed	Continuation of agreements beyond expiry
EL: 2011 law in effect suspends extension by restricting its application to employers' association member companies.	BG: Activation of hitherto unused extension procedures in some sectors.	EL: 2012 law introduced a three-month time limit on continuation of agreements.
IE: Extension via Registered Employment Agreements (concluded in some sectors) suspended following 2013 Supreme Court ruling.	DE: Increase in the number of sectors where minimum wages declared legally binding, under posted workers legislation.	ES: 2012 law introduced a 12-month time limit on continuation of agreements.
SK: Controversy over whether the consent of individual employers is required before extension procedure applied, resulting in three changes in legislation (2007, 2010, 2014).	IT: Court rulings confirming the legal validity of Fiat's new single-employer agreements call into question widespread practice of de facto extension of wage (and working time) clauses of sector agreements.	HR: 2012 law introduced a three-month time limit on continuation of agreements.
PT: 2012 Labour Code restricts extension procedures to sectors where employers' organization member companies employ >50% of the workforce.		PT: 2009 law introduced an 18-month time limit on continuation of agreements, extendable to 5 years by agreement between the parties.
RO: 2011 Social Dialogue Act curtails extension by restricting its application to employers' association member companies.		

Source: Eurofound, 2014.

3.4 Minimum wage setting and wage indexation

Changes to statutory minimum wage-setting procedures took place in 10 of the countries with these arrangements (Croatia, Cyprus, Greece, Hungary, Ireland, Poland, Portugal, Spain, Slovakia and Slovenia). In addition, in Germany – where a statutory national minimum wage was due to be introduced – there was change in the number of sectors specifying statutory minima. Changes to indexation arrangements featured in four (Belgium, Cyprus, Luxembourg and Spain) of the five countries where such mechanisms exist, with debate but no change in the fifth, Malta. In addition, the price index used as a reference for sector-level cost-of-living wage settlements in Italy was changed. Table 4 summarizes the changes involved.

Table 4. Changes to minimum wage setting and indexation mechanisms since 2008.

Minimum wage setting	Indexation mechanisms
CY: Memorandum of Understanding governing financial assistance package imposes restrictions on criteria for any increase in the minimum wage, and requires international approval.	BE: 2012 change in the method of calculation to temper effect of price increases on wage indexation.
EL: 2012 law changed minimum wage setting, and froze the minimum wage until 2016. Minimum wage no longer determined by the social partners through cross-sector negotiations, but by government following consultation with the social partners.	CY: 2012 tripartite agreement introduced temporary exemption for companies facing economic hardship. Further changes proposed by government, under the 2013 MoU, include reduced frequency of adjustments, possibility of suspension under unfavourable macroeconomic circumstances, replacing full with partial (50%) indexation.
ES: *De facto* change. Since 2011, government has discontinued previous practice of consulting the social partners before determining the minimum wage.	LU: following the failure of tripartite negotiations over reforming indexation, government suspended operation of indexation mechanism until 2014, imposing fixed-rate increase for 2012-2014.

Minimum wage setting	Indexation mechanisms
HU: Abolition, in 2011, of the tripartite body which had determined the minimum wage. The new tripartite body has consultative status only, with government now deciding.	ES: Wage guidelines agreed between the social partners no longer incorporate official inflation forecasts (since 2009). Sharp reduction in number of agreements including wage revision clauses, which adjust for deviation between anticipated and actual inflation.
IE: 2010 cut in the minimum wage under the Memorandum of Understanding governing its financial assistance package. Restored in 2012, but required international approval.	IT: 2009 cross-sector agreement introduced a new indicator of expected inflation as the reference point for sector wage negotiations.
PL: *De facto* change. Failure to agree on minimum wage level in Tripartite Commission, with result that government has unilaterally decided.	
PT: Memorandum of Understanding governing financial assistance package imposes restrictions on criteria for any increase in the minimum wage, and requires international approval.	
DE: Increase in the number of sectors with minimum wages declared legally binding.	
HR: Statutory minimum wage introduced in 2008, determined by government according to a formula. Annual uprating introduced in 2013.	
SI: 2010 legislation introducing indexation for the minimum wage.	
SK: 2008 legislative change enabling government to increase minimum wage above level indicated by cost of living formula.	

Source: Eurofound, 2014.

3.5 Volume of collective wage agreements

Estimates of the trend in the number of agreements were provided for all but three (Finland, Hungary, Ireland) of the 29 countries. As Table 5 shows, the majority reported either a decline in the number of agreements (13 countries, including Greece) or no change (10 countries). Four countries reported an increase, including Greece where numbers of company agreements increased while those of sector agreements declined.

Table 5. Changes in the number of collective wage agreements since 2008.

Decrease	*Small*	BE BG DE
	In-between	CY EE LT LV PL SK
	Steep	EL (sector) ES PT RO
No change		AT DK HR IT LU NL NO SE SI UK
Increase		CZ EL (company) FR MT

Source: Eurofound, 2014.

The steepest declines in the number of agreements were in Greece (sector agreements), Spain, Romania and Portugal. In Greece as compared to the 70 sector and 67 occupational multi-employer agreements concluded in 2010, only ten and two, respectively, were concluded in 2012. In Spain, the number of agreements in force (at sector, provincial and company levels) fell from almost 6,000 in 2008 to just over 3,500 in 2012. In Romania, no sector-level agreements have been concluded in the private sector since 2011 when legislation changing the basis of sector-level bargaining took effect. The number of company agreements fell from around 4,800 in 2008 to 2,400 in 2011 before increasing again to over 4,600 in 2013. In Portugal, the total number of collective agreements signed in 2008 stood at 295, whereas in 2013 only 94 agreements were signed. In 2008 the number of extensions was 137 and this figure dropped to only nine in 2013. The combined effect of the two developments was a decline in workers covered by renewed collective agreements from 1.9 million in 2008 to 242,000 in 2013 (UGT, 2014).

3.6 Summary

An overview of the different main types of change to collective wage-setting mechanisms, indicating the countries concerned, is provided in Table 6. Three clusters of country according to the number of changes which have occurred can be identified. There have been multiple changes in six countries: Cyprus, Greece, Spain, Ireland, Portugal and Romania, while there have been some changes in four countries: Croatia, Hungary, Italy and Slovenia. In the remaining 19 countries there have been fewer or no changes.

Table 6. Main types of change in wage-setting mechanisms.

Type of change	**Countries**
Main level(s) of bargaining:	
Decentralization	AT BG CY EL ES FR IE IT RO SI
Recentralization	BE FI
Linkages between levels of bargaining:	
Ordering between levels	EL ES PT
Opening and opt-out clauses	AT BG CY DE EL ES FI FR IE IT NO PT SE SI
Extending bargaining competence	EL FR PT RO
Reach and continuity of bargaining:	
Extension procedures	EL IE SK PT RO BG* DE*
Continuation beyond expiry	EL ES HR PT
Minimum wage setting and indexation mechanisms:	
Minimum wage setting	CY DE EL ES HR HU IE PL PT SI SK
Indexation	BE ES CY IT LU

Note: * Increased changed use of existing procedures.
Source: Eurofound, 2014.

The six countries featuring multiple changes have all received financial rescue packages from the troika of international institutions in the context of significant economic adversity. The impact of these rescue packages on the changes which have occurred in collective wage-setting mechanisms has been extensive (see below). In 2008, prior to the onset of the crisis, multi-employer bargaining constituted the prevalent bargaining regime in five of the six, whilst Cyprus had 'mixed' arrangements (see Appendix table). By 2012, multi-employer bargaining arrangements had been replaced by single-employer ones in Ireland and Romania. Amongst the other four countries, a distinctive characteristic of their multi-employer bargaining regimes up until 2008 was the weakness or absence of procedural provisions articulating bargaining across the different levels. Changes since then have further weakened the role of higher level (variously cross-sector, sector or provincial) agreements and accorded priority to those concluded at company level.

In the four countries featuring some changes – Croatia, Hungary, Italy and Slovenia – these changes have been primarily driven by domestic institutional actors i.e. governments and/or employers and trade unions (see Eurofound, 2014)). Amongst the 19 countries with few or no changes, four different kinds of reason were identified in the EIRO correspondents' reports (with more than one being cited for some countries). First, the absence of a major impact on economic activity under the crisis, and hence pressure on wage-setting mechanisms (AT, CZ, NL (until recently), NO, PL). Secondly, the capacity of existing wage-setting mechanisms to adjust to the changed economic conditions was indicated for several countries with multi-employer bargaining arrangements (DE, DK, NL, SE, NO), Slovakia with mixed arrangements and the Czech Republic and UK, with single-employer arrangements. Thirdly, three countries indicated that collective bargaining plays a (relatively) marginal role in wage setting (LT, LV, PL). Fourthly, governments and social partners can resist international pressure for change, as with the recommendation under the EU's new macroeconomic regime for abolition of Malta's indexation system (see below).

Discussion and Conclusion

Considerable variation has been found between countries both in the extent to which wage-setting mechanisms have been subject to change and in the nature of change. Towards accounting for both types of variation, variants of the framework proposed by Glassner and Keune (2010) were elaborated in the opening section. Accordingly, four main influences were expected to shape the extent and the nature of change: economic situation, political opportunity to effect change in public policy, institutional arrangements for collective bargaining, in particular capacity to adjust the balance between sector and company levels, and employer and trade union strategies.

Change has been concentrated amongst six countries, whose wage-setting mechanisms have each undergone multiple changes. All six have been in receipt of financial assistance packages from the troika. In a further four countries, there have been some changes to wage-setting mechanisms. Here change has been primarily driven by domestic actors – either governments or employers and trade unions. Wage-setting mechanisms in the majority of countries, 19, have seen fewer or no changes since 2008. In terms of the four influences, the most extensive change – found amongst the first six countries – is associated with significant economic adversity, the political opportunity which the conditions attached to financial assistance packages opens up for external actors to require, or internal actors i.e. government to impose, change, and lack of adaptive capacity amongst existing collective wage bargaining institutions. Any pattern arising from employer and trade union strategies is difficult to discern. In contrast, relatively small (in extent) or no change – evident amongst the 19 countries – is associated with one or more of absence of significant economic adversity, adaptive capacity of existing institutions (also marginalization of collective wage bargaining) and employer and trade union strategies. Political opportunity, in the shape of state intervention, has manifested itself in a minority of the countries concerned. The contrast between the two groups of countries is generally consistent with the expectations developed earlier.

The further finding of difference according to aspects of wage setting was not, however, foreseen. Some were more likely to be subject to negotiation; others to imposition. As noted, further decentralization of wage setting was more likely to result from negotiations between the social partners than from intervention by governments. The changes involved are consistent with 'marketization' (Crouch, 2014) of collective wage setting, and represent further movement along a trajectory which was well established before the onset of the crisis. In such cases the resulting marketization is evolutionary and internally driven by the parties concerned. In contrast, change involving government intervention tends to mark a departure from existing arrangements and trajectories of development. The marketization resulting is disruptive and enforced. Most notably, multiple government-imposed changes have substantially reconfigured wage-setting mechanisms in the six countries receiving financial assistance packages from the troika. Moreover, external actors i.e. the European and international institutions have played a prominent role: in all but Spain, most of the changes have been directly required under the associated MoUs. A key feature of this enforced marketization has been the removal or decisive weakening of long-established state supports to multi-employer (wage) bargaining, confirming that institutional settlements become open to change at times of economic and political turbulence.

Government imposition is also to the fore in the changes to minimum wage-setting and indexation mechanisms, which have featured in a wider range of countries than the six subject to financial assistance packages. Here another logic, of social partner exclusion, is apparent as well as that of marketization. The role of the social partners in determining the minimum wage has variously been reduced, temporarily circumscribed or removed altogether in several countries. Changes to indexation mechanisms also reflect an exclusion as well as a marketization logic: governments in three of the four countries concerned have side-lined the social partners and imposed change themselves. Increased government intervention in collective wage setting need not, however, always result in lower standards: in contrast to the weakening of minimum wage protection evident amongst the troika countries, the effect of recent interventions has been to augment minimum wage protection in three Central and Eastern European countries.

More generally, the reforms identified in CSRs are viewed by the European institutions as promising to enhance the capacity of labour markets to contribute to macroeconomic adjustment in the face of either imbalances (between countries) or changes in overall economic conditions (Erne, 2012; Schulten and Müller, 2013). In the context of the eurozone, where devaluation is no longer available to Member States as an adjustment tool, such enhanced capacity is deemed essential. However, both the diagnosis and the prescribed treatment from the European institutions (e.g. European Commission, 2012) are, arguably, wide of the mark because of failure to appreciate crucial differences in institutional arrangements amongst the countries where multi-employer bargaining still prevails. These divide into two broad groups. Amongst the first, including Austria, Belgium, France, Germany, Italy, the Netherlands and the Nordic countries, organized decentralization has led to bargaining arrangements which have increasingly opened up scope for company-level negotiation within the framework provided by sector and, in some, cross-sector agreements. Well-functioning articulation provisions govern the relationships between different levels, and have proved successful in facilitating adjustment in the balance between levels. For the most part state supports for multi-employer bargaining have remained in place, with Italy a partial exception, and in a few, including Germany, have actually been reinforced in recent years (Marginson, 2015). Put another way, multi-employer wage bargaining in these countries has demonstrated the capacity to adjust to changed economic conditions (Glassner *et al.*, 2011).

In contrast, among the second group of several southern European countries, prior to 2008 organized decentralization was altogether less developed. In Greece and Portugal formal scope for negotiation at the company level was noticeably limited, whilst in Spain scope for company-level negotiation had opened up but often outside the framework of multi-employer, sector and provincial, agreements (Molina, 2014). For these countries, an alternative reform path to that advocated by the European institutions, and enforced under the MoUs, would promote greater scope for company-level negotiation within the framework of multi-employer agreements, put in place effective mechanisms articulating bargaining at different levels, and retain or reinstate state supports for multi-employer bargaining. In short, there is an alternative to the current policy prescriptions for these countries.

Funding

This work was supported by Eurofound: the report on which it draws was commissioned under framework contract 10-3030-02.

Bibliography

Clauwaert S. & Schömann I. (2012). The crisis and national labour law reforms: a mapping exercise. *ETUI Working Paper* 2012.04. Brussels: ETUI, 2012.

Crouch C. (1993). *Industrial Relations and European State Traditions*. Oxford: Oxford University Press.

Crouch C. (2014). Introduction: labour markets and social policy after the crisis. *Transfer*, No. 20 (1), 2014, pp. 7-22.

Dufresne A. & Pernot J-M. (2013). Les syndicats européens à l'épreuve de la nouvelle governance économique (European trade unions in the test of new economic governance). *Chronique Internationale de l'IRES* 143–44 (Novembre, 2013).

Erne R. (2012). European industrial relations after the crisis. In: Smismans S. (ed.) *The European Union and Industrial Relations*. Manchester: Manchester University Press, 2012, pp. 225–35.

European Commission (2012). Labour Market Developments in Europe 2012. *European Economy*, No. 5, 2012. Luxembourg: Publications Office of the European Union.

European Commission. (2015). European Semester 2015. Retrieved September 25, 2016 from http://ec.europa.eu/europe2020/making-it-happen/country-specific-recommendations/index_en.htm.

Eurofound, (2014). *Changes to wage-setting mechanisms in the context of the crisis and the EU's new economic governance regime.* Dublin: Eurofound, 2014.

Glassner V. & Keune M. (2010). Negotiating the crisis? Collective bargaining in Europe during the economic downturn. *DIALOGUE Working Paper* 10. Geneva: ILO, 2010.

Glassner V., Keune M. & Marginson P. (2011). Collective bargaining in a time of crisis: developments in the private sector in Europe'. *Transfer*, No. 17(3), 2011, pp. 303–21.

Hancke' B. & Rhodes M. (2005). EMU and labour market institutions in Europe. The Rise and Fall of National Social Pacts. *Work and Occupations* Vol. 32 (2), 2005, pp. 196–228.

Ibsen C., Andersen S., Due J. & Madsen J. (2011). Bargaining in the crisis – a comparison of the 2010 collective bargaining round in the Danish and Swedish manufacturing sectors. *Transfer*, No. 17(3), 2011, pp. 323–339.

Jobert A. (2002). *Les espaces de la négociation collective* (Space for Collective Bargaining), 2nd ed., Toulouse, 2002.

Katz H. (1993). The Decentralization of Collective Bargaining: A Literature Review and Comparative Analysis. *Industrial and Labor Relations Review*, Vol. 47(1), 1993, pp. 3–22.

Kerckhofs P. (2011). Extension of collective bargaining agreements in the EU. *Eurofound Background Paper*. Dublin: Eurofound. 2011.

Keune M. (2011). Wage flexibilisation and the minimum wage. In: *European Commission Industrial Relations in Europe 2010*. Luxembourg: Publications Office of the European Communities, 2011, pp. 127–47.

Kohl H. & Platzer H-W. (eds.) (2004). *Industrial Relations in Central and Eastern Europe*. Brussels: ETUI.

Marginson P. (2015). Coordinated bargaining in Europe: from incremental corrosion to frontal assault? *European Journal of Industrial Relations*. Vol. 21(2), 2015, pp. 97–114.

Marginson P. & Sisson K. (2004). *European Integration and Industrial Relations. Multi-level Governance in the Making*. Basingstoke: Palgrave Macmillan, 2004.

Meardi G. (2012). *Social Failures of EU Enlargement. A Case of Workers Voting with their Feet*. London: Routledge, 2012.

Molina O. (2014). Self-regulation and the state in industrial relations in Southern Europe: Back to the future? *European Journal of Industrial Relations*. Vol. 20 (1), 2014, pp. 21-36.

Schulten T., Bispinck R. & Schaefer C. (eds.) (2006). *Minimum Wages in Europe*. Brussels: ETUI, 2006.

Schulten T. & Müller T. (2013). A new European interventionism? The impact of the new European economic governance on wages and collective bargaining'. In: Natali D. & Vanhercke B. (eds.) *Social Developments in the European Union 2012*. Brussels: ETUI, 2013, pp. 181–213.

Sisson K. (1987). *The Management of Collective Bargaining*. Oxford: Blackwell, 1987.

Traxler F. (1995). Farewell to labour market associations? In: Crouch, C. & Traxler, F. (eds.) *Organised Indus-trial Relations in Europe. What Future?* Aldershot: Avebury, 1995, pp. 3–19.

Traxler F. (1998). 'Collective bargaining in the OECD: Developments, preconditions and effects'. *European Journal of Industrial Relations*. Vol. 4 (2), pp. 207–226.

Traxler F., Blaschke S. & Kittel B. (2001). *National Labour Relations in Internationalized Markets. A Comparative Study of Institutions, Change, and Performance*. Oxford: Oxford University Press, 2001.

Appendix. Prevalent bargaining regime.

Country	Multi-employer (MEB) or Single-employer (SEB) bargaining prevalent	
	2008	**2012**
Austria	MEB	MEB
Belgium	MEB	MEB
Bulgaria	Mixed	Mixed
Croatia*	MEB	MEB
Cyprus	Mixed	Mixed
Czech Republic	SEB	SEB
Denmark	MEB	MEB
Estonia	SEB	SEB
Finland	MEB	MEB

Country	Multi-employer (MEB) or Single-employer (SEB) bargaining prevalent	
France	MEB	MEB
Germany	MEB	MEB
Greece	MEB	MEB
Hungary	SEB	SEB
Ireland	**MEB**	**SEB**
Italy	MEB	MEB
Latvia	SEB	SEB
Lithuania	SEB	SEB
Luxembourg	MEB	MEB
Malta	SEB	SEB
Netherlands	MEB	MEB
Norway	MEB	MEB
Poland	SEB	SEB
Portugal	MEB	MEB
Romania	**MEB**	**SEB**
Slovakia	Mixed	Mixed
Slovenia	MEB	MEB
Spain	MEB	MEB
Sweden	MEB	MEB
United Kingdom	SEB	SEB

Notes:
The coding as MEB or SEB is derived from the ICTWSS Database measure of 'Level', the predominant level(s) at which wage bargaining takes place.
– values of 3, 4 and 5 indicate that the sector and/or the cross-sector level is predominant: these correspond to multi-employer bargaining (MEB);
– a value of 1 indicates that the establishment or company level is predominant: this corresponds to single-employer bargaining (SEB);
– a value of 2 indicates an intermediate situation where sector and company negotiations each, respectively, account for at least one-third of those covered by collective wage-setting arrangements. ICTWSS codes five countries as 2: BG, CY, FR, LU and SK
– of these five countries, three are classified as 'Mixed' in the table: BG, CY, SK. Two countries, FR and LU, are classified as MEB: in the former, the wage provisions of sector agreements are almost universally subject to legal extension, whilst in the latter the cross-sector indexation mechanism accounts for an important component of wage increases.
*Croatia is not included in the ICTWSS, and for 2011 has been coded on the basis of the EIRO country profile.
Change in bargaining regime shown in bold.

Source: Visser J., ICTWSS Database, Version 4, 2013.

The Transformations of Employment Relations

What is the Role of Social Dialogue and Industrial Relations?

Daiva PETRYLAITĖ*

Abstract

This paper analyses the essential features of social dialogue and collective labour relations in the European Union and their role in strengthening the European social model. The analysis is based on the recent political, economic and social challenges faced by the European Union and its social model system as well as the systems of Member States. This paper does not pretend to propose cardinal solutions as it cannot be the result of one brief analysis. The author seeks to indicate the existing problems, to show their essence, and to encourage further academic discussions in this field.

Key words: social partnership, collective labour law, employment relations

Introduction

In a modern society, legal labour relations are very complicated and heterogeneous. They reflect both the existing situation in the market economy and general rules of social life. Even the smallest social or economic changes first of all send ripples through labour (industrial) relations and inevitably condition antagonism, disagreements and conflicts between/among the parties to such relations. The increasing role of labour relations and individual elements thereof are illustrated by new categories characterising contemporary social phenomena and processes. The reality of the twenty-first century determines new challenges for labour law. Increasing globalization processes, technological revolution,

---

* Daiva Petrylaitė is Professor, Head of the Institute of Collective Labour Law and Social Partnership at Faculty of Law Vilnius University, Lithuania. She is an expert on labour law, social partnership and civil service law in Lithuania. She has participated in research projects in the International Labour Organization as a national expert. Prof. Petrylaitė has authored numerous publications on labour law, social partnership, work and life balance issues, civil service law.

development of new forms of employment, business relocation to other countries or continents, nearly unlimited potential for using information technologies in labour processes – have all formed preconditions for the individualization of labour relations. Issues so relevant in the environment of industrial revolution and production relations lose their importance in the light of the technological revolution and settling relations of the consumer society. Therefore, today we should address not only the relations of the market economy and the commitment of the state to ensure free economic activities. We also face the inevitable necessity to take into account the social needs of our society requiring predetermined measures on the part of the state to restrict free market relations in order to implement social objectives and values arising out of the dialogue and cooperation of the social partners. The relations of the market economy should not only be free and independent, but they should be socially motivated at the same time. The state is given a possibility, and often a duty too, to restrict the relations of the market economy so as to achieve certain social goals. Therefore, there are new tasks for both social dialogue and collective labour law. A social context is no longer relevant for the protection of employees in a particular company or in the separate sphere of industrial relations. Today social dialogue and social partnership should have an important and maybe the most important place in all public decision-making processes.

1. European concept of collective labour relations and social dialogue

Social dialogue is a key part of the European social model, with European social dialogue having been launched at the historic Val Duchesse process initiated by Commission President Jacques Delors 30 years ago. However, since then, established approaches to social dialogue in Europe have been challenged by industrial and social change. Ongoing shifts towards greater decentralization of collective bargaining have resulted in a polarization of Member States and the crisis has resulted in an increased trend towards unilateral decision making by governments at the expense of social partners' autonomy. The modern European concept of collective labour relations is based on social dialogue, which represents an opportunity for ensuring permanent social peace. The social dialogue is regulated by the provisions of the primary European law, conducted at the supranational level by the social partners functioning in the European social area. It is also an important model for the social partners for conducting dialogue in the EU Member States, and for the authorities of particular EU Member States for establishing the principles and procedures for social dialogue in labour law systems. Freedom of association, collective bargaining, social dialogue and quality of collective labour relations are the fundamental elements of the European social model. Collective bargaining as part of this model should promote workplace democracy, redistribution of resources, and efficiency of employment relations.

Social dialogue, including collective industrial relations, have undergone dramatic change over recent decades, with a shift to predominantly service or knowledge economies, greater individualization in society, and the growth of female employment and changing gender roles bringing issues of work–life balance, care arrangements and working-time patterns. Also, economic change is a key driver of the role of social dialogue. After the financial crisis of 2008, the issue of European social dialogue slipped down the policy agenda in the face of more immediate economic concerns. At first sight, a direct relationship between collective labour law and the economic downturn seems to be hardly possible. However, it conditioned consequences such as: (i) diminution of the role or complete elimination (withdrawal) of social dialogue and its institutions; (ii) decentralization of collective bargaining by moving from bargaining at national/branch level to the enterprise level; (iii) application of the *in peius* principle in collective agreements; (iv) reduction of the status and role of trade unions *vis-à-vis* the role of other representatives of employees, e.g. labour councils. The crisis appears to have significantly affected industrial relations in the European Union. We only need to mention structural changes in the labour market, significant shifts in social relations, reducing the role of social partners and collective bargaining, and the increasing practice on the part of Member States to adopt unilateral decisions as proof of this. This concurrently created a climate of mistrust and denial; employees stopped feeling secure and relying upon representation of the social partners. Therefore, it can be stated with certainty that the Member States, in the long term, have to focus on labour market promotion measures that would not only contribute to higher employment rates and re-establishment of the role of collective bargaining and social partners, but that would also eliminate post-crisis psychosocial effects and prevent negative labour market phenomena such as job uncertainty, increasing pace of work, involuntary and undeclared work.

The development and coordination of collective labour relation at the European level still remains a great challenge. There is a very diverse situation of collective labour relations in Member States. In some countries, social dialogue is effective, efficient and representative, but in others, social partners have lost representativeness and credibility and even barely exist. While in some Member States strong social dialogue has been helpful in resisting the crisis, collective bargaining systems in others have undergone changes and remained weaker and fragmented, at times accelerating the shift to decentralized collective bargaining. The situation was announced and discussed during the high-level conference on social dialogue on 5 March 2015. During the meeting, the European Commission launched a new start for social dialogue and presented the main goal to reinforce competitiveness and fairness of the social market economy, which cannot be done without the social partners. President Jean-Claude Juncker added that the European Commission and the social partners should sit again around the table in the same spirit Jacques Delors sat with trade unionists and employers at Val Duchess in 1985, but with a greater vision[1]. The social partners' representatives expressed the need of a joint vision with all social partners on the challenges ahead, especially on the labour markets. The European social dialogue should be a facilitator for necessary reforms. Trade unions should acknowledge that European companies face severe global competition, and improved competitiveness alone will allow us to keep Europe's social model functioning[2].

The weakening situation by social dialogue is well illustrated by data and research done by Eurofound[3], the huge decline of trade union density starting from 1990s is very clear in most Central and Eastern European Member States, where in several cases from 1997 onwards, trade union confederations lost more than 40% or 50% of their members. The gap in trade union membership rates between the 'old' EU Member States (the EU15) and the Central and Eastern European countries that joined

1 See more: Vincenti D. (2015). Commission seeks to revive battered social dialogue. Retrieved August 22, 2016 from https://www.euractiv.com/section/social-europe-jobs/news/commission-seeks-to-revive-battered-social-dialogue.

2 So Business Europe President Emma Mercegaglia, cited by Vincenti D. (2015). Commission seeks to revive battered social dialogue. Retrieved August 22, 2016 from https://www.euractiv.com/section/social-europe-jobs/news/commission-seeks-to-revive-battered-social-dialogue.

3 *Eurofound: Collective bargaining in Europe in the 21st century*. Publications Office of the European Union, Luxembourg 2015.

in 2004 and 2007 (the EU10) had almost closed in 2000, when rates were 27.0% in the EU15 and 27.3% in the EU10. Developments in the number of social partner organizations, in other words changes resulting from mergers or the establishment of new organizations, have been much less pronounced than the changes in density. What stands out is an increase in the numbers of both employer and trade union organizations mainly in the EU10, reflecting changes in the structure of the economy, including the development of new sectors, the shrinking of traditional industries and sectors, and changing organizational structures resulting from privatization.

During the last decades, negative changes in tripartism and bipartism are visible as well. The Eurofound research mentioned above states this; the changes that have occurred since the late 1990s and, in particular, the negative effects of the crisis on tripartism and bipartism in some countries also illustrate that – perhaps even more today than 10 years ago – marked gaps between the main industrial relations models in the EU exist. On the one hand, tripartism, 'social partnership' and 'concertation' are strongly rooted in the Nordic and western-continental models; on the other hand, Central, Eastern and southern Europe is characterised by much more fragile and unsteady practice that depends far more on political cycles, changes and will[4]. These and similar situations in different spheres of the collective labour relations show that the economic crisis and its effects on industrial relations and working conditions are still changing the European labour world. The new EU economic governance tools had different consequences on individual Member States and their systems of industrial relations and working conditions. On the other hand, the situation in recent years has also revealed negative aspects, such as occasional demonstration of the limited practical interpretation of the ideas and objectives of social partnership, as well as attempts to satisfy the short-term and, unfortunately, often individual goals of social partner organizations. The public interest tends to be forgotten, whereas the opportunities offered by the proper implementation of social partnership relations and their outcomes in the strengthening of society and industrial democracy are underutilized.

The worsening situation and challenges for social dialogue growing all over Europe, stimulated the European Commission to present the draft recommendations for the social partners' forum which took place on 31 March 2015 in Riga. The Recommendations are recognizing

---

[4] *Ibidem.*

the importance of social dialogue in general and in both the economic and social governance conceiving the contribution of social dialogue at EU level for investment, competitiveness, economic growth and employment, particularly in quality job creation, and emphasizing the role and competences of social partners – employers' organizations and trade unions – need to activate involvement of social partners in achieving targets of the strategy Europe 2020, in implementation of macro-economic reforms and European investment plan, to support development of social dialogue at the EU, national, regional, sectoral and enterprise level[5]. The Recommendations clarify the principles and measures for all levels of the social dialogue. Speaking about the European level, the main idea is to promote active social dialogue in collaboration with the European social partners, effective governance of Economic and Monetary Union and aspects of social dimension of Europe ensuring timely and regular consultations of social partners on all related matters, facilitating involvement of social partners in setting country specific recommendations and supporting their implementation within the framework of the European semester process. Furthermore, the existing mechanisms of social dialogue should be strengthened by promoting social partners' agreements at the EU level and their implementation at national level.

With regards to national level, the Recommendation state that governments should provide substantive dialogue with social partners addressing macro-economic and social matters, including education, training and innovation related policies, by balancing the involvement of social partners' representatives. Regular consultations between social partners and government and conclusion of agreements should be promoted, while respecting the tradition of social dialogue in each EU Member State. Agreements reached within the framework of tripartite and autonomous social dialogue should be respected and implemented both by governments and social partners. Implementation of best practice of EU Member States should be promoted at national level. Governments should promote collective bargaining by setting conducive framework conditions and incentives, as well as realistic requirements regarding the representativeness of social partner organizations. The European Commission and governments of EU Member States should

[5] Role of Social Dialogue in Ensuring the Economic Growth and Qualitative Work Places. Retrieved 22 August, 2016 from https://eu2015.lv/images/Kalendars/Citi/rekomendacijas_eng_27.03.2015.pdf.

continue to support national capacity-building of social partners through a variety of funding resources.

Special principles and measures that need to be taken are described for regional, sectoral and even enterprise level (i.e. 'In order to facilitate balancing interests of employers and employees for business competitiveness and sustainability, consultations on all related matters, including education, training and modernization, as well as conclusion of collective agreements at enterprise level should be promoted. In particular – the benefits of employers' and employees' dialogue in micro and small enterprises should be promoted, while respecting the very specific characteristics of working relations and consequence on the mode of social dialogue organization in these enterprises')[6].

The above-mentioned situations of social dialogue and collective labour relations as well as the issues raised and solutions offered by the European Union institutions and social partners themselves reveal the importance of social cooperation in a contemporary society. The concept of social partnership is becoming more and more embedded in modern European conception. Social partnership is a concentration of diverse interests, especially for economic and social planning purposes. Social partnership became a key to the successful functioning of the European Union and to the strengthening of public democracy. The importance of social partnership was well pinpointed by Professor Marco Biagi near two decades ago when he said: 'The co-operative approach, in the spirit and the practice of partnership between the social actors is essential not simply to improve industrial relations across Europe. The need for a more intense and dynamic action at EU level is essential if the social partners want to ensure the progress of the future of Europe, employment as well social partnership will become a key to the successful functioning of the EU and to the strengthening of public democracy'[7]. The trademark of a dynamic modern European concept spreading around the world is the European social model. Its basic elements are: the idea of partnership and a regular, open social dialogue.

Active 'actors' of that process are social partners' organizations, government and non-government organizations representing social groups of the democratic local society interested in the maintenance

---

6 *Ibidem.*

7 Biagi M. The role of social partners in Europe: from dialogue to partnership. In: Tiraboschi M. *Marco Biagi: Selected writings*. The Hague: Kluwer Law International, 2003.

of social peace. The collective agreements, normative agreements and other agreements – social pacts that guarantee fair distribution of assets earned jointly by the social partners are one of the fundamental legal guarantees of social peace in labour relations. The material guarantees of social peace are: legally guaranteed balance of power of the social partners' organizations in the collective labour relations and transparent legal regulation of principles and procedures for collective bargaining and use by the social partners' organizations – under supervision of judicial authorities – of legal instruments, in particular means of mutual pressure.

2. Preconditions of social partnership in national law and practices

Central and Eastern European countries that joined the European Union in 2004 had to face the challenge of, *inter alia*, 'learning social democracy'. As it was then noted by Professor Manfred Weiss: 'In the countries of Central and Eastern Europe the development of industrial relations has not managed to keep pace with the emergence of democratic freedoms and the market economy, with highly individualistic neo-liberal values tending to prevail'[8]. Lithuania was to address these challenges, too. Moreover, it was the continuation of the already started construction of industrial relations of a new quality and, even, of social policy.

The Central and Eastern European countries, unlike Western countries with long-lasting traditions of social dialogue, had not lived in a stable social dialogue. In the 1990s, all of them had to create the first instruments of social dialogue and collective labour relations quickly and efficiently: not only to adopt necessary legal acts but also to declare labour relations with a new quality and content. This was a challenge for both states and participants of these relations – social partners. There was the beginning of 'discoveries' where some states tried to create something unique only for themselves while others tried to use good practices of other countries by transferring their models of collective labour relations. This is how next to the already existing models of collective labour relations, new ones began forming and these are difficult to attribute to any already existing groups.

8 Weiss M. Enlargement and Industrial Relations: Building a New Social Partnership. *The International Journal of Comparative Labour Law and Industrial Relations*, Vol. 20 (1), 2004, pp. 5-26.

Countries faced a new challenge for a second time when negotiations for accession to the European Union were opened. At that time it was necessary to take over the *acquis communautaire* and strengthen the role of social dialogue. However, regardless of all aims, investments, good wishes to strengthen the capacity of social partners and improve the infrastructure of social dialogue, a phenomenon not experienced by the western world was encountered – post-soviet mentality which denied and even ignored the importance of collective cooperation (because until 1990 collective cooperation was not linked to democracy and independent decision-making at all in the existing consciousness of individuals). It is no secret that many of these countries saw the negative aspects of social partners' activities: trade unions tried not to lose their held status and at the same time they could not change their mentality from being the state's official organ to the independent representative and defendant of employees' rights and interests. During this time employers' associations started to be formed, however, their confusion could be seen in several countries: they did not know what they were, what they were supposed to do and how to function properly. It was not clear whether they were to represent the interests of business and be negotiators between business and governments or be partners of trade unions representing employees. These challenges were a test for both social partners' organizations and governments, which had to respond effectively to changing political, economic and social circumstances. Besides, this situation was also a challenge for individual members of society – employees and employers. Therefore, in Central and Eastern Europe instead of a quick move to social democracy in the 1990s, the opposite phenomenon could be seen – individualization of labour relations, employees' scepticism, disappointment at trade unions, etc.

Despite labour law reforms, the transposition of European Union law and the common standards of behaviour to national systems, there was growing scepticism of collective labour relations and distrust of trade unions. Meantime trade unions themselves ignored and demonstrated the open distrust of employers' organizations and by-passing them, tried to bargain directly with governments. Neo-liberal ideas in labour relations have found many followers and little resistance. This explains that European social dialogue forms such as information and consultation, worker participation, basically, have never been successfully implemented in practice. As Professor Manfred Weiss notes the lessons of democracy have not been learned.

On the way to establishing values of democracy at work, strengthening the importance of social dialogue and achieving better results in social cooperation, there was a third challenge – the economic crisis which shocked Europe at the end of 2007.

The economic crisis which Europe and the world have experienced in recent years has negatively affected both civil and political as well as economic and social rights[9]. According to Thorbjørn Jagland, Secretary General of the Council of Europe, people's rights are threatened by the impact of the economic crisis and growing inequalities. European societies have suffered the effects of the recent economic crisis, which has deeply affected social cohesion in many Member States, and which may eventually threaten both the rule of law and democracy[10]. Indeed, statistical figures indicate that the economic crisis has had a dramatic effect on the European labour market. For example, total employment in the EU27 decreased by five million persons from the second quarter of 2008 through the second quarter of 2010. The global economic recession that started in the second half of 2008 has affected the entire European economy, impacting more on some countries than on others. This economic crisis and the related impact on industrial relations and working conditions are changing the world of work in Europe. The EU's new economic governance measures have had a varying impact on individual Member States and their system of industrial relations and working conditions. Despite country-level variations, the different European systems of industrial relations weathered the economic and social impact of the early phase of the crisis (2008–2010). Countries with strong social dialogue and/or industrial relations systems displayed better cooperation between the state, employers and employees. As for the second phase of the crisis (2010–2012), there have been many significant impacts of the crisis on a range of aspects of industrial relations, although in many cases it is difficult to disentangle the impact of the crisis from other longer-standing national industrial relations trends[11]. As pointed out by different

9 The Steering Committee for Human Rights (CDDH) of the Council of Europe. The impact of the economic crisis and austerity measures on human rights in Europe: Preliminary study on existing standards and outstanding issues, CDDH(2014)011, Strasbourg, 6 June 2014.

10 Report by the Secretary General of the Council of Europe. State of democracy, human rights and rule of law in Europe, (SG(2014)1- Final), Council of Europe, May 2014, 5, p. 40.

11 *Impact of the crisis on industrial relations and working conditions in Europe*. Eurofound, 2014.

authors, the following violations of collective labour rights were noticed and reported most often during the crisis[12]: (i) the abolition or diminution of the role of social dialogue and its institutions; (ii) the decentralization of collective bargaining on the level of enterprises; (iii) deviation *in peius* to a higher level collective bargaining/statutory rules; (iv) shifting trade union prerogatives to work councils or to the representatives of employees. At first sight, a direct relationship between collective labour law and the economic downturn seems to be hardly possible; however, freedom of association, collective bargaining, social dialogue and quality collective labour relations are fundamental elements of the European social model and key to European economic and social welfare[13]. Hence, the crisis appears to have significantly affected industrial relations in the European Union. It's enough to mention structural changes in the labour market, significant shifts in social relations (cardinal changes in the structure of collective labour relations and social dialogue), diminution of the role of social partners and collective bargaining, increasing practice on the part of states to adopt unilateral decisions. It is true that many countries managed to surmount the initial effects of the economic crisis by means of short-term drastic measures. However, this concurrently created a climate of mistrust and denial; employees stopped feeling secure and relying upon representation of the social partners. Therefore, it can be stated with certainty that the Member States, in the long term, have to focus on labour market promotion measures that would not only contribute to higher employment rates and re-establishment of the role of collective bargaining and social partners, but would also eliminate post-crisis psychosocial effects and prevent negative labour market phenomena such as job uncertainty, increasing pace of work, involuntary and undeclared work[14].

As a result, social partners, particularly in the analysed Central and Eastern European countries, where their position and expertise had not been as developed as in Western European countries, faced a new challenge – when their role and the level of social cooperation were

---

12 Lörcher K. Legal and Judicial International Avenues: The (revised) European Social Charter. In: Bruun N. *et al.* (eds.) *The Economic and Financial Crisis and Collective Labour Law in Europe*. Oxford, 2014, pp. 266–267.

13 Countouris N., Freedland, M. Resocialising Europe – Looking Back and Thinking Forward. In: Countouris N., Freedland M. (eds.) Resocialising Europe in a time of crisis, 2013, New York, p. 499.

14 Petrylaitė D. Decent Work in Times of Economic Crisis: Threats and Lessons Learned. VU mokslo darbai: *Teisė*, Vol. 94, 2015, pp. 149–162.

drastically reduced to a minimum. Formally, this situation was explained as an indisputable need to prevent the effects of the economic crisis. Consequently, governments were allowed to take unilateral decisions on economic, social and labour issues. It is obvious that such a situation had negative effects on the impact of social partners and the general disappointment in the principles of social partnership.

Instead of conclusions

Notwithstanding the importance of social dialogue and ideas of social partnership, the challenges of recent decades, which collective labour relations have faced at both the European and national level, have however, given rise to questions for discussion or at least for prospective reflections. The need to protect the social peace as an overriding common interest results in recognition of the supremacy of the modern European concept of industrial relations over the traditional concept based on permanent conflict between the parties to these relations. In addition, the introduction in labour laws of instruments inspiring the social partners to bargain collectively and to conduct a social dialogue for replacing the laws enacted by the state regulators with autonomous legal and political acts. With the consent of this, there still remains the question of confidence in social dialogue. As well as the question, which and what types of social partners can and shall represent the interests of participants of labour relations in a future Europe. Moreover, the other questions: whether there is still place for traditional trade unions; whether business organizations which are between shareholders, competitors, customers and staff requirements are capable of coping with their multidimensional tasks. Labour relations are transforming from traditional to new employment forms and standard collective labour relations cannot reflect these cardinal changes. Finally, today the working generation, which used to work together, could unite to find a solution to a problem and negotiate together, is changing to Generation Z. The employees of this generation have different values where collective interests are not of such importance and they tend to work and represent their interests individually. Therefore, beside economic and political challenges to collective labour relations and social dialogue, there are others of a social nature and changing values. This determines that with the aim of strengthening and giving new impulses to social dialogue, good will, compliance with principles of legal and moral mutual recognition and cooperation are not enough. It is necessary to take into account labour relations at the primary level, to assess what kind of cooperation can be expected from today's participants of labour relations, what needs their social partners can and should represent and defend. Only when social partners, first of all, trade unions understand and begin to speak the same language of needs which is spoken by the modern employee, can political and legal instruments be innovative and effective in the formation of the united European social model and collective labour relations at the European and national levels.

The Lithuanian Social Partnership Model and its Impact on the Development of Labour Law

Rytis KRASAUSKAS*

Abstract

The article presents the Lithuanian social partnership (hereinafter – SP) model. It reveals and analyses the SP system insofar as this system is related to social employment relations among employees (their representatives), employers (their representatives) and the state, the balancing of the interests of subjects involved in these legal relations, as well as its impact on the legal regulation of employment relations and on solving disputes arising in the area of these relations. The conclusion is drawn that, from 1990 until the present, the Lithuanian SP model has been undergoing transformation from quasi-partnership towards real SP. In order to assess the current situation of the functioning SP systems and their particularities, the main legal sources and the formally consolidated SP system, comprising the operating subjects, are addressed, and the forms and levels consolidated for implementing this system, as well as the established governing principles, are examined. The article presents a multifaceted cross-cutting assessment of the actual situation of SP. The article identifies and defines the key factors influencing the gap between the formal SP model and its actual condition. In the opinion of the author, this gap exists due to legal, economic, political and psychological reasons, which have a direct impact on the behaviour of social partners in balancing the interests of subjects involved in employment relations.

Keywords: social partnership model, social dialogue, employment relations, legal regulation, freedom of association.

Introduction

One of the major objectives of labour law is to define the boundaries of SP in legal terms and to consolidate an effective institutional system and methods enabling the reconciliation of different interests arising

* Rytis Krasauskas is Associate Professor of Labour Law of the Institute of Private Law, Faculty of Law of Mykolas Romeris University, Lithuania. He is acting judge of the Vilnius Regional Administrative Court of Lithuania and has almost ten years of experience working in different positions in the Constitutional Courts of the Republic of Lithuania. His particular research areas are collective labour law, social partnership and employment contracts.

from employment relations. In the course of implementing this objective, it is important to bear in mind the essence of the legal regulation of employment relations, i.e. achieving a balance between the flexibility and social security of employment relations to the satisfaction of all social partners. Therefore, it is not only important that laws in the area of labour would formally regulate SP mechanisms, or that the employees' guarantees laid down by the state-level (centralised) legal regulation would be artificially lowered in expectation that an agreement regarding them can be reached through the application of SP mechanisms; but it is also particularly important to analyse whether, based on such a legal regulation, there are adequate preconditions for the effective development of SP in the state. If no adequate account is taken of factors that affect the behaviour of social partners during social dialogue or lead to the avoidance of such dialogue on the whole, a legal regulation laid down in legal acts with the aim to construct the regulation of employment relations through SP mechanisms may remain a legal fiction, which creates no preconditions for achieving the raised objective to ensure an optimal balance between the flexibility of employment relations and the security of employees.

By means of comparative, logical, analytical and other research methods, this article reveals the major features of the Lithuanian SP model, identifies the reasons behind the development of this model and defines the factors preventing a smoother and more effective operation of SP systems in Lithuania. As presented in this article, the Lithuanian SP model is, in principle, based on the legal regulation that is laid down in the Labour Code of the Republic of Lithuania[1] (hereinafter referred to as the 2002 Labour Code) and other legal acts and is currently *de jure* in force in Lithuania. In the light of this, the article gives insights as to the initial objective of the drafters of the Lithuanian Social Model[2] to strengthen the impact of social dialogue on the regulation of employment relations.

1. The Lithuanian SP model and its elements

A national SP model represents an SP system in a particular state. Such a system is determined by the historical development of the given state, as well as by the legal, economic, political and even psychological

---

1 *Valstybės žinios* (State Gazette), 2002, No. 64-2569 (with subsequent amendments and supplements until April 1, 2016).

2 For more on the social model see http://www.socmodelis.lt.

conditions that have existed there. The development of this system is a dynamic and permanent phenomenon, to a large extent, indicating the maturity of civil society and reflecting the situation of democratic processes. In legal theory[3], depending on the motivation of partners involved in SP and on the effectiveness of SP, two extreme models of SP are distinguished: quasi-partnership (or formally enforced) model and real SP (or true proactive) model.

The quasi-partnership (or formally enforced) model was established in the USSR[4] and occupied Lithuania until 1990, and it was aimed at including (frequently merely formally) the greatest possible number of subjects in collective bargaining and collective agreements or arrangements at all levels. In this way, the actually existing problems were disguised, and real SP relations were disrupted. This SP model is identified by such features as enforced membership, the dominance of the state in creating and implementing quasi-partnership relations in employees' and employers' corporations, the undivided interest of an employer and the state, and a special role assumed by trade unions, which tend to be closed in nature and, among other things, are inclined to avoid confrontation with both employers and the state; in quasi-partnership, legal employment relations are characterized by paternalism (i.e. a false impression is created that, purportedly, care is taken of the rights of employees), the secondary role attached to material incentives to work, a closed labour market where an employee remains with the enterprise where he or she has started his or her working activity, etc. The quasi-partnership (or formally enforced) model, in its pure form, was in force in Lithuania from 1940 until 1990.

The real SP (or true proactive) model (which, for example, is typical of Denmark and Sweden) is a humanistic SP model, oriented towards the balancing of interests, solidarity, subsidiarity, alignment with the values of a social contract and a democratic social law-governed state, the needs of social partners and their initiative.

Both quasi-partnership and real SP models are relevant in analysing the Lithuanian SP model and the reasons for its formation, as well as for determining the directions for its improvement, since the former model was valid in Lithuania for nearly 50 years, and attempts were made to

---

3 Bagdanskis T., Guobaitė-Kirslienė R., Krasauskas R., I. Mačernytė-Panomariovienė (eds.) *Kolektyvinė darbo teisė. Vadovėlis* [Collective Labour Law. Textbook]. Vilnius: Mykolas Romeris University, 2013.

4 The USSR stands for the Union of Soviet Socialist Republics.

abandon it as soon as the restoration of Lithuania's independence, i.e. from 1990. In principle, the real SP model corresponds to what is sought in Lithuania with a view to improving SP systems. In the light of these circumstances, the Lithuanian social model can be defined as gravitating from the quasi-partnership model towards real SP.

In order to assess what kind of impact is still exerted by the former Soviet quasi-partnership model on the present-day Lithuanian SP model and to determine what Lithuania is lacking for the legal regulation of employment relations to be based on real SP, it is necessary to consider the following: (1) the actual situation regarding SP; (2) the factors behind the gap between the formally consolidated SP system and its actual situation.

2. The actual situation regarding SP

In order to identify the most characteristic features of the Lithuanian SP model, its actual situation should be analysed by revealing and assessing the legal status of employees' representatives, the role of employers and their organizations, the role of SP institutions, the effectiveness of information and consultation procedures, the situation regarding collective bargaining.

2.1 The legal status of employees' representatives and their impact on the development of SP

The legal status of trade unions in Lithuania is consolidated on the constitutional level[5]. In representing and defending the rights and interests of employees, trade unions also follow international treaties, other international legal acts, the Law on Trade Unions, the 2002 Labour Code, the Civil Code, other legal acts regulating the activity of trade unions and the articles (statute) of the trade union. Trade unions in Lithuania are recognized as having the right to represent and defend both their members and all the employees of a given enterprise who are not their members. The main and most considerable challenge faced by Lithuanian trade unions is the especially low number of members. Lithuania is 3rd from the bottom in the EU in terms of the percentage of employee membership in trade unions, and this percentage has seen consistent

5 Articles 35 and 50 of the Constitution, which have been interpreted from various aspects in the rulings of the Constitutional Court (see, e.g., rulings of 14 January 1999 and 30 September 2003, etc.).

decline since 2000, i.e. in 2000, it covered 18.4% of the employed and, respectively, in 2013 – 8.8%[6]. At the end of 2014, total membership in trade unions accounted for approximately 7.8% of all the employed[7]. Based on the calculations presented by trade unions themselves in 2016, their membership includes around 15% of Lithuanian employees[8]. Such a low membership in trade unions has a direct impact on the bargaining power of employees affiliated with trade unions, since employers and the state and, ultimately, employees themselves begin to lose trust in them[9]; it has been increasingly voiced that, in the Lithuanian Tripartite Council, which decides issues of relevant concern to all employees, trade unions have been representing merely the interests of a narrow group of employees.

Mainly, for the purpose of solving the problem of the insufficient representation of employees, the 2002 Labour Code established the institute of works councils. Under the legal regulation currently in force, a works council (or a representative of employees), in principle, has all the rights of collective representation and organizational rights. At present, only those rights that under laws, are recognised as the prerogative of trade unions, are not granted to works councils. This includes for example: the right to participate in collective bargaining and concluding collective agreements on the higher than enterprise level, also the right to call and lead a strike where there is a trade union operating in the enterprise or where a staff meeting has transferred the functions of employees' representation and protection to the trade union of the relevant sector of economic activity. In 2014, Lithuanian employees were represented in 36.7% of economic entities, including 3.5% represented by trade unions, 0.3% – by sectoral trade unions, 4.3% – by works councils and 28.6% – by a representative of employees[10]. The assessment of the indicated structure

6 Retrieved September 4, 2016 from http://www.ilo.org/ilostat.

7 At the end of 2014, Lithuanian trade unions had 94,200 registered members and 1,212,255 occupied jobs. Retrieved September 4, 2016 from http://osp.stat.gov.lt.

8 Retrieved September 4, 2016 from http://www.lpsk.lt/2016/02/26/lietuvoje-profesinems-sajungoms-priklauso-15-proc-darbuotoju.

9 The findings of the survey carried out on 1–11 April 2016 by the market and public opinion research company *Baltijos tyrimai* reveal that trade unions were trusted by 45% of the respondents, while distrust was expressed by 39%. See 'Be euforijos, tačiau palankiai' ['Without euphoria, but welcomed']. Federation of Lithuanian Forest and Wood Worker Trade Unions, Retrieved April 28, 2016 from http://www.lmpf.lt/be-euforijos-taciau-palankiai.

10 Ministry of Social Security and Labour. *Social Report 2014–2015*, Vilnius, 2015, pp. 16–19.

of employees' representation in enterprises shows that the employees of 32.9 out of 36.7% of economic entities were represented not by a trade union, but by a works council (or by a representative of employees); this means that, in as many as 90% of all the enterprises in which there were representatives of employees, these representatives were not from trade unions; thus, the conclusion should be drawn that the objective raised in the 2002 Labour Code was reached: works councils (representatives of employees) have sufficiently successfully filled the representation gaps appearing in the activity of trade unions due to inadequate participation by employees. In the light of the fact that, under the legal regulation currently in force, in cases where there is no operating trade union, works councils (representatives of employees) are entrusted, in principle, all the rights to participate in SP mechanisms, the above-indicated figures give grounds to be optimistic, and, at the same time, they also raise doubts as to whether it is reasonable to seek to deprive works councils and a representative of employees of the possibility of concluding collective agreements.

The effectiveness of the activity of employees' representatives and their ability to draw employees together while representing their interests is also revealed through how adequately use is made of the last resort, ultima ratio, collective self-defence measure – the right to strike. The use of the right to strike also reflects the clarity of the mechanism of the organization of strikes as consolidated in the 2002 Labour Code and, partly, the clarity of the legal regulation on strikes. Unfortunately, strikes in Lithuania are organized infrequently in a particularly narrow segment (i.e. in practice, only in educational establishments) and relatively ineffectively. Such a conclusion follows from the statistical data on strikes for 2001-2015: there were no legitimate strikes in Lithuania in 2002-2004, 2006, 2009-2011 and 2013; strikes organized in 2009 were declared to be unlawful; the year 2001 saw 34 strikes, including warning strikes (which drew the participation of 1,703 of the employed and approximately took 1.27 working days); in 2005, there was 1 strike (which drew 70 of the employed and approximately took 11.91 working days); respectively, in 2007 – 161 strikes (which drew 7,033 of the employed and approximately took 1.36 working days); in 2008 – 112 strikes (which drew 7,961 of the employed and approximately took 3.97 working days); in 2012 – 193 strikes (which drew 5,558 of the employed and approximately took 0.55 working days); in 2014 – 78 strikes (which drew 1,591 of the employed and approximately took 1.08 working days); and in 2015 – 296 strikes (which drew 7,126 of the employed and approximately took 0.34 working days[11]. In this context, it is worth mentioning that, although the total statistical data on strikes in Lithuania during 2001–2015 shows that employees were relatively active in exercising the right to strike, nevertheless, the absolute majority of strikes (i.e. 872 out of 875) were organized in the area of education; only on two occasions (in 2001), did strikes take place in the manufacturing sector, and once (in 2005) a strike was organized by employees engaged in artistic, entertainment and recreational activities. It should be assumed that a considerably high number (in particular, on the country-wide level) of strikes organized in the area of education is indicative of the activeness of employees' representatives in this area, as well as of the fact that social partners tend to conduct collective bargaining from positions of power. The provided statistical data make it clear that the duration of strikes in Lithuania is especially short (in 2001–2015, the average duration of the organized strikes was 2.9 working days; the average duration of the strikes in the area of education (872 out of 875 strikes, including warning strikes) was just 1.3 working days). These figures, if considered in connection with the circumstance that the demands of the employees' representatives were not satisfied (which, among other things, is evident from the large number of strikes called in the area of education (872 out of 875 strikes)), suggest the conclusion that the employees and organizers taking part in these strikes lacked sufficient trust in this ultima ratio instrument of collective action or were unable (lacked determination) to use it more efficiently, or that they faced pressure from state authorities (or society) to end the strikes.

2.2 The role of employers and their organizations in SP

In addition, the Lithuanian SP model is directly influenced by the structure of employers. At the beginning of May 2016, as many as 80% of enterprises operating in Lithuania, i.e. 79,490 out of 99,200, had less than 10 employees; enterprises with 10 to 100 employees made 18%; and there were around 2% of enterprises with more than 100 employees.[12] Taking account of these figures and seeking to attain real SP in small enterprises, both social partners (i.e. employers and representatives of employees) and the legislature should aim at activating SP processes on the higher than enterprise level, while the affiliation of employers

[11] Retrieved September 4, 2016 from http://osp.stat.gov.lt.

[12] *Ibidem.*

with associated organizations and effective joint action in the area of employment relations should become a priority. However, similarly to employees, employers are slow in joining associations. For example, at the end of 2014, the associations of entrepreneurs and employers comprised 15.3%[13] of enterprises as their members.

It should be mentioned that the representation of the interests of members in SP in the area of employment relations (in collective bargaining on the national, sectoral and territorial levels; in participating in the activity of bipartite and tripartite SP institutions; etc.) is not a priority action for employers' organizations, since they devote greater attention to lobbying, mainly in relation to the improvement of business conditions. And this is natural. Therefore, trade unions, whose principal activity is the protection of the interests of employees in the area of employment relations, have to understand that the activeness of employers' organizations in SP with regard to employment relations is directly proportionate to pressure from the representatives of employees.

2.3 The role of SP institutions

Lithuanian SP systems involve the participation of SP institutions operating on the basis of tripartite and bipartite partnership. The system of these institutions comprises: (1) the Tripartite Council of the Republic of Lithuania (hereinafter also referred to as the Lithuanian Tripartite Council); (2) permanent and temporary commissions and committees under the Lithuanian Tripartite Council; (3) specialised councils and commissions (which are formed according to the procedure established by laws or collective agreements); and (4) regional councils and commissions.

The effectiveness of the activity of SP institutions and their impact on the development of SP are, among other things, also affected by the fact that, inevitably, regardless of the efforts to reconcile the interests of all employees and employers, the representatives of employees and employers in these institutions, first of all, listen to the position of their members, which, due to a rather considerable specificity of employment relations in separate sectors, is frequently divergent. As is clear from the composition of the Lithuanian Tripartite Council, employees are

[13] At the end of 2014, entrepreneurs' and employers' associations united 13,900 members and 90,790 registered economic entities. Retrieved September 4, 2016 from http://osp.stat.gov.lt.

represented by the representatives of six trade union organizations, and employers are represented by the representatives of four employers' organizations[14]. It can be possible to discuss why specifically these employees' and employers' representatives form the composition of the Lithuanian Tripartite Council, as well as whether they satisfy the criteria of the representative organization, such as the qualitative criterion (i.e. whether they are sufficiently independent and experienced and have operated for a long time), the institutional criterion (i.e. whether they participate in the representations of functional institutions and are elected to institutions representing employees (staff of an enterprise)) and the functional criterion (i.e. whether they have experience in representing employees on the higher than enterprise level). However, it is evident that, regardless of which representatives will represent employees and employers in the Lithuanian Tripartite Council operating on the national level, all of them will face serious problems due to the compliance with the quantitative criterion (i.e. society will always raise reasonable questions regarding the number of members of these organizations). This problem, which remains of relevant concern to SP institutions operating on all levels, is predetermined by the low activeness of employees and employers in joining associated bodies. All of this raises public distrust in the legitimacy of the activity carried out by these institutions, which inevitably serves to weaken the influence of these institutions on the regulation of employment relations and undermines the effectiveness of SP as such.

2.4 The effectiveness of information and consultation procedures and the situation regarding the participation of employees in the management of the enterprise

Article 47 of the 2002 Labour Code lays down the general rule that, in Lithuania, the right to information and consultation is granted to employees' representatives (Paragraph 1) and, in the absence of any employee representatives, an employer must inform employees and hold consultations with them directly only in the cases specifically indicated in the Code (Paragraphs 3, 4 and 10). Consequently, the effectiveness of overall information and consultation is directly dependent not

[14] Retrieved September 4, 2016 from http://www.socmin.lt/lt/veikla/trisale-taryba.html.

only on the goodwill of employers in providing information and holding consultations, but also on whether, in general, employees are represented in a given enterprise; in this respect, considering the previously mentioned common problem of employee representation in Lithuania, the conclusion should be drawn that real preconditions for providing information and consultation are created only in 36.7% of enterprises[15].

Article 47(9) of the 2002 Labour Code indicates that the specific features of information and consultation procedures in Community-scale undertakings, Community-scale groups of undertakings, European companies and European cooperative societies are established by special laws. In this context, it should be noted that the Law on European Works Councils (wording of 22 June 2011)[16], which has been in force in Lithuania since 2004, legitimizes the possibility of forming European Works Councils, and establishes their legal status. However, so far no single European Works Council has been established. Such a situation shows that Community-scale undertakings with a controlling undertaking located in Lithuania are not numerous, and that the level of social dialogue in such undertakings has not matured enough for a complicated form of information and consultation through European Works Councils.

Item 2 of Article 43(1) of the 2002 Labour Code *expressis verbis* provides that SP in Lithuania can be implemented through one more form – the exercise by employees' representatives of other rights of participation in the employer's decision-making processes; however, in reality, these rights are directly related to employees' participation in other forms of SP, i.e. in the information and consultation process, in the conclusion of collective agreements, in realising the right to join trade unions or be a member of a works council. The compulsory participation of employees or their representatives in the management bodies of enterprises is as yet just an issue under discussion, and the position of employers in this regard is relatively hostile[17].

---

15 Ministry of Social Security and Labour. *Social Report 2014–2015*, Vilnius, 2015, pp. 16–19.

16 *Valstybės žinios* (State Gazette), 2004, No. 39–1271, 2011, No. 86–4149.

17 See, e.g., Free Market Institute of Lithuania. Employees' involvement in the management of the enterprise must remain a voluntary agreement between employees and the enterprise (in Lithuanian). July 29, 2014. Retrieved 28 April, 2016 from http://www.llri.lt/naujienos/ekonomine-politika/ekspertize-darbuotoju-isitraukimas-i-imones-valdyma-turi-likti-savanorisku-susitarimu-tarp-darbuotoju-ir-imones/lrinka.

2.5 The situation regarding collective bargaining and the effectiveness of the legal regulation laid down in concluded collective agreements

The best indicator of the situation regarding collective bargaining is the coverage of regulation through collective agreements, i.e. the percentage of employees covered by legal regulation through collective agreements. Rated against this indicator, Lithuania is at the bottom compared to all EU states. Under the currently applicable provisions of the 2002 Labour Code, it is not required that the collective agreements of an enterprise be registered; thus, there is no precise data on the number of collective agreements on this level. The coverage of collective agreements in Lithuania in 2002 and 2003 was 15%, respectively, and in 2013 – 9.7%, i.e. rated by the coverage of collective agreements, Lithuania occupies the last position in the whole EU[18].

In assessing the coverage of regulation through collective agreements, as well as its dynamics in Lithuania, it is pertinent to note that, according to the data provided by the Ministry of Social Security and Labour[19] concerning the 2007–2013 projects co-funded by the European Social Fund and the Republic of Lithuania under the Measure 'Promotion of Social Dialogue', 25 territorial collective agreements and 16 sectoral collective agreements were signed and registered in the Ministry of Social Security and Labour starting from the end of 2012 until April 2015. Collective bargaining for sectoral and territorial collective agreements took place and resulted in the conclusion of respective collective agreements also after April 2015[20]. Thus, a significant breakthrough in concluding territorial and sectoral collective agreements should, undoubtedly, promote the development of social dialogue in Lithuania. On the other hand, the number of sectoral and territorial agreements is only a quantitative expression of collective bargaining on the higher than enterprise level and, in itself, does not determine the effectiveness of SP, which is equally directly dependent on the quality of the legal regulation laid down in the concluded collective agreements, i.e. on the content of the legal regulation established in these agreements. The assessment of the content of several publicly accessible territorial and sectoral

18 Retrieved April 9, 2016 from http://www.ilo.org/ilostat.

19 *Ibidem.*

20 See, e.g., resolutions of the Government granting powers to bargain for the conclusion of sectoral and territorial collective agreements (Registry of Legal Acts, No. 2015-19691, No. 2015-19635, No. 2015-15727, No. 2015-11970, No. 2015-09272, No. 2015-07089, No. 2015-06151, No. 2015-05546; No. 2014–10344).

collective agreements concluded in 2007–2013 makes it clear that some of them are limited to the establishment of informational content terms, the striving to strengthen social dialogue and the consolidation of certain insignificant conditions concerning the information and consultation of employees' representatives[21]. Other territorial collective agreements contain such conditions as the obligation of the employers' organization 'to promote payment of remuneration to employees in accordance with the laws and sub-statutory legal acts of the Republic of Lithuania'[22]. Such loose and devoid of more substantive content territorial and sectoral collective agreements raise a certain degree of scepticism and give rise to no real preconditions for assuming that the Lithuanian SP model will substantively move towards real SP in the foreseeable future. On the other hand, the breakthrough in the conclusion of collective agreements on the level higher than the enterprise level should be regarded as a good opportunity for social partners (in particular, the opportunity for employee representatives to make use of the already concluded collective agreements, even though they lack specific substantive content, as a platform with a view to making them have more real impact on employment relations). Consequently, at the present moment, it is rather difficult to assess the impact of the territorial and sectoral collective agreements signed in 2007–2013 on the development of the Lithuanian SP model; however, it is already obvious that employee representatives, employers (their representatives), as well as the state, should exploit these collective agreements for strengthening social dialogue, gradually replacing them with more enriched, in terms of content, instruments of legal regulation.

3. Factors behind the gap between the formally consolidated SP system and its actual situation

Factors behind the gap between the formally consolidated SP system and its actual situation should be regarded as *legal*, *economic*, *political* and *psychological* reasons that have direct influence on the behaviour (action and/or inaction) of social partners, i.e. the behaviour of employees (their

[21] Retrieved April 30, 2016 from http://www.klaipedos-r.lt/go.php/lit/Pasirasyta-Klaipedos-rajono-savivaldybes-administracijos-ir-Svietimo-istaigu-profsajungos-kolektyvine-sutartis/1672.

[22] For example, such a condition is stipulated in Item 3.1 of the territorial collective agreement signed on 29 May 2013 between the Kaunas Chamber of Commerce, Industry and Crafts and the Kaunas Regional Centre of the Lithuanian Trade Union Confederation.

representatives), employers (their representatives) and, in separate cases, the state, in balancing the interests of subjects involved in employment relations.

The gap between the formally consolidated SP system and its actual situation results due to the following *legal factors*:

- *the balance between the state-level (centralised) and collective contractual legal regulation is unfavourable to SP*. It is not fully clear what content can be included in collective agreements concluded in budgetary establishments or institutions; the state retains a monopoly in regulating the essential work conditions of civil servants and employees remunerated from the state budget. In legal acts, a casuistic legal regulation of employment relations prevails. Consequently, laws not accepted by social partners have increasingly proved to be inefficient, while social partners have been left with little room for negotiation. In this context, attention should be drawn to the fact that reducing state-level legal regulation is a complicated task, since, in seeking to reduce employee guarantees established by labour laws, it is necessary to take account of the particularly low membership of employees in trade unions, as well as of other aspects impeding the smooth development of SP in Lithuania;
- *over-formalised legal regulation of collective labour disputes.* Due to this reason, the right to strike, for weakened trade unions, has become hardly implementable in practice, whereas employers (their organizations) are provided with the possibility, through exploiting minor procedural infringements, to seek in a court that strikes be declared unlawful. One of the most effective means of collective self-defence action, strikes and the relevant legal norms have been approached by Lithuanian courts of general jurisdiction in rather formal terms[23]. In deciding disputes related to collective employment relations, as a general rule, courts follow the universal principles of justice, fairness and reasonableness; however, the interpretation of specific principles of SP remains fragmented and inadequate.

---

[23] E.g., in a civil case subsequent to an action brought against trade unions by *UAB Švyturys-Utenos alus* seeking to declare an indefinite-term strike as unlawful, in principle, due to procedural infringements, the strike was declared to have been unlawful, while the courts started assessing the content of the dispute regarding the interest (for more, see the order passed by the Civil Division of the Supreme Court of Lithuania on 6 March 2012 in civil case No. 3K-3-81/2012).

The gap between the formally consolidated SP system and its actual situation is also significantly affected by the *economic factor*. The Lithuanian economy can still be regarded as a low-wage and low-productivity economy, characterized by high-level exploitation of labour[24], since as many as 80% of employers have a staff of less than 10 employees, while taxation of labour is among the highest in the EU. Consequently, most employers (including the state or municipalities where they act as an employer or a dominant shareholder) do not contribute to the development of SP. This has a direct impact on the situation in which employers are economically able to bear additional financial obligations, which leads to collective agreements lacking proper content, avoidance of collective bargaining or even its imitation (such imitation can be assumed to include collective agreements in which laws are practically copied and the obligations assumed by employers are non-binding and declarative).

The existing gap between the formally consolidated SP system and its actual situation can further be associated with *political factors*, such as:

- *reluctance by the state to launch a real process of promoting SP through the regulation of employment relations involving civil servants and employees remunerated from the state budget.* Regardless of the earlier mentioned objective officially declared by the state to promote SP, the state, in reality, does not abandon its monopolist position in the state-level regulation and, whether deliberately or not, by acting so, takes an unfriendly approach towards SP. It can be assumed that the state should gradually reduce the monopoly in the regulation of employment relations, thereby opening the possibility for moving closer towards the real SP model;
- *governmental negotiators are granted abstract powers.* Article 24(4) of the 2002 Labour Code provides that employers that are enterprises, establishments or organizations financed from the state and municipal budgets, the budget of the State Social Insurance Fund and resources of other funds established by the state are represented in the SP on the national, sectoral (production, services, professional), territorial (municipality, county) level by the Government or an institution authorized by it. However, as is evident from the resolutions of the Government under which

[24] Woolfson Ch., Calite D. Darbo aplinka ir socialinis dialogas Europos Sąjungos naujojoje valstybėje Lietuvoje [Working Environment and Social dialogue in the New Member State of Lithuania]. *Pinigų studijos,* No. 2, 2008, pp. 73–92.

individual institutions are empowered to bargain[25], no specific powers are granted; therefore, such collective bargaining is comparable not to real bargaining, but to its imitation.

Furthermore, the influence of *psychological factors* on the development of the SP model cannot be underestimated either:

- the most critical psychological factor is *Soviet legacy*, which, even after more than 25 years, continues to exert influence on the Lithuanian SP model. Due to this, Lithuania lacks a social dialogue culture[26], strong resentment is extremely obvious especially among the managers of private sector small and medium-sized enterprises against any kind of collective 'empowerment of employees'; the representation of employees is viewed as a return to the former regime, thus, also as a potential threat to authority[27]; the post-communist social environment of 'low confidence' prevails[28];
- *reluctance to act and fear of agreement*. For example, in Lithuania, including the Lithuanian Tripartite Council, discussions continued for a long time on whether it was necessary to increase the minimum monthly salary of LTL 800 (EUR 231.7), which was established from 1 January 2008 until 1 August 2012 under the relevant resolution of the Government[29], although, as confirmed by the research conducted in 2012[30], the minimum

---

25 See, e.g. these resolutions of the Government: Resolution No. 1274 of 9 December 2015 (TAR, 11/12/2015, No. 2015-19691); Resolution No. 1263 of 9 December 2015 (TAR, 10/12/2015, No. 2015-19635); Resolution No. 1084 of 14 October 2015 (TAR, 19/10/2015, No. 2015-15727); Resolution No. 395 of 23 April 2015 (TAR, 23/04/2015, No. 2015-06151).

26 Krasauskas R. Kolektyvinių sutarčių normatyvinės sąlygos, susijusios su darbuotojų teisine padėtimi: *in favorem v in peius*' [The Normative Conditions of Collective Agreements Relevant to the Legal Situation of the Employees: in favorem v in peius']. In: *Labour Market of 21st Century: looking for flexibility and security*. Vilnius: TIC, 2011, pp. 536–52.

27 Woolfson Ch., Calite D. Darbo aplinka ir socialinis dialogas Europos Sąjungos naujojoje valstybėje Lietuvoje ['Working Environment and Social Dialogue in the New Member State of Lithuania], *Pinigų studijos,* No. 2, 2008, pp. 73–92.

28 Woolfson Ch. Darbo formalumų nesilaikymas pokomunistinėse Europos Sąjungos naujosiose šalyse [Informalization" of Labour in Post-Communist New European Union Member States], *Pinigų studijos,* No. 1, 2007, pp. 62–73.

29 Resolution of the Government No. 1368 of 17 December 2007 on increasing minimum work remuneration. *Valstybės žinios* (State Gazette), 2007, No. 137-5592.

30 Zabarauskaitė R., Gruževskis B. *Sisteminis skurdo problemos tyrimas Lietuvoje* [The Systematic Study of the Problem of Poverty in Lithuania]. Kaunas: Lithuanian Social Research Centre, Lietuvos 'Caritas', 2015.

monthly salary virtually equalled the at-risk-of-poverty rate. Even though calculated based on the methodology according to which the poverty threshold, compared to other EU countries, is one of lowest, the poverty risk threshold in Lithuania, in 2012, was LTL 749 (EUR 216.9) monthly per person living alone and LTL1,572 (EUR 455.3) monthly per family consisting of two adult persons and two children under the age of 14 years.

4. The Lithuanian SP model and the directions for improvement of the legal regulation of employment relations

While currently undergoing a reform, employment relations in Lithuania have also been caught in a certain turbulence zone, where a tense clash is taking place over naturally conflicting interests of employers, employees (their representatives) and the state. New labour legislation has raised an objective to align formal legal regulation with actual employment relations, as well as to take account of the court-made legal regulation, which is frequently independent. However, in combining all of this, it is necessary to bear in mind that an objective of this legal regulation (in particular, concerning such a socially sensitive area of social relations as employment relations) is not only to give thought to the actual behaviour of employers, which at times is at odds with the imperatives consolidated not only in national, but also in international legal acts, or to have regard to the relevant case law, which frequently 'seals' the existing gaps in the legal regulation of employment relations by means of the application of civil law legislation[31]; but, more importantly, this legal regulation must also pursue the objective to construct a model of socially responsible behaviour of subjects involved in these relations.

It should be admitted that drafters of the social model have rightly enough identified that, currently, Lithuania is witnessing the stagnation of social dialogue and the absence of collective agreements. The following solutions were proposed by the drafters in order, as believed by them, to give fresh impetus to social dialogue and collective agreements:

---

31 For more, see Krasauskas R. Teismų kreipimasis į Konstitucinį Teismą kaip darbo teisės konstitucionalizacijos prielaida' *[Application of Courts to the Constitutional Court as Precondition for Constitutionalisation of Labour Law]*. *Jurisprudence: research papers*, No. 20 (4), 2014, pp. 1329–1348; Krasauskas R. Kai kurie Konstitucijos ir Darbo kodekso sąveikos aspektai [Some Aspects of Interface between the Constitution and Labour Code]. *Jurisprudence: research papers*, No. 22 (1), 2015, pp. 9–29.

(1) to liberalize the institute of collective labour disputes; (2) to introduce compulsory information and consultation in large enterprises; (3) to authorize participation by employees in the management of the enterprise; (4) to demarcate the competence of trade unions and that of works councils by leaving strikes and collective agreements as the prerogative of trade unions; (5) to facilitate the procedure for calling strikes; (6) to consolidate that a collective agreement applies only to members of the trade union[32].

In principle, most of the proposed solutions can be accepted. Liberalizing the institute of collective labour disputes, as well as streamlining the procedure for calling strikes, is likely to be particularly effective, since these steps are linked to strengthening the power (including bargaining power) of trade unions and their right to collective self-defence. A more cautious approach should be taken towards the attempt of the social model drafters to separate the competence of trade unions from that of works councils and to leave strikes and collective agreements as the exclusive prerogative of trade unions. On the one hand, this proposal is aimed at strengthening the institute of trade unions (which is welcomed); but, on the other hand, another employee representative – works councils – is weakened, which (in particular, given that works councils lose the possibility of concluding collective agreements) can lead to the disappearance of this channel of employee representation. In addition, it might be called into question whether the legal regulation proposed to be consolidated in the new Labour Code by the social model drafters regarding the application of collective agreements concluded by a trade union exclusively to members of the trade union is consistent with Article 50(1) of the Constitution, irrespective of the fact that this proposed regulation encourages joining trade unions with a view to improving work conditions through collective agreements. In its ruling of 14 January 1999[33], the Constitutional Court emphasized that the provision of Article 50(1) of the Constitution, under which trade unions defend the professional, economic, and social rights and interests of employees, in principle, expresses the dual mission and function of trade unions: first, primarily to represent and defend members of the trade union and, second, in the cases and by means provided for by law, to defend all employees of a given enterprise, establishment or organization.

32 Draft Labour Code of the Republic of Lithuania. Retrieved May 6, 2016 from http://www.socmodelis.lt.

33 Constitutional Court of the Republic of Lithuania case No. 8/98.

Conclusions

The Lithuanian SP model, basically, has a sufficient legal framework for the development of SP; however, it is characterized by particularly low employee membership in trade unions, a small number of employers' organizations, SP institutions lacking influence, the lowest coverage among EU states in terms of legal regulation through collective agreements, collective agreements devoid of substantive content, rare and ineffective strikes and the dominance of state-level legal regulation in the area of the regulation of public employment relations. All of this does not provide grounds to rate Lithuania as one of the states where real SP models are operative. In the light of the existing Lithuanian SP model, a radical reduction of employee guarantees established by law, in expectation that a new legal regulation will provide appropriate preconditions for employees to 'reclaim' these guarantees (i.e. security of employment relations) by means of social dialogue, may bring no desired results.

In seeking to establish a real SP model in Lithuania, social partners (i.e. employees (their representatives), employers (their representatives) and the state (municipalities)) must be well aware of the factors behind the gap between the formally consolidated SP system and its actual situation and, accordingly, make an effort to minimize the possible effects. Action should be taken both to improve the legal regulation and to make use of the force of soft law. It is vital that all parties concerned have a clear understanding that SP and contractual law making by social partners are essential for the effective regulation of employment relations.

It can be proposed that the legislature should accept the solutions proposed by the social model drafters regarding the liberalization of the institute of collective labour disputes, compulsory information and consultation in large enterprises, and the legitimization of the participation of employees in the management of the enterprise. However, there should be no rush in deciding on the proposals to separate the competence of trade unions from that of works councils and to leave strikes and collective agreements as the exclusive prerogative of trade unions, or to apply collective agreements exclusively with regard to members of trade unions, since the implementation of the first of these proposals would weaken one of the alternative channels of employee representation – works councils, and the second proposal may possibly contradict the Constitution.

The activity of trade unions should be directed towards changing their image and strengthening their real bargaining power through active and targeted action in order to ensure increased employee participation in their activity. Trade unions should make active use of strikes, which are one of the most effective means of collective self-defence. Also they should actively seek to use the breakthrough of 2007–2013 in concluding collective agreements on the level higher than the enterprise level for the benefit of strengthening social dialogue, as well as to pursue replacing these as yet loose and devoid of more substantive content territorial and sectoral collective agreements with more enriched, in terms of content, instruments of legal regulation.

Employers and the state should change their attitudes towards SP and trade unions and to break through one of the most serious psychological barriers – the Soviet quasi-social partnership construct. Attempts must be made to promote SP on the higher than enterprise level. The Government and other responsible institutions should, in a timely manner, identify the areas with a sufficient representation of employees and create real conditions in those areas for substantially enriched and meaningful collective bargaining.

Standards for Employee Participation in Decision-Making Processes (Information and Consultation Rights) and their Implementation in Candidate Countries for EU Accession in the Western Balkans

The Case of Albania

Otmar SEUL*

Abstract

European minimum standards, for individual and collective involvement in the workplace and at the company level, are the aim of the Directive 2002/14/EC of the European Parliament and the Council of 11 March 2002 establishing a general framework for informing and consulting employees in the European Community. National legislation and industrial relations' practices determine how these participative processes are applied. As a candidate country for EU accession, Albania is orientated towards the current models of good corporate governance with its delegated employee participation: the rights of the employees are either exercised by unionized representations or by elected representatives in the companies. The establishment of labour councils marks the real beginning of this process, in compliance with EU Directives introducing new forms of employee participation as an indispensable European social norm. However, the applicability of these rights is very low. So far, the involvement of employees in companies seems to be ensured above all by the councils on occupational safety and health at work. Overall, the practice of social dialogue and the efficiency of this participative system of decision-making are still far behind the expectations of the ILO and the EU standards.

Key words: Industrial relations, social dialogue, employee participation in decision-making, information and consultation, board-level representation, work councils

---

* Professor Emeritus of legal German at the University of Paris-Nanterre; co-founder of the integrated French-German law study programme Paris-Nanterre/Potsdam (1994–1995), founder of the Nanterre Network, a European Academic Network for legal studies (1995); initiator of French-German Summer Universities in Law, with third countries in Central, Eastern and South-Eastern Europe (2004). His extensive research on industrial democracy and employee participation in decision-making reflects this French-German and European intercultural dimension.

Introduction

In the context of the globalization of markets, corporate governance has emerged 'as a key point' in the debate on reform and new policies throughout the world, by 'redefining academic concepts' (Blerta Aliu, 2014). It is legitimate to question whether countries applying for an adhesion to the European Union already comply with the Copenhagen Criteria (1993) imposed by the Union on its future members – high democratic standards that also influence the decision-making processes in companies.

This contribution focuses on the involvement of employees in decision-making in companies in Albania. In the First Part, the Directive 2002/14/EC of the European Parliament and the Council of 11 March 2002 will be presented, establishing a general framework for informing and consulting employees in the European Community under the title: 'Corporate Government and Employee involvement: minimum requirements of the European Union.' The findings regarding employee participation in the special case of Albania will be presented in the Second Part of this contribution: 'Delegated "Employee Participation" in Albania: unions and elected bodies.'

In the phase of transition to democracy and social market economy, the political, economic, social and mental structures of this country are marked – like no other country of the region with a Communist past – by the stone age Communism of the Enver Hoxha era. Albania's neighbouring countries (Macedonia, Kosovo, Montenegro), though successor republics of the former Yugoslavia, can at least make use of their self-management experience inherited from the socialist system which was implementing forms of corporate governance – an innovation that distinguished Yugoslavia from the Stalinist version of communism in Albania.

With a 'plea for a participative social dialogue in the workplace and at the company level' in the Third Part of this contribution, it will be up to Blerta Aliu and other Albanian experts to consider how to achieve greater economic efficiency and social justice, by improving the effectiveness of human capital.

1. Corporate Government and Employee involvement: minimum requirements of the European Union

Through the Copenhagen Criteria (1993), the European Union imposes on its future members high democratic standards that also influence the decision-making processes in companies. Processes which, in today's modern economic world, must follow the concept of a good corporate governance[1]. This requirement should serve as a reaction to the numerous cases of mismanagement, corporate crises and collapses in this country and abroad. In addition, the globalization of the economy and the liberalization of capital markets also give weight to the discussion on efficient and transparent forms of corporate governance. Therefore, the previous forms of governance are particularly questioned in the course of the financial and economic crisis. The term is more than a new buzz word, and rather represents a code of conduct, or even designates the 'legal and actual framework of a company for management and surveillance on national level'[2].

As opposed to the corporate institution, which most importantly concerns the internal rule of a company, corporate governance also deals with issues such as the integration of a company in its environment (especially within the capital market). Corporate governance is commonly understood as a system in which there is an interplay of different regulations and market forces. Hence, it deals with multiple issues in the field of corporate law, securities regulation, corporate finance and industrial relations. The narrow definition of corporate governance focuses on the control of management by shareholders. The broader definition concerns the role of stakeholders in making and implementing strategic decisions in the company. So for countries like Germany, this is not really a new issue: dealing with questions such as the (lacking) efficiency of leading bodies like the supervisory board (Aufsichtsrat) and the fundamental discussion on employee participation and codetermination (Mitbestimmung) has been a long-held tradition. Especially from the perspective of trade unions, employees should have a 'voice' in the decision-making process,

---

1 The term *Corporate Governance* (CG) was introduced by Bob Tricker. See Tricker B. *Corporate Governance: Practices, Procedures and Power in British Companies and their Board of Directors*. London: Gower Pub Co, 1984. His latest publications: Tricker B. *Corporate Governance – principles, policies and practices,* Oxford: Oxford University press, 3rd ed., 2015; *Business Ethics* (with G.Tricker), London, New York: Routledge, 2014; *The Economist Essential Director,* London: Profile books, 2003.

2 See Werder von A. *Corporate Governance*. Retrieved September 12, 2016 from http://wirtschaftslexikon.gabler.de/Definition/corporate-governance.html.

to ensure that a reasonable balance is achieved in the goals pursued by the company, and not just the maximization of corporate profits and shareholder value[3]. Many corporate institutions seem to have met this ideal: in 17 of the 27 EU Member States, employees are represented in the companies' supervisory or administrative board. In fact, the acquis communautaire (Community acquis) has certain concerns in labour law, in particular regarding the protection of individual and collective rights, employees' health and safety at the workplace. Each time legislation proposals are made to create company structures on a European level or to regulate cross-border company restructuring, the issue of employee involvement is raised. The legislations proposed or already passed contain significantly variable provisions for information, consultation and participation rights for them. So, for example, the Employee Involvement Directive 2001/86/EC is an EU directive concerning the right of employees to elect members of the board of directors in a European company (Societas Europaea: SE) who do not participate in day-to-day decisions – which are a matter for the management – but in the supervision and strategic development of the company. The European minimum standard for employee involvement, which would apply to all European companies' legal structures and to cross-border restructurings regulated on the European level, was particularly the aim of the Directive 2002/14/EC of the European Parliament and the Council of 11 March 2002, establishing a general framework for 'informing and consulting' employees in the European Community. It establishes general principles on the minimum rights for employees in companies based in the EU, and wants to guarantee a continuous social dialogue between management and labour, even and above all, in small and medium-sized enterprises: to advance opportunities to obtain decent and productive work in conditions of freedom, equality, security and human dignity.

More precisely, information and consultation cover data on a company's recent and probable development, including economic situation, employment structure, especially if there is a threat to jobs, and on decisions that could lead to substantial changes in the way work is organised or in contractual relations. But employee representatives and their advisors are bound not to make public any information they have received in confidence. Consultation must take place at the relevant management and employee representation level depending on the issue

[3] Tischer L. *Corporate Governance: do employees count too?* Retrieved September 12, 2016 from https://www.linkedin.com/pulse/corporate-governance-laura-tischer.

being discussed, and on the basis of the information the employer supplies. These consultations should enable employee representatives to meet their employer and receive an answer, with the aim to reach agreement on decisions that could lead to substantial changes in the way work is organised or in contractual relations.

National legislation and industrial relations' practices determine how these participative processes are applied individually. So EU countries may choose whether the legislation applies to companies with at least 20 or 50 employees, or establish special rules for companies essentially involved in political, professional, religious, charitable, educational, scientific or artistic fields. They may even determine that employers do not need to inform or consult employee representatives at all, in cases where doing so would seriously harm the company's activity.

Does this mean that precise terms for information and consultation are predetermined for the Member States when it comes to implementing Directive 2002/14/EC and that they are assigned generic terms for participation? This does not seem to be the case. Of course, on a national level, the terms of information and consultation can be clearly defined and adapted to one another, as, for example, in the German Works Constitution Act (*Betriebsverfassungsgesetz*). But Germany does not follow the logic of the Community Charter of the Fundamental Social Rights of Workers (1989) which juxtaposes 'information, consultation and participation of workers' (Title I, Articles 17, 18)[4]. Does this not suggest that information, consultation and participation are three distinct, although complementary phenomena? It is considered, on the contrary, that participation is the generic term for information and consultation, in

4 The Charter was adopted in accordance with the preamble of the Treaty establishing the European Economic Community, which recognized the need to continually work towards improving the living and working conditions of European citizens. The Charter was only adopted by the United Kingdom in 1998 as part of the integration of the principles of the Charter into the Amsterdam Treaty. The Charter establishes the major principles on which the European labour law model is based. It applies to the following areas: free movement of workers; employment and remuneration; improvement of working conditions; social protection; freedom of association and collective bargaining; vocational training; equal treatment for men and women; information, consultation and participation of workers; health protection and safety at the workplace; protection of children, adolescents, elderly persons, and disabled persons. These social rights represent a foundation of minimum provisions common to all the European Union (EU) Member States. The provisions of the Charter were kept by the Lisbon Treaty (Article 151 of the Treaty on the Functioning of the European Union) and by the Charter of Fundamental Rights.

the same sense as the German Works Constitution Act: the appropriate German terms *Unterrichtung* and *Anhörung* are participation rights, as opposed to rights to co-determination, in the decision-making process on the board-level and workplace-level[5].

These are terminological disagreements and contradictions which the European Commission is aware of, and which encourage it to consolidate the different regulations on employee information and consultation – directives respectively on collective redundancies, transfers of undertakings and a general framework for information and consultation of workers[6]. The Commission actually started, in April 2015, a consultation with the EU-level social partners on whether to merge the aforementioned three directives into one single legislative text.

If, since 2002, the European Union supplements the Member States' activities regarding employees' rights to information and consultation by adopting minimum requirements by means of directives, it is legitimate to question whether States applying for an adhesion to the European Union already comply with the issues at stake in Directive 2002/14/EC or not, or if they are at least willing to implement it in the foreseeable future in their national laws. In November 2015, during our second Itinerant Summer University in the Balkans 'Accession to the European Union and Identity of Balkans', a workshop revolved around this question concerning the candidate states in the Western Balkans[7]. For Balkan States, the European perspective exposes them to the irreversibility of political, economic and social reforms that these countries must put in place, alongside peace and regional stability.

The findings regarding employees' participation in the special case of Albania[8] will be presented in the second part of our contribution. In the

5 Betriebsverfassungsgesetz part 4, §§ 74 et sqq.

6 Consultation document: First phase consultation of Social Partners under Article 154 TFEU on consolidation of the EU Directives on information and consultation of workers, COM (2015) 2303 final.

7 Itinerant Summer University in the Balkans coordinated by the Université Paris Ouest-Nanterre and the Westfälische Wilhelms-Universität Münster; Session II, Faculty of Law in Tirana, November 2015. Retrieved September 12, 2016 from http://www.droit-fr-all-paris-ouest.fr/universite-dete-itinerante-franco-germano-balkanique.

8 Seul O. *Critères de Copenhague et Gouvernance des Entreprises.* Retrieved September 12, 2016 from http://www.droit-fr-all-paris-ouest.fr/wp-content/uploads/2015/12/Atelier-Tirana-Albanie-30-oct-2015-Copenhagen-Criteria-and-Corporate-governance-European-minimum-standards-for-Employees-Participation-in-Decision-Making.pdf.

phase of transition to democracy and social market economy, the political, economic, social and mental structures of this country are marked here – like in no other country of the region with a Communist past – by the stone age Communism of the Enver Hoxha era. After a decade-long international isolation, compliance with the Copenhagen criteria is a particularly difficult task for the country. The countries neighbouring Albania (Macedonia, Kosovo, Montenegro), though successor republics of the former Yugoslavia, can at least make use of their self-management experience inherited from the socialist system which was implementing forms of corporate governance – an innovation that distinguished Yugoslavia from the Stalinist version of Communism.

2. Delegated 'Employee Participation' in Albania: unions and elected bodies

Without a doubt, Albania, as an aspiring country for integration in the European Union, is trying to adapt its legislation to the European Union standards. Employees' rights are guaranteed and protected by a series of legal mechanisms, starting with the Constitution of the Republic of Albania (Articles 46, 50 and 51), followed by the Labour Code (Chapter 16), the Civil Code, the law on 'Entrepreneurs and Companies', the law on 'Consumer Protection', the law on 'Cross-border Merge' as well as a number of other mechanisms, such as European Union directives, OECD principles, the Ethic Code of Good Governance and different ILO conventions ratified by the Albanian state (Conventions 29, 87, 98, 100, 105, 111, 138 and 182). These legal instruments are considered as 'becoming day by day a significant part of the practical application of employee rights in companies' (Livia Rrokaj, 2015) by the Albanian participants of our workshop in Tirana.

When it comes to discussing the nature, the content, the form and the impact of employees' rights – in whichever country – it must first be determined whether employees should exercise these rights directly or indirectly, and who, if need be, are their legal or de facto representatives. Albania is undoubtedly oriented towards the current EU model, with its mostly delegated participation: the rights of the employees are either exercised by unionized representations of interests or by elected representatives in the companies.

2.1 Unionized employees' representation and collective bargaining procedures at the national and branch levels

The Constitution and the Labour Code guarantee the right of every employee to be free to join Unions which are protecting his/her interests in the matter of job position, working and living conditions.

Just like many EU Member States, Albania is characterized by a trade union pluralism, with an impressive number of sectoral organizations: there are 83 established trade unions operating in the country. A characteristic feature is that trade unions have grown in the public sector and in private enterprises (former state enterprises), whereas representation is much lower in the purely private sector. They are mainly operational in the sectors of education and science, administration staff, retired workers, industry, agriculture, the food industry, public health, transportation, oil, construction, textiles, craftsmanship, trade, metallurgy, chemistry and telecommunications. Most of the unions operate under the umbrella of two confederations, representing about 90% of the members of trade unions in Albania, whereas the rest operate independently: the Confederation of Trade Unions of Albania (KSSH) and the Union of Independent Trade Unions of Albania (BSPSH)[9]. These confederations are represented with 5 members in the National Labour Council, which constitutes the tripartite social dialogue in Albania between government, business associations and trade unions, in particular in order to fight unemployment (current unemployment rate is officially 16.9%)[10]. There is no doubt that trade unions are the main representative authorities of the labour force. Their bodies practice the highest possible form of employee participation, which is comparable to a form of 'co-determination' (Mitbestimmung): they enter into negotiations and sign collective bargaining agreements with the employers. Branch-collective agreements are mainly signed at the national or the regional level. They cover minimum salary, remuneration in case of dismissal, overtime work, terms of contract and the free activity of trade unions. According to data from the Ministry of Labour, collective agreement coverage in the public sector – in which union membership

---

9 Doçi N. Albania. In: *Annual Review of Labour Relations and Social Dialogue in South East Europe 2013*, Belgrade: Friedrich-Ebert-Stiftung, January 2014, p. 4. Retrieved September 12, 2016 from http://library.fes.de/pdf-files/bueros/belgrad/10535.pdf.

10 Retrieved September 12, 2016 from http://fr.tradingeconomics.com/albania/unemployment-rate.

rate is 18% – is 69%, 29% in the private non-agricultural sector (10%) and only 1%[11] in the private agricultural sector.

A low rate of unionization does not necessarily have a negative impact on the collective agreement coverage, as depicted in a comparison with France. Just like in Albania (7%), the French membership average (8%) is under 10%. But as opposed to Albania, France has one of the highest collective bargaining coverage in Europe, close to 98%! There are two major reasons for this: the extension of collective bargaining agreements by the Ministry of Labour and – considering an increasing union pluralism – the legal form of union recognition, according to which each of the confederations recognized by the government as 'representative' at the national level is entitled to sign collective agreements at any level. Since 2013, in order to be valid, collective bargaining agreements at industry level currently need to be unopposed from a majority of representative union organizations[12]. In countries with a low rate of unionization, it is of course extremely significant for the development of industrial relations and social dialogue, to show that bodies other than trade unions could represent the employees. This development would fully achieve the goal of Directive 2002/14/EC, by establishing a general framework for 'informing and consulting' employees. Does the Albanian legislation allow for elected representatives of employees, if there are no member of organized trade unions in the company, and thereby prove that the country is currently transposing Directive 2002/14/EC into national law?

---

11 Doçi N., *op. cit.*, p. 13.

12 Rehfeldt U. The French System of Collective Bargaining. In: *Social Europe*, Retrieved September 12, 2016 from https://www.socialeurope.eu/2010/08/the-french-system-of-collective-bargaining. 'Legislation adopted in 2008 introduced new criteria for determining whether a union is representative and therefore allowed to participate in collective bargaining at national, industry and company level. The new law requires a union to win at least 10 percent of the votes at the workplace level, 8 percent of the votes at industry level and 8 percent of votes at national 'inter-professional' level to be considered representative. The new legislation will only come fully into effect at national and industry level in 2013 (…). It will only be valid if it has been signed by unions with at least a 30 percent support in the industry, based on works council and similar elections, and if it is not opposed by unions with majority (more than 50 percent) support. These rules have already started taking effect at the company level where elections under the new rules have taken place' (August 29th, 2010).

2.2 Workplace and board-level representation: elected bodies for informing and consulting employees

In Albania, there could be bodies, other than the trade unions, representing the employees. This is the case of the procedure which is currently implementing Law No. 10237 of 18 February 2010, allowing for the establishment of Occupational Health and Safety Councils with representatives of employees[13].

The establishment of labour councils in companies with more than 50 employees, provided by Articles 19, 20 and 21 of Law No. 9901/2008, revised, for 'Entrepreneurs and the companies', marks the real beginning of this process. It is in compliance with EU Directives introducing new forms of employee participation as an indispensable European social norm. All the costs of the election and the functioning of the councils are to be borne by the companies[14].

Decision-making transparency firstly enables the councils to exercise control rights, that is to monitor the observance of laws, statutes, regulations and instructions and, in particular, to monitor the implementation of collective labour contracts. This means that employee participation is based, firstly, on the right to be comprehensively and regularly informed, i.e. to be able to follow company policies regarding work conditions, salaries, safety at work, the potential sharing of profits, any possible future amendments to the statute, the pension system restructuring of the corporation participation in other companies. In other words, the council must be given, at any time, full information on the economic activities and performances of the company, by having access to all the accounting documents, if they are not published on the company's website.

Employee participation means, secondly, the right to be consulted and to offer comments, opinions and suggestions to the management staff, including on economic and financial matters, whenever, for example, the company starts a new project, or decides on the use of special funds, or for the distribution of profits which the general shareholders meeting decides to allocate. If the employees' concerns have not been taken into account, the legal representative of the company has to inform the

---

13 See the presentation of Livia Rrokaj. Retrieved September 12, 2016 from http://www.droit-fr-all-paris-ouest.fr/wp-content/uploads/2015/12/Atelier-Tirana-Albanie-30-oct-2015-Copenhagen-Criteria-and-Corporate-governance-European-minimum-standards-for-Employees-Participation-in-Decision-Making.pdf.

14 *Ibidem.*

council about the reasons for the rejection of its suggestions. But on the board level, employee information and consultation rights are, all in all, weakly defined and very often limited to reporting periodically in the general shareholders meeting.

In the case of anonymous companies, the legal representative of the company and the labour council may agree to appoint a person to represent the employees in the management staff (executive board or administrative board). Inspired by the company law of other EU Member States, the Albanian companies are structured according to the so-called dualistic (two-tier) system – with the corporate bodies of the executive board, the supervisory board and the general shareholders meeting – or according to the so-called monistic (one-tier) system, with the corporate bodies being the administrative board and the general shareholders meeting.

Just like in France and other EU Member States, in Albania, coordination of the activities of the elected bodies of employee representation are incumbent on the trade unions. The legislator thereby prevents competitive situations between union representatives and elected representatives, and thus situations in which the management could be tempted to act within its own interests by playing the elected employee representatives off against the unions. But it must be in the union's interest to use the cooperation with the new bodies of employee participation as a way to put the company forward, by proving its efficiency: 'Trade unions should use this additional instrument in order to increase their competences in labour relations and strengthen the protection of workers' interests'[15]. This is exactly what the unions suggest doing, by promoting the establishment of labour councils and trainings for candidates and elected members as much as possible.

3. Economic efficiency and human capital: a plea for a participative social dialogue in the workplace and at the company level (Conclusions in the light of new research)

Do those observations confirm or contradict the perception of Employee Participation in Decision-Making Processes in Albania? A workshop for Masters students with comparative law elements, which

---

15 Doçi N. *op. cit.* p. 14.

must necessarily give due consideration to pedagogical and didactical aspects, cannot – understandably – seize the topic as thoroughly as theoretically and empirically grounded long-term studies.

An insightful analysis was presented in 2014 and 2015 by Blerta Aliu from the European University of Tirana. While comparing our results with those of the Albanian researcher, we will limit ourselves to two observations:

1. Blerta Aliu starts from premises similar to ours. She confirms the interdisciplinary interest in Corporate government by referring to the sense of ownership and 'profit' in times of globalization of markets in relation to traditional concepts: 'Today, are seen new definitions dealing with the fragmentation of capital or management issues, which are related to principles, such as the obligation of loyalty, executive compensation, social responsibility of business, etc.'[16]. The discussion on the importance of human rights in corporations, as well as the main strategies for their implementation focus on three objectives, according to Blerta Aliu: 'Respect protective legal minimums established by the lex specialis for each category of stakeholders, building dynamic dialogue (dynamic stakeholder dialogue) and the engagement in corporate decision-making (stakeholder engagement)'[17]. The main objective would be to increase transparency in the relationship between ownership and management structures, but also between the administrators and the dominant owner – especially with regard to the means of compensation. In other words, Blerta Aliu's approach on corporate governance is based on the nature of the employment relationship. She wants to bring further the prism of representation 'by looking at human capital and elaboration of the concept of human assets of a corporation productivity and involvement of employees in decision making'[18]. She argues that human resources, often, find difficulties in the working conditions but also, in the selection and training conditions or the relation of payment with performance: 'Results from a juridical analysis show problems with contract enforcement,

16 Aliu B. Potentials and limits of Corporate Social responsibility in Albania. *European Journal of Research in Social Sciences*, Vol. 3 (1), 2015, pp. 69–75; Aliu, B. Dimensions of Employee protection in Albanian corporations and harmonization with EU. *European Journal of Research in Social Sciences.* Vol. 2 (4), 2014, pp. 66–77.

17 Aliu B. (2015), *op. cit.*, p. 69.

18 *Ibidem.*

but especially immediate and abusive contract disposals'[19]. The hypothesis is the following: the protection and respect of the rights of stakeholders in Albania, especially employees, is achieved through their 'participation in the decision-making of the company, which guarantees sustainable development of the company, making it competitive on the international market'[20].

2. Blerta Aliu confirms our impression: the protection of employees' rights in corporations is 'very low' in Albania compared to the EU level. It is still a fact that even after more than 25 years of transition, for example 'enforcement of contracts still takes quite a long time and thus the efficiency of the system in Albania is persistently problematic. Jurisprudence similar to the CJEU, on aspects of discrimination or equal treatment remain embryonic'[21].

Basing her research essentially on the analysis and interpretation of the legal framework, Blerta Aliu also wants to investigate to what extent the directives drawn up by the European Union regarding employee participation (as a form of corporate social responsibility) are applied or will be applied as soon as possible in the Albanian context. When it comes to granting information and consultation rights at the workplace level, she notices in particular that although Albanian law has provided for the establishment of labour (employees') councils, the applicability of these rights is 'very low'. This is not surprising: all the costs of the election and the functioning of the councils are borne by the company! This means that financial reasons alone can impair the creation or continuity of such councils.

On the other hand, the involvement of employees in Albanian companies seems to be more secure than the councils on occupational safety and health at work, not only on a legal basis, but also in practice. The councils actively contribute to state politics, regarding the improvement of physical and mental health protection, the safety of employees and the improvement of working conditions: they 'participate in the evaluation, design and implementation of programmes to prevent risks to the enterprise; [they] promote initiatives on ways and procedures for the effective prevention of risks'. And their proposals are binding: the employer is obliged to implement the proposals made

19 *Ibidem.*

20 Aliu B. (2014), *op. cit.*, p. 66.

21 Aliu B. (2015), *op. cit.*, p. 69.

by the council, cooperating with the Occupational Health Sector State Labour Inspectorate State and the State Sanitary Inspectorate. The latest conclusions submitted by the State Labour Inspectorate explains the momentary improvements of physical and mental health protection, safety of employees and the improvement of working conditions in a few firms[22]. through first approaches of the social dialogues. In other words, the 2008/2010 reforms mentioned by the International Labour Organization (ILO) are starting to take effect. Until now, Albania could only show embryonic forms of labour participation at national, sectoral and enterprise level. In other words, the examination report on the national profile on Occupational Safety and Health[23], commissioned by the ILO and publicized in 2007, is to a great extent still valid today.

First of all, the report gives an overview of the general participative frameworks in Albania, in so far as they implement trade unions, the employees' representatives that are dominant in Albania (excluding more direct forms of employee participation through elected bodies):

– Participation in tripartite commissions for occupational safety and health that are part of the National Labour Council. The commissions transmit opinions to the Council on: a) orientating and implementing government policies in the field of occupational safety and health; b) drafting government laws

---

22 Aliu B. (2014), *op. cit.*, p. 75.

23 See Beqiri E. The role of the State Labour Inspectorate in matters of Safety and Health at Work, Presentation for the 2nd Tirana Gas Pipelines Safety Workshop. Retrieved September 11, 2016 from http://agora.mfa.gr/agora/images/docs/radD497A2nd%20Safety%20Workshop%2020042016-PRESENTATIONS.pdf. During 2015, the awareness of employers is increased significantly in taking measures regarding the health and safety at work where concretely, compared with 2014, there was an increase in the number of Councils for Health and Safety at Work (CHSW). In 2014 there were 521 CHSW, in 2015, we have 562 CHSW. We have an increased number of entities that are covered with medical service; in 2014 about 1,187 entities had an enterprise doctor while in 2015 about 1,327 entities had an enterprise doctor, as a result of the orientation of the process of inspections and awareness meetings with the business in order to improve the labour conditions in entities that pose a risk for the safety and health of employees. The number of entities which use individual protective equipment is 2,944 (compared to 2, 344 in 2014), while the number of entities which use collective protective equipment is 2,763 (compared to 2,363 in 2014). We have also a significant increase in the number of entities which use collective and individual protective equipment, as a result of the increase of inspection number in entities that pose risks for the health and safety of employees at work, as well as awareness and information meetings with business in order to improve the working conditions, especially for the usage of protective individual and collective equipment to decrease the number of accidents and professional diseases.

and decrees that are related to occupational safety and health and their respective implementing institutions, c) consulting and discussing occupational safety and health issues which the Council has addressed for consultation and drawing up opinion. Albania therefore aligns with European standards: in a growing number of countries, labour inspection is organized under a tripartite body, 'which in turn supervises the inspectorate proper, sets policy, monitors its implementation, evaluates the results, attribute resources and assumes overall responsibility for the proper running of the inspection service'[24].

– Bilateral Committees of employers' representatives and employees function in an ad hoc manner when Collective Contracts are drafted and signed. To conclude collective bargaining is obligatory between the employer and employees at company and sectoral branch level. A significant number of the contracts comprise issues related to working conditions, occupational safety and health, work time duration, holidays, vacations, and wages. For the OSH issues, in companies with over 100 employees, a bilateral trade union-employer commission operates. The trade union councils in each company monitor the provision and inspection of working conditions related to OSH, which derive from the collective contract and from the individual labour contracts. The appointed trade union representatives keep account of the completion of employers' duties regarding OSH and inform employees, in some companies, about parts of the collective contract which have to do with OSH. For the partial or full incompletion of obligations that stem from the collective bargaining, the parties are obliged to pay to one another, as a disciplinary measure, an amount of money that is defined in the collective contract signed by them.

In other words, like some other European countries, Albania has introduced legislation that requires joint committees to be established in industrial, commercial and even non-commercial companies above a certain size[25].

---

24 Balliu O. National Profile of Occupational Safe and Health in Albania, Tirana (International Labour Organization), March 2007, p. 48. Retrieved September 12, 2016 from http://www.ilo.org/wcmsp5/groups/public/---ed_protect/---protrav/---safework/documents/policy/wcms_187886.pdf.

25 *Ibidem.*

However, the practice of social dialogue and thereby the efficiency of this participative system of decision-making on branch and company level are still far behind the expectations of the ILO and the EU standards (a global tendency to associate the social partners more closely with the work of the inspectorate). In its Situational Analysis, the report notes in particular that:

- 'Cooperation of trade unions and employers' organizations at institutional level is weak: the only governmental institution is the *National Labour Council*, in the OSH Commission […]
- At economic sector level, the cooperation is inconsiderable […].
- The number of Albanian enterprises that apply good OSH conditions is very limited […].

Trade Unions that operate in various sectors of the economy in the framework of the two big confederations are powerless to prevent the unacceptable work conditions that are often dangerous to life […]. Employers' organizations are very interested in economic, legal and financial gains from the government, but their devotion and care for OSH is not satisfactory […]'[26]

Concerning the implementation of a real social dialogue through improved information and consultation rights of the employees and their union representatives, the report recommends three *structural* measures:

1) Representation of regional employers' organizations and trade unions sections in the national body on occupational safety and health;
2) Expansion of the representation of trade unions and employers' organizations at district level, in order to improve representation and close supervision of problems in the OSH area;
3) Creation of bilateral committees on occupational safety and health, in order to review more specifically problems in various sectors like agro-processing, construction, mining, metallurgy and manufacturing sectors.

Recommendations that ought to accompany four complementary measures in improving the efficiency of the social partners:

1) Enactment of annual activity programmes of trade unions (related to OSH in the country and for specific sectors) and of employers'

---

[26] *Ibidem.*

organizations (in relation to Albanian company policies and strategies for the prevention of occupational accidents and diseases and the improvement of working conditions);

2) Creation of a bilateral committee of trade union/employer organizations for various sectors of the economy;
3) Improvement of the drafting of collective bargaining at both levels, where the obligations to meet OSH requirements, especially in the private sector, are particularly stressed;
4) Participation of trade union and employers' organization representatives in international meetings for occupational safety and health to exchange experience and best practices[27].

---

[27] *Ibidem.*

Part Three

Individual Employment Law

Individual Labour Law Reforms in Belgium and the Role of Certain Socio-Economic Factors

Wilfried Rauws* and Evelien Timbermont **

Abstract

The economic problems in Belgium, as analysed by the Belgian and European authorities, caused a number of measures, especially around the reducing of labour costs and controlled flexibility of work. Social policy in Belgium also aims at further improving transitions in the labour market. Moreover, Belgium intensified the policy against bogus self- employed workers.

Keywords: socio-economic factors, individual labour law, Belgium.

Introduction

Law plays an important role in our Western society. The main purpose of law is to create a fair and legally secure society. Since law and society are intrinsically linked, they cannot be separated. As previously mentioned, law serves to prevent disorder in society. Law should thus keep pace with society, changes to law occur when society evolves. In addition to this existing mutual influential relationship, it should be noted that law also constitutes certain social institutions (e.g. property, family, etc.). This partly explains why socio-economic factors play an important role in the development of law. Belgium, like most of the other EU countries experienced a double-dip recession in both 2009 and 2012[1]. Since 2014, there have been signs of

---

* Wilfried Rauws is full professor at the Vrije Universiteit Brussel and part-time professor at the University of Maastricht for labour law and comparative labour law. Prof. Rauws is deputy judge in the Court of Appeal of Antwerp and member of the editorial board of the main Flemish legal journals such as the *Rechtskundig Weekblad* (Weekly Journal of Law) and the *Tijdschrift voor Privaatrecht* (Journal of Private Law).

** Evelien Timbermont is a teaching and research assistant at the Vrije Universiteit Brussel. She focuses mainly on individual and collective labour law. Her PhD deals with the legal status of teaching personnel within the Flemish Community

1 European Commission. Employment and Social Developments in Europe 2015. Retrieved September 1, 2016 from http://ec.europa.eu/social/main.jsp?catId=738&langId=en&pubId=7859&furtherPubs.

economic recovery, although unemployment remains high in Belgium at around 8.6%[2].In other words, law begets social change.

These general observations are also applicable to Belgian (individual) labour law as socio-economic factors often affect employment and thus (individual) labour law. In the past two decades, some significant changes have occurred as a result of several socio-economic factors, such as the economic crisis, new forms of commerce, etc. Both temporary and permanent measures were adopted.

In this paper, the most important temporary and permanent reforms in Belgian individual labour law due to socio-economic factors over the past two decades will be examined. Additionally, a number of measures which the government intends to implement in the framework of 'workable and flexible work' will be briefly discussed[3].

1. Permanent and temporary reforms in Belgian individual labour law due to socio-economic factors

1.1 Permanent reforms

1.1.1 Wage norm

The first important permanent measure is the introduction of the so-called wage norm, which was adopted in 1996[4]. This biannually determined norm defines the increase of wages for the next two years[5]. It was introduced because the government wanted to secure the competitiveness of the Belgian economy. Moreover, this regulation should ensure the elimination of the wage gap. In principle, the social partners set the wage norm by entering into a cross-industry agreement every two years. In order to determine the wage norm the technical report of the central council for the economy on the maximum available margins for wage cost development is taken into account. The maximum available margins are calculated taking into account the expected evolution of

---

2 Nationale Bank van België. Economische projecties voor België. Retrieved September 1, 2016 from www.nbb.be/doc/ts/publications/economicreview/2016/ecotijdi2016.

3 In Dutch 'werkbaar en wendbaar werk', in French 'travail faisable et maniable'.

4 Act of 26 July 1996 to promote employment and the safeguarding of competitiveness. *Belgian State Gazette,* 1 August 1996.

5 The wage norm concerns the average wage cost per employee within a company. Please note that certain benefits are not taken into account in order to calculate the wage cost (e.g. the employer's contribution in social pension systems).

wages in three reference countries, namely France, Germany, and the Netherlands, as well as the development over the past two years. If the social partners are unable to reach an agreement on the wage norm, the government will have the final say.

The following scheme shows the evolution of the wage norm over the past years:

Period	**Wage norm (%)**
1997-1998	6.10
1999-2000	5.90
2001-2002	6.40–7.00
2003-2004	5.40
2005-2006	4.50
2007-2008	5.00
2009-2010	250 EUR
2011-2012	0.30
2013-2014	0.00
2015-2016	0.50 + 0.30

As one may notice, in the last few years the wage norm has been static. This was a result of the economic crisis.

With regard to the current wage norm set out for 2015–2016 it is important to underline that the government determined the wage norm in an act of 28 April 2015[6]. Moreover, it is remarkable that the wage norm is split up per year. For 2015 the wage norm is 0%, which means the gross average wage cost per full time equivalent employee may not increase. Please note that this results in a three-year long salary freeze, since the wage norm for 2013-2014 was also set at 0%[7]. With regard to 2016, a small increase of 0.5% of the total salary cost for the employer (in certain cases increased by 0.3% of the net salary cost) is provisioned.

The effect of the current wage norm is aggravated by the simultaneous application of the index jump, i.e. a one-time skipping of automatic (2.00%) wage indexation[8].

6 Act of 28 April 2015 on the salary freeze. *Belgian State Gazette,* 30 April 2015.

7 However individual wage increases are possible as long as the average wage cost does not increase. Moreover, wage increases as a result of for example a job change remain possible.

8 Act of 23 April 2015 on wage indexation. *Belgian State Gazette,* 27 April 2015.

With regard to the wage indexation, please note that in Belgium wages are linked to the health index. This monthly index differs slightly from the consumer price index and excludes for example alcoholic beverages. The automatic wage indexation applies when the health index reaches a certain level. Thus, wages will increase automatically. This mechanism exists separately from the wage norm. However, the Act of 23 April 2015 defines a new term, the smoothed health index which is the arithmetic mean of the last four health indices. The index jump is effectively enforced in three stages. In the first stage (until March 2015) the smoothed health index was calculated as described above. In the second stage (as from April 2015) the smoothed health index remains at the same level as March 2015. In other words, the smoothed health index is suspended. In this stage a reference index is calculated by multiplying the smoothed health index by 0.98. Once this reference index transcended the level of the smoothed health index for March 2015 the 2% index jump was achieved. At this point, the suspension of the wage index is abolished. The month in which the above occurs is called the reference month[9]. Please note that this point was reached in April 2016. This implies that from May 2016 onwards the sectoral indexation mechanism could in theory enter into force again. In order to give a more permanent effect to the index jump, the smoothed health index is calculated by multiplying the arithmetic mean of the last four health indices by 0.98 departing from the reference month (i.e. April 2016). Thus, the enforcement of the one-time skipping of the automatic wage indexation reinforced the effect of the 0% wage norm. With this measure, the government wanted to bring the wage cost evolution to the same level as France, Germany, and the Netherlands in order to improve the competitiveness of the Belgian economy.

1.1.2 Reduced social security contributions for employers[10]

These recent social security measures are designed to reduce the overall wage costs of employees. From 1 April 2016, the percentage of the basic social security contributions will decrease from 33% of the gross salaries to +/- 30%. From 1 January 2018, the percentage of the basic social security contributions for employers will be reduced to +/- 25% instead of 30%. Moreover, as from 1 January 2016 a new employer

9 The act expressly excludes the possibility of negative wage indexation as from April 2015 until the reference month.

10 Act of 26 of December 2015 adopting measures for enhancing job creation and purchasing power. *Belgian State Gazette,* 30 December 2015.

will enjoy full exemption on the basic social security contributions for the first recruitment between 1 January 2016 and 31 December 2020. This benefit applies to the entire period of employment and thus for an indefinite time.

1.1.3 Employment relationship

Further measures were taken in order to fight the phenomenon of false self-employment[11] or false employment[12] and thus social contributions fraud.

In this context, an Act was adopted in December 2006[13] which introduced four general criteria in order to assess the existence of an employer's authority (and thus an employment contract). This Act mainly confirmed the jurisprudence of the Belgian Supreme Court and wanted to counter the proliferation of interpretations in the decisions of the lower courts. The legislator especially wanted to create more legal certainty, promote employment and economic growth and provide more guarantees against false employment, but above all false self-employment, which would result in unfair competition.

As a basic principle, the qualification of the agreement by the parties (i.e. the intention of parties) takes priority. Thus, parties can freely choose the nature of their employment relationship. However, when the actual execution of the relationship shows sufficient elements which are not compatible with the qualification by the parties, the relationship will be requalified. Therefore three general criteria, besides the will of parties, are taken into account: the freedom to organize the working time, the freedom to organize the work and the possibility to exercise hierarchical control. These four general criteria are not cumulative; the importance of each criterion is assessed on a case by case basis. Note that some criteria are in themselves insufficient to classify the employment relationship, e.g. the title of the agreement, the way in which income is reported to the tax authorities, etc.

Furthermore, since 2012 nine specific criteria are applied with regard to false self-employment sensitive sectors, such as the transport sector, the

---

11 In order to evade higher social security contributions for employees, payment of a statutory indemnity in lieu of notice in case of termination of an employment contract, etc.

12 In order to open unlawful social security benefits.

13 Title XIII Programme Act (I) of 27 December 2006. *Belgian state Gazette,* 28 December 2006.

construction industry, security activities and the cleaning sector[14]. The specific criteria are the following:

- the absence of any financial or economical risk for the person performing the work, such as (for example):
  - absence of a personal and substantial investment with own resources in the company; or
  - absence of a personal and substantial part in the profits or losses of the company;
- the absence of responsibility and decision-making authority in respect of the company's financial resources;
- the absence of power of decision in respect of the company's purchasing policy;
- the absence of power of decision in respect of the company's price policy, unless prices are statutory fixed;
- the absence of a commitment to achieve a certain result with regard to the agreed work;
- the guaranteed payment of a fixed remunerations without prejudice to the result of the company or the extent of the performed work;
- not being an employer of personally and freely recruited employees or the absence of the possibility to recruit employees to carry out the agreed work or to be replaced in order to perform the agreed work;
- not acting as a an enterprise towards other individuals or working principally or usually for only one co-contractor;
- working at premises of which one is not the owner or tenant, or working with materials provided, financed or secured by the co-contractor.

In the aforementioned sectors the existence of an employment contract is refutably presumed when the execution of the employment relationship shows that more than half of the specific criteria are fulfilled. When less than half of the criteria are fulfilled, the employment relationship is considered a self-employed agreement[15]. The presumption can be reversed by all means of law.

[14] These changes were mainly implemented due to the fact that the expectations of the 2006 Act were not met and had not had the hoped-for effects. The legislator opted for a more specific and sector-wide approach.

[15] However, in certain cases the presumption is not applicable (e.g. in case of a professional relationship between family members).

Please note that although for the assessment of the employment relationship priority is given to the actual implementation of the agreement, parties have the possibility to submit their agreement for review to a ruling commission prior to the execution of the contract. The ruling commission will determine the nature of the employment relationship (i.e. the so-called 'social ruling'). The social ruling will be effective for a three-year period and will be binding for the social security authorities. However, (labour) courts are not bound by the decisions of the commission.

1.1.4 Economic unemployment for white-collar employees

The third permanent measure we would like to bring to the reader's attention is economic unemployment for white-collar employees, which was first introduced in 2009 as a temporary measure to avoid job losses due to the economic crisis but later on – in 2011 – was adopted as a permanent measure[16].

This measure provides for a suspension of the execution of the employment contract due to economic reasons. In order to apply this system of suspension, the company must be recognized as a company in difficulty[17]. Moreover a collective bargaining agreement[18] or a company plan should be in place, which includes a number of statutory entries as well as the modalities of the suspension.

If the above-mentioned conditions are met, the employer may either decide to proceed to a full suspension (up to 16 weeks per calendar year[19]) or a partial suspension of the execution of the employment contract (at least two days a week for a maximum of 26 weeks per calendar year[20]).

---

16 Article 77/1-77/8 of the Act of 3 July 1978 on employment contracts. *Belgian State Gazette,* 22 August 1978. Please note that a similar system of economic unemployment already was in place for blue-collar employees.

17 A company in difficulty is a company which meets one of the following criteria; a substantial reduction (i.e. at least 10% compared to the same quarter of calendar year 2008 or one of the two calendar years preceding the application) in turnover, production or orders, or, a substantial use (i.e. at least 10% of the total days reported to the National Social Security Office) of temporary unemployment for blue-collar employees.

18 On sectoral or company level.

19 The collective bargaining agreement or the company plan could provide for a shorter term.

20 The collective bargaining agreement or the company plan could provide for a shorter term.

The notification of the suspension system must be done at least seven days in advance by displaying them on the company premises in a visible place. This may be replaced by a written notice to each employee concerned. The National Employment Office shall be informed about the reasons that have caused the crisis electronically within the same time frame, as the same applies to the works council[21].

In case of suspension of the execution of the employment contract, the employee obtains an unemployment benefit and an additional compensation[22] paid by the employer per non-working day.

1.1.5 Outplacement

The next important permanent measure is the generalization of outplacement. In order to reduce unemployment – and public expenditure – outplacement was generalized for dismissed employees in 2014[23]. Up to 31 December 2013, only employees aged forty-five years or more at the time of their dismissal or employees dismissed by a firm in restructuring could benefit from outplacement. As from 1 January 2014 every dismissed employee with a notice period (or a corresponding severance pay)[24] of minimum 30 weeks[25] is entitled to outplacement. The aforementioned outplacement schemes that existed before 2014 became residual systems (i.e. they only apply if the employee is not entitled to a notice period or a corresponding severance pay of at least 30 weeks)[26].

The modalities of the general outplacement scheme depend on the mode of termination of the employment contract. If the employment contract is terminated with a notice period, the employee will be entitled to 60 hours of outplacement deducted from his application leave[27]. In this

---

21 Or in absence, the union representatives.

22 The amount is determined by the collective bargaining agreement of the company plan.

23 Act of 5 September 2001 to improve the employment rate of employees. *Belgian State Gazette,* 15 September 2001.

24 Under Belgian law, employers can freely chose to terminate the employment contract with a notice period or with severance pay.

25 Taking into account the new notice-period rules (i.e. for employment contracts entered into as from 1 January 2014) this corresponds to nine years' seniority.

26 Please note that both the general as well as the residual scheme is not applicable if the employee is dismissed for serious cause.

27 I.e. during the performance of the notice period every employee has the right to leave from work (retaining his salary) in order to seek new employment. If the employee is entitled to outplacement the application leave amounts to one day a week throughout the duration of the notice period. If the employee is not entitled to outplacement, the application leave amounts to one day a week during the last 26 weeks of the notice period and half day a week in the previous period.

case, the employer's outplacement offer must be made within four weeks after the start of the notice period. The employee has four weeks to accept the offer. If the employee does not respond within this period, he shall be deemed to have accepted the offer. Should the employment contract be terminated with severance pay, the employee will be entitled to 60 hours of outplacement as well, at the value of 1/12 of the gross annual remuneration of the calendar year that precedes dismissal[28], with a minimum value of EUR 1,800 (excl. VAT) and a maximum value of EUR 5,500 (excl. VAT)[29]. In this case, the outplacement offer must be made within 15 days after the termination of the employment contract. The employee has four weeks to accept the offer. If the employee does not respond within this period, he shall be deemed to have accepted the offer. Up to 31 December 2015 the employee who refused the outplacement offer regained his four weeks' salary that had been taken into account for outplacement. However, in order to encourage employees to actually commit themselves to the outplacement and quickly find a new job, as from 2016 four weeks' salary may be deducted from the severance pay regardless of their acceptance or refusal of the outplacement offer by the employee[30].

Finally, please note that specific modalities exist in order to begin or resume outplacement should the employee lose his new job.

1.1.6 Early retirement[31]

Additionally specific measures were taken with regard to early retirement whereby the major aim was to activate early retirees to find a new job. In fact, in the last few years the government took several measures in order to discourage the use of early retirement[32].

---

28 I.e. the wages and benefits acquired in the context of the employment agreement and to which the employee is entitled on 31 December of the year preceding his dismissal.

29 These amounts are prorated in case of part-time employment.

30 This is just a possibility (and not an obligation) for the employer.

31 In Dutch '*Stelsel van werkloosheid met bedrijfstoeslag*', in French '*chômage avec complément d'entreprise.*'

32 Royal Decree of 3 May 2007 on the early retirement schemes. *Belgian State Gazette,* 8 June 2007. See also: collective bargaining agreement No. 17 of 19 December 1974 introducing a system of additional compensation in favour of some elderly dismissed employee (*Belgian State Gazette,* 31 January 1975); collective bargaining agreement No. 105 of 28 March 2013 laying down the conditions for the granting of additional compensation as part of the unemployment benefits for some elderly disabled dismissed employees and dismissed employees with severe physical problems (*Belgian State Gazette,* 24 October 2013).

First of all, the age and career requirements in order to be entitled to early retirement have become several times more strict. The last changes in this respect date from 2015[33].

Please find below an overview of the different types of early retirement:

Type	Age requirement[34]	Career requirement[35]
General system	62	Men: 40 Women: 32 (2016) – 40 (2024)
Arduous occupation[36]	58	35[37]
Medical reason[38]	58	35
Long career	58	40
Night work	58	33[39]
Work disability[40]	58	33
Company in difficulties	55	10/20[41]
Company in restructuring	55	10/20[42]

As one may notice, in general an employee dismissed at the age of 62 years and a professional career (in 2016) of 40 years (for men) or 32 years (for women)[43] is entitled to early retirement. However, several exceptions to this general rule are in place[44].

33 First time with the so-called '*Generatiepact*' of 2005, which consist 66 measures countering aging. The next big reform dates from 2012. Finally, in 2015 the latest reforms were introduced.

34 Expressed in years.

35 Expressed in years.

36 I.e. night work, shift work or continuous work.

37 Arduous occupation for five years in the last ten years or seven years in the last fifteen years.

38 Disabled or serious medical problems (assessed by a physician of the Occupational Accidents Fund or the Occupational Diseases Fund).

39 With at least 22 years of night work.

40 Proved by a certificate of the occupational physician. Moreover, please note that this system is only applicable in the construction industry.

41 Professional career of 10 years in the last 15 years in the same sector or of 20 years in general.

42 Professional career of 10 years in the last 15 years in the same sector or of 20 years in general.

43 Please note that the length of the career for woman increases annually until they reach the same level of men (40 years) in 2024.

44 E.g. arduous occupations.

We would like to emphasize that early retirement is not a right for employees; it is only the result of the dismissal of the employee by the employer. This entails that an employee cannot claim his dismissal in order to be entitled to early retirement. The early retiree receives unemployment benefits as well as an extra company allowance paid by his former employer.

Secondly, there were some major changes with regard to the status of early retirees. Before 1 January 2015, early retirees had the unemployed status but were exempt from the requirement to be available for the job market; they did not for example have to find new employment or accept a job offer.

As from 1 January 2015, a so-called adapted availability for the labour market applies for early retirees until they reach the statutory retirement age (i.e. 65 years). It should however be noted that the definition of this new type of availability, as well as how this concept relates to the (full) availability for (ordinary) unemployed, remains quite unclear. In any case, the early retiree has to register himself as a jobseeker. Furthermore, adapted coaching based on an individual action plan is provided for. If suitable employment is offered, the early retiree should accept this offer. However, he is exempt from actively having to seek a new job.

In certain cases, one could also be exempted from this adapted availability (e.g. if an early retiree meets certain age ore career requirements). Please note that the aforementioned rules with regard to the adapted availability also apply for unemployed persons as from the age of 60 years.

1.1.7 Candidate-refugees

The current refugee crisis also had an effect on several measures. In order to give candidate refugees the chance to be employed their waiting period was shortened from six to four months after the introduction of their asylum application[45]. After this four-month period the candidate refugee may apply for a work permit (type C). This type of work permit is valid for one year (but is renewable) and for any employment with any employer.

A candidate refugee may in any case be employed until a decision is taken regarding their asylum request by the Commissioner General for Refugees and Stateless Persons (CGRSP) or, in case of appeal, by the

45 Royal Decree of 9 June 1999 on the employment of foreign employees. *Belgian State Gazette*, 26 June 1999.

Council for Alien Law Litigation (CALL). If a positive decision is taken by the CGRSP or the CALL, they can be employed further without a work permit. In the opposite case, the foreign employee no longer meets the conditions to be allowed to work (and to stay) in Belgium.

1.1.8 Flexi-jobs

In 2015 flexi-jobs were introduced for hotels, restaurants and cafés to combat the wave of bankruptcies and to discourage the undeclared work in this sector[46].

An employee can only be employed with a flexi-job on the condition he is employed by (an) other employer(s) for at least 80% of a full-time equivalent.

Preliminary to the execution of the first flexi-job employment agreement, parties should enter into a written framework agreement for definite or indefinite term. This agreement merely establishes the framework within which one or more employment agreements may be concluded. However, this does not constitute an obligation to do so. The framework agreement should include a number of compulsory statements, such as the identification of the parties, the flexi wage, a short description of the tasks, etc. If parties do not enter into a framework agreement or this agreement does not meet the statutory requirements, the employment agreements concluded within this context cannot be considered as flexi-job employment agreements. Thus, the specific consequences associated with flexi-jobs will not be applicable.

With regard to the employment agreement, parties could enter into an (oral or written) fixed-term employment agreement or an employment agreement for a specific project. In general, the Employment Contracts Act of 3 July 1978 applies. The flexi wage amounts to an hourly minimum of EUR 8.82 and is subject to the consumer price index[47]. The flexi vacation pay amounts to 7.67% of the flexi wage and has to be paid along with the flexi wage. This results in an hourly minimum wage of EUR 9.50. The employer only has to pay a special contribution of 25%; no social security contributions or taxes are due. Finally, the

[46] Act of 26 November 2015 concerning various provisions on social affairs. *Belgian State Gazette,* 26 November 2015.

[47] In addition, sectoral allowances are due to the employee (e.g. clothing allowances, public holiday allowances, night allowances, eco vouchers, etc.). These allowances are also subject to vacation pay.

termination of the employment agreement does not affect the existence of the framework agreement.

1.1.9 Night work

The last permanent measure which deserves attention is the possibility to perform night work in the distribution sector given the rise of e-commerce and the necessity to perform this type of work[48].

In general, night work (this means work performed between 8 pm and 6 am) is prohibited in Belgium. Exceptions on this general prohibition can be determined by law or royal decree.

In March 2016, a royal decree was adopted in order to set an exception for e-commerce activities in companies of the distributions sector. In this context, several collective bargaining agreements on sectoral level were concluded[49]. If a company wishes to introduce night work a legal procedure should be followed. Negotiations at company level should be started covering at least the identification and listing the activities and functions covered by the e-commerce activities, the kind of night work which is necessary to develop e-commerce activities within the company, the type of employment contracts, work regime and work schedule of the employees recruited for e-commerce activities and the regulation of student work. This should result in a collective bargaining agreement at company level (signed by all trade union represented in the trade union delegation) or an adjustment of work rules (if there is no trade union delegation).

Furthermore, several collective bargaining agreements on night work must be concluded. It concerns specific rules with regard to, amongst other things, the specific conditions of night work[50].

---

48 Royal Decree of 13 March 2016 on night work for e-commerce activities. *Belgian State Gazette,* 18 March 2016.

49 Collective bargaining agreements of 14 January 2016 concerning the introduction of night work for e-commerce activities entered into by the Joint Committee for the independent retail (JC No. 201), the Joint Committee for white-collar employees in the food retail (JC No. 202), the Joint Subcommittee for medium-sized food business (JC No. 202.01), the Joint Committee for the large retail business (JC No. 311) and the Joint Committee on the department stores (JC No. 312), *Belgian State Gazette* 12 February 2016.

50 Collective bargaining agreement No. 49 of 21 May 1991 relating to the guarantee of a specific financial compensation for employees performing shift work combined with night work or any other type of work combined with night work. *Belgian State Gazette,* 28 August 1991. See also collective bargaining agreement No. 46 of 23

1.2 Temporary reforms[51]

1.2.1 Working time reduction

The first temporary measure reduces the working time[52] of all employees or a category of employees by a quarter or one fifth[53]. The major aim of this measure was to provide employers with the ability to cope with a decrease in working volume without having to dismiss employees.

As previously mentioned, the working time reduction was to be applied to all the employees or a specific category of employees of the company. In the latter case, the company was free to determine the criteria for the delineation of the specific category of employees to which the reduction of working time was applicable (e.g. all employees of a particular department). However, these criteria could not affect the collective nature of the measure. Moreover, it was impossible to base the application of the working time reduction on an individual decision of the employee or the employer. Logically, the criteria were required to be relevant, objective and sufficiently precise. Only a collective bargaining agreement entered into at company level could introduce this type of working time reduction. If working time was reduced, the employer obtained a target-group reduction on the social security contributions.

This system was applicable up to 31 March 2011[54].

March 1990 on accompanying measures for shift work combined with night work, as well as any other type of work combined with night work. *Belgian State Gazette,* 13 June 1990. E.g. employees performing night work are entitled to an hourly additional compensation of at least EUR 1.12 (younger than 50 years) or EUR 1.35 (older than 50 years).

51 Since at this time no temporary measures are in place, only the two most recent temporary measures will be discussed.

52 Working time is defined as the average weekly working time of full-time employees, calculated over a one year period, as resulting either from the working time schedule set out in the work rules (possibly applied over a cycle), or from the working time schedule combined with working time reduction days granted within the framework of the working time reduction.

53 Act of 19 June 2009 concerning various provisions on employment in times of crisis. *Belgian State Gazette,* 25 June 2009.

54 Please note that at this time several other types of career break exist. See for example: collective bargaining agreement No. 103 of 27 June 2012 on the introduction of a system of career break, career reduction (for older employees). *Belgian State Gazette,* 31 August 2012.

1.2.2 Career break[55]

The second temporary measure was of an individual nature as it allowed to reduce the working time of a full-time employee by half or by one fifth for a period of one to six months[56] in order to avoid job losses[57]. Only so-called 'companies in difficulty'[58] could apply this measure.

The reduction had to be introduced by an individual agreement between the employee and the employer. The employee was entitled to part-time salary, benefits paid by the government and in certain cases additional compensation paid by the employer.

This system was also applicable up to 31 March 2011.

2. Future reforms (?)

The Belgian government, in particular the Minister for Work K. Peeters, indicated that from 2016 onwards priority will be given to certain measures in the framework of workable and flexible work, more specifically employment plans for older employees, the career account and career savings, the modernization of working time, tackling stress and burn-out and the reintegration of disabled employees[59].

In the context of this paper, only the most eye-catching measure will be discussed briefly, in particular the modernization of working time and the reintegration of disabled employees. The main aim of this measure is to give companies the opportunity to adapt working time to the necessities of the company and to give employees the possibility to balance work and private life. Therefore, the reference period in order to determine the average weekly working time shall be set at one year. Currently, in

---

55 In Dutch '*tijdskrediet*', in French '*crédit-temps*.'

56 This period was however renewable.

57 Act of 19 June 2009 concerning various provisions on employment in times of crisis. *Belgian State Gazette,* 25 June 2009.

58 I.e. a company that either could prove (i) that turnover or production was reduced by 15% compared to the corresponding quarter of 2008, or (ii) an economic unemployment of blue-collar employees of at least 20% compared to the total working days reported to the National Social Security Office, or (iii) a substantial decrease of orders with 15% compared with the corresponding quarter of 2008.

59 Algemene beleidsnota Werk (3 November 2015), *Parl.St.* Kamer 2015-2016, No. 1428/003. Retrieved September 23, 2016 from http://www.dekamer.be/FLWB/PDF/54/1428/54K1428003.pdf. See also http://www.krispeeters.be/sites/krispeeters/files/wwww_tekst_nederlands.pdf.

general, the reference period is set per quarter. Unless conflicting sectoral provisions exist, the daily and weekly working time limits will be set at respectively nine hours and forty-five hours. However, at sectoral or at company level there will be some room for small adjustments. At sectoral level, for example, working time could be extended up to 11 hours a day and 50 hours a week, subject to compliance with an average weekly working time of 48 hours on a yearly basis. Moreover, the reference period of one year can be extended to six years[60].

With regard to the reintegration of disabled employees, the government intends to implement a framework for a partial work resumption and a reintegration programme. According to the government it is important to give employees the chance to go back to work at an early stage, and to provide modified or other work (when necessary). In the context of reintegration, there must be smooth cooperation between the various physicians[61]. In the reintegration programme the prevention consultant – occupational physician will play a key role in enabling the employee to re-integrate into the working environment under the best possible conditions. The main aim of this programme is to provide both the employer and the employee legal certainty and to eliminate obstacles that may arise during his/her return to work. A procedure that offers legal certainty with regard to long-term or permanent disability to work will also be included.

Conclusion

This paper showed that a wide range of socio-economic factors influenced the law, more specific Belgian individual labour law. This resulted in both the introduction of new regulations as well the adaptation of already existing regulations.

The economic problems in Belgium have provoked a series of measures, with a central purpose to combat unemployment. Belgium has a centre-right majority government at the federal level. This government majority analyses the problems in a way that is similar to the social policy within the European Union. The policy of the

60 At this time, certain activities within the Joint Committee for the metal, mechanical en electrical constructions (No. 111) already apply such reference period.

61 This could be organized electronically, obviously respecting the sensitivity and the protection of medical data.

Union, also previously driven under the influence of the financial crisis and fiscal problems in EU countries, is based on economic motives more than on social ideals. The latest permanent measures as well as the possible future measures often relate to working longer and more flexible hours, while the latest partly temporary measures date from the economic crisis of 2009 and 2012.

From Dismissal Law to Re-Employment Law

A Culture War

Marc De Vos*

Abstract

This article takes stock of the flexicurity agenda from both a general perspective and from the perspective of Belgian labour market reforms. It argues that, notwithstanding the difficult crisis period and also because of it, the European Employment Strategy (EES) has succeeded in inspiring reforms along flexicurity lines. It focuses on dismissal law modernization as a case in point. However, it stresses the limits of ad hoc and piecemeal reform. Flexicurity requires commitment from partners and stakeholders. This commitment does not sufficiently materialize through limited reforms, making flexicurity increasingly a cultural challenge. The article applies this reasoning to dismissal law. It advocates a full reform of dismissal law towards re-employment law. In the absence of such a comprehensive reform, marginal reforms modernize at the surface but fail to change dismissal culture, limiting reform effectiveness, which in turn further erodes cultural confidence in Flexicurity's promise.

Keywords: dismissal, flexicurity, European Employment Strategy, work-to-work transition

1. Structural labour market reforms: dream or nightmare?

For decades, extensive research and policy work from academia and international institutions has advocated overhauling employment regulation as an integral part of a broad strategy to combat persistent underemployment and unemployment in Western European countries as well as in post-communist European countries. Under the aegis of the European Union, the European Employment Strategy (EES) and its

* Marc de Vos is Professor of Ghent University Law School, Curtin University Law School and Itinera Institute. He is the author and co-author of a large number of publications on issues of labour and employment law, European integration, labour market reform, pensions, healthcare, ageing and the welfare state.

successive Employment Guidelines have crystallized a consensus approach to structural labour market reform. This formal institutionalization of European labour market modernization emerged from and with the so-called 'Flexicurity' movement that sought – and continues to seek – an appropriate blend of flexibility and security in globalized contemporary economies.

The standard European or EU approach to structural labour market reform has thus been an attempt to systemically bridge the perennial tension between economic or market logic and social protection. As this philosophy requires proponents of old school job security to abandon some of their job protection for the organization of new but uncertain employment and career potential, this was never going to be an easy sell. Today, approximately two decades after its inception, it is easy to dismiss the original pan-European consensus drive as cynical or meaningless[1].

Indeed, in the cauldron of the euro-crisis much regulatory reform in ailing debtor states, including for the labour market, has been or is perceived as 'imposed' 'austerity'-driven logic from Brussels. Modernization is then portrayed as a cynical byword for an alien power grab that favours business interests while crushing the weak, fuelling populism while failing to solve the crisis woes. In other countries, on the other hand, the momentum of employment law modernization seems lost in a miasma of frustrating economic stagnation. Meagre initiatives introducing small doses of flexibility are always heavily contested and are never part of a comprehensive reform agenda. Modernization then indeed becomes meaningless, a fig leaf barely hiding political improvization without much strategic orientation except a rather anaemic desire to stimulate economic growth and employment creation. Isolated flexibility is easily vilified as contributing to labour market polarization: the disease, instead of the cure. Flexicurity, with some exaggeration, is seemingly the new F-word.

There is much to be said for this gloomy assessment, unfortunately. Perhaps labour market regulation only really ever responds to economic pressures, making the resulting process inevitably messy and reactive, rather than deliberate and proactive. Yet this contribution will attempt to offer a more positive appraisal. It will seek the value of the overarching EU policy framework more in fostering the biotope of policy debate,

---

1 For recent critical overviews, see, e.g. Eichhorst W., Marx P., Wehner C. Labor Market Reforms in Europe: Towards More Flexicure Labor Markets? *IZA* DP, 2016, No. 9863; *Inventory of labour market policy measures in the EU 2008–13: The crisis and beyond.* Geneva: ILO, 2015

policy preparation and policy implementation, rather than in bold and systematic domestic policy change. It will look at the EES and Flexicurity as an overall beacon, rather than as a fixed roadmap.

My limited prism is the Belgian scene. Belgium is a notoriously difficult country for structural policy reform. Institutional complexities, different regional political orientations, cultural differences, and deep regional economic asymmetries, make Belgium perhaps – as it is sometimes labelled by international media – 'the world's most successful failed state'. In recent years, moreover, Belgium – like many other European countries – has gone through a dismal succession of institutional, financial, economic, budgetary, immigration, and security crises. There was simply no time or energy to mobilize democratic forces around a long-term employment strategy.

And yet, notwithstanding all these structural and cyclical handicaps, this contribution will demonstrate that Belgium has made genuine progress towards the flexicurity ideal in an area that is perhaps the most sensitive of all: dismissal law. Not through bold leadership but through diverse and gradual policy steps, indirectly inspired but not directly guided by flexicurity policy convictions, Belgium has moved markedly towards a more modern approach of employment termination. It has not reached a fully-fledged 2.0 of flexible and secure career-oriented job transition protection, but it has clearly evolved in that direction. And it is possible today to see the contours of the mature status of what could be called 're-employment law' instead of dismissal law.

2. Belgium's labour market at a glance[2]

Traditionally, the Belgian labour market is characterized by a below EU-average overall activity rate, currently at 67.6% underneath this national average lie profound and very persistent differences in labour market performance, for regions and provinces within Belgium and for subgroups within the working age population. For instance: the Flemish region typically has a substantially better track record in employment rate and unemployment rate than Wallonia, while non-European immigrants and older workers typically fare substantially worse in labour market prospects than other workers and jobseekers.

---

[2] Figures from the 2016 Annual Report of Belgium's High Council of Employment (Hoge Raad voor de Werkge-legenheid, *Digitale economie en arbeidsmarkt*).

In the crisis years after 2007, Belgium's labour market showed some of the tell-tale signs of serious economic stress. Temporary workers bore the brunt of initial job cuts, working-time reductions reduced job losses among insiders, job creation fell, and unemployment levels rose. However, a combination of macro-economic luck – particularly the absence of a bursting housing bubble and close economic ties with Germany – and a dose of deft crisis policy – particularly generous temporary unemployment benefits – lowered the immediate labour market costs of the economic crisis in comparison with many other Eurozone countries.

As a result, the overall labour market situation of Belgium has not dramatically shifted through the recent crisis years and is now showing signs of a relatively modest post-crisis recovery in line with pre-crisis structural trends. In terms of job growth, Belgium has added about 20,000 net new jobs per year on average in the last five years, though now accelerating to roughly 40,000. Reaching its EU2020 overall employment rate target of 73.2% would require more than two or three times as much net job growth per year, respectively. However, since 2014 and in stark contrast with the preceding crisis years, the good news is that job creation has restarted in the private sector, particularly in the services industry, and has particularly benefited jobseekers younger than 25 years. This is a critical shift since almost all net job creation post-2007 had been government subsidized and since crisis policy was aimed more at keeping workers in their existing jobs than at promoting job opportunities for newcomers.

The post-crisis world thus leaves the Belgian labour market with many of its age-old structural shortcomings. The unemployment rate in Wallonia (around 12%) is more than double than that in Flanders (around 5%). The employment rate of immigrants (and their descendants) from outside the EU is dismal. At more than 16%, the difference in overall employment rate for nationals and non-EU nationals is nowhere bigger in the EU than in Belgium, with the exception of Sweden, although the difference has started to slowly trend downwards. On the plus side, the employment rate in the age group older than 50 has increased from 27% in 2000 to over 46% in 2015. This marked improvement is partially a demographic transition as active baby-boomers age, but is also tied to successive measures by successive governments to delay early retirement and to strengthen job search requirements for the unemployed in that age group.

The reality of job polarization and insider-outsider segmentation notwithstanding, people in employment in Belgium on average continue to enjoy a relatively high level of stability. At 11.4 years, average seniority is among the very highest in the entire OECD[3]. Moreover, Belgium's level of employment protection, using the standard OECD indicators, is also among the most stringent, particularly as regards collective dismissal. Overall employment security, as measured by transitions in employment status, has constantly remained over 85% since 2006 and is now almost at pre-crisis level[4]. However, while the overall market share of temporary work remains relatively low at below 9%[5], its share is more than three times that for workers younger than 25, an indication of how temporary work has become a matching and transition station on the road to more stable employment, bypassing dismissal law almost entirely along the way.

3. Flexicurity in Belgian stealth mode

From the perspective of the so-called 'Wilthagen Matrix', Belgium's flexicurity profile is traditionally more oriented towards job security and income security than it is towards employment security and combination security. As such, Belgium is part of a continental cluster of countries that have historically emphasized job security and relatively low external flexibility in their labour market organization.[6] The formal adoption, since 2006, of Flexicurity as a pan-European policy aim has not (yet) fundamentally altered this reality. In the run-up to the global financial crisis, Flexicurity failed to unite Belgium's social partners and political parties behind an ambitious reform agenda[7]. The subsequent crisis years have understandably focused energies on crisis measures while not favouring fundamental policy reflections.

By and large, Belgium's powerful labour unions still remain largely to be convinced of flexicurity's win-win potential, essentially seeing increased flexibility as its only security. Belgian employer organizations, on the other hand, remain suspicious of increased costs associated with

---

3 OECD Statistics. Retrieved September 28, 2015.

4 Eurostat, Labour transitions by type of contract – Changes in employment security. Retrieved September 30, 2015.

5 Eurostat, Temporary employees as percentage of the total number of employees. Retrieved September 30, 2015.

6 See, recently, Wilthagen T. *Flexicurity in bedrijf: het beste van twee werelden?* [Flexicurity in business: the best of both worlds]. Itinera Institute, No. 6, 2014.

7 See De Vos M., Konings J. *D'une sécurité d'emploi vers une sécurité du travail sur le marché du travail belge* [From job security to employment security in the Belgian labor market]. Anthémis, 2007.

flexicurity at the HR level, particularly against a back-drop of wage cost handicap and loss of market share in exports. Finally, Belgium's politicians have been stuck in a cycle of institutional, financial, budgetary and economic crises since 2006, with predictable mixed results.

Belgium's automatic stabilizer is not a labour market organization that actively supports transitions, but rather the passive income security of the welfare state. Much of Belgium's immediate crisis response was directed at providing income security, especially through generous temporary unemployment and subsidized job creation schemes, the short-term impact of which was to avoid layoffs and unemployment respectively. The long-term impact, both as regards economic growth potential and insider/outsider entrenchment on the labour market, remains unclear.

While subsidized job creation thus stands out as the hallmark of Belgium's labour market reality since the advent of the crisis, only to give way to cyclical private sector job creation in the most recent years, Belgium's labour market policy has evolved in directions more familiar to a flexicurity agenda as well. Working time flexibility in Belgium has been increased by raising the maximum amount of overtime within a reference period of one calendar year: from 65 to 91 hours by law, or to 130 hours if a collective bargaining agreement can be reached[8]. In the same vein of favouring flexible work, the possibility for companies to use temporary agency workers has been extended beyond peaks and illnesses to vacancies. Essentially formalizing a widespread pre-existing practice, the new rule allows employers to use temporary agency work to test potentials for job openings, while also restricting the possibility to use day contracts[9].

Systemic wage moderation has been an official Belgian policy since 1996, with a bi-annual cycle of maximum wage growth margins that reflect expected wage cost increases in Belgium's neighbouring economies. Aiming to boost competitiveness and improve job creation, the federal government has frozen wage-growth altogether for 2013-15 in the private sector, while allowing for only minimal overall wage increase in 2016[10]. This wage freeze does not cover Belgium's well-known automatic wage indexation tied to consumer price inflation, however.

---

8 Act of 17 August 2013. *Belgian State Gazette*, 29 August 2013.

9 CBA No. 108, 16 July 2013.

10 Decree of 28 April 2013, *Belgian State Gazette,* 2 May 2013 and Law of 28 April 2015, *Belgian State Gazette,* 30 April 2015.

Whereas the bulk of Belgium's active labour market policy or ALMP has remained focused on subsidies for job creation, activating measures for improving employability were also on the menu of Belgian crisis responses. Here, the combination of federal and regional policy – the result of Belgium's decades-long devolution process – comes into play. A new nation-wide programme for paid internships for young jobseekers (younger than 25) with no high-school degree was launched with an ambitious target of helping 10,000 people into their first jobs. So far, it has not lived up to expectations.

Belgium has also tinkered with its unemployment insurance with an aim to increase labour supply and willingness to work. Belgium famously provides unemployment benefits of unlimited duration, making the activation of the unemployed a pressing need from a perspective of labour market participation. For a number of years, Belgium's official employment agencies – first in Flanders, then also in Wallonia and Brussels – have increasingly embraced follow-up policies towards the unemployed, complemented with a more systematic supervision and sanctioning at the level of benefit payment[11]. The crisis and post-crisis periods have seen the continuation of this process.

On the one hand, personal follow-up has been extended to cover the unemployed until age 58 (first in Flanders). On the other hand, the employment agency in charge of verifying benefit eligibility, has extended its process of screening labour market availability to include the unemployed up to age 54, en route to full coverage. This screening process is based on initial interviews, followed by personal agreements with the unemployed who show insufficient job-finding efforts.

Since 2012, two target groups of unemployed have moreover seen a change in their benefit system, again with an activation purpose. For the long-term unemployed, a new system of accelerated gradual benefit reduction has been designed. After one year of continuous unemployment, unemployment benefits are gradually reduced, the tempo depending on the years of previous employment. After a period of no more than five years, all the unemployed fall back on a fixed-sum benefit. The reform was adopted to encourage re-employment but is highly contested by the labour unions. Its statistical impact is as yet unclear, although there is evidence of both labour market reinsertion and labour market exit. Finally, for first entrants on the labour market the unemployment

11 See also OECD, *Enhancing the inclusiveness of the labour market in Belgium*. 2013.

insurance has been adjusted to avoid immediate entitlement to benefits. They now need to wait an entrance period of 310 days, after which time they are entitled to insertion benefits for no longer than 36 months. Aided by a more favourable economic climate and the re-emergence of job creation, this measure has led to a decline in young people claiming insertion benefits.

Both the previous and the current federal Belgian government has also gone further than mere 'activation'. The concept of 'suitable work' which unemployed jobseekers are required to accept has been broadened. More contentious is the ambition, of both the current federal and Flemish governments, to impose compulsory 'societal service' for categories of long-term unemployed, in the shape of two half-days of unpaid work, as a condition for continued unemployment benefit eligibility. This political ambition has not yet come to fruition and is the subject of intense opposition, raising questions whether the ambition will actually become reality[12].

Overall, these changes reflect a growing concern for extending careers and boosting labour market participation, against the backdrop of demographic ageing and rising pension costs. Other reforms have gone in the same direction. Early retirement schemes have, once again, been restricted and made more onerous, but they have nonetheless remained standard practice in the big company restructurings of the recent crisis period[13]. A complementary rule requiring employers to follow the age pyramid of their companies when selecting personnel for collective redundancy was adopted in 2012 but its implementation has been stalled[14].

An increased emphasis on career development has also led to the adoption of a career voucher system in Flanders, providing people who have at least one year of professional experience with a counselling package of four hours at an authorized career centre[15].

---

12 See, e.g., Schepers W, Nicaise I. *Chinese vrijwilligers: nu ook in België? Naar een verplichte gemeenschapsdienst voor langdurig werklozen?* [Chinese volunteers now in Belgium? To compulsory community service for long-term unemployed]. HIVA, 2015.

13 So-called 'bridge pensions' have been re-baptised 'unemployment with a surplus', reflecting their nature but intended to emphasize the need for continued labour market availability.

14 Act of 29 March 2012. *Belgian State Gazette*, 30 March 2012 and CBA No. 104 of 27 June 2012.

15 Flemish Government Decision of 17 May 2013. *Belgian State Gazette,* 11 July 2013.

The latest phase of Belgium's protracted state reform has devolved almost the entire competence for ALMP to its three regions. The competences for rehabilitation, activation, and sanctioning of the unemployed, are now together in one single hand. In principle, this should allow for a tailored and intelligent approach that maximizes employability. Moreover, a substantial part of the job creation schemes has also been regionalized.

Both the new Flemish and Walloon regional governments have committed themselves to streamlining and concentrating existing ALMP funds. In the same vein, the current federal government has embraced working time flexibility and career accounts as a policy goal, albeit with severe union protest. In view of these institutional changes and political intentions, Flexicurity's moment may actually be about to arrive in Belgium after all. This brings me to the symbolic case of dismissal law and its evolution from a Flexicurity perspective.

4. Modernized Belgian dismissal law

Irrespective of the burden of long notice periods and the proliferation of specific protections against dismissal for specific groups, the key characteristic of Belgium's dismissal law is one akin to 'employment at will'. As a matter of principle, a Belgian employer who wants to dismiss can also dismiss, either through a notice period or by a payment in lieu of notice. Violation of specific dismissal protections translates into yet more redundancy cost but not into forced reinstatement. Important recent dismissal law modernization in 2013 (hereinafter – the 2013 Act) has not focused on work-to-work transition per se but has primarily sought to harmonize notice periods for blue collar and white collar workers[16].

However, this does not mean that work-to-work transitions are not on the radar of Belgian dismissal law, quite the contrary. First and foremost, at least from a historical and formal point of view, notice periods themselves offer a dismissed employee the time to adjust and explore reemployment opportunities while still remaining in the employment relationship that is in the process of unwinding. While still bound to work during the notice period, employees are entitled to job-search leave. This gives the employee the right to be absent from work once or twice per week, provided the total duration of this absence does not exceed one full day of work per week.

16 Act of 26 December 2013. *Belgian State Gazette,* 26 December 2013.

Notice periods are prescribed by the 2013 Act and are substantial. During the first 3 months of employment, the notice to be observed is 2 weeks. Thereafter, the notice period increases from 4 weeks for an employee with a seniority of 3 to 6 months and up to 64 weeks for an employee who is in his 23rd year of seniority. After the 23rd year, the employee is entitled to 1 additional week per additional year of seniority. In practice many notice periods are often curtailed and replaced by (partial or full) payment in lieu. This leaves the dismissed worker with income and full liberty to explore reemployment opportunities, but is recognized to also present a risk of passivity, increasing the likelihood of long transition periods.

Besides the 'passive' component of notice or payment in lieu of notice, Belgian dismissal law has long contained an 'active' element of work-to-work transition in the shape of outplacement services. As a rule, outplacement consists of 60 hours of services, worth 1/12 of the yearly salary of the calendar year that precedes the dismissal with a minimal value of 1,800 EUR and a maximal value of EUR 5,500[17]. The employer is obliged to make a valid outplacement offer, either within a short period of the termination by in-lieu payment or within four weeks after the commencement of the notice period.

The 2013 Act has extended and generalized the outplacement obligation. Prior to 2014, outplacement services were a right only for dismissed workers older than 45. It now covers anyone with a notice period or in-lieu payment of at least 30 weeks, irrespective of age. As of 2016, employees are obliged to participate in the outplacement, turning a right into a duty.

Outplacement services are also an integral part of Belgian's legal framework of collective dismissal. In case of a collective dismissal as defined by law (that is with a sufficient number of dismissals taking into account the number of employees of the company), the employer is obliged to constitute a re-employment cell. The employer must do so at the moment of the announcement of the collective dismissal. The employer, at least one of the trade unions, the regional employment agency and, as the case may be, the training fund of the company's sector of industry are all part of the cell. The regional employment agency has the leading role in offering outplacement to every employee registered in

17 2016 figures, exclusive of VAT, in proportion for part-timers.

the cell. Employers who recruit a registered employee, temporarily pay less social security contributions on that employee's salary.

Moreover, both Flanders and Wallonia (but not yet Brussels) complement the institutional fabric of collective dismissal with an independent and complementary framework for local 'reconversion cells' that can be established in the wake of a company closure or collective dismissal at the request of unions. The purpose of these publicly funded ad hoc cells is to offer a local platform for personal support and assistance to the workers who have lost their jobs, with an aim of increasing their mobility and employability.

The 2013 Act also attempts to modernize the law of individual dismissal by fully integrating an active component. Sectoral collective bargaining agreements are expected, by 2019, to provide that dismissed workers who are entitled to a notice period or in lieu payment of at least 30 weeks will receive a third of their dismissal package through measures that increase the employability of the dismissed worker. It remains to be seen whether the bargaining will follow if workers favour hard cash over services: failure will only result in the employer having to top up notice pay with a contribution of 4%[18].

The Belgian case demonstrates how incremental policy changes can gradually add up to upgrading the institutional framework, here the framework of dismissal, in a direction that amounts to a Flexicurity orientation. Of course, it remains to be seen whether the various new components beside the old monetary protection will amount to more than simple decoration. New elements of the dismissal process need to take root and help the dismissal culture evolve. The balance between old-school monetary payments and new-school career enabling should gradually be found and is now still heavily tilted towards passive payments.

Overall, I personally continue to believe that dismissal law should emphasize work-to-work transition. We should treat dismissal as a bridge to the next job. We should use dismissal law, not really as protection against dismissal but as protection with dismissal. Dismissal law should become, and indeed be called, re-employment law[19]. For this paradigm shift to become reality I will now suggest few points for broad policy consideration.

---

18 Articles 92 and 93 of the Act of 26 December 2013. *Belgian State Gazette*, 26 December 2013.

19 See De Vos M. *Welke prioriteiten voor arbeidsmarktbeleid?* [What Priorities for Labour Market]. Itinera Institute, 2013.

5. Reinventing dismissal law as re-employment law

First and foremost: if the economy is in the doldrums and no jobs are being created, any focus on work-to-work transition will be powerless, except through targeted services or investment that shepherd persons to sectors or places where jobs are available. That is true for the macro-level of the labour market in general but also for lower levels: every general employment trend hides sectoral, regional or local differences. It can be advisable to prioritize transitions from declining to growing segments, particularly to avoid damaging long-term unemployment. It is also advisable to facilitate entrepreneurship: the end of a job can be the beginning of a self-employed business activity, also where suitable job vacancies are lacking.

From a viewpoint of re-employment, it is both advisable and efficient to limit the actual notice period to the period of shock-adjustment subsequent to dismissal, to be followed by a general framework for personal guidance towards new work, including a budget for investment in education and training. This reduces to near-zero any distance between the actual dismissal and the follow-up of the employee, on the one hand, and the 'activation' of jobseekers in the context of the unemployment insurance, on the other hand. In many cases, the very same case workers or service providers can serve both groups. They have a good relationship with employers seeking new employees. Since nearly everyone will or can be assisted, there is no stigma attached to it for prospective employers. Denmark comes to mind as the country that most closely resembles the ideal intimate connection between fluid dismissal and fast transition, with immediate support where needed.

From the perspective of re-employment, it is useful to be quick on the ball: to avoid starting with 'activation' support when the moment of dismissal is already imminent or has already arrived. When the shock of dismissal is upon a worker, he or she will naturally focus on income certainty and hence on passive protection, while his or her real interest is to proceed and progress career-wise. The ideal template is a 'holistic' career approach that is already cultivated and nurtured during employment and through the human resources policies of the then-employer, anticipating career changes well before they become reality. A second best is early risk detection and preventive investment upstream from the actual dismissal, at least during the notice period as such: notice should not mean wait and see. Preventive and proactive support will definitely improve chances for quick re-employment. However, it will also generate 'dead weight' loss because it will help people that may have made the next step easily themselves. Since budgets are limited it will be important to prioritise investment for active transition on the basis of objective needs.

A mundane but unavoidable question is how the means for investment into work-to-work transition will actually be raised. Arcadia is not upon us and budgets are under pressure everywhere. Those countries that already have sizeable ALMP budgets can opt to emphasize spending on threatened or dismissed workers who are not yet unemployed and entitled to unemployment insurance. The same prioritization can be achieved from a company perspective. The budget represented by passive dismissal costs, particularly in case of negotiated packages for mass redundancies, can at least be partially redirected towards the re-employment of affected workers. This will make the actual spending more progressive, enabling more efforts for those workers who need it. This is the outplacement philosophy in its mature stage. It is also possible to build transition packages up-front, for instance through a career account that is filled by contributions during employment periods. One can also consider 'mutualization' formulas where companies and/or workers contribute collectively to a fund that is applied individually in case of dismissal. In all of this it is advisable to factor in the size of companies since SMEs will often lack resources or sophistication.

It is crucial to ensure that the means are used where they are needed and useful, i.e. to really focus on real re-employment needs. A policy tool in this regard is earmarking, where the regulator or legislator reserves certain budget items for certain activation goals. Passive payment is then excluded, or at least forbidden. A similar goal can be obtained by adding dismissal as a fixed component of a career account, ensuring that part of the assembled funds are tied to dismissal as a career event. There too, it will be important to ensure that funds are spent in accordance to their career purpose, because the temptation of the extra short-term income can be real. A connected step is to tailor spending to needs, ensuring that needier workers get more. This is a type of solidarity that can be made intrinsic to collective mechanisms of work-to-work transitions. Their very purpose entails that people with more transition risks will receive more support, within a transparent framework that sets the rights and duties of all. Addressing needs also implies identifying needs. An apparatus for data finding and identification will be needed. This sounds cold but it is very warm: it requires personnel and personal contact. This again implies more budget, which is not always easy. At the same time it is important to allow for a period of adjustment and not force transition too early, avoiding rash career choices with perverse long-term effects. The only solution is personal and tailored.

If we want to promote transitions between jobs we also must remove obstacles on the transition path. A possible obstacle are employer-based rights: entitlements tied to a particular employment or to a particular sector of industry. Personalization and transferability of rights should be a transversal policy goal. The already mentioned career account can serve as tool to guarantee this, as currently considered in France[20]. Portability of rights will become more important as people will have to become more mobile to lengthen their careers in view of demographic ageing.

Always and everywhere financial incentives can play a role in stimulating dismissal and career behaviour in a desired direction. Tax incentives can be devised to promote employment and avoid dismissal. Where budgets can be spent freely, it can still be possible to tax differently in view of its actual usage. Employers who already invest generously and generally in career development and training prior to dismissal can be taxed differently and less when they actually dismiss workers. The formation and the funding of career accounts can be stimulated through taxation. And so on, and so forth.

Psychology and culture matter greatly. Countries or companies can be a paragon of 'active' regulation in theory, while a basket case of passive payments in practice. Outplacement can be central on paper but will result in little more than extra payments when the willingness and commitment for actual transition investment is lacking. The general corporate culture in HR and career development will influence the behaviour and wishes of everyone when an incidence of dismissal arises. The step from passive dismissal payments to active reemployment assistance is also a mental switch, also formed by language and behaviour. We all together forge the biotope that will either induce or restrain job mobility.

In times of scarcity it is important to set priorities. Supporting work-to-work transitions for dismissed workers and generally supporting the career development of workers can definitely be beneficial for their employability and for the labour market. However, it will bypass workers who are not so fortunate as to have an employment contract

[20] See Commission Compte personnel d'activité. Retrieved July 4, 2016 from http://www.strategie.gouv.fr/commission-CPA.

the termination of which requires a formal dismissal. Dismissal law is really for 'insiders' with a job, while 'outsiders' make do with precarious contracts. Modernizing dismissal law is desirable and necessary but it can also increase the gap between insiders and outsiders by helping insiders to remain insiders longer. That is one reason why it is advisable to allow for a buffer period during which desired workers can take the next step on their own, why collective redundancy should focus more on tailor-made solutions for actual career needs, and why career support in general should ideally extend well beyond the scope of dismissal to all workers irrespective of contractual status.

There are many different countries and many differences within countries, but one thing is common: it is critical to collect transparent and reliable data to gauge the impact and cost effectiveness of measures for career transition. Such data should not only trace the immediacy of transition subsequent to dismissal: it is also important to assess effects in the longer run. Only by adopting a career perspective can one really determine what works and what does not. There is still some doubt whether and which ALMP actually presents added value vis-à-vis more laissez-faire alternatives[21]. The only way to settle that debate is by striving for impact and best practices, through a governance culture of measurement and transparency.

Which of these attention points are relevant and priorities will depend on the situation of the country and on the labour market reality. Not all of the points are necessarily fully inescapable or compatible. One does not need to do everything to make progress. But having an overarching framework does allow to transcend the zero-sum discussion of piecemeal change with a more holistic and long-term strategy to take dismissal towards re-employment.

Conclusion: Flexicurity as a culture war

Notwithstanding years of EU coordination and consensus building, it is fair to argue that Flexicurity has not (yet) fully entered the DNA of European labour market regulation. But it is hard not to see its invisible

[21] For a recent survey of literature, see Card D., Kluve J., Weber A. What Works? A Meta Analysis of Recent Active Labor Market Program Evaluations. *NBER* WP No. 21431, 2015; Martin J. Activation and active labour market policies in OECD countries: stylised facts and evidence on their effectiveness. *IZA Journal of Labor Policy*, No. 4:4, 2015.

hand behind much of the piecemeal and crisis-driven reforms that have gradually emerged in several EU Member States. This may in part attest to the flexibility of the Flexicurity concept itself, but it also suggests that the intellectual framework of Flexicurity has indeed managed to survive and inspire during what has been the most difficult economic period in more than a generation.

To what extent do piecemeal reforms organically yield a strategic whole? To what extent will they succeed in mobilizing the commitment of stakeholders on which the Flexicurity philosophy depends? From the Belgian vantage point, these critical questions yield only tentative and hesitant answers. Belgium's crisis and post-crisis policy measures, irrespective of their intrinsic compatibility or incompatibility with Flexicurity principles, are more patchwork than strategy. They are more reactive in the face of pressure than proactive as a consequence of vision. Indeed, the crisis has not enabled the decision-makers and the stakeholders of the Belgian labour market to coalesce around a shared ambition for improvement and reform. Quite the contrary, social partners are profoundly divided and many of the reforms described above were and remain politically highly contested as well.

The shortcomings of ad hoc and incremental reform are evident in the symbolic case of dismissal law. Will partial modernization succeed in truly modernizing the institutional framework of dismissal, and will it succeed in converting attitudes during the dismissal process towards re-employment? The age-old notice period and its in lieu payment are age-old examples of an active protection aimed at enabling alternative employment. In reality they have mostly become passive payment guarantees. The very same legal protection can be used in both directions: what makes the difference is culture, more than rules and institutions. Will a passive culture shift towards an active alternative when reforms are marginal and partial?

Belgium – not unlike other EU Member States – has added layers of new and 'activation'-oriented obligations around the core of 'passive' financial compensation for dismissal, with a particular focus on outplacement. More than modernizing dismissal law itself, old dismissal law and old dismissal culture have thus become surrounded by and embedded in additional procedures and entitlements tilted towards work-to-work transitions.

This is nowhere more evident than in the case of collective dismissal, where the activation record of the aforementioned re-employment cells is disappointingly poor. Belgium's procedure for collective dismissal is very slow and involves a long and drawn-out negotiation process over additional dismissal fees, between the employer and the company unions. Workers often prefer to wait and cash in on these generous dismissal bonuses, rather than fully commit to outplacement and move on prior to being able to receive the payment from the deal[22].

This touches a raw nerve of work-to-work transitions subsequent to dismissal: the role of unions or social partners. There can be no 'active' dismissal culture if unions do not advocate or support it. More generally: who are the stakeholders of modern dismissal law, and how to get them all aboard are key success questions for anyone seeking to promote a work-to-work philosophy.

How do we succeed in mobilizing all the relevant actors around a shared goal of employability and work-to-work transition? What role has to be given to which actor? Where do unions fit in? What is the proper role of governments, of the public sector and of the private sector, particularly the HR service providers and temporary work agencies? How do you succeed in incorporating work-to-work transition into HR-policies well before any immediate risk of dismissal presents itself? Will we not have to nurture and develop a life-cycle approach to employment and complement dismissal rules with such instruments as career accounts or time saving accounts for new dismissal rules to really become effective when the critical time of a dismissal is upon a contracting party?

Achieving societal acceptance and stakeholder commitment, avoiding a 'witch-hunt' perception or culture, making increased activation a success in terms of employability, will all be keys to sustaining and finding support for a more work-oriented regulatory framework. Whether changes currently adopted or considered will suffice, or whether dismissal law and unemployment insurance must join forces to forge an even stronger tool for work-to-work transitions constitutes one of the deciding success factors.

Finally, as with ALMP and indeed as with all new policy orientation, there remains the issue of data and transparency. Work-to-work is no miracle. We will need to develop its best practices. We will need to understand the limits of what it can achieve. We will need to show the reality of what it does achieve and what it does not achieve, both for the

---

22 See, e.g., Annual report of Belgium's High Council of Employment, 2011. Retrieved from www.employment.belgium.be.

short-term employment status of the persons involved and for their long-term careers. What perspectives do we integrate? What measurements and data collection do we have to develop in order to gauge the impact of new dismissal rules on a career and labour market level correctly? How do we compare outcomes in the search for good and bad practices? A culture of performance, targets, and results, must animate and permeate the entire fabric.

Outcomes are the proof of the flexicurity pudding. Hard data and reality on the ground, more than any policy report, are needed to convert – or, perhaps, affirm – sceptics. But eating the pudding is not easy. It requires a sophisticated governance culture, which is often underdeveloped. It requires research able to compare group outcomes with different policy contexts, which is often difficult or near impossible in practice.

Overall, we have made more progress, albeit somewhat haphazardly, in flexicurity policy culture than in governance and stakeholder culture. However, winning that cultural war will be necessary if institutional flexicurity reforms are to become truly successful. Timid policy reforms are potentially counterproductive in this regard. As their impact will be limited and potentially one-sided, they create the risk of alienating rather than converting flexicurity opposition. Hence, unless we find the courage and vision to achieve more substantial reforms, limited reforms may actually prevent ambitious reforms from ever becoming possible.

Dismissal by Reason of Redundancy for the Company's Needs in the latest Labour Reform in Spain

Cristina Aguilar GONZÁLVEZ*

Abstract

Economic, technical, organizational or production-related reasons as justifications for a company's decision to dismiss workers (Article 52, c of the Workers' Statute) are studied from jurisprudential and legal perspectives according to their definition after the 2012 labour law reform in Spain and from the standpoint of the general principle of causality in dismissal. The aims of the reform were to adjust the volume of employment to the economic and organizational changes taking place in companies, to establish the cost of dismissal at a similar level to other European countries and to abolish fast-track dismissals. We also examine the effects of the labour reform on other related aspects such as procedure, the legal description of fairness of dismissal, the amount of compensation and the intervention of the Social Guarantee Fund.

Key words: dismissal by reason of redundancy for the company's needs, economic, technical and production-related reasons, 2012 Labour Law reform, fast-track dismissal

Introduction

The object of our study is the type of dismissal known as individual redundancy, which may, in fact, affect up to five workers (in which case it would be plural), occurring for economic, technical, organizational

* Cristina Aguilar is a Doctor in Law and a Professor in the Labour Law and Social Security Department at Cádiz University, Spain. She was previously Head of the Research Management Secretariat at the Research Vice-rectorate at this University, and the Student Vice-dean, Teaching Innovation and Mobility at the Faculty of Labour Science. She has done some research at the European University Institute in Fiesole, Trinity College in Dublin, Bordeaux University and at Siene University, and has also taught for short periods of time at Vilna, Siene, Brescia, Napoli, Budapest, Coimbra. She has taken part in a large number of seminars and international congresses. Her research focuses on European Community collective negotiation, professional education aimed at finding a job, telework as a means of labour, family and professional conciliation, retributive discrimination, psychosocial risks, labour relationships in micro firms – In general, matters related to European Community Social Law, Equality and Employment Law.

or production-related reasons, regulated in Article 52 of the Workers' Statute (Texto Refundido de la Ley del Estatuto de los Trabajadores) [Recodified Text of the Workers' Statute Law] (hereafter – TRLET)[1], in the light of the most recent major structural reform carried out in Spain in February 2012 by Royal Decree 3/2012 of 10 February, which was replaced by Law 3/2012 of 6 June containing urgent measures for the reform of the labour market[2].

More specifically, Article 52 of TRLET regulates the 'extinción del contrato por causas objetivas' [termination of contract by reason of redundancy] brought about, apart from the causes already mentioned (and on which we will focus), by other causes such as the worker's ineptitude, either existing or occurring after being hired by the company; absences from work, albeit justified but recurrent[3]; the worker's failure to adapt to the technical modifications occurring in his/her job, and, in the case of open-ended contracts agreed directly with non-profit organizations for the carrying out of public plans and programmes, having no regular funding and being financed by Public Administrations.

At first sight it may appear that the judicial framework surrounding dismissal did not receive special attention in the 2012 reform, since the references to it are included in the chapter on 'medidas para favorecer la eficiencia del mercado de trabajo y reducir la dualidad laboral' [measures to favour the efficiency of the labour market and reduce the duality of this market]; in spite of this, it did undergo profound changes, made directly through the measures adopted regarding hiring of workers. There is no doubt that making changes in dismissal procedures provokes feelings of fear, given their importance for workers and their families, which has made it a taboo subject[4]. This is reflected even in the term used

---

1 Royal Legislative Decree 2/2015, 23 October 2015 in approval of the recodified text of the Workers' Statute. *BOE* [Official State Gazette] 255, 24 October 2015, p. 10024.

2 *BOE* 162, 7 July 2012, p. 49113; RDL 3/2012, 10 February (*BOE* 36, 11 February 2012, p. 12483).

3 The 2012 reform revises this cause, focusing only on individual absenteeism of each worker, having no regard for the average level of absenteeism in the whole workforce. Absences due to medical treatment for cancer or serious illness have also been added to the list of exceptions. See Moreno Gené J., Burillo Romero A.M. El despido del trabajador por motivo de sus ausencias al trabajo tras las últimas reformas laborales [The dismissal of the worker because of his absences from work under the last labor reforms]. *Revista Internacional de Organizaciones*, No. 8, 2012, pp. 31–62.

4 Cruz Villalón J. Los cambios en materia de extinciones individuales en la reforma laboral de 2012 [Changes in individual dismissal in the labor reform of 2012].

in the Workers' Statute for the figure that concerns us; when it occurs for objective reasons, in no case is it referred to as dismissal, but rather, it is included under the more generic term termination of contract[5].

It is true that, on the one hand, the causes that are the subject of this study are only affected because they are common to those of collective dismissals, since the 2012 reform touches sections b), d) and 3) of Article 52 of TRLET, but the basic reason is the same. Labour relations depend on the viability of the company, which, in turn, depends on, among other variables, the economic situation, which determines whether or not it can compete in the market. Both objective and collective dismissal are used as instruments of adjustment in the face of situations of economic crisis or of changes in production.

Having established this, we can affirm that the general aim of this recent reform as regards redundancy was to adjust the volume of employment to the economic and organizational changes taking place in companies. Once this situation has been observed and can be proved, the focus must be on the reasonableness of the measure.

As alternative measures to dismissal, and for the same reasons as those which are the object of our study, that is, economic, technical, organizational and production-related, Spanish labour legislation contemplates suspension of contract[6] and reduction of working

---

Relaciones Laborales, No. 23/24, 2012, pp. 121-147; Munín Sánchez L. Las causas económicas, técnicas, organizativas y de producción en los despidos objetivos y colectivos [Economic, technical, organizational and production causes in objective and collective dismissals], *AFDUC*, No. 16, 2012, p. 141. Likewise Del Rey Guanter S. El despido por causas empresariales en la Ley 34/2010: los nuevos artículos 51 y 52 c) del ET [The dismissal for business reasons in Law 34/2010: new Article 51 and 51 p. c)]. *Relaciones Laborales*, No. 21/22, 2010, p. 117.

5 Contrary to previous reforms, such as that produced by Law 11/1994, see the Explanatory Statement and comments in Fernández-Lomana García. M. La extinción de la relación de trabajo por causas económicas, técnicas, organizativas o productivas: un análisis jurisprudencial [The termination of the employment relationship for economic, technical, organizational or productive reasons: a jurisprudential analysis]. *Revista del Ministerio de Trabajo*, No. 38, 1998, p. 286.

6 Company proprietors may opt for suspension of contract when economic causes exist due to a persistent decrease in the level of regular income or sales; that is, when, for two consecutive quarters, the level of regular income or sales for each quarter is inferior to those of the same quarter of the previous year. Article 8 of Royal Decree 1483/2012, 29 October, which approves the regulation of procedures for collective dismissals, suspension of contracts and reduction of working hours (*BOE* 261, 30 October 2012), contemplates as a choice of accompanying social measures, to be determined during the consultation period, that it can be reduced to functional

hours (a reduction of between 10 and 17%: Article 47 TRLET). Nevertheless, the adoption of these measures only proceeds if the problem experienced by the company is temporary or circumstantial, which means that the reason must be linked to a specific circumstance and therefore subject to a time limit[7]. In addition, logically, in the existence of a suspension of contract it is not possible to make a dismissal for the same reason.

Both individual and collective dismissals (regulated in Article 51 of the Workers' Statute, characterized by the number of workers dismissed, calculated over a period of 90 days) share the same reasons for termination of contract as those that concern us here, to the point that in the regulation of individual redundancies there is an indication to remit 'a las causas previstas en el Article 51.1' [to the reasons mentioned in Article 51.1]. In addition, since the 2012 labour reform, in which the need for the authorization of the Labour Department before making collective dismissals was eliminated, requiring only a notification and a report from the Inspectorate of Labour and Social Security on the circumstances surrounding them, it is clear that they now have two characteristics in common[8].

1. Normative evolution of the causes of dismissal for reasons of the company's needs, through labour reforms

In Spain, since the promulgation of the Workers' Statute in 1980, there have been more than 25 labour reforms. Specifically, as far as the object of our study is concerned, after the major reform that took place in our labour law in 1994, revised in 1997[9], in which the factor of causes was introduced but there was still no clear definition of the causal element

---

and geographical mobility, substantial modification of working conditions, non-application of conditions etc. Dilla Catalá M.J. Suspensión, reducción temporal de jornada y fuerza mayor [Suspension, temporary reduction of work and force majeure]. In: *Comentario a la Reforma Laboral de 2012* [Commentary of the Labour Reform of 2012]. Civitas, Thomson Reuters, 2012, pp. 151 and seq.

7 In this regard, Hidalgo Espinosa I. Reestructuraciones laborales: un estudio práctico sobre las medidas de flexibilidad en la empresa [Labor restructurings: a practical study on flexibility measures in the company], *Ediciones CEF*, 2014, p. 297.

8 Munín Sánchez L., *op. cit.*, p. 140. Fernández-Lomana García M., *op. cit.*, p. 302.

9 Law 11/1994, 19 May 1994. *BOE* 122, 23 May 1994; Law 63/1997, 26 December 1997. *BOE* 312, 30 December 1997.

that justified a company's decision to make workers redundant for needs originating from the company, either individually or collectively (via Article 51 in the latter case), two types of dismissal which, as we have mentioned, shared the same causes, it is noteworthy that, in the case of collective dismissal, the 1994 reform added the reasons of organization and production to the economic and technical reasons already cited in the Workers' Statute.

Nevertheless, although the reasons for which redundancies could occur within a company were enumerated as part of the regulation, they were not defined; this task was left to jurisprudence. In this regard, the work of the Supreme Court ruling of 14 June 1996 is of vital importance, as it identified the causes on the part of the company[10].

It was in the 2010 reform that the legislator incorporated the definition of the reasons for redundancy according to this Supreme Court ruling: 'economic reasons are related to the results of the company's operations, organizational reasons are related to the working systems, technical ones to the sphere of the tools or instruments of production, and production-related reasons are linked to the products or services that the company wishes to place on the market'[11].

For its part, the labour reform of 2012 is comparable in its scope to the first great reform of the labour market which was carried out in 1994. It turned out to be so controversial that the Constitutional Court verdicts were necessary when the constitutionality of some of its measures was questioned, although the appeals regarding its unconstitutionality were all resolved by declaring it to be in accordance with the Spanish constitution[12]. This is a reform that was carried out unilaterally by the right-wing government in power at the time, having no regard for the existing scenario that would have been of tripartite social dialogue or

---

10 STS 3662/1996, concerning the dismissal for economic reasons of the director of Cadena COPE radio station. Martín Rivera L. La influencia de la sentencia del Tribunal Supremo de 14 de junio de 1996 en la configuración del elemento causal del despido económico [The influence of the judgment of the Supreme Court of June 14, 1996 in the configuration of the causal element of economic dismissal]. *Tecnos*, 2015.

11 See also on Law 35/2010 Del Rey Guanter S., *op. cit.*

12 STC 119/2014, 16 July 2014 (*BOE* 198, 15 August 2014), Appeal of Unconstitutionality 5603-2012, presented by the Parliament of Navarra regarding Law 3/2012, 6 July 2012, STC 8/2015, 22 January 2015 (*BOE* 47, 24 February 2015) Appeal of Unconstitutionality 5610-2012, presented by over fifty MPs belonging to Socialist and Broad Left parliamentary groups regarding different precepts of Law 3/2012.

social concertation, and making use of a norm, the Decree, coming from the government, to which it resorts as if it were a law with immediate effect, although the Constitutional Court considers it incorrect to use emergency legislation to carry out this type of reform[13].

It was declared in the Explanatory Statement or preamble to the reform that it responded to the need to fight against the Spanish model of labour relations, characterized by a high level of temporary employment[14] and, therefore, by precarious contracts; in carrying out technical training in the sense of permanent re-training for employees, and the need to improve the internal flexibility of the workforce (by means of functional mobility, geographical mobility, significant modification of the working conditions for contractual labour, suspension of contracts and reduction of working hours) as a viable alternative to the external flexibility of entering and leaving the labour market. The latter aim led to the establishment of means of simplifying dismissals, through the flexibilization of the company's objective reasons for individual or collective redundancies, which has resulted in a rise in redundancies and, consequently, increased unemployment.

It is therefore necessary to redress the balance of the causal treatment of internal-external flexibility as regards alternative measures. In addition, this flexibility of entering the labour market, considered to be an advantage for companies that wish to make use of the mechanisms of temporary employment, or, as it is called under the reform 'contrato de apoyo a los emprendedores' [support contract for entrepreneurs] is characterized by a one-year probationary period which is, in practice, a causal temporary contract which can be terminated at no cost[15], if we bear in mind that in periods of probation the employer may decide to dispense with the employee's services without this being considered

13 Sala Franco T. Puntos críticos para un debate sobre la reforma laboral de 2012 [Critical points for a debate on the 2012 labor reform]. *Relaciones Laborales*, No. 10, 2013, pp. 31-33. See also *La reforma laboral en el Real Decreto-Ley 2/2012* [The labor reform in the Royal Decree-Law 2/2012]. *Tirant lo Blanch*, 207, 2012. *Colección Laboral*, 11-15.

14 Rate of temporality in Spain in 2011 was 25.1% (in EU – 14%, in Lithuania – 2.3%) and in 2015 was 24.2% (in EU – 14.1%, in Lithuania-2.5%). See Hispabarómetro. Indicadores económicos, sociales y sindicales'. Retrieved June 14, 2016 from http://www.1mayo.ccoo.es/nova/NPortada?CodPortada=1155.

15 This is a newly-created figure in the 2012 reform, which is presented as a means of fostering stability in employment with the intention of alleviating the high level of temporality characterizing the Spanish labour market and designed for the small businesses predominating in the manufacturing area in Spain. *La reforma laboral en el Real Decreto-Ley 2/2012*, *op. cit.*, p. 26.

a dismissal. Likewise, the flexibility of leaving the market or of the termination of work contracts has contributed to disguising the extent of the effects of the 2012 labour reform on redundancy, because, strictly speaking, the flexibility of leaving the labour market includes measures that are related to entering it, inasmuch as the latter are only measures that make the fact of leaving flexible: an increase or decrease in the prerequisites for temporary contracts, greater or lesser permissiveness regarding the company's right of waiver through a broad regulation of the probationary period. These are simply ways of making it easier to abandon the labour market; that is the regulation of termination of contract[16].

When a company proceeds to carry out a reduction of its workforce, this is due to a situation of restructuration in which the option of collective dismissal is more viable than resorting to the adoption of individual measures. However, in Spain there are more individual than collective dismissals, due to the small size of its companies; although the fact that administrative authorization is no longer necessary since 2012 can make collective dismissals easier[17].

Let us now examine the current panorama of the Spanish labour market regarding collective dismissals, suspension of contract and reduction of working hours:

Workers affected by collective dismissals, suspensions of contract and reduced working hours.

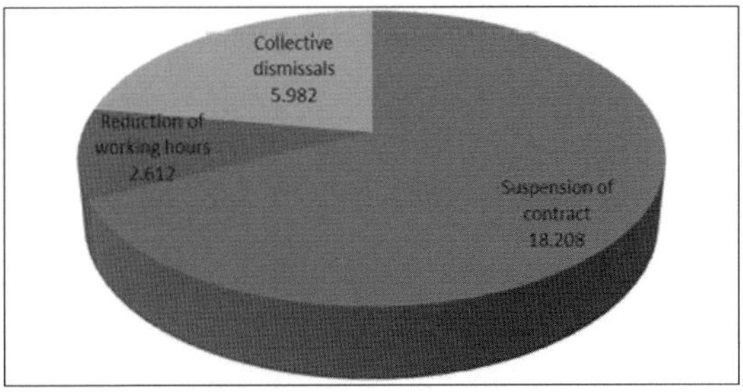

Source: Ministry of Employment and Social Security (Data Jan–Mar 2016)

16 Cruz Villalón J. *op. cit.*, p. 1. See also *La reforma laboral en el Real Decreto-Ley 2/2012, op. cit.*, p. 28 et seq.

17 Ministerio de Empleo y Relaciones Laborales. Estadística de regulación de empleo [Employment regulation statistics]. Retrieved from http://www.empleo.gob.es/estadisticas/reg/welcome.htm. '64.600 empleos menos en el mejor primer trimestre desde 2007. *Cinco Días*, 28 April 2016. Retrieved 23 June 2016 from http://cincodias.com/cincodias/2016/04/28/economia/1461825439_709708.html.

Workers affected according to autonomous community.

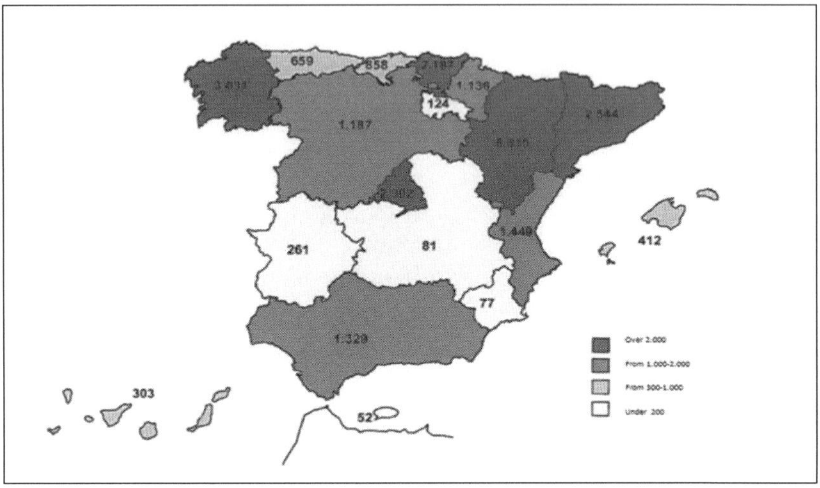

Source: Ministry of Employment and Social Security (Data Jan–Mar 2016)

Completing the interpretation of the first graphic the number of companies affected by collective dismissal procedures, suspension of contract and reduction of working hours was 1,407. Of the 26,802 workers affected, 5,982 (22.3%) workers were affected by collective dismissals, 18,208 (67.9%) by suspension of contract, and 2,612 (9.7%) by reduction of working hours.

It is difficult to obtain data on the number of individual dismissals, among other reasons because if the worker affected does not appeal in court we have no information about the adoption of this procedure, neither have we data according to type (disciplinary/objective reasons), and it is absolutely impossible to obtain information regarding the company's needs in this second type of dismissal.

In any case, the Spanish labour market, with such a high level of temporality, offers the employer the 'advantage' before resorting to dismissals, of opting for not renewing temporary contracts, which means that 'la temporalidad se utiliza como bolsa de regulación de empleo' [temporality is used as a means of regulating employment][18], or for different types of retirement measures (forced, early or for reasons of ill health).

[18] Cruz Villalón J., *op. cit.*, p. 11.

2. Economic, technical, organizational or production-related reasons as justifications for the company's decision to dismiss workers

In accordance with the demands of the Community Charter for the Fundamental Rights of the European Union, as well as Convention No. 158 of the International Labour Organization regarding termination of contract on the part of the employer, based on the operational needs of the company, establishment or service, in Spanish labour law the general principle of causality in dismissal applies.

As we know, in the 2010 reform, the legislator included the definition of the causes, according to the paradigmatic Supreme Court ruling of 14 June 1996, and in 2012 adjustments were made, under a wider perspective, permitting termination of contract on the part of the company to the point of reducing the importance of the proof of the reason justifying the dismissal. This is also because the reform did not attempt to reformulate the reasons but rather, it delimited them as causes justifying these dismissals in order that 'el control judicial de los mismos se ciña a una valoración sobre la concurrencia de unos hechos' [judicial control should be limited to an assessment of the existence of the facts][19].

The economic, technical, organizational and production-related reasons that legitimize the act of dismissal of workers on the part of the company for external reasons which are no fault of their own have in common that they arise unexpectedly, must be considered objectively and must be current and sufficient or proportional to the situation, as established by jurisprudence.

As far as economic reasons are concerned, these are considered to exist when the company's results indicate a negative economic situation, in the case of the existence of current or foreseeable losses, or a persistent decrease in regular income or sales. In any case, losses will be considered to be persistent if the level of regular income or sales for each quarter is inferior to that of the same quarter of the previous year.

---

[19] Gil Plana. J. Despido colectivo: Aspectos sustantivos [Collective dismissal: Substantive aspects]. In: *Comentario a la Reforma Laboral de 2012* [Commentary of Labour Reform of 2012]. Civitas, Thomson Reuters, 2012, p. 256; Cruz Villalón J., *op. cit.*, p. 3. See the recent Castilla y León High Court ruling of 22 March, AS/2016/585, on termination of contract for economic and production-related reasons in which dismissal is declared unfair because the cause, lack of building contracts, is not considered to have been proved.

Thus, there must exist a cause or trigger which affects the company's profits unfavourably (negative economic situation) or which has a negative effect on its efficiency. (a lack of or need for a more efficient organization of resources)

The modifications included relative to this reason refer to the fact that dismissals can be made not only in the case of reduced income, but also when there is a downturn in sales. Furthermore, the legislator specifies that that the reference is to regular income.

According to jurisprudence, economic reasons require the existence of four prerequisites in the company's results: objectivity, currency, sufficiency and persistence. In practice this means that, in different cases, dismissal is justified even when it is not absolutely necessary as long as it assists in overcoming negative economic situations; the relevant losses do not in themselves justify the measure, but reasonableness, functionality and proportionality must be taken into account; the negative situation must affect the whole company; company closure (with the established limit on the number of workers in this case); there is no need for a company viability plan when significant losses are made over an extended period and when business turnover is reduced, even when there are positive future prospects[20].

The aforementioned Supreme Court ruling established a connection of functionality or instrumentality between the termination of contracts and overcoming a demonstrably negative situation of unprofitability in the company or lack of efficiency of its productive elements; that is, we are dealing with a type of dismissal with special demands in the sense that it is not enough for the company owners simply to prove their reasons

---

20 Sempere Navarro A.V. La permanente reforma del despido: últimos hitos [The permanent reform of the layoff: last milestones]. *Revista Internacional de Ciencias Sociales*, No. 32, 2013, pp. 47-48. See Del Rey Guanter, S., *op. cit.*, p. 3, who criticises the delay in the consolidation of less demanding criteria regarding the justification of reasons by the Supreme Court, along with the disparity of criteria in High Court rulings. All this brings about a situation of legal insecurity. As regards the requirement for currency, the Galician High Court ruling 3155/2011, 22 June 2011, AS/2011/1884, declares the dismissal of an employee who was head of Human Resources and had been President of the Board of Directors of the Company being sued to be unfair, since in the letter of dismissal it is stated that this was for economic reasons 'que usted, por razón de su puesto de trabajo, conocía perfectamente' [which you, due to your position, were perfectly familiar with], owing to the lack of proof of the existence of the negative economic situation in 2010, not in 2009, and that this has been so before and after the reform (of 2010). In the first plea it is stated that in the normative modification the material and formal requirements of objective dismissal have been reduced.

for terminating contracts, but they must also show that with this measure they will achieve the aim established by the Workers' Statute; that is, a relationship of cause and effect[21].

However, since 2012 concerns centred on whether to eliminate the requirement for the company to justify the reasonableness of the decision to terminate contracts in order to avoid the negative evolution of the company or improve its situation through a more adequate organization of resources. By doing this, as well as reducing the importance of the proof on the part of the employer, the reform questions the need for the requirement of proportionality, that is, the fact that the reason must be serious enough to justify the number of workers affected by this measure. The company simply has to prove that it is going through a negative economic situation, whatever the reason may be 'sea o no un sobredimensionamiento del empleo en la empresa' [whether or not it is due to an excessive number of employees in the company][22].

The 2012 reform does not affect technical reasons for redundancy. Technical causes are understood to exist when there are 'cambios en el ámbito de los medios o instrumentos de producción' [changes in the area of tools or instruments of production], which means that these instruments have become obsolete. It is therefore necessary to invest in replacing them and this investment affects the jobs of those who use them.

In order to allege organizational reasons, there must be changes in the company's working systems and methods, or in the organization of production, this latter aspect having been introduced in this reform. The following points, taken from jurisprudence, constitute pertinent guidelines. Some of the most important ones are that the assessment must be carried out within the independent productive unit or section in which the redundancies are necessary, and not in the context of the whole company; it is necessary to give evidence of current management problems or losses of efficiency in the case of the decentralization of part of the productive process; decentralization in order to increase profits is not a valid reason, it must be linked to the correct functioning of the company; termination

---

21 Martín Rivera L., *op. cit.*, pp. 575 et seq.

22 Cruz Villalón J., *op. cit.*, pp. 3-4. See also Lahera Forteza. J. Medidas de contratación laboral y despido en la Ley 3/2012 [Measures of labor recruitment and dismissal in Law 3/2012]. *Relaciones Laborales*, 2012, No. 15-18, p. 3. See Gil Plana J., *op. cit.*, pp. 262 et seq. See also the Andalusian Supreme Court ruling 841/2015, 21 May 2015, AS 2015/1081 regarding termination of contract for economic reasons. In relation with the non-suppression of the criterion of proportionality, Catalan High Court Ruling No. 6270/2014, 29 September 2014, AS/2014/3113.

of contracts resulting from the fusion of commercial networks following a merger between two companies does not proceed.

Production-related reasons arise from, among other things, changes in the demand for the services or products that the company wishes to place on the market. In the National High Court ruling No. 49, 29 March, on contract termination for organizational and production-related reasons, invoking reiterated jurisprudential doctrine, the example of service companies is given, in which 'la pérdida o disminución de encargos de actividad ha de ser considerada por su origen una causa de este tipo en cuanto que significa una reducción del volumen de producción contratada, y por el ámbito en el que se manifiesta una causa organizativa, en cuanto que afecta a los métodos de trabajo y a la distribución de la carga de trabajo entre los trabajadores' [the loss or reduction of orders must, by definition, be considered a cause of this type since it means a reduction in the volume of work contracted, and, because of its context, it is an organizational cause, since it affects working methods and the distribution of the workload among the workers][23].

Furthermore, due to the connection with reduced sales, considered to be an economic cause, there would seem to be an overlap of reasons, although, in fact it has been argued that this phenomenon is the result of the process of production. This reason is linked to the premature termination of cleaning contracts and to terminations of contracts with no provision for vacancies in the company in which to redeploy workers, as well as a reduction in the functions included in the contract; to the termination of rental contracts with the difficulty of finding other suitable premises, and in cases of the legal annulment of public service selection processes[24].

Before this reform, dismissal for economic reasons was not contemplated by law in the public sector. Indeed, the jurisprudence of the time opposed this. However, it was now permitted with regard to the workforce, giving priority to the continuation of those workers who had obtained permanent contracts according to the principles of equality, merit and abilities, by means of a selection process organised to this end.

---

23 AS/2016/623, plea 4.

24 Sempere Navarro A.V., *op. cit.*, pp. 47–48. In this regard, in the Canary Islands High Court ruling of 18 June 2015, AS/2015/ 2004, on termination of contract for economic and production-related reasons, the succession of figures is interesting: voluntary termination of contract, tacit dismissal, and the subject of our study, objective dismissal or redundancy.

However, the above-mentioned alternatives of suspension of contract and reduction of working hours specified in the Workers' Statute are not contemplated for the public sector, so there are no palliative measures for avoiding dismissal, and therefore there is no other means of adjusting the hired workforce[25].

Similar, to what has occurred in the public sector, with the incorporation of Additional Provision No. 16 in the Recodified text of the Workers' Statute, it would seem necessary to take action with regard to other cases, such as in labour relations in the sphere of foundations. Given the peculiarities of their legal nature, a specific regulation of economic causes legitimizing the objective dismissal of staff working for non-profit foundations, based on a decisive and persistent insufficiency of patrimony and funding, meaning that it would not be able to carry out the work for which it was constituted, would help avoid legal insecurity and varying judicial interpretations. This could even determine the percentage variation that could justify exceptional measures of dismissal[26].

3. Effects of the reform on other aspects apart from reasons for dismissal

As regards the effects of the 2012 labour reform on other aspects, it is important to mention again a relevant change in the procedure for collective dismissals, which are now similar to individual dismissals.

In the latter case, the period of 30 days' advance notice, responding to the concession to the affected worker of a period of time in which to seek a new position, was reduced to 15 days (Article 53, 1, c ET)[27].

Furthermore, the legal description of fairness of dismissal was modified in Article 53.4 of the Workers' Statute, declaring it to be lawful provided that the reason alleged for the termination of contract could be

---

25 Additional Provision 17 of the Workers' Statute excludes the application of suspension of contract and reduction of working hours in Public Administrations and in legal entities linked to or depending on these and in other public bodies, excepting those that are mainly financed by income obtained from market operations.

26 Sánchez Peña. I. El despido objetivo por causas económicas respecto del personal laboral al servicio de fundaciones [The objective dismissal for economic reasons with respect to the workforce at the service of foundations]. *Trabajo y Derecho*, No. 16, 2016, p. 6.

27 Del Rey Guanter S., *op. cit.*, p. 3.

proved and having fulfilled all the prerequisites, otherwise it would be considered unfair[28].

In cases of unfair dismissal, the amount of compensation to which the worker is entitled, when he opts for this instead of being reinstated, has been reduced to 33 days' pay per year of service, prorating periods of less than a year by the month, up to a maximum of 24 months' pay. The argument in favour of this measure was the alleged need to establish the cost of dismissal at a similar level to that of other European countries. The quantity was calculated to equal the compensation that was previously contemplated only in cases of termination of contract for objective reasons in order to promote indefinite contracting, abolished in this reform. For this reason, that quantity is now applied for all unfair dismissals, regardless of the type.

In cases of fair dismissal, compensation will be of 20 days' pay for each year of service, up to a maximum of 12 months' pay. There has been a reduction of the difference between fair and unfair dismissal, which means that the employer has the possibility of calculating the cost of dismissal before acting, and may decide accordingly.

The formula of fast-track dismissals has been the main means of termination of indefinite contracts, rather than through collective or objective dismissals, occupying the opposite end of the spectrum to flexicurity[29]. It consists of the company's admission of unfair dismissal, after considering the financial benefits of fair or unfair dismissal depending on the employee's years of service. Not even the new guidelines for procedural salaries, according to which these will only be paid if the employer opts to reinstate the worker or if the person sacked is the workers' legal representative, have helped to reduce this type of dismissal. Only economic costs are considered, leaving aside the very basis of employment policy, that is, the workers' productivity and the need for their services, their personal and professional competences, in times of crisis during which, in cases of economic, technical, organizational and production-related reasons, there would be a genuine justification which would lead to cheaper lawful dismissals[30].

---

28 Sempere Navarro A.V., Martín Jiménez R. *Claves de la Reforma Laboral de 2012*. Thomson Reuters Aranzadi, 2012, p. 236. See also Cruz Villalón. J., *op. cit.*, p. 8.

29 *La reforma laboral en el Real Decreto-Ley 2/2012, op. cit.*, pp. 16 et seq.

30 Cruz Villalón. J., *op. cit.*, p. 9.

The Social Guarantee Fund, since the first version of the Workers' Statute, helps to reduce partially the cost of dismissal as it is responsible for part of the compensation in the case of dismissal for economic reasons, regardless of whether the employer is in a position of insolvency. The 2012 reform has had the effect of minimising its intervention, limiting it to companies with fewer than 25 employees. This occurs in cases of termination of indefinite contracts and only when the dismissal is considered fair. However, it is applicable to all cases of dismissal for objective reasons, not only for those caused by economic, technical, organizational and production reasons, as was the case before. The non-refundable amount paid by the Fund is still 40% of the total compensation. The employer is responsible for paying the full amount to the worker, and must subsequently apply to the Fund for the corresponding sum[31].

As can be expected, the employer's decision to terminate the contract in this case means that the dismissed worker is legally unemployed.

Conclusions

Since 1994 the termination of contract due to the company's needs, within the general catalogue of objective reasons, can arise from the existence of economic, technical, organizational or production-related reasons. In the 2010 reform the legislator included the definition of the reasons, which were reformulated – making them more flexible – in the 2012 reform as a measure with the aim of improving the efficiency of the labour market, as well as being an attempt to crystallize the jurisprudential criteria deriving from these causes, resorting to the establishment of exemplifying standards and, in this way, simplifying, but, naturally, not eliminating, judicial control.

In a field such as that which concerns us here, it is jurisprudence that shows what conclusions can be drawn regarding the potential of a labour reform, and even more so with the passing of time since its promulgation[32]. It has been affirmed by jurisprudence that 'el concepto y la finalidad de la extinción del contrato por causas objetivas con base en razones económicas, técnicas, organizativas o de producción no se ha

31 Cruz Villalón. J., *op. cit.*, p. 10.

32 Castilla y León High Court ruling 218/2012, 28 March 2012, AS/2012/867, in a case of termination of contract for economic reasons, the dismissal being declared unfair, and analysing the consequences in the face of the implementation of the 2012 labour reform.

modificado'[33] [the concept and the purpose of termination of contract for objective causes based on economic, technical, organizational or production-related reasons have not been modified], although it is understood that there has been a move towards simplifying the system of termination of contract for objective causes[34].

Jurisprudence even enumerates the variations introduced by Law 3/2012 in the preceding text (when dismissal derives from economic reasons, it emphasizes the fact that persistent decrease, that is, for three consecutive quarters, must be in the 'regular income'); and without doubt the most controversial question is the aforementioned judicial control of these dismissals, to the point that jurisprudence states that, in the case of economic reasons, it is necessary to be 'especialmente riguroso en los supuestos en los que la empresa siga obteniendo beneficios y no haya entrado aún en pérdidas' [specially strict in cases in which the company continues to make a profit and has not yet begun to make losses][35].

In ruling 1681/2014, of 24 November 2015, on objective dismissal and the selection of workers to be affected, the Supreme Court, in line with STC 8/2015, does not deny judicial control of objective dismissal starting from the evaluation of reasonableness, but rather, this is limited to an abstract suitability of the alleged cause and the agreed measure of termination, without considering the specific connection as regards the functional relationship between the cause of redundancy and the specific choice of the worker to be dismissed, recognizing a great freedom of choice among all the affected workers equally with the exact cause of dismissal having been alleged and proved.

In turn, the Catalan High Court ruling 6270/2014, 29 September, in its ruling on termination of contract for objective causes in the case of a company linked to the public sector, (carrying out electrical installation and maintenance work for local authorities) declares that the legal reform introduced in Law3/2012 in no way means the elimination of the evaluation of reasonableness that the judicial body is obliged to make in all cases of termination of contract for objective causes. In these dismissals the company must demonstrate the existence of one of these

---

33 In this regard, Catalan High Court ruling 6270/2014, 29 September 2014, AS/2014/3113, plea 2. See Gil Plana J., *op. cit.*, p. 256.

34 Asturian High Court ruling 1681/2014, 25 July 2014, AS/2014/219631, regarding termination of contract of a sales assistant in a furrier's shop for economic reasons, in plea 2.

35 In this regard, Catalan High Court ruling AS/2014/3113, plea 3.

causes and justify that the reasonableness of the decision to terminate arises from this cause[36].

Therefore, the key is that the justification of the reasonableness of the decision to terminate should be an adequate mechanism to attempt to overcome the situation[37]. We consider that in no case should one lose sight of the causal relationship between the company's economic situation and whether or not this is due to an excessively large workforce, and of the proportionality that justifies the termination of contract.

---

36 In this regard, Catalan High Court ruling 6270/2014, 29 September 2014, AS/2014/3113, plea 2.

37 Asturian High Court ruling 1681/2014, 25 July 2014, AS/2014/219631, plea 2.

Labour Law Reform

The Emergence of a New Concept of Employment Relationship in Poland

Andrzej Marian Świątkowski*

Abstract

The amendment of the Act of 25 June 2015 to the employment relationships based on the contracts of employment presented in this article show a tendency to the convergence of two opposite tendencies: stability and flexibility of employment under contracts of employment of definite duration. In the amendment Act, the following results were achieved in respect of the contracts of employment of definite duration: automatic conversion of a contract of definite duration into a contract for an indefinite term obligates the employer who intends to end the employment relationship – concluded under the amended contract of employment – to give notice of termination of such contract. The automatic change of the type of the contract from a fixed-term contract into a contract for an indefinite term obligates the employer to issue an employment certificate to the employee, which should include a note on the change of the basis of employment and the date of legal conversion of the contract as prescribed by the legislature.

Key words: employment relationship, fixed-term contract, contract for an indefinite term, labour law reform, Polish Labour Code, stability and flexibility of employment

Introduction

In 2015, the Labour Code was amended three times. The first was an amendment to the provisions governing employment relationships. The second was an amendment concerning employees' rights in respect of parenthood. Third, the maternity rights were amended by social security

---

* Andrzej Marian Świątkowski is Jean Monnet Professor of European Labour Law and Social Security Law, Jesuit University in Cracow. He is former Vice President of the European Committee of Social Rights of the Council of Europe. Professor Andrzej Marian Świątkowski is an expert for the European Union Commission in the field of labour law. He is the author of more than 650 publications dealing with Polish, comparative and international labor and social security law and social policies.

provisions. As regards the social security laws, amendment was made to the act on the social security cash benefits in respect of sickness and maternity, certain maternity rights provided for in chapter VIII of the Labour Code were complemented[1]. As regards the collective labour law – provisions concerning the social dialogue were codified[2]. The purpose of this article is to present and perform a legal analysis of the first of the mentioned amendments to the employment relationships in terms of the contracts of employment of definite duration: contracts for a probationary period and fixed-term contracts, made by the legislature in the provisions of the Labour Code.

1. Amendment of employment relationships

1.1 Contract of employment for a probationary period

The most significant changes were made in the provisions governing conclusion of fixed-term employment contracts. A fixed-term employment contract (umowa na czas określony) is one of the three types of contracts of employment currently provided for in the Labour Code[3]. Two other contracts: a contract for a probationary period and a contract for an indefinite term in fact remained unchanged. As regards the list of contracts of employment included in Article 25 § 1 of the Labour Code, a contract for the period of performance of a specific work (umowa na czas wykonywania określonej pracy) was deleted. Article 25 § 2 of the Labour Code was also amended. The previous, unnecessary statement confirming the freedom of employment under a contract for a probationary period before each employment relationship under one of the contracts listed in the catalogue included in Article 25 § 1 of the Labour Code was replaced by specifying the purpose of the contract for a probationary period. Moreover, the freedom of re-employment and successive employment of employees previously employed under contracts for a probationary period

1 The act of 15 May 2015 amending the act on the social security cash benefits in respect of sickness and maternity *(ustawa z dnia 15 maja 2015 o zmianie ustawy o świadczeniach pieniężnych z ubezpieczenia społecznego w razie choroby i macierzyństwa). Journal of Laws* [Dz.U.] of 2015, item 1066.

2 The act of 24 July 2015 on the Council of Social Dialogue and on other social dialogue institutions *(ustawa z dnia 24 lipca 2015 o Radzie Dialogu Społecznego i innych instytucjach dialogu społecznego). Journal of Laws* [Dz.U.] of 2015, item 1240.

3 Mitrus L. Projekt nowelizacji Kodeksu pracy dotyczący umów terminowych [Proposal for an amendment to the Labour Code in respect of contracts of definite duration]. *Monitor Prawa Pracy* [Labour Law Gazette], No. 6, 2015, pp. 285 et seq.

was restricted (Article 25 § 3 of the Labour Code). The length of the applicable probationary period was not changed. Article 25 § 2 of the Labour Code retained the principle according to which the maximum period of employment under the contract for a probationary period should not exceed three months. The mentioned article is one of the few provisions in the Labour Code in which the legislature laid down the maximum and not (as in most of the labour law provisions) the minimum standards of employment from which the parties to individual employment relationships may derogate in favour of an employee. The favourability principle laid down in Article 18 § 1 of the Labour Code is fully applicable since it is generally accepted that reduction of the probationary period is more favourable to an employee than its extension within a maximum period of employment during which the employer may verify the professional qualifications of an employee and decide on his employment under a contract of employment for an indefinite term or under a contract of definite duration. The completely amended wording of Article 25 § 2 of the Labour Code is justified by the meaning and purpose of employment under the contract for a probationary period. Such a contract may be concluded in order to verify the qualifications of an employee and the possibility of his employment for a specific job. The right to verify the qualifications and professional skills is granted to every employer. The subject of such verification may be the qualifications and skills of all job candidates. The above also applies to a candidate for a job who submits documents confirming long or sufficient period of employment in the position or at work for which the candidate applies. The employer who is recruiting employees has the right to evaluate whether a job candidate meets the prescribed expectations. Employment for the probationary period is a classic example of conclusion of a fixed-term employment contract, not exceeding the period set out by the legislature. A job candidate with whom such contract was concluded has no rights (except the right to file an appropriate request) in respect of reduction (within the limits allowed by the legislature) of the maximum, three-month probationary period of employment. The parties to a contract concluded for a probationary period may enter into an agreement on the reduction of the term of such contract. Extension of the probationary period is possible only within the maximum limits of employment for a probationary period prescribed by the legislature and laid down in Article 25 § 3 of the Labour Code. Expiration of any employment for a probationary period agreed upon between the parties, even this not exceeding three months, must be identified with negotiations between the parties to the contract for a probationary period aimed at re-employment under an identical contract. In such case the freedom of the parties to choose the basis for the successive employment is subject to restrictions laid down in Article 25 § 3 of the Labour Code. A renewal of the contract of employment for a probationary period is possible only in two cases. First, where an employee seeks to take up work with the same employer which is different from the work previously performed under a contract for a probationary period. Second, where an employee returns to work with the same employer within a period of at least three years following the end of the previous contract for the performance of such work for which the employee would be reemployed. The reservation made in the last fragment of Article 25 § 3 (2) of the Labour Code, according to which in the second case mentioned above the contracts for a probationary period may be renewed only once, was unnecessary. It is impossible to imagine that after at least three years from conclusion or expiration of a previous contract of employment a candidate for the same job with the same employer could be lawfully, two or more times, subject to verification by the employer in terms of his qualifications or the possibility to perform work. This is because the contract of employment for a probationary period is a type of contract of definite duration which may be concluded between the same parties to an identical employment relationship only once after a three-year break. No public institution, in particular the National Labour Inspectorate (Państwowa Inspekcja Pracy, PIP) performs a formal or material supervision over the conclusion of contracts of employment for a probationary period. The legislature does not consider breach of the prohibition of re-employment of an employee under a contract for a probationary period to be as serious as breach of the prohibition to employ employees under fixed-term employment contracts beyond the time limits laid down in article 25^1 § 1 of the Labour Code.

1.2 Fixed-term employment contract (umowa o pracę na czas określony)

The new version of employment under a fixed-term contract stipulated in Article 1 of the Act of 25 June 2015 is another attempt (more effective than under the amendment to the Labour Code in 2003)[4] at convergence

4 *Journal of Laws* [Dz.U.] No. 213, item 2081. Pisarczyk Ł. Nowy model zatrudnienia terminowego w prawie pracy – Część 1? [New model of Fixed-Term Employment in a Labour Law – Part One?]. *Monitor Prawa Pracy* [Labour Law Gazette], No. 4, 2016, p. 175.

of two opposite tendencies: stability and flexibility of employment. The first is supported by employees and trade unions representing the interests of the former while the second is of major importance for the employers. The Union institutions have encouraged the European social partners to negotiate agreements enabling achievement of the necessary balance between flexibility of the principles of labour law and the legal and social security of the employed persons. A legal consequence of the framework agreement on fixed-term work is the Council Directive 99/70/EC of 28 June 1999[5]. According to this directive, contracts of indefinite duration are considered the general form of employment relationship. Whereas fixed-term employment contracts are a feature of employment in certain sectors, occupations and activities. Therefore, conclusion of such contracts may meet the interests of both the employees and the employers. The Directive 99/70/EC was adopted to prevent abuse by employers of fixed-term employment contracts. The use of fixed-term employment contracts 'based on objective reasons' is 'a way to prevent abuse' in the labour relations (general provisions, points 5–8). Clause 4 of the normative agreement provides that fixed-term workers shall not be treated in a less favourable manner than comparable permanent workers solely because the former are not working under the legal framework of a 'typical contract of employment'. In order to prevent discrimination in employment based on the type of employment contract concluded, the European social partners recommend that the authorities of the EU Member States should introduce, in the national labour law system, one, two or even three legal measures prescribed in clause 5 (1) to prevent abuse: 1) objective reasons; 2) the maximum total duration of successive fixed-term employment contracts or relationships; 3) acceptable number of renewals of such contracts[6]. The amended Article 25^{1} of the Labour Code provides for the application of the first (supplemented) and the third of the legal techniques mentioned in directive 99/70/EC. Article 25^{1} § 1 of the Labour Code provides that the period of employment and the total period of employment under fixed-term employment contracts concluded between the same parties may not exceed 33 months and the total number of such contracts may not exceed three.

---

5 *Official Journal*, L 175, p. 43. See Świątkowski A.M., Wierzbińska H. *Kodeks pracy i zabezpieczenia społecznego Unii Europejskiej, wybór i opracowanie* [The Code of Labour and Social Security of the European Union, selection of documents]. Cracow, 2011, pp. 359 et seq.

6 Świątkowski A.M. *Prawo pracy Unii Europejskiej* [Labour Law of the European Union]. Warsaw: Beck C.H., 2015, pp. 194 et seq.

Based on the previous experience where all the arrangements between the parties to an individual employment relationship in respect of extension of the term of such contracts (annexes) were considered, under law, to be conclusion of a successive contract of definite duration, Article 25^1 § 2 of the Labour Code applies a legal fiction of termination of a fixed-term employment contract despite its extension by the parties to an employment relationship. Since according to the amended provisions none of the fixed-term contracts, or a short-term contract, ends ex lege, upon expiry of its term, the legal fiction consists in recognizing that on the next day following the end date of the contract, the contract 'is terminated' and a new contract is concluded[7]. While there is no doubt that extension of the previous contract may be classified as conclusion of a new contract of definite duration, it is difficult to accept the term 'termination' used by the legislature in the case where the contract ends as a result of expiration of its term. The term 'termination' of a contract of employment or employment relationship is an expression used by the legislature to designate a unilateral or bilateral legal act. The situations where a contract of employment or an employment relationship ends as a result of events other than a legal act are designated with such terms as: 'end', 'expiration' or the impersonal statement of consequences of an event such as that the employment relationship 'terminates'. However, in principle, a lawyer specializing in labour law is able to accept a concept of 'termination' of the contract of employment despite extension of its term by the parties and accept that – because of the legal limitation of the number of fixed-term contracts allowed under the amended Article 25^1 § 1 of the Labour Code – extension of the current contract may be considered equal to concluding a new contract of definite duration. If the parties to a fixed-term employment contract do not comply with the limitations laid down in Article 25^1 § 1 of the Labour Code and exceed the total maximum period of employment under a fixed-term employment contract or conclude, within a period of 33 months, a successive contract for a fixed term, the employee – starting from the first day following expiration of 33 months or from the date of conclusion of the fourth contract – will be employed under a contract of employment for an indefinite term (Article 25^3 § 3 of the Labour Code). Therefore, the legal construct applied previously by the legislature in Article 25^1 § 1 of the Labour Code, amended by the Act of 26 June 2015, was not significantly

---

7 Świątkowski A.M. *Kodeks Pracy. Komentarz* [Commentary to the Labour Code]. Warsaw: Beck C.H., 2012, pp. 152 et seq.

changed. The new provision, applicable from 22 February 2016, obligates the parties to an employment relationship to treat the contract named by the parties a 'fixed-term employment contract' as a contract concluded for an indefinite duration as from the first day of employment on which the parties to an individual employment relationship lost their right to continue employment under a fixed-term employment contract[8]. The automatic conversion of a contract of definite duration into a contract for an indefinite term obligates the employer who intends to end the employment relationship – concluded under the amended contract of employment – to give a notice of termination of such contract. The act terminating the converted contract of employment should be served upon the employee on the last day preceding commencement of the statutory period of notice of a contract of employment for an indefinite term. If the parties conclude a fixed-term employment contract exceeding the total acceptable period of employment of 33 months by three months, the employer will be obligated to apply the three month notice period prescribed in Article 36 § 1 (3) of the Labour Code. However, the length of the notice period will not change in the case of employment of an employee under the fourth successive fixed-term employment contract, concluded within the first six or twelve months of employment. The automatic change of the type of the contract from a fixed-term contract into a contract of indefinite duration obligates the employer to issue to the employee an employment certificate, which should include a note on the change of the basis of employment and the date of legal conversion of the contract as prescribed by the legislature.

The former Article 25^1 § 1 of the Labour Code provided for a time limit – a period of one month in compliance with the right to employ employees under fixed-term contracts. At present, it is unclear whether upon expiry of the currently applicable maximum period of employment under one or three successive fixed-term contracts the parties to the employment relationship(s) may – after a period of break – return to the previous practice and conclude one, long-term (33 months) contract of definite duration or three successive fixed-term contracts. It seems that in the amended Article 25^1 of the Labour Code the legislature deliberately omitted the previously applicable requirement of a monthly break between termination of the previous and conclusion of the successive

[8] Świątkowski A.M. Nowelizacja zobowiązaniowych stosunków pracy [Amendments of contractual employment relationships], *Roczniki Administracji i Prawa*, Vol. 1, 2016.

contract of employment. A specific 'barrier' against continuance of a long-term employment under a contract or contracts concluded for a fixed term is the abovementioned legal mechanism of conversion of a fixed-term contract into a contract for an indefinite term (a fixed-term contract exceeding thirty-free months or the fourth fixed-term contract concluded within a period of 33 months running from the first day of the contract of definite duration). It seems that under the amended provisions of the Labour Code the function of the notice period is the same as the function of the previous Article 25[1] § 1 of the Labour Code. However, there is an essential difference between the previous and the current legal mechanism which was introduced into the Labour Code with a view to protect the rights of employees and limit the abuses by the employers. Previously such 'barrier' was a monthly break in the legal relationship between the parties to the contracts of employment concluded for a fixed term. Following the amendment of Article 25[1] of the Labour Code, there is no reason why, after termination upon notice of a fixed-term employment contract converted by operation of law into a contract for an indefinite term (a contract for a fixed term exceeding thirty-free months or the fourth fixed-term contract), the parties to the previous employment relationship (long-term employment under one fixed-term contract or three shorter contracts concluded within a period of 33 months from the date of conclusion of the first of those contracts) should not conclude (on the next day following expiration of the statutory notice period) another long-term, 33 months contract for a fixed term or start a new cycle of free, although limited in terms of the number of contracts of definite duration (three within 33 months), employment under lawful fixed-term contracts. According to the presented interpretation of the amended article 25[1] of the Labour Code, the legal mechanism of conversion of the fixed-term contract (after exceeding the thresholds established by the legislature) is no longer applicable after the employer terminates the automatically converted contract. Conclusion of a fixed-term employment contract on the next day following termination of the converted employment relationship opens another cycle of employment under the contract or contracts of definite duration.

The arguments in support of such interpretation of the amended Article 25[1] of the Labour Code are: repeal by the Act of 25 June 2015 of Article 33 of the Labour Code and establishing, in the amended Article 36 § 1 of the Labour Code, uniform notice periods for contracts of definite and indefinite duration. The legislature eventually dropped the former legal concept according to which employment under a fixed-term employment contract guaranteed the employee greater stability than that guaranteed by the provisions on the relative protection of sustainability of employment relationship for an indefinite term. A contract concluded for a fixed term of six months could not be terminated. The repealed Article 33 of the Labour Code allowed the parties who concluded a contract of employment for a period exceeding six months to introduce a clause enabling termination of such contract upon two weeks' notice. The principle of stability of employment under the fixed-term employment contract was significantly limited. It goes as far as to say that it was practically not known in the Polish labour law governed by the Labour Code in force for more than 40 years (since 26 June 1974). The situation was different as regards the labour law of the interwar period. The laws in force at that time – two regulations of the President of the Republic of Poland of 16 March 1928 on the contracts of employment of: blue-collar workers[9] and white-collar workers[10] provided for the following types of contracts of employment: for a probationary period, for a period of performance of a specific work and for an indefinite term (Article 4 of the regulation of the President of the Republic of Poland on the contracts of employment of blue-collar workers; Article 5 of the regulation of the President of the Republic of Poland on the contracts of employment of white-collar workers). The contracts of definite duration were terminated only upon completion of work for which they were concluded (a contract for the period of performance of specific work) or upon expiration of the term of the contract (a fixed-term contract). Therefore, termination by notice applied only to the contracts for an indefinite term and contracts for a probationary period. An essential characteristic of employment under a contract of definite duration was the absolute stability of the employment relationship. The labour laws in force at that time did not provide for the possibility to terminate such contract upon notice by any of the parties. The notice periods were fixed. They could not be reduced; however, a notice of termination not in compliance with the statutory notice period was effective. An employee was entitled to compensation in the case of non-observance by the employer of the statutory notice period. The case law provided that if the time limit and the conditions of termination were observed, it was of no importance why each of the parties to an employment relationship, the employee or the employer, terminated the

9 *Journal of Laws* [Dz.U.] 35/28, item 324.

10 *Journal of Laws* [Dz.U.] 35/28, item 323.

contract of employment upon notice[11]. While assessing the past Polish labour laws from the current perspective, it should be noted that the contracts of definite duration as compared with a contracts of indefinite duration guaranteed to the employees absolute stability of employment since they could not be terminated upon notice. On the other hand, the level of the relative stability of the employment relationship ensured by a contract of employment for an indefinite term was lower than under the currently applicable laws. However, neither the contemporary labour law literature discussing the provisions of the Labour Code governing the contracts of employment (Articles 25-29²) nor the interwar labour law doctrine, emphasized the absolute stability of employment under a fixed-term employment contract.

Article 25¹ of the Labour Code amended by the Act of 25 June 2015, includes an extended list of exemptions to the legal mechanism of automatic conversion of a fixed-term employment contract into a contract for an indefinite term as prescribed in article 25¹ § 3 of the Labour Code. They apply to four types of contracts of definite duration concluded for the purpose of: 1) replacement of other employee whose absence from work is excused; 2) performance of casual or seasonal work, 3) performance of work during a term of office; 4) in the case where the employer interested in conclusion of a fixed-term contract proves existence of 'objective reasons on his part' (Article 25¹ § 4 (1)-(4) of the Labour Code). I should now analyse each of the above-mentioned situations which justify lawful derogation from the principles laid down in Article 25¹ § 1-3 of the Labour Code, according to which employment under fixed-term employment contracts should be subject to certain limitations in respect of the time and number of the concluded contracts in order to minimise this (atypical and not ensuring stability of employment relationship) form of performance of work.

1. According to the amendment Act of 25 June 2015, a contract for replacement may be concluded so that the employer may, during the 'excusable absence of an employee from work', lawfully employ another employee, under another fixed-term contract, who should temporarily replace the previously employed employee now unable to continue employment for justified reasons. The contract for replacement of an absent employee was not mentioned in the list of contracts of employment included in Article 25 § 1 of the Labour Code. In fact, this is not necessary since such a contract is

[11] SN Zb. Urz. 658/34. See Bloch J. *Kodeks pracy. Ustawy, rozporządzenia, dekrety, orzecznictwo, komentarz* [The Labour Code. The laws, regulations, decrees, case-law, commentar]. Warsaw, 1936, p. 43, note 82.

treated as a fixed-term contract in such cases where the end date of the contract is known. In most cases, the contracts for replacement are concluded during an employee's incapacity for work where the employer must replace the latter with another employee. A continued excusable absence of an employee replaced by another employee employed for a fixed term obligates the employer to conclude contracts of definite duration for the replacement of the absent employee, and submission by the replaced employee of successive certificates of incapacity for work justifies renewal of the fixed-term contract for the successive period of his excusable absence from work. The parties to an individual employment relationship established under a fixed-term employment contract for replacement of an absent employee incapable of work are not obligated to renew the contract concluded 'for replacement'. Such contract ends upon expiration of its term. The contract 'for replacement' cannot be concluded for the period of absence of the replaced employee since in such case it would be a contract concluded for the performance of a specific job. Such work, from the perspective of the persons concerned (the replaced employee, the employee replacing the absent employee, the employer or an entity if the employer is not a natural person but an organizational unit) is work which – because of the excusable absence – cannot be performed by the absent employee. Article 25 § 1 of the Labour Code, amended by Article 1 (1) of the Act of 25 June 2015, unlike Article 25 § 1 of the Labour Code in its original wording, does not mention the contract for replacement in the list of the contracts of employment. Also a contract for the period of performance of a specific job was not mentioned. Therefore, under the current wording of Article 25^1 § 1 and 3 of the Labour Code, the previous contract 'for replacement' is now a fixed-term employment contract to which the legal mechanism stipulated in Article 25^1 § 1-3 of the Labour Code does not apply. Therefore, it is necessary to present the legal consequences of conclusion of such a contract and of the end of the term of such contract. Since the legal nature of the contract 'for replacement' may be considered practically identical to the nature of a fixed-term contract, the contract 'for replacement' will not be converted into a contract for an indefinite term except for the automatic conversion of the contract 'for replacement' into a contract for an indefinite term as a result of exceeding the time and number limits laid down in Article 25^1 § 1 of the Labour Code. In all other situations, all the provisions of the Labour

Code applicable to fixed-term employment contracts will apply to a fixed-term contract 'for replacement'. Such interpretation of the provisions of the Labour Code on the contracts of employment is most visibly confirmed by Article 1 (5) of the Act of 25 June 2015. This provision of the amending act to the Labour Code repealed, among others, Article 33[1] of the Labour Code which allowed the parties to a contract 'for replacement' to terminate such contract upon three days' notice counted in working days. Exclusion of the legal mechanism laid down in Article 25[1] § 1 of the Labour Code guarantees to the parties to fixed-term employment contracts – concluded for replacement of another employee previously employed by the employer concerned whose employment relationship was suspended because of, and for the duration of his excusable absence from work – the full freedom to conclude fixed-term employment contracts for replacement of the absent employee. Therefore, neither the maximum period of employment (33 months under such contract) nor the total period of employment under successive contracts of that type concluded between the same parties or the maximum total number of such contracts (three) restrict the freedom to conclude fixed-term contracts for replacement of an employee – a person absent from work who remains in an employment relationship but is granted leave from work during the excusable absence. Therefore, the legislature is consistent as regards matters relating to the legal construct of an employment relationship as a legal bond which is not broken by justified reasons for an employee's absence from work and the resulting justified non-performance of the statutory and contractual (laid down in the contract of employment) obligation to perform work agreed upon by the parties to a contract of employment.

A fixed-term contract of employment for replacement of an employee during his excusable absence from work may be concluded for replacement of any employee. The exception laid down in Article 25[1] § 4 (1) of the Labour Code applies to employees employed under a contract of employment for an indefinite term and fixed-term employment contracts. However, in the latter case the exemptions to the principle laid down in Article 25[1] § 1 of the Labour Code will apply only to the total number of contracts of definite duration which may be concluded within the maximum time limit of 33 months. An academic example is a good illustration of the above argument. An illness contracted by an employee employed under a fixed-term employment contract of employment, concluded for a period of 33 months, allows the employer to conclude thirty-two monthly agreements of definite duration 'for replacement' with another employee, if the replaced employee regularly, on a monthly basis, presents to his employer thirty-two medical certificates of incapacity for work. And a precondition for overcoming the additional limitation of the parties' freedom in respect of conclusion of fixed-term employment contracts is employment of the absent employee under a contract of employment for an indefinite term during his excusable absence from work.

An important preventive measure against abuse of the freedom of employment of employees under fixed-term employment contracts for replacement of another employee not available for work or unable to perform work for justified reasons is the reservation of the possibility to derogate from the principle laid down in Article 25^1 § 1 of the Labour Code only in the case where a contract of definite duration 'for replacement' is concluded during the excusable absence from work of the replaced employee. It is left to the legislature to decide whether the above condition was met or not. Article 298^2 of the Labour Code provides for a delegation of legislative powers to a competent minister for labour, currently the Minister for Family Affairs, Labour and Social Policy, to issue regulations concerning the methods for excusing absences from work. According to a regulation of the Minister for Labour and Social Policy of 15 May 1996 on the method of excusing absences from work and on granting leaves of absence (rozporządzenie Ministra Pracy i Polityki Socjalnej z dnia 15 maja 1996 w sprawie sposobu usprawiedliwiania nieobecności w pracy oraz udzielania pracownikom zwolnień od pracy)[12], an employee's absence from work is justified in situations where the employer must grant the employee leave from work since the above obligation is prescribed by the Labour Code, the regulations implementing the Labour Code and other laws. A list of events where the above obligation must be fulfilled is included in § 5-15 of the said regulation. The reasons justifying absence from work are events and circumstances specified by law which prevent reporting to work and performance of work as well as other events of inability to perform work indicated by the employee and considered by the employer to

12 A Notice of the Minister for Labour and Social Policy of 16 September 2014. *Journal of Laws* [Dz.U.] of 2014, item 1632.

be reasons justifying the absence. The evidence to justify the absence may be medical certificates, decisions of public authorities and statements of employees. The latter allow justification of a short-term absence from work. They are of no significance in the situations described in the present article. It is difficult to imagine that the employer apparently concludes a fictitious contract of employment for an indefinite term with a person not interested in the performance of work who submits certificates justifying the absence from work during the entire term of the established employment relationship in order that the employer may freely conclude with other persons real, however contrary to the Labour Code, contracts of employment 'for replacement'.

2. Casual or seasonal work means employment whose duration is determined by the type or specifics of the work performed. In the event of casual work, there are more possibilities to circumvent the provisions governing the time and number limits to employment. The legislature does not provide for a legal definition of the term 'casual work'. Casual work is non-permanent work, a casual employment, usually dependent on demand. The difference between the term 'seasonal work' and 'casual work' is that casual work may be performed on any day during a calendar year and seasonal work depends on the season of the year. Agricultural work, saving hay, harvesting and other similar work is typical seasonal work which in our climate conditions may be performed during the season of harvesting agricultural and horticultural crops. Repairs of roads are both casual and seasonal work. Usually they are performed after the end of the winter season. The purpose of such work is to bring the communication routes damaged during winter to a usable condition.
3. The term 'work performed during the term of office' is a legal term the meaning of which was not defined in the labour laws. For a lawyer specializing in labour law this term is associated with a descriptive expression used to denote work performed by a person whose employment relationship is based on the election to a public or social function. The election is one of the legal bases of employee employment listed in Article 2 of the Labour Code. Where an employment relationship is dependent on the election, the person elected to a post may need to enter into an employment relationship, take up and perform work. However, the legal relationship by election may only be a public law relationship. Persons elected to the post of councillor, deputy or senator may,

but do not have to, enter into employment relationships with the local government institution or state legislative authority to which they were elected. The term of office for each public or social function is specified by applicable laws governing the legal relationships between persons elected to a post and a public or social institution to which they were elected. A legal guarantee of compliance with applicable laws and with the legal restrictions of the freedom of employment for a fixed term are provisions governing the legal status of a person employed under election as an employee of a public or social institution.

4. The least precise is the situation specified in Article 25^1 § 4 (4) of the Labour Code. According to the legislature, the employment under a fixed-term contract above the time and number limits laid down in Article 25^1 § 1 of the Labour Code and without the consequences stipulated in Article 25^1 § 2 of the Labour Code may happen in an unspecified event where the employer indicates objective reasons 'on his part' which justify (because of the need to meet the 'actual periodic demand' for employment under a fixed-term contract or contracts) non-compliance with the time and/ or number limitations laid down in Article 25^1 § 1 of the Labour Code. I will try to describe the essence of the latter, the fourth exception to the generally applicable principle of limited freedom of parties to individual employment relationships to enter into fixed-term employment contracts. To illustrate the scale of difficulties encountered by an interpreter of Article 25^1 § 4 (4) of the Labour Code, I should quote this legal norm which includes several vague expressions and which has incorrect grammar construction. 'The provisions of § 1 shall not apply to fixed-term contracts […] 4) in the case where an employer specifies objective reasons on the employer's part – if conclusion of such contracts [sic!][13] in an individual case serves to meet the actual periodic demand and is necessary in this respect in the light of all the circumstances attending the conclusion of the contract'. I quoted Article 25^1 § 4 (4) of the Labour Code mainly to draw attention to the vague specification of the conditions justifying conclusion of, partly 'banned' by the legislature, fixed-term employment contract. My understanding of the statutory exemption to the restrictions of the freedom to conclude such contracts of employment (that is a vague and general exemption

13 The quoted provision lacks the expression "such contracts".

to prohibition on concluding a fourth contract in a period of 33 months or a contract or contracts of definite duration for a period exceeding 33 months) is that it means permission for the employer who faces exceptional situation and is forced not to comply with the generally applicable prohibitions laid down in Article 25^1 § 1 of the Labour Code, without fear of automatic conversion into contracts of employment for an indefinite term. In order that my understanding may be accepted, it is necessary to specify the conditions laid down in the analysed Article 25^1 § 4 (4) of the Labour Code on which a decision of a competent regional labour inspector – on compliance or non-compliance of a contract of employment of definite duration with applicable laws – depends. This is not simple since there are a large number of general clauses and vague expressions used in the provision in question. One thing is certain: the legislature imposed on the employer who concludes a fixed-term employment contract in breach of the principle of limited freedom of contract, an obligation to prove that there exist: 1) objective reasons, 2) on the part of the employer, 3) regarding a decision on employment of an employee or employees in breach of the provisions of Article 25^1 § 1 of the Labour Code. Indication of such causes may be difficult since the Article in question further provides that it (the legislature uses a vague term 'if their conclusion') shall depend on: 1) a particular case ('in individual case') and 2) 'serves to meet a periodic demand' of the employer for seasonal workers and, moreover, 3) is necessary ('in this respect'); 4) 'in the light of all the circumstances attending the conclusion of the contract'.

The total risk of the decision to violate the principle of the limited freedom of contracts for a fixed term and to conclude such contract above the limits laid down in Article 25^1 § 1 of the Labour Code is borne by the employer facing a 'forcible' situation (in the economic sense). The employer must notify, within five working days, a regional labour inspector at the seat of the employer or at the place of employment (this has not been specified in this article), of the conclusion of such contract. Such notification is made after 'conclusion of the contract of employment' described in Article 25^4 § 4 (4) of the Labour Code. The notice should also include information on the reasons for conclusion of such contract (Article 25^1 § 5 of the Labour Code). Therefore, it is in the employer's interest to: 1) provide a precise description of the situation faced by his undertaking, including specific examples;

2) provide arguments to illustrate the sudden and previously not expected necessity to employ an additional employee or employees under a fixed-term contract or contracts of employment; 3) prove that the period for which the contracts were concluded corresponds with the demand for employment of additional employees under contracts of employment of definite duration; 4) provide a precise and convincing (well founded) summary to the decision-maker concerning the necessity to employ additional employees for a fixed term in breach of the principle of limited freedom of the parties to conclude fixed-term contracts of employment.

A decision-maker is a territorially competent regional inspector of the National Labour Inspectorate. Article 1 (21) of the Act of 25 June 2015 – a provision amending Article 281 of the Labour Code in which point 1a was added after point 1, provides that failure to notify a competent regional labour inspector, in writing or electronically, of the conclusion of a fixed-term contract of employment (in the situations specified in Article 25^4 § 4 (4) of the Labour Code) and the reasons for conclusion of such contract, within five working days of such conclusion, shall constitute breach of an employee's duties and be subject to a fine. Given the exact repetition in the amended Article 281 (1a) of the Labour Code of the formal obligation laid down in Article 25^4 § 4 (5) of the Labour Code, we are justified in considering the possible number of infringements on the part of an employer breaching the obligation laid down in Article 281 (1a) of the Labour Code. The employer's infringement can involve: 1) failure to notify of the conclusion of a contract of definite duration; 2) failure to comply with the required form of such notification and/or 3) failure to meet the statutory deadline for the notification; 4) failure to specify the reasons for conclusion of such contract.

In general, the legislature does not demand the employer to specify the basis for conclusion of any contract of employment. A bilateral act of conclusion of an obligation relationship of employment under a contract of employment does not have to specify a *causa*. A sufficient reason for conclusion of a contractual employment relationship is the mutual intention of the parties to an agreement called in the Labour Code a contract of employment. As regards a fixed-term contract of employment, the situation is specific.

According to a view established in the Union[14] and national[15] case law, specification by the employer of the factual grounds for conclusion of a fixed-term contract of employment allows him to avoid being accused of circumventing the law in all the situations where conclusion of the contract of employment of definite duration is permitted by law[16]. As regards the exception laid down in Article 25[1] § 4 (4) of the Labour Code, specification of causes of such contract is based also on the general exceptions to the principle of employment under a contract for an indefinite term laid down by the legislature.

The labour inspector should assess the value and accuracy of the information contained in the notification of employment of an employee under a fixed-term employment contract. He should use his own judgement as to the facts presented by the employer. The above is not equal to interference by the labour inspector with the freedom of business guaranteed to all entrepreneurs by the Constitution. The labour inspector does not take any business

---

14 CJEU case C-38/13. A judgment of 13 March 2014 issued in Małgorzata Nierodzik v. Samodzielny Publiczny Psychiatryczny Zakład Opieki Zdrowotnej im. Dr Stanisława Deresza w Choroszczy, LEZ No. 1433647; LEX/El. 2014 with a commentary of Derlacz-Wawrowska M., Latos-Miłkowska M. Kodeks pracy komentarz w perspektywie europejskiej i międzynarodowej *[Labour Code. European and international perspective]*.

15 Judgments of Polish Supreme Court (SN) of 27 May 2014 (II PK 225/13, OSNP 2015, No. 11, item 146), 25 October 2007 (II PK 49/07, OSNP 2008, No. 21-22, item 317, OSP 2009, No. 7-8, item 76 with a commentary of A. Kosut), 14 June 2012 (I PK 222/11, LEX No. 1222145 with a commentary by K. Stepnicka).

16 In this case, the circumvention involves the exercise by the employer, formally in compliance with the repealed Article 33 of the Labour Code, of the right (guaranteed to each of the parties to an individual employment relationship) to terminate a fixed-term contract of employment concluded for a period exceeding 6 months. The meaning of this legal issue was noted by the Polish Supreme Court. In the reasoning of the judgment of 5 June 2014 (I PK 308/13, OSNP 2015, no. 11, item 149) the Supreme Court held that circumvention of law occurs where the parties to an individual employment relationship formulate the terms of an act in such a manner that formally it is not contrary to Article 33 of the Labour Code. By concluding a long-term fixed-term contract of employment the employer created in the employee a false conviction that he is guaranteed a greater stability of employment than in the case of the contract of employment for an indefinite term. An example of circumvention of law in the labour relationships may be lack of any reasonable grounds for conclusion of a long-term fixed-term contract of employment apart from the 'activities undertaken by the employer to facilitate redundancies in connection with the ongoing restructuring of his business' (Judgment of the Polish Supreme Court (SN) of 7 September 2005, II PK 294/04, OSNP 2006, No. 13-14, item 207).

decisions which are subject to legal protection resulting from the principle of freedom of business. He only evaluates whether, in the light of the general statutory restrictions on conclusion of the contracts of employment of definite duration, there was a case of legally unjustified conclusion of such contract. However, certain doubts may arise as to whether the restrictions on the freedom of economic activity laid down in general terms in Article 25^1 § 4 (4) of the Labour Code are in compliance with the Constitution. The provision in question allows a public administration body – the labour inspector – to evaluate certain activity of the employer. If the inspector finds a non-compliance with the general restrictions on the freedom of contract and imposes an administrative fine, it will have the same legal consequences as the conversion of the concluded contract of employment. The applicable labour laws do not allow for the substantive verification by the employer of the administrative decision adopted by the labour inspector and the resulting civil law and economic consequences.

5. Other statutory exceptions to the principle of limitation of the freedom to conclude fixed-term contracts of employment were laid down in Article 2 of the Act of 25 June 2015 amending certain other (apart from the Labour Code) acts allowing conclusion of such contracts. The view presented by the legislature is that the legal mechanisms laid down in the amended Article 25^1 of the Labour Code, restricting the freedom of the parties to conclude fixed-term employment contracts, do not apply to the employment relationships governed by the following acts: 1) Act of 16 September 1982 on the employees of public agencies (ustawa z dnia 16 września 1982 o pracownikach urzędów państwowych)[17]; 2) Act of 27 July 2001 on the foreign service (ustawa z dnia 27.7.2001 o służbie zagranicznej)[18]; 3) Act of 9 July 2003 on the employment of temporary agency workers (ustawa z dnia 9.7.2003 o zatrudnianiu pracowników tymczasowych;)[19]; 4) Act of 21 November 2008 of the local government staff (ustawa z dnia 21.11.2008 o pracownikach samorządowych)[20]. In all the above-mentioned acts the amendment Act of 25 June 2015 introduced an identical provision according to which 'Article 25^1 of the Labour Code does not apply', in the wording given by the

17 *Journal of Laws* [Dz.U.] of 2013, item 269 and of 2014, item 1199.
18 *Journal of Laws* [Dz.U.] No. 128, item 1403 as amended.
19 *Journal of Laws* [Dz.U.] No. 166, item 1608 as amended.
20 *Journal of Laws* [Dz.U.] of 2014, item 1202 and of 2015, item 1045.

amendment Act of 25 June 2015, to the contracts concluded for a fixed term. The Act of 25 June 2015 amending the Labour Code and certain other acts introduced in the Polish legal system a principle established in the case law according to which Article 25^1 of the Labour Code does not apply where an act exhaustively specifies the circumstances in which the parties may conclude a fixed-term contract of employment[21].

2. Interim provisions

The Act of 25 June 2015 on the amendment of the Labour Code and certain other acts entered into force on 22 February 2016. As regards contracts for the period of performance of specific work concluded under the previous article 25^1 of the Labour Code applicable before the date of entry into force of the Act of 25 June 2015, the previous provisions continue to apply (Article 13 of the Act of 25 June 2015). As regards all fixed-term employment contracts in force on the date of entry into force of the amendment Act of 25 June 2015, as well as those which were terminated by notice before 22 February 2016, the previous provisions continue to apply (Article 14 (1) of the Act of 25 June 2015). The period of employment under a fixed-term contract includes the periods of performance of work under Article 25^1 of the Labour Code after the entry into force of the amendment Act of 25 June 2015. A fixed-term employment contract in force on 22 February 2016 is considered by the legislature as the first or the second contract of employment within the meaning of Article 25^1 of the Labour Code before the amendment under the Act of 25 June 2015 if it was concluded as the first or the second contract within the meaning of the previously applicable Article 25^1 of the Labour Code (Article 14 (4)). Therefore, the previous provisions apply also to the fixed-term employment contracts not exceeding six months or exceeding six months in which the parties did not provide for the possibility to terminate such contracts upon two weeks' notice and which are in force on the date of entry into force of the amendment Act of 25 June 2015. As regards the possibility to terminate such contracts,

---

[21] Judgments of the Polish Supreme Court (SN) of 29 June 2000 (I PKN 709/99, OSNAPiUS 2001, No. 24, item 716), 10 October 2002 (I PKN 546/01, OSNP 2004, No. 10, item 169), 14 October 2004 (I PK 693/03, OSNP 2005, No. 11, item 158), 6 October 2005 (II PK 77/05, OSNP 2006, No. 17-18, item 266), 21 September 2011 (II PK 36/11, Legalis; 28 August 2013, I PK 46/13, OSNP 2014, No. 8, item 115), 9 April 2015 (I PK 213/14, MoPr 2015, Vol. 11, p. 586).

the previous provisions continue to apply (Article 14 of the Act of 25 June 2015). This means that upon expiration of the maximum period of employment for a fixed term allowed by the amended Article 25^1 § 1 of the Labour Code, all contracts of employment for a fixed term, the end date of which falls on 22 February 2016 or on successive days after the date of entry into force of the amendment act of 25 June 2015, end automatically upon their end date. A similar mechanism of automatic end of a fixed-term contract of employment is also provided for in Article 14 (6) of the Act of 25 June 2015. It provides that Article 14 (4) of the act of 25 June 2015 shall not apply to contracts concluded for a fixed term before 22 February 2016 if the scope of application of any of such contracts was – during the period of operation of the amended Article 25^1 of the Labour Code – after the expiration of the maximum allowed period of employment under a fixed-term contract (33 months), but the employment relationship did not end because of the special protection of sustainability of employment relationship granted during the period of operation of the amended Article 25^1 of the Labour Code. In such case the legislature considers that a contract of employment terminates upon expiration of its term (Article 14 (6) of the Act of 25 June 2015).

Although Article 25^1 of the Labour Code amended by the Act of 25 June 2015 allows the parties to conclude three fixed-term contracts of employment during a term of 33 months, Article 14 (5) of the amendment Act of 25 June 2015 provides that the third fixed-term contract, after the entry into force of the amendment act – on 22 February 2016 – and on the following days in a period of one month from conclusion of the second contract for a fixed term governed by the provisions of the previously applicable Article 25^1 of the Labour Code, is considered a contract of employment concluded for an indefinite term if the period of monthly break between the second and the third contract started running before or on the date of entry into force of the Act of 25 June 2015 (Article 14 (5) of the Act of 25 June 2015). As regards the fixed-term contracts which may be terminated by the parties upon notice, they will be subject (on 22 February 2016 and on the subsequent days) to the current, introduced under Article 1 (6) of the amendment act, notice periods laid down in Article 36 § 1 of the Labour Code (Article 14 (3) of the Act of 25 June 2015). The above expression by the legislature does not mean excluding the possibility of conclusion by the parties of a successive fixed-term contract of employment and the following contracts of that type after exceeding the maximum periods of employment (33 months) and the number of contracts of definite duration between the same parties (three contracts). The parties to binding contracts concluded for a fixed term, in force on the date of entry into force of the Act of 25 June 2015 (22 February 2016), concluded under the provisions establishing an exception to the principle (laid down in the previously applicable Article 25^{1} of the Labour Code) of limited freedom of employment under fixed-term contracts of employment, were obligated to supplement these contracts, within three months from the entry into force of the Act of 25 June 2015, with information listed in the amended Article 29 § 1^{1} of the Labour Code. Under this provision the employer who concluded a fixed-term contract of employment before 22 February 2016 based on one of the reasons mentioned in the currently applicable Article 25^{1} § 4 (1)-(3) of the Labour Code or in the case referred to in Article 25^{1} § 4 (4) of the Labour Code, was obligated to include information on the objective reasons for concluding such contract. The legislature amending the laws requires, without specifying the obligated party, to inform the National Labour Inspectorate of the causes of conclusion of each of the four additional (exceeding the allowed legal limits) fixed-term contracts of employment, while no such obligation was established under the provisions applicable before 22 February 2016. When comparing the wording of Article 25^{1} of the Labour Code before and after the amendment, it can easily be seen that in the previous version the catalogue of exceptions to the principle of limited freedom to conclude contracts of definite term included two causes while the version currently in force includes four causes. However, this does not mean that previously it was not possible to lawfully conclude contracts of employment to perform work for the period of the term of office (Article 25^{1} § 4 (3) of the Labour Code amended by the Act of 25 June 2015) or for 'objective reasons on the part of the employer' in order to 'meet the actual periodic demand' of the employer which is 'necessary in this respect in the light of all the circumstances attending the conclusion of the contract' (Article 25^{1} § 4 (4) of the Labour Code amended by the Act of 25 June 2015). Each of the currently applicable exceptions to the principle of limitation of freedom of contract could be the basis, under the previous laws, for conclusion of fixed-term employment contracts. A precondition for the validity of the previously concluded contract was that the same parties did not conclude a third contract of definite duration before the end of the monthly period. A contract of employment for a fixed term was not, and still is not a causal contract. Therefore, any attempt by the legislature to demand that the parties to a contract concluded before 22 February 2016 provide explanations as to the purposes for which such contracts were concluded, is groundless.

An interesting example is another obligation, laid down in Article 15 (2) of the Act of 25 June 2015, imposed on the employer. If the parties conclude a fixed-term contract of employment before the entry into force of the Act of 25 June 2015 amending Article 25[1] of the Labour Code, in the case specified in Article 25[1] § 4 (4) of the Labour Code (applicable from 22 February 2016), the employer who is a party to such contract was obligated to notify, in writing or electronically, a competent regional labour inspector 'of such contract', including specification of the causes for which it was concluded. Because of the lack of the precise specification of the obligation imposed by Article 15 (2) of the act of 25 June 2015, the obligation is fulfilled by the employer who notifies the National Labour Inspectorate that he is a party to a fixed-term contract of employment or notifies of the date of conclusion, the term and the terms and conditions of such contract. In the notification of the existence and effectiveness, on the date of entry into force of the Act of 25 June 2015, of a fixed-term contract of employment, the employer does not have to specify the reasons of such contract. This obligation was laid down separately in the latter part of Article 15 (2) of the Act of 25 June 2015. The time-limit of five working days during which the employer should notify a competent regional labour inspector of the above-mentioned contract starts running after the contract of employment is supplemented with the information on the reasons for such contract. Given that Article 29 § 1[1] of the Labour Code added by Article 1 (2) of the Act of 25 June 2015 does not impose on the parties to an employment relationship any obligation to submit to anyone, except the employee concerned who is a party to the contract, a copy of the concluded contract, it should be noted that the legislature did not specify the running of the period laid down in Article 15 (2) *in fine* of the Act of 25 June 2015. Article 29 § 2 of the Labour Code provides that the contract of employment shall be made in writing. The above requirement is not subject to any condition. In the Polish labour law, the freedom to conclude contracts of employment means also the freedom of the parties to the employment relationship to choose the method of documentation of the established obligation relationship. If a contract is concluded in oral or a form other than the written form, the legislature imposed on the employer an obligation to confirm in writing the arrangements concerning: the parties to the contract, the type of the contract and the terms and conditions of the contract. The employer must fulfil this obligation not later than on the date the employee commences work. It should be noted that the above obligation laid down in Article 29 § 2 of the Labour Code applies only in relation to the period between conclusion of the contract of employment by the parties and commencement of performance of work by the employee. The situation in the case referred to in Article 15 (2) of the Act of 25 June 2015 is different. It provides for an additional obligation of the employer in a situation when the work has not yet been commenced by the employee. The situation referred to in that article is completely different. The employee was employed under a fixed-term contract of employment and performs that work. According to the Polish laws, a contract of employment of definite duration does not have to specify the factual grounds (*causa*) enabling competent public bodies (National Labour Inspectorate) to determine the legality of such contract. If the amended Article 29 of the Labour Code, in the added § 1^1, included a clause worded in Article 15 (2) *in fine* of the Act of 25 June 2015, there would be no doubt that the running of the time-limit of five working days refers to the date of supplementation of the written contract of employment or – if the parties fail to comply with the written form requirement *ad probationem* – it refers to the date of confirmation of the terms and conditions by the employer. *De lege lata,* in the lack of detailed specification of the time-limit for compliance by the employer with that obligation in relation to a fixed-term contract concluded under the previously applicable laws, the situation of the parties to an individual employment relationship established under the previously concluded contract is less complicated. Now let us consider the possible legal consequences which may arise if the National Labour Inspectorate questions the grounds of a fixed-term contract concluded in the past, worded in Article 25 § 4 (4) of the Labour Code. Generally speaking, *lex retro non agit.* The above fundamental Roman principle is fully applicable in the legal relationships governed by the labour laws. Conclusion by the parties of a long-term fixed-term contract (and the provisions of Article 25^1 of the Labour Code both in the previous and current version are to prevent abuse by the employers of the contracts of definite duration) which is further questioned by a regional labour inspector, is a threat to the legal transactions in the individual and collective labour relations. The *ex post* introduction of a legal mechanism enabling a public institution to efficiently undermine the legal compliance of the established and existing employment relationships does not serve to strengthen the legal relationships in the past, presence and future. Therefore, it cannot be considered compatible with law, all the more so since it is in conflict with the *lex retro non agit* principle. The non-compliance with the principle of non-retroactivity may be seen in Article 16 of the act of 25 June 2016 which lays down a principle according to which in determining the length of a notice period of fixed-term contracts of employment which are in effect on the date of entry into force of that act, the periods of employment with the employer concerned preceding the date of entry into force of that act should not be taken into account. On the other hand, Article 17 of the Act of 25 June 2015 is in compliance with the *lex retro non agit principle.* It provides that disputes relating to termination or expiration of a contract of employment should be resolved under the labour laws in force on the date of performance of the questioned legal acts, if the contracts of employment were terminated upon notice, terminated without notice or expired before the date of entry into force of the act amending the Labour Code.

3. Partial alignment of contracts of employment concluded for a fixed term and for an indefinite term

Other regulations provided for in the Act of 25 June 2015 show that the intention of the legislature is to align the fixed-term contracts with contracts for an indefinite term. The amendment of the Labour Code in force as of 22 February 2016 proves that such alignment was achieved in matters relating to: 1) notice periods (Article 36 § 1 of the Labour Code); 2) rights of employers to reduce the maximum, three months' notice periods to one month in the case of declaration of bankruptcy or liquidation of the employer or for other reasons not attributable to employees (Article 36 § 1 of the Labour Code); 3) right of an employer to grant an employee a leave of absence with pay during a notice period (article 36^2 of the Labour Code); 4) repeal of article 41^1 § 2 of the Labour Code, a provision which allowed for termination of a contract of employment in the case of declaration of bankruptcy or liquidation of the employer; 5) uniformization of the period of compensation in the case of termination of a contract of employment without notice by the employee because of gross violation by the employer of fundamental obligations in relation to the employee (Article 55 § 1^1 of the Labour Code), amount of compensation for the notice period (Article 58, 61^2 § 1, 63^2 § 2 of the Labour Code) and an optional entitlement to compensation in the case of violation by the employer of the provisions on termination of the contracts of employment without notice (Article 59 of the Labour

Code). Uniformization of the length of the notice period, making such period conditional upon the seniority at an establishment concerned and making the amount of the compensation conditional upon the remuneration payable to the employees employed under fixed-term contracts and contracts for an indefinite term is – in my opinion – most characteristic for the amendment of the Labour Code of 25 June 2015[22].

Conclusion

The amendments to the employment relationships based on the contracts of employment presented in this article show a tendency to convergence of two opposite tendencies: stability and flexibility of employment under contracts of employment of definite duration. In the amendment act, the following results were achieved in respect of the contracts of employment of definite duration:

1. Automatic conversion of a contract of definite duration into a contract for an indefinite term obligates the employer who intends to end the employment relationship – concluded under the amended contract of employment – to give notice of termination of such contract. The automatic change of the type of contract from a fixed-term contract into a contract for an indefinite term obligates the employer to issue to the employee an employment certificate which should include a note on the change of the basis of employment and the date of legal conversion of the contract as prescribed by the legislature.
2. According to the presented interpretation of the amended Article 25^1 of the Labour Code, the legal mechanism of conversion of the fixed-term contract (after exceeding the thresholds established

[22] I do not share the views of J. Stelina, who thinks that the act of 25 June 2015 renders the fixed-term contract of employment similar to a contract for a probationary period. In my opinion both of these contracts of employment represent the same type of contracts of employment of definite duration. However, basically different from any contract of employment of definite duration is a contract concluded for an indefinite term. Therefore, the uniformization of the periods of employment in respect of two separate types of contracts: for a fixed term and for an indefinite term and granting identical value to the periods of employment of two separate types of contracts is far more important aspect of the amendment than the liquidation of the symbolic absolute stability of employment established by conclusion of a short-term fixed-term contract of employment. See Stelina J. Nowa koncepcja umowy o pracę na czas określony [A new concept of a fixed-term employment contract]. *Państwo i Prawo*, Vol. 11, 2015, pp. 41 et seq.

by the legislature – 33 months, three fixed-term contracts) is no longer applicable after the employer terminates the automatically converted contract. Conclusion of a contract of employment for a fixed term on the next day following termination of the converted employment relationship opens another cycle of employment under the contract or contracts of definite duration.

3. The legislature eventually dropped the former legal concept according to which employment under a contract of employment for a fixed term guaranteed to the employee greater stability than that guaranteed by the provisions on the relative protection of sustainability of the employment relationship for an indefinite term.
4. The amended Article 25^1 of the Labour Code includes an extended list of exemptions to the legal mechanism of automatic conversion of a contract of employment for a fixed term into a contract for an indefinite term as prescribed in Article 25^1 § 3 of the Labour Code.
5. The statutory exemption to the restrictions of the freedom to conclude such contracts of employment should be interpreted as a permission for the employer who faces exceptional situation and is forced not to comply with the generally applicable prohibitions laid down in Article 25^1 § 1 of the Labour Code, without fear of automatic conversion into the contracts of employment for an indefinite term. The firm character of the above statement is weakened because of imprecise powers of the labour inspection and their legal consequences in respect of employment relationships;
6. Contract of employment for a fixed term was not and still is not a causal contract. Therefore, any attempt by the legislature to demand that the parties to a contract concluded before 22 February 2016 provide explanations as to the purposes for which such contracts were concluded is groundless. The employer who is a party to such contract was obligated to notify, in writing or electronically, a competent regional labour inspector 'of such contract', including specification of the causes for which it was concluded. The *ex post* introduction of a legal mechanism enabling a public institution to efficiently undermine the legal compliance of the established and existing employment relationships does not serve to strengthen the legal relationships in the past, presence and future. Therefore, it cannot be considered compatible with law, all the more so since it is in conflict with the *lex retro non agit* principle.

7. Other regulations provided for in the Act of 25 June 2015 show that the intention of the legislature is to align the fixed-term contracts with contracts for an indefinite term. Uniformization of the length of the notice period, making such period conditional upon the seniority at the establishment concerned and making the amount of the compensation conditional upon the remuneration payable to the employees employed under fixed-term contracts and contracts for an indefinite term is – in my opinion – most characteristic for the amendment of the Labour Code.

New Forms of Work

An Austrian Perspective

Robert REBHAHN*

Abstract

This paper focuses on the recent development of Austrian labour law where – although the 'traditional' forms of work still prevail – new forms are becoming increasingly more significant. These new forms such as on-demand work, posting of workers, solo workers, and increasingly, more cases of undeclared work from the perspective of the lack of control from the state side are analysed from an Austrian perspective, taking into account peculiarities of its labour market and assessing the EU regulation in this field as well.

Key words: on-demand work, posting of workers, social dumping, solo workers, independent contractors, employee-like workers, undeclared work.

Introduction

Austrian Labour Law[1] is characterized by two features. At the macro level, the Austrian system is quite rigid, especially because collective agreements cover nearly all employment contracts and prescribe inter alia a minimum wage[2]. At the same time, the regulation at the micro level was rather flexible, especially as far as the protection against dismissal is

---

* Robert Rebhahn has been full Professor of Labour Law and Social Security Law at the University of Vienna since 2003 and was previously Professor of Civil Law and Labour Law at the Humboldt University Berlin. He has published about labour Law (including comparative law), non-discrimination law, civil law (torts and contracts) and European Union Law.

1 See Risak M. E. Austria. In: Blanpain R., Hendrickx F. (eds.) *International Encyclopaedia for Labour Law and Industrial Relations*. Kluwer, 2010; Neumayr M., Reissner G-P. (eds.) *Zeller Kommentar zum Arbeitsrecht* [Zeller Commentary on Employment Law]. Vienna: Manz, 2011.

2 Rebhahn R. The Austrian pattern of Flexicurity in a comparative view. In: *Labour Market of 21st Century: Looking for Flexibility and Security*. Vilnius: TIC, 2011, pp. 100–111.

concerned; however, the regulation of working time is rather complex and strict. Works councils exist in most of the bigger establishments. Their competences are wider and stronger than in most other Member States, although less far reaching than in Germany. Strikes are still a rare occurrence.

The main features of Labour Law have not changed for a long time, and even the legislator has not much altered the details during the last decade. Austrian Labour Law is thus rather stable. This applies especially with regard to Collective Labour Law, where neither the structure nor the details changed. The only amendment that is worth mentioning is that now an enterprise (collective) agreement may regulate (with normative effect) all forms of performance-linked payments, whereas it must not regulate time-wages[3]. Also regarding the regulation of the employment contract (individual labour law), only minor changes were introduced. The most important among them is a new regulation about 'all-inclusive' contracts. Such contracts provide that overtime cannot be paid in addition, although the all-inclusive payment has to respect the minimum wage as well as the surcharge for overtime, which the statute fixes at 50%. Since 2015, such a contract has to stipulate the basic time-wage, so that one can assess whether the employer pays enough with respect to minimum wage and surcharges. Only in one respect, was there a major change; this regards the enforcements of the due payments; I will deal with that later.

Nevertheless, the situation of employment has changed much during the last years. Ten and even five years ago, Austria had the lowest unemployment rate in the Union. Today, this rate is much higher and tends towards 10%, especially if one includes hidden unemployment by premature retirement, training and 'voluntary' abstention. However, the number of jobs, and of employed persons has increased. Thus, the reason for the rise in unemployment is that the number of persons willing to work increased faster. According to experts, an important, if not the main reason therefore was immigration, permanent or temporary, from other Member States[4].

---

3 Article 97 of the Arbeitsverfassungsgesetz [Statute on Labour Constitution].

4 Sator A. Arbeitslosigkeit in Österreich: Das Ende eines Musterschülers [Unemployment in Austria: The End of a model student]. *Standard*, 9 May 2015; Staudacher A. Fünf Gründe, warum die Arbeitslosigkeit weiter steigt [Five reasons why the unemployment rate is increasing. *Kurier*, 1 March 2016.

Thus, a labour lawyer might inquire about the role of Labour Law in this evolution and the importance of the underlying changes for Labour Law. An appropriate way to do this is to have a look at the different forms of work.

1. The 'traditional' forms of work

The standard form of employment, that is full-time work based on an open-ended employment contract, is still the predominant form in the Austrian Labour market. This applies not only for the public sector and semi-public services, but also with regard to most private enterprises, especially the bigger ones. Statistics show that a fairly large number of employees change their employer every year – however, it seems that over time this affects mainly the same persons.

Besides, there are the well-known forms of atypical work, namely part-time, fixed-term and agency work. Without going into details, regarding these forms not much has changed during the last decade. Part-time work is a social problem only insofar as the persons concerned wish to work full time. According to a recent Eurostat survey, 16% of part-time workers in Austria would like to increase their working hours[5]. This also includes people who do not want a full-time job.

Regarding fixed-term work, its deviation from the standard form depends in fact mainly upon the strictness of the protection against dismissal. In Austria, this protection is less strict than in many other Member States. Thus, fixed-term work is 'less atypical' in Austria. Further, Austrian law provides that two or more consecutive fixed-term contracts with the same employer are licit only if the employer has a good reason for this. If there is no such reason, the contract is held to be open-ended[6]. Both facts may explain why the share of fixed-term work has not gone up much, although this type of work is used often if not regularly at the beginning of an employment relation.

---

[5] Eurostat. Press release 99/2016. Retrieved 11 September 2016 from http://ec.europa.eu/eurostat/documents/2995521/7311566/3-19052016-BP-EN.pdf/35ed90ae-24ab-4d0b-b42f-f267f7490a9d.

[6] Reissner G-P. Artikel 19 Angestelltengesetz [Act on White-collar Workers]. In: *Zeller Kommentar*, *op. cit.*, pp. 22 et seq.

A Directive regulated agency work some years ago[7]. The Austrian legislator has transformed the Directive, but no substantive changes were necessary to adapt to its provisions. Further, only less than 2% of all employees work as agency workers.

Thus, the 'old' forms of atypical work do not pose any real new legal problems in Austria.

2. 'New' forms of work

Therefore, we should look instead at 'new' forms of work in order to evaluate how far their legal status contributes to the present state of the labour market.

2.1 Work on demand

In some Member States, work on demand or zero-hour-contracts have increased a lot. In Austria, the legal situation of this type of work has been rather clear for a long time. If the person is obliged to work, then the contract has to determine the number of hours due. If the contract fails to be explicit on this, the courts assume that the parties stipulated the number of hours that were actually worked after the beginning of the contract during a longer period[8]. The employer is obliged to pay for this amount of work even if he does not dispose of it. If, on the contrary, the working person is not obliged to work when asked to do so, then the contractual relation will be assessed according to the general criteria applied to the work actually done. Normally, it will show that the work is done in subordination and thus as an employee based on consecutive fixed-term employment contracts[9]. The CJEU has ruled in this direction recently in the Kunsten judgment dealing with substitute musicians[10]. Since, the Dutch court that referred the Kunsten case ruled that the substitute musicians are employees as long as they perform during rehearsals and concerts[11]. However, Union law does not require that in

---

[7] Directive 2008/104/EC. See Rebhahn R., Schörghofer F. Directive 2008/104/EC. In: Franzen M., I. Gallner I., Oetker H. (eds.) *Kommentar zum europäischen Arbeitsrecht* [Commentary on European Labour Law]. Munich: Beck C. H., 2015.

[8] Rebhahn R. Artikel 1151 ABGB [Austrian Civil Code] In: *Zeller Kommentar, op. cit.*, p. 194.

[9] Ibidem, pp. 94 et seq.

[10] CJEU case C-413/13.

[11] Gerechtshof Den Haag 1.9.2015 ECLI:NL:GHDHA:2015:2305.

the case of consecutive fixed-term contracts the employee be entitled to an open-ended contract. Austrian law does impose such a contract if the employer has no good reason for consecutive contracts.

2.2. Posting of workers

Another form of work, that has risen in importance during the last decade, is posting of workers, especially from Middle and East European countries. The Posting Directive 96/71/EC allows the host state to prescribe particularly the minimum wage of the working site, but does not allow imposing the full range of Labour Law. Two years ago, the CJEU ruled that the full scale of minimum wages might be prescribed[12]. For several years, Austria has obliged the posting employer to pay the wages that the Austrian collective agreement for the branch provides for; Austria has no statutory minimum wage.

The Directive's model fits well for postings over a short period as far as labour law is concerned. However, even in the case of short-time postings many see a problem in the different levels and amounts of social contributions in the origin and host state. Regarding labour law, the model enshrined in the Directive fits rather badly for longer postings, because it is hardly convincing that the centre of the employment relationship then still relates to the country of origin. The Commission recently came forward with a proposal for amending the Directive[13] specifically on this point: If the anticipated or effective duration of posting exceeds 24 months, then the Labour law of the host state shall be applicable in full. The Parliaments of several Member States have objected that this proposal contravenes the principle of subsidiarity (which is as such not wholly understandable).

Further, many criticize that effective enforcement of the rules regarding posting is not possible. Observers in Austria say that the rise of unemployment among people living there – longer residents as well as migrants – results, to a great extent, from the replacing of this workforce by posted workers (and independent contractors whom I will deal with later). Even leading exponents of the ruling Social-Democratic party recently demanded that postings in critical branches (such as construction) should be forbidden – presumably knowing that this would contravene the interpretation the CJEU has found regarding the freedom of services.

[12] CJEU case C-396/13.

[13] COM (2016) 128 final.

For a long time, one of the main problems of posting seems to be the effective control of the rules that the host state rightly imposes, particularly if the enforcement of wages is left to the initiative of the employee. This was the case in Austria, where only the employee was able to enforce the employer's duty to pay by suing the employer. In order to control postings more effectively, Austria enacted a new statute in 2011, which according to its title should combat social dumping[14]. It brought a fundamental change in this area. Since then an administrative authority is empowered to control the due payment of minimum wages and fine the employer quite heavily if he does not comply. According to the ban on discrimination in Union law, the new regime applies to mere internal cases as well. This has not increased the sympathies for postings even among business people. The new regime has shifted an important part of Labour Law from pure private law to public law – which is an important structural change not from a purely legal perspective, but also regarding the structure of the employment relationship.

The provisions against social dumping have been tightened since; in May 2016 the Government proposed other amendments that are currently under discussion in Parliament[15]. In practice, the implementation of the new regime has turned out to be rather difficult. The best indicator therefore is that the Government's proposal tremendously increased the number of paragraphs that deal with the topic. The first regulation in 2011 contained only a few paragraphs; the proposal comprises 72! However, more than half of them deal with the enforcement of administrative acts against employers that reside in another Member State – obviously, because some Member States are very 'reluctant' to cooperate with the host state or to control their nationals.

An important material problem of the statute on social dumping is that the authority controls whether the employer abides by all the details of the applicable collective agreement, although these are in most cases very complicated. This increases the probability of infractions and fines accordingly. Many of the employers concerned would more easily accept administrative control of a statutory minimum wage. A possible solution might be that the collective agreement provides for an additional

---

14 Lohn- und Sozialdumping-Bekämpfungsgesetz (LSDB-G) [Pay- and Social dumping Act], *BGBl* I No. 24/2011, since amended Sozialbetrugsbekämpfungsgesetz (SBBG) [Act on controlling social fraud], *BGBl* I No. 113/2015.

15 Lohn- und Sozialdumping-Bekämpfungsgesetz [Pay- and Social dumping Act], 189/ ME 25.GP.

'minimum wage' that serves solely as the purpose of administrative control and is set in a less complicated way then the 'real' minimum wages.

Art 12(2) of the Enforcement Directive provides that the Member States prescribe for subcontracting chains in the construction sector that the contractor of which the employer is a direct subcontractor is (in addition to or in place of the employer) liable to the posted worker with respect to any outstanding minimum pay. The government's proposal dutifully implements Art 12(2) with the speciality, that the contractor may withhold payment to the subcontractor as far as he is liable and as long as he might be liable. The liability presupposes that the employee informs an authority within six weeks that the employer has not paid the due wages, thus the contractor may pay the amount withheld after some weeks. Art 12(1) of the Enforcement Directive would allow that Member States prescribe a similar liability as that mentioned in Article 12(1) also for subcontracting chains in other branches. However, the Austrian legislator has not made use of this possibility.

The effectiveness of the Posting Directive as well as that of the new Austrian regime just mentioned depends further on the possibilities of the authority to control postings as such. The CJEU has often ruled that control measures enacted by host Member States go too far because they infringe upon the freedom of services[16]. There is a new Directive on Enforcement[17], but some ask if it might encroach upon more effective control rather than support it.

This leads to a crucial question regarding the role of labour and social law in the Union: How and how far are these areas of law meant either to stabilize the differences in conditions that exist between different regions and countries or meant to help equalize these conditions. The Treaties do not give a clear answer. It might be an argument in favour of the first position that the Treaty in Article 153 TFEU allows minimum standards solely (and thus excludes Directives that set minimum as well as maximum standards at the same time) as a means of harmonization. The question cannot be discussed here. Regarding posting, a rather rigid regulation, which ensures that the working conditions at the place of work have to be respected, serves the first aim (stabilizing differences), whereas a regulation that allows to 'export' the working conditions of the country of origin serves the second aim (equalizing differences).

---

16 CJEU case C-168/04.

17 Directive 2014/67/EU.

Understandably, different Member States might have different views on the problem. However, the legal regulation in this area should at least be coherent. This does not seem to be the case if it is said that the higher social standards of a country should be maintained, whereas this is undermined by impeding those controls that would be necessary to enforce the higher standards. It would be then wiser to argue more frankly at the forefront.

The control problems that I have mentioned also affect the possibility to detect bogus-employment – not only in internal cases but also in inter-state cases. Both aspects undermine the efforts to fight bogus employment, and those of the Commission. A particular problem seems to be the A1 Declaration as far as some think that it is also relevant for the contractual relation. However, nobody can say in advance if the work in the host state is performed in a dependent or in an independent manner.

2.3 Solo workers

Another type of work that should be mentioned here is that of solo workers, who in fact do not fulfil the criteria of an employee and thus perform their work as an independent contractor. The number of solo workers has increased sharply in Austria. Most of them are registered as an 'undertaking' with the Austrian Chamber of Commerce; this registration does not hinder a specific work relation from being qualified as an employment relationship if the work is done in a subordinated manner. A rather big share of the new solo workers came from other Member States.

Many of the solo workers, however, do not offer their services on the market, but work in fact for a longer period for one or two clients only. Legally, they are nevertheless independent contractors and self-employed, in fact they are rather workers that are economically dependent on their client(s); one might call them 'independent workers.'

Only some Member States have enacted special rules for such working persons, among them Austria and Germany[18]. There they are called employee-like workers. Under Austrian labour law some rules apply to independent contractors if they are employee-like, mainly because they

---

18 Perulli A. *Economically dependent / quasi-subordinate (parasubordinate) employment: legal, social and economic aspects.* European Commission, 2002; Pottschmid D. *Arbeitnehmerähnliche Personen in Europa [Employee-like persons in Europe].* Baden-Baden: Nomos, 2006; Rebhahn R. Arbeitnehmerähnliche Personen – Rechtsvergleich und Regelungsperspektive [Employee-like persons – comparison of laws and perspective]. *Recht der Arbeit,* 2009, pp. 236–253.

economically depend on the client. However, the most important rules do not apply, such as collective agreements with their minimum wages, working time rules and dismissal protection. On the other side, since 1997 all solo workers are included in the mandatory Austrian social security system and have to pay contributions – except those solo workers who post themselves from another Member State.

Union law has not yet regulated employee-like work, because 10 years ago many stakeholders objected thereto[19]. The CJEU seems to see the employee-likes as independent contractors and therefore as undertakings, as the Kunsten case showed. Another qualification is, however, possible if the work is actually performed in a subordinated manner[20]. In all other cases, a legal problem at Union level might arise if a Member State applies to employee-like solo-workers rules that are typical for employees. The application of any such rule by Member State A makes it less attractive to exercise the economic freedom in A starting from another Member State B. In consequence, the application of these rules needs to be justified. One could consider two different ways of justification. The first one asserts that the special rules for employee-likes aim at the protection of employees because they shield them from unfair competition. The second way would assert that the special rules are necessary for the protection of the employee-likes themselves. However, both efforts to justify might turn out to be difficult – especially as long as many Member States do not have special rules for employee-likes.

Article 101(1) TFEU raises another problem related to employee-like solo workers. Said provision forbids all agreements between undertakings, which may affect trade between Member States and which have as their object or effect the prevention, restriction or distortion of competition. The CJEU ruled in the Kunsten case that a provision of a collective labour agreement, which sets minimum fees for self-employed service providers falls within the scope of Article 101(1) TFEU unless the self-employed are 'false self-employed', namely 'service providers in a situation comparable to that of workers'[21]. There is doubt as to what exactly the CJEU means by this wording. It could either extend the notion of non-undertaking beyond the traditional scope of 'employee' in Union law or leave this notion of 'employee' untouched. In the second case, 'false self-employed' covers only those working persons that are employees

19 SEK (2007) 1373.

20 CJEU case C-413/13.

21 *Ibidem.*

according to the criteria of Union law, but that are either qualified as independent contractors by national law or falsely treated as independent contractors in the contractual relationship. It seems that the ruling uses 'false self-employed' with this meaning and thus exempts only these working persons from Article 101(1) TFEU. Then, the ban in Article 101(1) would apply also to collective agreements that cover employee-like workers. This would hinder Member States from providing for such collective agreements, which however, may be necessary in the future in order to improve the situation of the rising number of employee-like workers. One might perhaps avoid this result claiming that most such collective agreements concern a purely internal situation and do not affect trade between Member States[22]. An argument in favour of this position is that the collective agreement as such (without an extension by the State) binds only the members of the federation of employee-likes; it then does not hinder any competition by working persons from another Member State[23].

3. Undeclared work

The last form of work I want to address is undeclared work. It is naturally quite difficult to assess how large the share of undeclared work is. The share in Austria is undoubtedly much smaller than in some other Member States, but it seems to be bigger today than 10 years ago. In the past, undeclared work in Austria was – as far as workers are concerned – mainly performed by people who had official employment; it was thus additional work. Now undeclared work quite often seems to be the main occupation.

Here again we are confronted with the control problem, as in the cases of underpaid posting and of false independent contractors. The reasons are similar: If an authority is not allowed to effectively control the declared exercise of an economic freedom, this might and often will impair the control of undeclared work, also in internal cases – because before the control you ignore whether the work is done legally or undeclared. It might be a consequence of these difficulties that the fines, which Austrian authorities nowadays impose in case of postings or falsely

22 The Kunsten ruling has answered the referred question because the provisions of the national Dutch law adopted the same approach as that provided for under EU law.

23 The less the collective agreement excludes an undertaking from another Member State, as it was in the CJEU cases C-271/08 and C-437/09.

declared work, are rather high and harsh. It is however, a well-established insight, that the low rate of detection raises the severity of the sanctions.

Conclusions

One has to ascertain that Austrian labour law system has become more rigid also at the micro-level. This diminished the important competitive advantage of Austria – however, we cannot be convinced that the increased possibilities to control will ensure over-all effective control. As regards the Union level, it seems that Union law still deals mainly with those atypical forms of work that were new 30 years ago, but does not address those forms that are new today, namely solo workers. Then, Union law at least should not hinder the Member States from efficiently addressing the problems these new forms pose. The broader social-economic perspective should be discussed more openly, and in particular – how far labour law and social security either should stabilise the differences in conditions that exist between different regions and countries or help to equalize these conditions.

Occupational Health and Safety Requirements and Flexible Organisation of the Working Time

Legal Regulation of Labour Relations in Estonia

Gaabriel Tavits*

Abstract

New forms of employment have raised the question of how labour law should regulate those new forms. Although the idea of flexibility of labour relations is one important aspect of labour law, one should ask how far we can go with flexibilization? New types of employment like crowdsourcing or sharing services raise the question of whether there is an applicable labour law and where the occupational health and safety rules must be applied. One aspect of flexibilization of labour relations concern working time (e.g. zero-hour contract). The article analyses the legal regulation of working time for flexible labour relations and the necessity to apply occupational health and safety rules also for the new forms of employment.

Key words: flexible employment relations, new forms of employment, flexible working and rest time, occupational health and safety rules.

Introduction

Changing economic circumstances inevitably bring about a situation which requires the implementation of changes in the legal regulation of labour relations. Labour relations are a part of economic relations and therefore cannot be kept apart from the development of economic relations. When labour relations are too rigid, it causes a situation in which the development of economic relations may become restricted. At the same time it is important that flexible labour relations guarantee the

---

* Gaabriel Tavits is a University Lecturer and Researcher at the Faculty of Law, University of Tartu, Estonia. His main areas of research include labour law and social security law (at European and international level). He has published many articles on issues relating to labour law and flexible labour relations, as well as on European social security law.

protection of employees' rights. It is important to follow the occupational health and safety requirements. The guaranteeing of occupational health and safety requirements is foreseen in the national legislation and by the EU directives and the Social Charter of the Council of Europe. Therefore, occupational health and safety requirements have to be ensured irrespective of how flexible the labour relations are.

The developments of recent years show that platform-based work[1] and work under the conditions of the sharing economy[2] are becoming more important. In both cases occupational health and safety requirements have to be guaranteed. In order to establish whether the occupational health and safety requirements have to be followed, it has to be clear whether it is possible to conclude an employment contract or any other civil law contract due to the new altered forms of employment.

The current article analyses the possibility of changing the flexibility of labour relations under economic conditions and the requirement of following the occupational health and safety requirements. In addition to the general discussion of the topic, the legal regulation of labour relations in Estonia is discussed and the impact of flexible working time and the consequences for the occupational health and safety requirements are analysed.

1. Is the flexicurity of labour relations still important?

The flexicurity of labour relations is a concept or rather a policy, which has been discussed in the European Union since 2005-2006[3]. The idea of the concept is rather simple – in changing economic conditions the employer should be able to change labour conditions quickly. If, under the changed circumstances, an employee loses their job, they are guaranteed payment of compensation while they search for a new job. The European Union does not prescribe to the Member States how they should implement the ideas of flexicurity. The EU activity programme

1 *Mobile Crowdsourcing Platforms: Transforming How Work and Research are Done.* Retrieved June 29, 2016 from http://crowdsourcingweek.com/blog/mobile-crowdsourcing-platforms-transforming-work-research-done/.

2 *The rise of the Sharing Economy.* Retrieved June 29, 2016 from http://www.economist.com/news/leaders/21573104-internet-everything-hire-rise-sharing-economy; *The Sharing Economy.* Retrieved June 29, 2016 from https://www.pwc.com/us/en/technology/publications/assets/pwc-consumer-intelligence-series-the-sharing-economy.pdf.

3 *Flexicurity.* Retrieved June 29, 2016 from http://ec.europa.eu/social/main.jsp?catId=102.

Europe 2020[4] also states that the flexicurity of labour relations is currently an important aspect of the labour market and in connection with that also in the regulation of the economy. Although Europe 2020 states flexicurity, today the idea of the flexicurity of labour relations remains in the background. At the same time the topic of flexibility of labour relations is still the important one.

The flexibility of labour relations has become important under the new forms of employment. Today we can speak about so-called platform-based work and employment in the sharing economy[5]. In the case of platform-based work the main question has always been: which restrictions have to be followed when an employment contract has been concluded with an employee? Another important aspect is related to restrictions of working time. The current regulation of working time establishes the maximum limit of working time and the minimum limit of the rest period, which have to be guaranteed to the employee[6]. The new forms of employment raise the question of whether the restrictions can always be followed? In this context, we can refer to the example of the zero-hours contract[7] in which there is no agreement on a fixed working time and the employee's working time largely depends on how much work the employer can provide to the employee.

Solutions are required to the questions: whether and to what extent occupational health and safety requirements have to be followed under these conditions? When the employee does not know the amount of work to be performed, it is not possible to ensure that the occupational health and safety requirements are followed.

The European Union has so far paid a lot of attention to the following of and maintenance of occupational health and safety requirements. The framework directive on occupational safety was adopted in 1989[8] and since then continuous and balanced development to establish different occupational safety requirements has been carried out.

---

4 COM(2010) 2020.

5 *The platform economy and the disruption of the employment relationship.* Retrieved June 29, 2016 from https://www.etui.org/Publications2/Policy-Briefs/European-Economic-Employment-and-Social-Policy/The-platform-economy-and-the-disruption-of-the-employment-relationship.

6 See e.g. ILO Convention No. 47 (1935). On EU level – Directive 2003/88/EC.

7 See e.g. A Study on the Prevalence of Zero Hours Contracts among Irish Employers and their Impact on Employees 2015. Retrieved June 27, 2016 from https://www.djei.ie/en/Publications/Publication-files/Study-on-the-Prevalence-of-Zero-Hours-Contracts.pdf.

8 Council Directive 89/391/EEC of 12 June 1989 on the introduction of measures to encourage improvements in the safety and health of workers at work.

Flexible labour relations denote that an employee's working time can be adjusted according to the requirements of the enterprise and the employee's needs. Generally speaking this means that if the employer can provide work to the employee, the former invites the latter to work and the employee works as long as the employer provides work. When the employee works he receives a salary. When the employer has no work for the employee, the employment contract is still effective but the employee does not have any work to do and the employer has no obligation to pay the employee any salary or to guarantee any other possible compensatory payments or compensations.

The organization of flexible working time in the Estonian legislation may prove to be complicated. According to the Estonian Employment Contract Act (hereinafter ECA) the employee's employment contract must establish whether the employee is employed part-time or full-time[9]. When there is no provision concerning the working time in the employment contract, it is assumed that the employee is employed full-time. Full-time employment assumes a forty-hour week over seven days or eight hours a day, whereby, the employee has five working days a week. Although the ECA includes certain restrictions related to the working time, the ECA sets no restrictions on the flexible regulation of the working time.

If working time has been agreed in the employment contract, the employer is obliged to provide work to the employee during the working time. If the employer fails to provide work to the employee, the employer is obliged to pay the employee the average salary pursuant to the ECA§ 35. Based on the case law of the Estonian Supreme Court, the abovementioned principle has been changed: according to the case law of the Supreme Court the employee himself/herself has to be active and interested in working for the employer[10]. When the employer has work to provide and the employee is prepared to work, the employer is obliged to pay the average salary. However, if the employee has shown no interest in working and fails to request work from the employer or ask when he/she can start to perform his/her duties of employment, the employer is not obliged to pay the average salary as the possible work stoppage is not caused due to the employer's non-activity and fault and because the employee is subject to joint liability.

---

9 § 5 of the Employment Contracts Act (Töölepingu seadus), RT I 2009, 5, 35. English translation may be retrieved from https://www.riigiteataja.ee/en/eli/520062016003/consolide.

10 Estonian Supreme Court, case 3-2-1-176-12 (I.M. vers AS LTH-Baas).

When the employee's working time is not definitely established and the employee does not know how many hours a week or day he/she is obliged to work, actually no work stoppage occurs; and additional remuneration for overtime work is excluded. The Supreme Court of Estonia has already once decided that in case of certain forms of work performance no restrictions have to be followed in regard to the performance of overtime work and night work. Namely, the Supreme Court ruled that if the remuneration is based on piece work, the implementation of restrictions established for working time is not required or obligatory[11]. However, the Supreme Court failed to give an answer on how to behave in regard to the occupational health and safety requirements. If, in the case of piece work, it is not necessary to follow the working and rest time restrictions, then why is it necessary to adjust the occupational health and safety requirements in full scope (e.g. prepare a risk assessment analysis of the working environment to establish whether and how many night work shifts or shifts of over twelve-hours may be applied).

The development of new forms of work performance raises the necessity for new regulation of labour relations. Therefore, it may be stated that the flexibility of labour relations is still actual, even if the European Union does not consider the approach a priority in the social policy. At the same time the topic of flexible labour relations (and the idea of flexicurity) confronts the legal regulation of occupational health and safety with important choices. New forms of employment and possibilities must be subject to the currently valid occupational health and safety requirements.

2. New forms of employment and the flexibility of labour relations

Different surveys have pointed out new work forms and the need to regulate them[12]. Although the sharing economy has been discussed over the last few years, platform-based work has only been an issue only the last couple of years[13].

---

11 Estonian Supreme Court, case 3-2-1-6-08 (O.S vers OÜ Arliten).

12 See e.g. *New Forms of Employment.* Retrieved June 29, 2016 from http://www.eurofound.europa.eu/et/publications/report/2015/working-conditions-labour-market/new-forms-of-employment.

13 Prassl J., Risak M. Uber, Taskrabbit, & Co: *Platforms as Employers? Rethinking the Legal Analysis of Crowdwork*, 2016. Retrieved June 28, 2016 from http://papers.ssrn.com/sol3/papers.cfm?abstract_id=2733003.

Sharing of different services and the legal regulation of those persons involved in sharing of services is related to the sharing economy and platform-based employment. In this context, the entrance of the driving service provider Uber onto the European service market has to be pointed out[14]. This new type of service sharing has raised questions among the so-called traditional taxi drivers: if and to what extent should the status of the sharing service providers be legally regulated. The same question arises in connection with other new forms of employment like crowdsourcing[15]. How to deal with crowdsourcing and whether the participants in crowdsourcing are employees or not?

The Estonian parliament – the *Riigikogu* has prepared draft legislation, which aims to regulate the legal status of sharing service providers. The so-called 'draft legislation of Uber'[16] establishes that sharing service providers shall be subject to contract provisions established in the Law of Obligations Act. The aim of such regulation is to avoid applying employment contracts for participants of the sharing economy. According to the wording of the draft legislation the application of the provisions of the ECA cannot be avoided. According to the ECA the provisions of the authorization agreement are applied in the employment contract. Hence – at least the abovementioned draft legislation does not exclude the possibility of also applying the employment contract regulation to the participants of the sharing economy.

For better legal regulation of new forms of employment, Estonian employers made proposals on how and under which conditions it is possible and necessary to change the working and rest time regulations in order to use project-based and short-term working on a wider scale. According to the vision of the Estonian employers the employment contract provision according to which the establishment of working time is requested by the legislation should be eliminated. The working

---

14 Digitalisation and working life: lessons from the Uber cases around Europe. Retrieved June 29, 2016 from http://www.eurofound.europa.eu/observatories/eurwork/articles/working-conditions-law-and-regulation/digitalisation-and-working-life-lessons-from-the-uber-cases-around-europe.

15 Felstiner A., *Working the Crowd: Employment and Labor Law in the Crowdsourcing Industry*, 2011. Retrieved June 29, 2016 from http://papers.ssrn.com/sol3/papers.cfm?abstract_id=1593853.

16 Ühistranspordiseaduse muutmise seadus 188 SE [Act amending the Public Transportation Act]. English translation may be retrieved from http://www.riigikogu.ee/tegevus/eelnoud/eelnou/17074c56-bf09-477f-befb-a6e4ea86461f/%C3%9Chistranspordiseaduse%20muutmise%20seadus/.

time shall be based on the mutual agreement of the parties. Alteration of the abovementioned provision would cause uncertainty primarily to the employee because the employee cannot plan his/her working and rest time. At the same time, the situation cannot be avoided in which an employee may work more than 40 hours per week and the maximum working time and the minimum rest time are not guaranteed to the employee.

Although Estonian employers made proposals in regard to the regulation of working time, the employers and the trade unions could also agree on how to make labour relations and the working time more flexible. The alteration of legislation might be a proper and necessary solution but it is not very quickly achieved if working time has to be made more flexible in a short time.

With the application of new forms of employment, the main question is whether and in which amount the legal regulation foreseen in the ECA should expand to such forms of employment? At this point we return to the features of labour relations via or by which it is possible to define the labour relations. In the case of labour relations an important aspect concerns the subordination of another person's orders during the work performance and the other party's obligation to pay remuneration for the performed work. This is where personal subordination is important; it means that the employee does not decide during the working time which work assignments have to be carried out by him/her. This definition of labour relations may be considered traditional or classical.

In the case of telework the employer cannot track how the employee uses his/her labour force. In the case of telework usually the aim is most important – an assignment has to be accomplished by a certain deadline. How and when the work assignment is completed by the employee remains beyond the employer's actual control. In case of crowdsourcing, employees themselves decide whether they want to contribute or not. Application of such work form (crowdsourcing) may require a certain kind of subordination because the product developer expects a certain input and prescribes activities that have to be carried out by the 'crowd'. As mentioned above, according to the Estonian ECA, the payment of remuneration is not a primary obligation. The primary aspect is to obey another party's orders in regard to the work performance. In the case of crowdsourcing such subordination can be established. If zero-hour contracts are applied, the work is also performed in subordination. Zero-hour contracts do not establish the number of hours per week the employee has to work. The actual need to perform work depends on the circumstances and the employer's needs. In the cases of zero-hour contracts also, to some extent the employee himself/herself decides upon the application of his/her labour force but is not totally free to do it. Namely – the employee never knows when and how much of his/her contribution is required by the employer.

In the presence of modern ways of doing work (teleworking, crowdsourcing, sharing service (e.g. Uber), it is difficult to define personal dependence from the employer. In the case of a sharing service, the question arises whether an employer exists at all, and if an employer exists, how and on which conditions can the platform be regarded as an employer? Thus, in the case of the ride-sharing service or accommodation-sharing service, the employer is not exactly definable. Both a client and service provider meet via an internet platform. It is not possible to define who exactly is behind the internet platform. Furthermore, it is also impossible to define whether a provider of opportunity to use such platform is a qualified employer or their legal representative. Therefore, the question now arises that if we are to handle a platform as a potential employer, then how can we inspect the health and safety rules at the employer's site, and what can we consider as the workplace, where occupational health and safety should be ensured and the working environment risk analysis performed. The spread of new ways of doing work and their actual application, to a great degree, needs specification and amendment of the occupational health safety requirements with the aim to ensure employees' occupational safety and mitigate health risks resulting from inappropriate working environments and dangers of accidents at work.

In the presence of modern forms of employment, it is no longer possible to draw on personal dependence on an employer. Since in the new circumstances employees are free to decide when they perform their work tasks (e.g. crowdsourcing), the assessment of economic dependence becomes significantly relevant. Therefore, in different countries, a new category of employee characteristics is available, i.e. economic dependence[17]. Thus, for instance, in the case of a sharing service or crowdsourcing no personal dependence can be expressly provided as an

---

[17] Economically dependent workers' employment law and industrial relations. Retrieved June 27, 2016 from http://www.eurofound.europa.eu/observatories/eurwork/comparative-information/economically-dependent-workers-employment-law-and-industrial-relations.

example. On the other hand, at least, indirect economic dependence is available. In the case of a sharing service, a platform administrator provides people with an opportunity to earn income. If the quality of service is not good enough, a ride-sharing service provider will be removed from the platform. So, there is an expressly defined relation with earning income.

Estonian legal literature also contains references to the usefulness of bringing in a category of employees regarded as economically dependent employees[18]. Validation of an economically dependent employees' category will bring about the situation when all such employees, who are mainly dependent on one employer will get the same protection that is provided for all employees who work under an ordinary employment contract, and against whom there are no doubts that this means an employee within the legal meaning of employment contract. A definition of economically dependent employee provides the aforesaid employee with the opportunity to get protection in compliance with the occupational health and safety requirements.

3. Occupational health and safety and legal regulation of the working time

In addition to the legal regulation of working time, ensuring the occupational health and safety requirements is significantly relevant. If the working time and rest time rules become more flexible (more unclear), it imposes specific limits to the occupational health and safety rules. It is more complicated to ensure the occupational health and safety rules, and the control over ensuring such rules is difficult too. The problems mentioned above are important, first of all, in the use of modern ways of employment. It is problematic to ensure safe working conditions in teleworking situations. In a situation, where an employee does most of his work in home conditions, the employer cannot control whether the employee takes the required rest time and whether all the required work equipment is sufficiently ergonomic. In addition, the competency of the labour inspectorate in performing checks over work conditions remains unresolved – whether and to what extent a labour inspector can enter the residential rooms of an employee when he needs to control

18 Haljasmäe R. Extension of Guarantees for Economically Dependent Workers. *Juridica Abstract*, No. 4, 2009, pp. 217–223; Haljasmäe R. Legal Protection of Economically Dependent Workers. *Juridica Abstract*, No. 4, 2007, pp. 274–280.

that occupational safety requirements are being fulfilled and ensured in a workplace?

There is a direct relation between flexible working time and ensuring occupational health and safety. Although, at first glance, it may seem that such relation is missing, it still exists. If an employee's work days become too long or working time is irregular, and the long working hours are not compensated by the necessary rest periods, it will result in work accidents caused by fatigue or, in the long term, by getting an occupational illness. Based on the Estonian Occupational Health and Safety Act (hereinafter OHSA), the main responsibility for meeting the occupational health and safety requirements rests with the employer[19]. However, the employer alone should not be liable for meeting all the occupational health and safety requirements. The OHSA also contains employee's obligations which they should follow in the course of doing their work.

Apart from general obligations in ensuring safe working conditions, the OHSA also contains more specific obligations for ensuring working time and rest time regime. In compliance with § 9 OHSA, an employer is obliged to ensure additional breaks for an employee in the case of monotonous or routine work. The abovementioned additional breaks are included in the working time. For instance, this situation may arise in the case of those who are constantly sitting at work or constantly standing (e.g. sales persons in shops). An employer should ensure additional breaks for a pregnant employee if they are necessary to ensure the health of both the mother and her child.

A separate document, based on the OHSA, which contains the requirements for computer use also provides for the necessity of additional breaks. Thus, the computer use requirements stipulate that an employee should take periodic breaks and the total periodic breaks during a working day should be not less than 10% of their working time[20].

The obligation of ensuring all the abovementioned requirements and compliance with them thereon is imposed on the employer. If an employee gets an occupational disease or an accident occurs that are caused by excessively long working hours or fatigue, the employer shall bear the main liability. The Estonian legal system lacks a separate insurance

19 § 13 of the Occupational Health and Safety Act (Töötervishoiu- ja tööohutuse seadus), RT I 1999, 60, 616. English translation may be retrieved from https://www.riigiteataja.ee/en/eli/520062016004/consolide.

20 Kuvariga töötamise töötervishoiu ja tööohutuse nõuded [Requirements for working with personal computer], RT I 2000, 86, 556.

mechanism which could protect employees or employers against different risks, caused by accident or occupational disease. Therefore, in the event of potential damage, an employee may and should submit a claim against their employer.

As for applying responsibility on the part of the employer, liability under public law has an important function in the Estonian legal system. In compliance with § 125 and 126 of the ECA, an employer shall be liable in an administrative way if they fail to comply with the requirements stipulated by the law and related to ensuring working time and rest time. In addition, the employer shall be liable under the public law if the night-time working requirements are not complied with. This liability under the public law means, first, a situation where the labour inspector may impose a public law fine. A public law fine may be adjudged both against a physical person, who acts as a representative of an employer or against a company as a legal body.

With the aim of ensuring occupational safety requirements, an employer should carry out a risk analysis on a workplace. The main task of a workplace risk analysis is to detect such risks that may impair an employee's health. According to Estonian labour legislation, an employer may not operate night shifts or shifts longer than twelve hours without compiling a workplace risk analysis. Should an employer not compile a working environment risk analysis he/she is liable to a monetary fine and, in addition to the private law, claims are possible on the part of employee, which relate to incorrect working time records and wrong application of the working time.

The abovementioned requirements to the working time organization can be found both in domestic law and the requirements imposed by the European Union. Taking into account, that the occupational health and safety directive was adopted in 1989, the new forms of employment were not widely spread (e.g. agency work, telework, crowdsourcing). In conformity with the Directive of 1989 it was, and is possible to meet such requirements, and the labour inspectorate can also control their performance.

With the new forms of employment, there is an inadvertent problem where all occupational health and safety requirements cannot be complied with, and meeting them cannot be ensured. In the case of a ride-sharing service, no working environment risk analysis can be performed, or no control guaranteed over the scope in which the occupational health and safety requirements are ensured. As far as no working environment risk analysis being performed, it is also impossible to control if, and to what extent one may talk about ensuring the occupational health and safety requirements in the case of the new forms of employment (e.g. remote working, crowdsourcing, platform working, etc.). Consequently it can be said that in the case of the new forms of employment it is not always possible to ensure that the occupational health and safety requirements are met to the full extent. Using flexible employment relations and, first of all, ensuring flexible working hours will lead to the situation where employers cannot ensure the current applicable occupational health and safety requirements, and the health inspector cannot control how and to what extent an employer performed such requirements at all. Consequently, amendment to the regulation of working time is not only related to ensuring employment contract conditions or payments made to the labour force, but to a significant degree it refers to ensuring the occupational health and safety requirements and ensuring control over meeting them. In the legal regulation of the new forms of employment it is important to ensure that employees are ensured primary occupational health and safety requirements. Even in a case when, for instance, no legal regulation against Uber's managers will lead to the provider of a ride-sharing service being regarded as an employee, the occupational health and safety requirements must be ensured.

The new forms of employment have failed to find significant legal regulation in the Estonian private labour law. Among the unusual ways of working, we can consider agency work and telework. Though both ways of doing work are provided for by the ECA, the legal regulation of the these ways of doing work has been poor. There is a reference to the fact that if work is done in this way there should be a separate agreement. In the case of agency work, attention is paid to subsequent conclusion of fixed-term employment contracts.

The OHSA also fails to stipulate the new opportunities for doing work. In terms of ensuring occupational safety, an important factor is shared liability in agency work in a situation where an accident occurs or occupational disease is diagnosed. The OHSA stipulates a requirement where employers agree on who,, and to what extent they shall be liable when a potential accident occurs. If such agreement is missing, employers who operate on the same object shall be jointly and severally liable for damages caused by accidents and occupational diseases.

In terms of other forms of employment, the OHSA provides no special requirements. So, general requirements shall apply. The labour inspectorate can only control the occupational health and safety requirements when the OHSA provides for such competence. The corresponding competence is defined through the employment relationship. Whereas a term of employment relationship is defined in Section 1 of the ECA, according to which if one person performs work for another, for which it is reasonable to assume payment of a fee, the question is in the employment relationship. In order to ensure meeting the occupational health and safety requirements in relation to the new forms of employment, firstly, it is necessary to clarify the existence of an employment relationship with regard to such ways of working, and, next, to check whether and to what extent the occupational health and safety requirements can be met. As previously mentioned, the existence of an employment relationship is accepted for two new ways of employment – telework and agency work. Other new ways of doing work have not been handled in Estonian legal literature or the case law.

Conclusions

The existence of new forms of employment poses a considerable challenge to working time regulation and the occupational health and safety requirements regulation. With the new forms of employment, it is not always possible to ensure currently applicable occupational health and safety requirements. This means that the legal regulation should be amended in the area of occupational health and safety so as to provide assurance of occupational safety requirements with regard to the new forms of employment, too. Alongside this, it is irrelevant whether an employee can and should always be qualified as an employee in the legal meaning of the employment relationship. With respect to ensuring the occupational health and safety requirements, it is important that employees who do work for someone else and who get paid for that work are protected with occupational health and safety requirements and that the labour inspectorate can carry out the corresponding control.

In most cases, the new ways of employment and flexible organization of employment relationships are related to making working time organization more flexible. Flexibility in employment relationships anticipates that an employee would be able to use their labour in a manner that is most profitable for the employer, and the employer could use the employee's labour whenever it is needed. When deciding about flexibility of working time regulation, there is a risk that an employee's labour may be misused and the danger of forced work occurs. Therefore, time limits for the purposes of the occupational health and safety requirements must be set. Such limits are necessary when working or another person and orders of another person are executed.

The formation and spread of new forms of employment are inevitable, and consequently the employment relationship regulations and occupational safety requirements must be amended. First of all, the scope of occupational health and safety should be expanded, beginning with execution of the requirements and increasing the list of persons, who should be responsible for executing the occupational health and safety requirements. The purpose should be established where any kind of doing work that is not expressively defined as doing work pursuant to a contract of services or authorization contract, is covered by occupational health and safety requirements.

New Limits of ICTs at Work

The Right to Disconnect from Them

Lourdes Mella MENDEZ*

Abstract

This study addresses the impact of the latest information and communication technologies, particularly smartphones and tablets, provided by companies to workers for professional use. It studies the impact it has on the employees' working hours and rest periods. In most cases, an extension of working hours (voluntary or forced) is observed, with the consequent negative impact on the physical and mental health of workers and their right to reconcile work and family life. This result forces companies – especially in France and Germany so far – to react with specific agreements establishing a series of measures to protect workers, including a right and duty to technological disconnection.

Keywords: new information and communication technologies, worker health, right to disconnect

Introduction

The new information and communication technologies (ICTs) applied to the employment relationship introduce flexibility in the services provided by the worker. These new working tools give way, from a classic and rigid working model, in the traditional workplace, to a new model, in which work can be carried out – thanks to technological instruments – in any place outside of the traditional business centre. This place can be

---

* Lourdes Mella Mendez is a Professor *(Acreditado)* of Labour Law and Social Security at the Faculty of Law, University of Santiago de Compostela (Galicia, Spain). She is the author and co-author of a large number of books on collective agreements, disciplinary sanctions, termination of employment, etc. She has published more than a hundred articles in various fields of labour law. Lourdes Mella Mendez is running projects of national and regional research and is the recipient of many national awards for Legal Research. This paper is a result of the National Research Project carried out by MINECO (Spain), titled 'Legal analysis of telework in Spanish and Comparative Law' (DER2013-43615-R), lead by Prof. Lourdes Mella.

the worker's home or any other place available to him. In addition, this ability to work anywhere is also accompanied by the freedom to do so at any time deemed appropriate by the worker. Certainly, the massive and unstoppable use of new ICTs, especially those that permit interactive communication, such as smartphones[1] electronic tablets and laptops, allow any worker to have all possible information over the internet and contact, at any time and place, with co-workers, employers, customers, suppliers and the general public.

The advantages of this new way of working are clear to the employer and employee. The latter can organize their personal and family interests with the professional ones better. An example of this is being able to adjust a schedule or working hours to meet family or personal requirements.

With these advantages there are also disadvantages arising from excessive and uncontrolled use of new technological tools. Certainly, the elimination of the rigid border between working time and rest may end up creating a situation in which work (labour services provided by the worker or certain tasks related to it) is present everywhere and the worker no longer has a fixed and authentic time of rest. In this sense, the previous rigid – and safe-border between times becomes increasingly porous and insecure, allowing filtration of work or, at least, of one activity of labour content in a temporary area that is not its own, and whose value is difficult to quantify[2].

The blurring of boundaries between work and rest time may lead to – in the extreme cases – the on-site or remote worker being forced to be a specific type of worker: the employee 24/7, on call worker who is always available to the employer and the new requirements of flexibility in working time (lexi-time work)[3]. As it is noted, the techno-invasion suffered by the ordinary citizen, leading to hyper or almost permanent connectivity (always online), has its inevitable reflection in the field of employment and the employee cannot escape it, leading to situations of 'digital labour exploitation or harassment'.

---

1 Mettling Br. *Transformation numérique et vie de travail.* Retrieved June 12, 2016 from http://www.franceculture.fr/2015-09-16-rapport-mettling-ce-que-le-numerique-change-au-travail.

2 Parent-Thirion A. *et al.*, *Fifth European Working Conditions Survey (2012).* Retrieved June 12, 2016 from https://www.eurofound.europa.eu/lt/publications/report/2012/working-conditions/fifth-european-working-conditions-survey-overview-report, p. 33.

3 *Ibidem*, p. 96. See also Mettling Br., *op. cit.*, p. 18; Pompa J. *Techno-stress and the right to disconnect.* LLRN Conference, Amsterdam, June 2015 *(first draft,* p. 4).

Thus, when the worker concludes their official working hours they are still involved in work and feel compelled to keep in touch with the company, and enters into a *sui generis* time[4]. The problem arises because, generally, this time of extraordinary labour is not considered as working time and, therefore, neither remuneration nor compensation[5] is made for it. This is despite the fact that the worker may feel obliged or compelled to be attentive to ICTs and respond accordingly if work is required.

This excessive connectivity can seriously affect their right to reconcile work and private life and health. Physical risks are due to poor body posture and continued use of a technological device in one fixed posture for a lengthy time. This manifests in headaches and pain of other body parts or even in deformities of limbs or other diseases related to physical inactivity[6].

However, the most important and emerging risks have a psychosocial nature, such as, on the one hand, the general work-related stress[7] or more specifically, the techno-stress, or its opposite, techno-addition, or even the broader addiction to work or to the habit of working (workaholics). Specifically, in relation to new technologies, technostress is generated when the worker subjectively perceived a mismatch between the high demands required and the scarce personal resources available for the proper use of the new technological tools at work.

On the other hand, the lack of labour disconnection can lead to the psychosocial risk of addiction to new ICTs. Therefore, we talk about the techno-addiction, which is configured as a kind of technological stress related to an uncontrollable compulsion to use new technology for long periods of time. Undoubtedly, the continuous work or business connection discussed here can contribute to the aforementioned dependence on the pretext of work motivation. Both types of psychosocial risks are often accompanied by specific and common side effects such as techno-fatigue,

---

4 *Work-Life Survey of American Psychological Association* (September 2015), pp. 7, 16. Retrieved June 1, 2016 from http://www.apaexcellence.org/assets/general/2015-work-life-survey-results.pdf.

5 In France, the trade union UGICT-CGT claims the labour character of this working time http://ugict.cgt.fr/deconnexion/a-propos-de-la-camapgne/.

6 Pompa J. *The Janus face of the 'New Ways of Work'. Rise, Risks and regulation of nomadic work. Working Paper.* Brussels: European Trade Union Institute, 2013, pp. 10 et seq.

7 Salanova M. Working with technologies and addressing Technostress: the role of efficacy beliefs. *Journal of industrial and organizational psychology,* 2003, No. 19, pp. 225-247. See also Article 3 of the European Framework Agreement of 8 October 2004 on work-related stress.

techno-anxiety[8], techno-phobia or information overload[9]; the latter generates the so-called 'informative fatigue' syndrome[10].

Currently, it is undeniable that the employer has a duty to take the necessary measures to ensure workers' health, protecting them from all risks, including the psychosocial ones derived from interaction with communication technologies. In this regard, although Directive 89/391/EEC of 12 June 1989 on the introduction of measures to encourage improvements in the health and safety of workers at work (Framework Directive), does not directly refer to such risks, its broad terms allow us to understand that the employer should still be concerned about them, because their duty of protection refers to '*all* aspects related to work' (Article 5.1).

The framework agreements negotiated by the European social partners have also been increasingly alluding to the risks arising from new technologies and, in general, the psychosocial ones. So, it is arguable that the European Framework Agreement on Telework of 16 July 2002 requires the employer to ensure extensive worker protection against all types of risk, even without specific mention of those. More specific in the matter is the European Framework Agreement on work-related stress, already mentioned, which, although it does not expressly refer to technological stress, is emphatic about the employer duty of preventing and, if necessary, solving the issue of work stress, whatever its cause.

Recently, in a very specific sector, Directive 2010/32/EU of the Council of 10 May 2010, implements the Framework Agreement on prevention of injuries caused by sharp instruments in the hospital and healthcare sector, concluded by HOSPEEM (European Hospital and Healthcare Employers' Association) and EPSU (European Federation of Public Services Union). This Directive already provides expressly that: 1) the employer is obliged to ensure the health and safety of workers in every aspect related to work, including 'psychosocial factors and work organization' (clause 4.3) and 2) the risk assessment must take

8 Mettling Br., *op. cit.*, p. 35.

9 Agreement on the prevention of psychosocial risks of the Association of French Executives (APEC) of 28 February 2013. Retrieved June 23, 2016 from http://www.wk-rh.fr/actualites/upload/Apec-accord-RPS.pdf. See also Mettling Br., *op. cit.*. p. 52.

10 This term was used for the first time by the British psychologist David Lewis in the 1990s, in its report *Dying for information?* The company commissioned by Reuters. See *The Reuters Guide to Good Information Strategy*. Retrieved June 24, 2016 from http://jmab.planetaclix.pt/GesInf/Aula5/.

into account various elements such as, for example, technology, work organization and psychosocial factors (clause 5.3).

The new European Strategy for Health and Safety at Work (2014-2020) insists on this and highlights the need to improve the prevention of work-related diseases to address new and emerging occupational hazards. More specifically, it is specified that changes in work organization that have been enabled by the new information technologies, particularly those that enable seamless connectivity, open up enormous possibilities for flexible and interactive work, which manifests itself in a multiplicity new ways of working and types of workers.

On the other hand, the protection of the health of workers can also come through the specific working time regulations, by requiring in this regulation strict compliance with all maximum working time and minimum rest periods. Thus, it is of extreme interest to Directive 2003/88/EC of the European Parliament and of the Council of 4 November 2003, concerning certain aspects of the organization of working time, and it establishes – linking both aspects – 'minimum provisions on safety and health for the organization on the matter of working time' (Article 1). In order to ensure the health of workers, including those who work outside of the working time and the traditional workplace, it is essential to respect the rights under the Directive in relation to the daily, weekly and annual minimum, uninterrupted breaks and, with the limitation of the maximum working week of forty-eight hours[11].

Any rest period interrupted by work should be added in calculations of the maximum duration of daily and weekly working hours and remunerated for[12].

1. The Technological Disconnection as a New Worker Right and Duty of the Employer

Given the clear importance of ensuring the safety and health of workers, Directive 2003/88/EC, calls on Member States to take measures to guarantee that the worker has an adequate and effective rest period

---

11 On the importance of respecting the maximum duration of 48 hours, see CJEU case C-243/2009, since this cap is a non-derogable minimum.

12 Judgment of the Court of Appeal of Grenoble (France) of 30 January 2014. See *Du meilleur usage des outils de communication numérique dans les entreprises*. Observatoire de la Responsabilité Sociétale des Entreprises, January 2015, p. 52.

(Arts. 3-6). Logically, those states do not assume this responsibility directly, but they assign it to the employer. At this point, it is worth noting the interesting transposition of this in the UK. The original *Working Time Regulations 1998 (No. 1833)* were accompanied by a guide developed by the Department of Trade and Industry, whose sections 5 and 6 established that obligation of the employer was observed to give the worker a chance to rest. The employer needs to present employees with the opportunity for rest without the obligation to ensure that the worker effectively rested[13]. The legislator understood that the worker was ultimately responsible for what was done with periods of rest and, in any case, the employer could not go further, and so the latter did not have the obligation to ensure that such periods were really enjoyed. However, the CJEU disagreed with this position and stated that such provisions have an adverse reinterpretation of the rights enshrined in the EU Directive and left them without effect violating the ultimate purpose of that Directive[14].

It is concluded that the employer has a duty to ensure that the worker (also the one who has some autonomy to organize themselves) effectively observes their right to rest, and it may be necessary to perform special surveillance of the workers' health and, where appropriate, take the necessary and appropriate measures of protection. In any case, it seems clear that the attitude of the employer must be active in the control and monitoring of employee work time; because the responsibility for ensuring the safety and health of workers is an obligation of result.

In order to avoid the specific risks arising from excessive use of new technologies that prevent the enjoyment of rest periods, in some European countries – especially in Germany and France – some agreements or specific measures are being adopted in order to limit or avoid the excessive use of technologies, especially recognizing the right of workers to turn off their cell phones and laptops outside working hours. In other words, the right of workers to the technological disconnection or to be un-reachable or out of contact is being recognized, despite having a technological device that allows them interactive and immediate communication with

---

13 Sections 5 and 6 of the aforementioned guidelines: 'employers must make sure that workers can take their rest, but are not required to make sure they do take their rest". Retrieved June 25, 2016 from

http://webarchive.nationalarchives.gov.uk/20070603164510/http://www.dti.gov.uk/employment/employment-legislation/employment-guidance/page28979.html.

14 CJEU case C-484/04, paras 40, 42, 44 and 47 of the judgement.

the company at any time. All this with the ultimate goal of controlling the limits of the working day and preventing the invasion of this in the sacred minimum rest periods of workers.

In the case of Germany, Volkswagen pioneered an agreement of this nature in 2011. It was then followed by its competitors Daimler-Benz and BMW.

In France, trade unions are demanding measures to improve working conditions, especially in order to avoid work overload (physical and mental), which has been leading to a high number of sick-days caused by stress, exhaustion and depression, and even in the telecommunications sector (especially France Telecom, now Orange), to an abnormal and alarming number of suicides. Thus, the growing awareness of the scale of the problem by enterprises has begun to slowly lead to the negotiation and signing of specific agreements to control the excessive use of new technologies as tools, as well as the effective enjoyment of rest time by workers.

We can also refer to, for example, Article 7.3 of the Agreement in favour of professional equality between women and men and gender diversity within companies of the Renault group, of 16 May 2012, which establishes no obligation on the worker to respond to messages received outside working hours (especially in the evenings and weekends)[15]. Similarly, Article 17 of the French Inter-professional National Agreement on a policy of improving life at work and professional equality, of 19 June 2013 (valid for three years), states the need to 'promote a smart management of information and communication technologies at the service of the competitiveness of enterprises, respectful with the privacy of workers'. In this regard, this agreement adds that the company should choose the means of reconciling personal and professional life more suited to the characteristics of it, being able to establish 'a few timeouts, as already practiced in some companies'[16].

More important is a sectoral collective agreement of 1 April 2014, concluded between the employer SYNTEC and CINOV and CFDT and CFE-CGC trade *unions*. This agreement amends Article 4 of Chapter 2 of the National Agreement of 22 June 1999, on the duration of working time in the field of technical consulting, engineering, computer services,

15 Retrieved June 27, 2016 from http://www.cfdtrenault.com/content/archives/3811_Accord_du_16_mai_egalite_hommes_femmes_V_signee.pdf.

16 Retrieved June 27, 2016 from http://www.cfecgc.org/content/externals/docs.php?action=open&id=1356.

human resources and consulting[17]. The new paragraph 8 of that provision is especially interesting as, in a novel way it sets off an obligation of disconnection for the worker, although the employer is affected too, as will be seen below[18].

Meanwhile, the aforementioned Mettling report of September 2015, commissioned by the Ministry of Labour, Employment, Vocational Training and Social Dialogue, in order to develop a bill to reform the labour market, strengthens trade union arguments by stating that technological disconnection is a matter to be seriously assessed for its implications on the health and privacy of the worker. The right of workers to technological disconnection is configured as a different right to the other right to have a minimum rest period, although, in a certain way, one can say that that one has an instrumental character with respect to the latter, as it facilitates its achievement and effectiveness[19].

2. Specific Collective Agreements for the Protection of Workers against the Abuse of New ICTs

2.1 General features

The first agreements which are being negotiated in order to regulate the use of technological tools of communication and guarantee the rights to the maximum working time and rest time, through the right to disconnection, are, as already noted, mostly of enterprise level. In this regard, the most important are those adopted in the already mentioned countries of Germany and France (for example, in the first country, the aforementioned companies in the automotive sector and, in the latter, Areva, Sodexo, Atos, Orange or O'zone), although gradually some agreements are beginning to be negotiated at the sectoral level. In France, besides the SYNTEC agreement, it is possible to refer to other similar recently achieved ones in the fields of jewellery and metalwork[20];

[17] IDCC 1486.

[18] Retrieved June 27, 2016 from http://ugict.cgt.fr/deconnexion/.

[19] Judgment of the French Court of Cassation of 17 February 2004 (No. appeal 01-45889). Also cited in the report *Du meilleur des outils de communication usage numérique dans les entreprises, op. cit.* Judgment of the French Court of Cassation of 29 June 2011 (No. resource 09-71.107). Retrieved June 27, 2016 from http://www.legavox.fr/blog/maitre-haddad-sabine/juin-2011-conditions-forfait-jours-5980.pdf.

[20] National collective agreement of 31 January 2014, concerning working time (Brochure No. 3051; NOR: ASET 1450315M, IDCC: 567). See Mettling Br., *op. cit.*, p. 31.

general insurance agencies[21], oil industry[22] and brokerages insurance and reinsurance[23].

In general, the negotiating initiative belongs to the social part, i.e. the unitary representatives (works council) or the sectoral unions. However, as a case in which the initiative of the agreement arises from the business side, we can mention the Daimler-Benz case. On this occasion, in order to increase workforce productivity, the employer commissioned a study on the situation of the reconciliation of work and private lives of their employees and, in view of its disturbing results, he decided to introduce technological disconnection measures in order to protect their health and thereby fulfil their duty in this matter.

As regards the subjective scope of the right or the measures to technological disconnection, most of the agreements analysed are naturally cautious, and start recognizing that right only to ordinary employees, excluding senior ones, who enjoy powers and autonomy, and who are required to have greater availability due to the responsibility assumed or position held within the company. In front of this restrictive position, the ambition of the SYNTEC agreement must be praised; it is applied to all employers and workers in the sector concerned, even to those in positions of management or administration and who enjoy full autonomy to organize their working time. More clearly, the latter are workers with powers of command, who perform executive or management within the company and are subject to a flexible annual working time that, even if agreed with the employer, they can manage freely, particularly with regard to the time dedicated to performing the work activity. For such workers, the said

21 Article 7 of the National collective agreement of 30 October 2014 (IDCC 2335), amending the national collective agreement of 20 December 2000 concerning working time. See Mettling Br., *op. cit.*, p. 31.

22 In a similar direction, may also be highlighted the national collective agreement in 'the oil industry', recently amended by Article 7 agreement of 27 November 2014 (effective from January 1, 2015), which adds to that national agreement the article 1114 bis, entitled 'use of information and communication tools'. Under that provision, in principle, the professional use of information and communication tools made available to workers by the employer is limited to working time. The worker is not subject, in general, to an obligation of connection to the servers of the company outside of working hours, except in exceptional cases.

23 Article 3, paragraphs 6 and 7, the national collective agreement of 19 November 2014, amending the previous agreement of 12 May 1999, on the reduction and development of the time work of the companies in the insurance brokerage and reinsurance industry (Brochure No. 3110; NOR: ASET1550212M, IDCC: 2247). See Mettling Br., *op. cit.*, p. 31.

Agreement also provides, expressly, the right to enjoy the minimum rest periods established – with general character – in Directive 2003/88/ EC, namely those of eleven hours of rest between working days and thirty-five (twenty-four plus eleven) hours between weeks. Thus, although the Agreement is applied to all workers and entrepreneurs, it is remarkable as it focuses on the worker who enjoys full autonomy to organize itself. The agreement wants to protect this type of worker, first, recognizing for him the same minimum rest periods as any other worker and then making him responsible for the exercise and effective enjoyment of it.

Moreover, most of these specific agreements are not binding on the parties, but they act as codes of conduct or recommendations for those, reflecting the will to introduce measures of technological disconnection slowly. Sometimes, the company only offers some opportunities for disconnection to the worker and then he can use them at will (as in the Daimler case) or establish a clause according to which it is not expected that the worker respond to electronic messages outside of working hours, but it is left to him to decide on the importance of the message.

In order to protect the worker, the other agreement (such as SYNTEC) is better; it clearly and conclusively establishes the obligation to disconnect both the worker and the employer, as will be seen below. In addition, this agreement is legally binding, since it is based on the right to health and safety of workers and enshrined in Article 4 of a general agreement of 1999. This latter agreement implements the French law on working time 1998.

2.2 The right and the duty of disconnection of the worker

As regards its content, these agreements typically provide a general statement of rights, especially for the worker, and then in some cases – most interesting – certain measures are detailed to try to ensure their effectiveness. The obligations established in this regard often affect both the worker and the employer, which is valued as the ideal approach. In the following pages, the basic points of the content of such collective agreements are discussed. Thus, from the point of view of the worker, note that:

a) *The recognition of the right to disconnect also entails the duty to disconnect from technology tools*. In this sense, one of the first companies to regulate the intelligent and rational use of new information and communication technologies was French Areva. It does this in an agreement of 2012, in which the right of the worker to disconnect is recognized, whatever their position in the company. This agreement also provides the duty of the employee to disconnect from the network and for the prohibition of sending emails outside working hours[24].

In relation to the sector level, the aforementioned SYNTEC agreement, first, recognizes the right of workers to enjoy minimum rest times laid down in the EU Directive, and then it remembers that these minimum rest periods do not have to define a regular working day of thirteen hours per day, but the possible 'maximum and exceptional breadth' of a working day. After setting the normal working day – usually less than thirteen hours – and the working week, the need to respect rest times indicated is repeated and, for this purpose, in order to ensure compliance, it sets – in a new form – *the worker's obligation to disconnect* from remote communication tools (Article 4.8.1, fifth paragraph).

Thus, the right to rest also carries a secondary or instrumental duty to the beneficiary, as the disconnection of the technological apparatus (with which the employee works) seems the first and essential step for the observance of that right (although it should not be forgotten that, indeed, the worker can continue performing other tasks, such as reading or studying reports, manually writing and similar activities). But it is necessary to insist on the danger that seems to be especially found in the excessive use or addiction to a technological device, and which keeps the workers connected with the company and facilitates that it can send them ongoing labour tasks.

b) *The employee must inform the employer of the problems that prevent the enjoyment of minimum rest.* As an example of the reasonable and prudent conduct that the employee must adopt, it is expected that, in the case of having a subjective assessment that they will not respect the minimum rest times, he or she can go to their employer and warn them about this, in order to find a solution that allows him or her to remedy the situation and enjoy some time of rest. Article 4.8.1, tenth paragraph, of the modified SYNTEC agreement establishes this information to the employer as a mere

---

24 Article 20 of the collective agreement on the development of the quality of life at work in the AREVA group in France from May 31, 2012. Retrieved July 2, 2016 from http://yves.lasfargue.pagespersoorange.fr/03Teletravail/accordAREVA2012.htm.

Similarly Thales Group expressed on the quality of life at work in its Agreement of February 4, 2014. See *Du meilleur des outils de commication usage numérique dans les entreprises*, *op. cit.*, p. 49.

possibility or right to the worker ('*il peut*' and not 'must', according to the autonomy enjoyed). The article 8.2 third paragraph of that agreement reinforces this action and it is imperative, by providing for the need for the worker to have informed their superior of the elements or circumstances that may arise with an increase of work load, which may indirectly prevent the enjoyment of their leisure time.

In cases of exceptional difficulty regarding organizational aspects, workload or a problem linked to professional isolation, the worker can send a written notice (or written warning) to the employer or his representative, who will meet with them within the following eight days and, thereafter, the employer will draw up in writing the measures to be taken to solve the problem posed (Article 4.8.2, fifth paragraph). In order to ensure its effectiveness, it is expected that these measures are the subject of a written report and evaluated, and although it is not stated by whom, it seems that such obligations may lie both in the business, or left with the worker [25].

2.3 Specific protection measures to be taken by the employer

Regardless of the obligations required of the worker, the analysed agreements usually also establish obligations to be observed by the employer, after all they are the holder of the managerial and organizational power apart from the responsibility for the safety and health of workers. Accordingly, the commented agreements require:

a) *The employer exerts his management and control to ensure proper compliance with the maximum working hours, without excesses, by the worker himself.* Thus, a collective agreement provides that the employer has 'an obligation to remind the worker that the professional equipment made available (computer, mobile phone) should not be used during break time'[26].

---

[25] In a similar sense, Article 8 of Agreement No. 3 of 30 October 2014, amending the national collective agreement of December 20, 2000, in relation to the staff of the general insurance agencies.

[26] *Convention collective nationale des hôtels, cafes restaurants (HCR) du 30 avril 1997 – Textes Attachés – Avenant No. 22 du 16 décembre 2014 relatif aux cadres autonomes* (IDCC 1979). Article 2.4. Retrieved June 27, 2016 from https://www.legifrance.gouv.fr/affichIDCC.do;jsessionid=D9D9E2086E281D132591BD5A8091243B.tpdila08v_1?idConvention=KALICONT000005635534&cidTexte=KALITEXT000030590674&dateTexte.

More incisive is the renewed SYNTEC Agreement, repeatedly cited, which states that 'in order to guarantee the right to health, security, rest and work-life balance', the employer who has entered into a labour agreement with a worker must ensure the regular monitoring of their work organization, especially 'the workload and the extent of their working hours'. The latter two aspects should allow workers to reconcile work and private life (Article 4.8.2).

In order to complement the obligation to disconnection of the worker, as already mentioned, it is required that the employer install *a* monitoring tool to ensure that the employee complies with his right and duty regarding rest periods. For the sake of effectiveness of such monitoring, it is also indicated that such a technical tool should allow activation of an alert when the worker exceeds the working time or starts to default on – by continuing working – what should be the rest (Article 4.8.1 sixth paragraph and 2, fourth paragraph). Therefore, it seems that this instrument helps or guides the employee, by indicating to them that they have already fulfilled their maximum working hours and must start to rest. It also guides the employer, as it refers to the exercise of their power of control and supervision of labour activity. In short what is relevant is that the employer takes the necessary measures to ensure that the worker has the possibility to disconnect technologically from the interactive communication tools at their disposal (ibid., seventh paragraph).

On the other hand, among the technical measures to help the worker in the enjoyment of their time of rest, are:

1) Switching off the sounds and vibrations that notify of incoming emails or electronic messages. The elimination of these immediate and simultaneous sounds of arrival of information via electronic do not prevent the worker from communicating – even in an asynchronous or delayed way – with the message sender[27].
2) Blocking the technical and work-related functions installed on the mobile device at the end of the day or from a certain time onwards. In this case, what is sought is complete disconnection, preventing the worker-company contacts – even with nuances – once the workday has finished and during the time off or between labour days. As an example, the agreement of the German Volkswagen Company establishes the disconnection of the electronic servers

[27] Renault Agreement, at Mettling Br., *op. cit.*, p. 31.

and prevents the connection of the worker with the company and vice versa from 18:15 (end of working day) until 7 am the next morning, and during the weekend. The measure is referred to the professional smartphones provided by the company to the worker to perform their work task, leaving the simple operational function to send and receive phone calls. Due to its success, this measure, although initially addressed only to the group of managers, from 2011 has been spread to the entire workforce. However, other German companies reject the measure, as the managers want to be contacted outside working hours, receive and read messages at their own pace, which is very difficult during working hours[28].

In France, the company Gie Réunica recognizes, first, in an enterprise agreement (of 28 February 2013) that both work outside of working hours and the use of new technologies have psychosocial risk factors, and then it proceeds to implement (the 29 January 2014) a similar measure to avoid these factors. Thus, the main electronic server of the enterprise blocks incoming messages on emails of the workers from 8 pm in the evening to 7 am in the morning of the next day and the weekend (8 pm on Friday to 7 am the following Monday). During these imposed electronic closures, the worker can send messages, but cannot receive them, thus, somehow, the possibility of doing some work is left with the worker, but without pressure from the other side. However, certain exceptions to this information blockade are allowed in relation to some senior positions[29].

b) *The employer exerts their management and control to ensure the correct behaviour of the directors and subordinates of the company in this matter.* The management and control of power can be addressed to control not only the worker, but also the rest of the managers of the company, preventing them from falling into abusive behaviours with regard to workload and working time that the worker must comply with. In this regard, it is recommended to give clear orders on the need to respect the maximum working hours and, correspondingly, the rest time, which can be accompanied by the wording of some written rules about it,

28 *Du meilleur des outils de communication usage numérique dans les entreprises, op cit.*, p. 13.

29 Article 3.3 of the Amendment No. 7 of the protocol agreement of working time. Retrieved July 3, 2016 from http://www.wk-rh.fr/actualites/upload/Avenant-reunica.pdf.

as a code of conduct on the proper use of email or electronic messages in general[30]. Thus, the content of these references may refer, for example: 1) to that electronic messaging should not be the only possible way of communication between managers and employees, so there is the need to restore and enhance verbal communication before electronic communication 2) the use of electronic messaging responsibly, which means the limitation, on one hand, of its use to the strictly necessary, and, on the other hand, of the number of recipients of a message to those that are essential, without saturating in an inappropriate and unnecessary way the companions' mailbox; or, finally, 3) the ban on sending messages during the time of daily rest (for example, from 8 pm. to 8 am), days off, on vacation or the suspension days of the contract for other reasons (illness, accident)[31].

To demand that managers become examples in the proper management of the new digital tools with regard to the respect for the rest rights of the users, the employer can install a device: 1) to generate an automatic response on the computers of issuers (managers, peers) when they intend to contact a worker in the hours of rest or in the final minutes of the working day; so the system will ask him about the real need to send an email at that moment[32]; 2) to control the number of emails received by the employee during the working day and the still pending tasks at that time, which will allow access to the actual workload that do not support the opportunity to send a new message with a new assignment[33]; 3) to send an automatic notice that the recipient of the email is simply out of office or, more precisely, enjoying their time off.

---

30 See, in this regard, the letter of recommendation from use of email (Charte des 9 principes de l'email-attitude) of the company SODEXO. Retrieved July 2, 2016 from http://fr.sodexo.com/frfr/Images/Les_9_principes_de_l_email_attitude334-669924.pdf.

31 See Article 3.1.3 of the agreement on prevention of psychosocial risks of the Association of French executives (APEC) of 28 February 2013 and Article 3.3 of Amendment No. 7 of protocol agreement replacing the working time of the company Gie Réunica. See also Article 5.3 of the collective agreement signed on establishment of nomadism BNP Paribas on September 24, 2013. Retrieved 3 July, 2016 from http://gps.teletravail.free.fr/BDDaccords/2013%20Accords%20TW/2013-09-17accord%20nomadisme%20BNP% 202013.pdf.

32 Article 20 of the collective agreement on the development of the quality of life at work in the AREVA group in France from May 31, 2012.

33 Mettling Br., *op. cit.*, p. 31. See also Article 20 of the collective agreement on the development of the quality of life at work in the AREVA group in France from May 31, 2012.

To ensure no interruption of annual leave, we can send out automated messages such as 'mail on holiday' installed by the German company Daimler-Benz in digital tools given to their workers. In this case, the aim is to guarantee that the minimum annual leave of the employee is not disturbed with labour issues, so when employees are enjoying their holidays and receive an email, the mechanism sends an automatic reply message to the sender advising him of the absence of the worker and its reason. At the same time, the mechanism redirects the sender to other available colleagues or invites them to reconnect with the recipient after the rest period has ended; to such effect the return date is indicated. The device has the ability to enable, at the wish of the employee, an option for automatic deletion of all emails received during the holidays[34].

c) *The employer is to take preventive measures involving hearings with the worker.* The worker may inform the employer of the anticipated difficulty of respecting rest periods, the latter can also take the initiative too and organize a meeting with the employee concerned. In this regard, the French Agreement SYNTEC insists on several occasions of this type of preventative measure, which consist of a personal and individual interview with the worker and seems the most direct and effective way of finding effective solutions to this type of problem. On the one hand, Article 4.8.2, sixth paragraph of this Agreement provides that an employer can make an appointment with a worker when they recognize that the organization of work adopted by the employee – within their autonomy to do so – can lead to 'abnormal situations' and it is in order to take corrective measures to prevent those situations. On the other hand, Article 4.8.3 of the Agreement provides that the employer must convene at least two individual interviews a year with the worker, in order to monitor the compliance with the rules on working time and rest, as well as their health and safety, without prejudice to other specific interviews in case of 'unusual hardship'[35].

These provisions make it clear that the role of the employer is not passive, so they do not have to limit themselves to responding to the present problems, but they can anticipate them and act to solve the first sign of the worker's inability to respect their minimum rest periods.

34 Mettling Br., *op. cit.*, p. 22.

35 Article 8 of the Agreement of 30 October 2014 amending the national collective agreement of December 20, 2000 for the staff of the general insurance agencies.

d) *The employer to adopt preventive measures involving awareness and specific training regarding the proper handling of digital instruments used as working tools.* Without a doubt, the new challenges and labour risks arising from new technologies must be evaluated seriously with regards to their potential impact on worker health. Such analysis may allow for an indication of groups or individuals at risk and compulsive and dangerous behaviours, which require corrective and preventive urgent measures for the future. Therefore, after obtaining this data and objective results, it is essential to carry out specific information, training and awareness actions in this matter targeted at individuals or groups at risk of suffering serious problems of technological addiction. At the preventive level, the same or similar information and training actions must be open to all employees and directors of the company, as well as the unitary and union representatives and members of prevention of occupational hazards[36] teams.

Such training should be comprehensive, addressing all physical, psychological and even ethical aspects of the use of the new technologies – according to the rules of each country and company – that affect the development of work and private and social life of all employees. The inclusion of the deontological and ethical aspects is justified as the aim is not only to teach the simple handling of the device, but rather 'a digital awareness' about the meaning and limits of that use[37]. In order to raise awareness of all personnel in the proper use of new technologies, including the directors of the company, different measures or campaigns, even symbolic, such as those relating to the establishment of a day or half day a month without mail, or, more generally, without electronic messages, can be taken. The goal is to remember the importance of traditional, personal and direct oral communication, promote the exchange of information and ideas and creative and collaborative group work, while facilitating relaxation or technological 'detoxification' or even the breakdown or the decrease of the dependence on technological apparatus, which, as already noted, carries significant risks for the worker[38].

---

36 Mettling Br., *op. cit.*, p. 52.

37 Mettling Br., *op. cit.*, p. 33. See also agreement of February 4, 2014 on the quality of life at work in the Thales Group, in: *Du meilleur des outils de communication usage numérique dans les entreprises*, *op cit.*, p. 49. Also Article 9.2 of the agreement on telework in Thales. Retrieved July 26, 2016 from http://www.wk-rh.fr/actualites/upload/accord-teletravail-thales.pdf.

38 For several years some companies like INTEL instituted (even in a voluntary way) a measure with the motto 'zero e-mail Fridays'. Retrieved June 27, 2016 from

e) *The employer to report to the bodies responsible for prevention of the labour risks detected in the use of digital tools.* In this field, the SYNTEC agreement also provides the employer's obligation to inform the competent bodies in safety and health, namely the Committee of Hygiene, Safety and Working Conditions or, failing that, to staff representatives, about the number of alerts or notices sent by workers, as well as the measures taken to address the problem posed (Article 4.8.2 seventh paragraph).

Conclusions

In view of the new information revealed above, it is clear that the introduction of the latest ICT at work has a revolutionary importance in the transformation of the employment relationship and the lives of working people. Therefore, this rigorous and complete treatment through collective autonomy, both at a corporate and sectoral level. In this regard, it is clear that social dialogue and, particularly, the conventional route, are the most appropriate means of reconciling the interests of workers and social progress, especially in an open and new digital economy, with permanent and fast economic mutations. Thus, it is recommended that social partners are open – first – to a genuine process of reflection and debate on the overall impact of new technological tools in the company and in the lives of working people, in order to establish – after – codes of conduct or guides of good use of technological tools[39].

Regarding technological disconnection, this negotiation between social partners allows for an investigation of the most suitable solution for each case depending on the nature of the industry or business activity and responsibility, functions or tasks to be performed by the worker, which can even justify the inclusion of certain nuances or exceptions to that disconnection. If collective autonomy succeeds in negotiating on the impact of new technologies on the employment relationship and fills the gap that now begins to exist regarding worker protection, the legislator will no longer need to regulate the matter directly.

---

http://usatoday30.usatoday.com/tech/techinvestor/corporatenews/2007-10-04-no-email_N.htm and http://fr.atos.net/fr-fr/accueil/notre-profil/zero-email.html. See also Mettling Br., *op. cit.*, p. 32.

39 Guide for good use of technological tools in DG Trésor, in: *Du meilleur des outils de communication usage numérique dans les entreprises*, *op. cit.*, pp. 19-20; 40–42.

In this sense, it does not seem advisable to seek the recognition of the general right to technological disconnection in Directive 2003/88/EC, currently under review. Such consideration is based on the fact that the Directive, on the one hand, is sufficiently protective in its current Articles 3, 5 and 7 in relation to what should be a rest period for the worker (as it relates to minimum periods, consecutive and uninterrupted periods of rest), so rather than its modification, the next step is to demand the strict compliance in order to protect the health of workers. On the other hand, the objective of the Directive is to lay down minimum requirements for Member States, which allows for collective bargaining for the social partners, by understanding it the best choice to get specific protection measures adapted to each case (Article 15).

The commitment to collective bargaining as the most appropriate way to regulate the procedures for exercising the right to disconnect is the clear choice of the French legislator. Indeed, the current proposal for labour reform in France[40] includes a modification of the Labour Code (Article L. 2242-8, paragraph 2.7) to include, as a specific point to negotiate collectively and annually, within the aspects related to quality of life and work, 'the modalities of exercise by the worker of the right to disconnect from the use of IT tools to ensure the respect of rest and vacation time'. Thus, it is considered essential that collective bargaining focus its attention on the consequences, disadvantages or burdens that technological tools provided by the company entail for workers. Collective bargaining cannot be left out of this debate, because the issue is relevant and the aim is to ensure the effectiveness of the right to rest, especially for workers who are regular users of IT tools.

As the mentioned bill expressly stated, the objective is to get a significant increase in collective agreements in the matter concerning the use of new ICTs and that the parties concerned find the most appropriate solutions to reconcile the use of these tools with the health and private life of workers, therefore, the intervention of the legislator, although very important, is intentionally limited. The latter is satisfied by recognizing, first, the legal right to technological disconnection in the Labour Code, and secondly, allocating to social partners the responsibility and freedom to agree its various forms. Direct negotiation with workers and their representatives will be essential and will enable the social parties to

40 Article 25 of the Bill aimed at instituting new freedoms and new protections for businesses and assets, sent to the National Assembly on March 24, 2016.

develop the '*bien faire son travail*' and consequently reduce the impact of stress and other psychosocial risks.

As the varieties for exercising the right to disconnect are in direct correlation with the internal organization, the production process and the characteristics of each business entity and its employees, it is logical that its concretization is forwarded to *enterprise bargaining*, and not sector. It is presumed that this negotiating area is the ideal place to find the most appropriate measure for the circumstances of each case, as the impact of new ICTs is not the same for all workers and companies. Each company must build its own system of governance based on their particular circumstances.

In the absence of a collective agreement, the employer must unilaterally define these modalities of disconnection and communicate them, by all means, to their workers. Thus, if social dialogue fails, the solution is not the non-existence of the adoption of the measures, but that the employer, by virtue of his organizational and executive power, will be responsible for the implementation of that type of measure, in order to effectively protect the health and rest of workers.

In companies with a large workforce – of 300 or more workers – these modalities will be reflected in *a letter* drafted informing a work council or, in their case, to the appropriate delegates. This document states the implementation, among others, of training and awareness actions on the use of IT tools, especially targeted at the workers and training and management staff. If the reform succeeds, the entry into force of these provisions is planned for 1 January 2018, to give some time for collective bargaining to be effective.

When writing this, it was expected that the aforementioned bill would pass in the neighbouring country and increase the negotiating power to specific agreements to protect workers against excessive use of new ICTs. If achieved, this objective, in the French case will serve as an example in other European countries related to the adequate way of protecting the health of workers.

A New Approach of Flexicurity

The Importance of *Pacta Sunt Servanda* and *Clausula Rebus Sic Stantibus* in employment relationship

György Kiss*

Abstract

This study presents a possible new approach to so-called flexicurity. Starting points are two substantial attributes of the employment relationship, namely the legal subordination of the employee and long-term nature of this relationship. These attributes are correlated with each other. Labour law is the law protecting the employee, as a counterbalance to the employee's subordination. Nevertheless, the applicability of civil law principles in the labour law seems practically unquestionable. For this reason, it makes a difference how the legislator wants to provide this protection and with what tools. A new interpretation of the contract has appeared in commercial law: long-term contract as a 'relational contract'. The recent literature asks, 'how relational is the employment contract?' This study tries to analyse the possibilities of such solution.**

Key words: contract of employment, flexicurity, *Pacta Sunt Servanda Clausula, Rebus Sic Stantibus*

1. Significant attributes of an employment relationship

1.1 Correlation between the legal subordination of employees and the long-term character of the employment relationship

The two substantial attributes of the employment relationship are the legal subordination of the employee and long-term nature. The

* György Kiss is Professor at the National University of Public Service, Dean of the Faculty of Public Administration; Professor at the University of Pecs, Faculty of Law, Department of Labour Law, Hungary. He is also a head of the Association of Labour Law in Hungary, Chair of the MTA-PTE Research Group of Comparative and European Employment Policy and Labour Law.

** This volume is published within the framework of the MTA-PTE Research Group of Comparative and European Employment Policy and Labour Law [2011TKI435]. Head of the Research Group is Prof. Dr. György Kiss, University of Pécs, Hungary.

subordination of the individual employee is a fundamental matter of fact of labour law[1]. In any event, it was quite an effort to justify why there was no subordination in certain types of work performed for other persons, while it was self-evident in the case of the employment relationship. The initial explanations[2] were later replaced by legal dogmatic arguments such as the lack of agreement in a service subject to restrictions by a legal transaction[3]. This, in turn, implied that the cause of subordination had been the contract[4]. The long-term relationship may affect the ability to exactly define the content of the contract, although the parties are free to alter the legal relationship. The term 'incomplete contract' does not originate in labour law[5]; however, its interpretation is of increasing significance in labour law too. I shall return to this problem in detail later, but the preliminary issue is whether the long-term character of an employment relationship, in its substance, differs from other long-term private-law relationships, such as long-term assignment? Because, according to Freedland's evaluation, it is the unique long-term character of an employment relationship that creates the basis of the requirement for employee protection[6]. This character – based on a latent promise –

1 R. Richardi: 'Die Abhängigkeit des einzelnen Arbeitnehmers ist der Grundtatbestand des Arbeitsrechts'. See Richardi R. *Kollektivgewalt und Individualwille bei der Gestaltung des Arbeitsverhältnisses.* München: Beck C.H., 1968, p. 1.

2 Despite the fact that the theory of *economic* and *personal* dependence was dismissed later, Veneziani pointed out that freedom of employees – within the framework of contractual freedom (!) – was not to become a reality on the labour market due to their social status. See Veneziani B. The evolution of the contract of employment. In: Hepple B. (ed.) *The making of labour law in Europe.* London–New York: Mansell, 1986, pp. 31–72.

3 Richardi R. Der Arbeitsvertrag im Zivilrechtssystem. *Zeitschrift für Arbeitsrecht,* 1988, p. 252.

4 Wank R. Einvernehmliche Änderung von Arbeitsbedingungen. In: Hromadka W. (ed.) *Änderungen von Arbeitsbedingungen.* Heidelberg: Recht und Wirtschaft, 1990. pp. 40–41; Aubert-Monpeyssen Th. *Subordination juridique et relation de travail.* Paris: CNRS, 1988, pp. 7-51; Couturier G. *Droit du Travail.* Paris: Presses Univ. de France, Paris, Tome 1, préc. n-44-3; Collins H., Ewing K. D., McColgan A. *Labour Law.* Cambridge: Cambridge University Press, 2012, p. 94.

5 Tirole J. Incomplete contracts: where do we stand? *Economica,* No. 67 (4), 1999, pp. 741–81; Deakin S., Lane C., Wilkinson F. Trust' or law? Towards an integrated theory of contractual relations between firms. *Journal of Law and Society,* Vol. 21 (3), 1994, pp. 329–49; Hart O., Moore J. (). 'Incomplete contracts and ownership: Some new thoughts. 2007, pp. 182-186. Retrieved 5 April 2016 from https://www.aeaweb.org/annual.../0105_1015_1702; Collins H. Regulating the employment relation for competitiveness. *Industrial Law Journal,* Vol. 30 (1), 2001. pp. 17–47.

6 Freedland M. *The contract of employment.* Oxford: Clarendon Press, 1976, pp. 19–21.

differentiates the employment relationship from various relationships of work performed for other persons.

What is the basis of this correlation? It is nothing else but the employee's subordination. Labour law is contract-based, and as such, is part of the system of private law. It is hardly a coincidence that the general principles of private law are invoked and applied in labour law. At the same time, labour law also functions as employee protection law[7]. For a long time, after centuries of development[8], the traditional employment relationship was a legal relationship established for an indefinite period, with the purpose of providing full-time work. The continuous nature of the employment relationship is one of the fundamental requirements of employee protection – also under changed circumstances[9].

1.2 The reason and justification of subordination

The *locatio cunductio operarum,* referred to as the ancestor of the contract of employment, was in fact renting the work or service of a free man to another person. Essentially, at the beginning, this contract only differed from slave work in its legal base; this is well reflected in the term *se locare,* which in fact meant self-rental. In other words: the rental of the service and the person (the labour force) carrying it out were not dissociated. The term *operas suas locare* appeared only later, expressing that the person renting his labour is not totally under the rule of the person hiring his labour[10].

---

7 W. Friedmann: 'In other words, a contract must not become a disguised form of status'. See Friedmann W. *Law in changing society.* London: Stevens & Sons, 1972, p. 122. Referring to *Maine's* status versus contract analysis, see Main H. S. *Ancient law, its connections with the early history of society and its relation to modern ideas,* London: John Murray, 1908.

8 Deakin S. (2001). *The Contract of employment.* Cambridge: ESRC Centre for Business Research, University of Cambridge, Working Paper No. 203, 2001; Deakin S. *The evolution of the employment relationship.* Symposium. ILO, 2002, pp. 191-205; Veneziani B., *op. cit.*, pp. 31–72.

9 'The statutory concept of continuity of employment is therefore an important filter for employment protection'. See Deakin S., Morris G. *Labour Law.* London: Butterworths, 1998, p. 189.

10 The person renting his labour is not a subordinate member of the building community; further, not only the use of force, but also judicial enforcement could be applied for taking up and performing work. See Mayer-Maly Th. *Locatio conductio (Eine Untersuchung zum klassischen römischen Recht).* Berlin: Duncker & Humblot, 1982, p. 123.

In the era when modern labour law was born – as major codices went back to rental[11] – it was obvious to justify the employee's dependence with economic vulnerability. Later, it has become evident that although economic dependence is typical for the vast majority of workers, dependent work may not be regarded as a distinguishing feature[12]. In this context, it is necessary to refer to Flume's argument that in the course of private law transactions the unequal position of partners might almost be regarded as general. This does not mean, however, that the weaker party's right to self-determination, and thereby his bargaining position, would be compromised because the stronger party's economic power is usually balanced in an economy based on private autonomy[13]. It needs to be added that such balance was achieved in practice through the intervention of public law in contractual relationships, and this intervention was the strongest in respect of labour law.

Regarding dependent work, one of the most influential theories was that of personal dependence (*persönliche Abhängigkeit*)[14]. On the other hand, according to many, personal dependence is used rather figuratively; it serves as a benchmark for an employment relationship in respect of other contracts that also represent work performed for other persons[15].

Later, the legal nature of dependence came to the forefront of research primarily with regard to the concept of employee and the demarcation of its legal status. Wiedemann argues that an employee can be characterized

---

11 A good example is Code Civil which regulated the rental of labour as a type of labour contract. Brun A. *Droit du travail.* Paris: Dalloz, 1958, p. 66.

12 Zöllner W., Loritz K. *Arbeitsrecht.* München: Beck C. H., 1992. pp. 43–44.

13 Flume W. *Allgemeiner Teil des bürgerlichen Rechts.* Berlin: Duncker & Humblot, 1979, p. 10.

14 The concept represented by *Sinzheimer* and his school rested on the premise of opposition to civil law, and emphasized that workers also contributed to their performance with their personality, thereby they are in a dependent position. Sinzheimer H. *Grundzüge des Arbeitsrechts.* Jena: Fischer, 1972, pp. 7–9.

15 Molitor E. *Das Wesen des Arbeitsvertrages: eine Untersuchung über die Begriffe des Dienst- und Werkvertrags, sowie des Vertrags über abhängige Arbeit.* Leipzig–Erlangen: A. Deichertsche, 1925. p. 95. Personal dependence is also a point of connection from the perspective of other criteria, such as adaptation to the employer's organization/business/sphere of interest *(Eingliederungstheorie),* as well as being bound by command. Nikisch A. Die Eingliederung und ihre Bedeutung für das Arbeitsrecht. *Recht der Arbeit,* 1960, pp. 1–5. In connection with being bound by command, *Lieb* noted that, from the perspective of law judicature, this involved personal dependence if the command included conditions relating to time and location as well. See Lieb M. Unternehmerähnliche Arbeitnehmer. *Zeitschrift für vergleichende Rechtswissenschaft,* 1976, pp. 276–304.

by his incapability of participating in economic transactions because he has lost his free economic disposition. It is crucial, however, that after all he is party to a legal relationship deriving from an exchange-type contract, therefore it is important for him that protection is recognised *(Schutzbedürftigkeit)*[16]. In this context, Maschmann emphasizes that the employee is just as dependent as any other citizen. Personality dependence is in fact an unfortunate term for what is called work determined by others *(fremdbestimmte Arbeit)*[17].

Complexity of the employment relationship is expressed by the multiple test or multi-factor test applied in English labour law, developed through case-law in connection with the concept of employee[18]. Later the indicators were refined and, at the same time, expanded; a decade and a half after the case referred to in the footnote there were 18 relevant indicators recorded for classification of legal relationships representing performance of work[19]. Criteria of employment relationship were also developed outside the *Code du Travail* in French labour law. Among the criteria, *'subordination juridique'* is a starting point[20]. However, the evaluation of this subordination is not clear. Many authors consider voluntary, free commitment the dominant element of the contract of employment[21].

Richardi's view is that the reason behind dependent work is to be found in the law: it is simply the abstract definition of service[22]. The entrepreneur and commissioner perform a well-defined service. In other words: these services are limited by legal transaction. In these obligations, the recipient of the service (customer, agent) is not in the position to obtain a ruling position over the person providing the service in the course

---

16 Wiedemann H. *Das Arbeitsverhältnis als Austausch und Gemeinschaftsverhältnis.* Karlsruhe: C. F. Müller. 1996, pp. 15–19.

17 Maschmann F. *Arbeitsverträge und Verträge mit Selbständigen. Rechtliche Qualifizierung von Dienstleistungsverhältnissen als Abgrenzungs- und Einordnungsproblem.* Berlin: Duncker & Humblot, 2001, p. 59.

18 See *Ready Mixed Concrete (South East) Ltd. v. Minister for Pensions and National Insurance* (1968) 2 QB 497; Reference in Deakin S., Morris G., *op. cit.*, pp. 57–60.

19 See *O'Kelly and others v Trusthouse Forte* (1984) 1 QB90. Reference in Deakin S., Morris G., *op. cit.*, p. 160. About the different tests see Collins H., Ewing K. D., McColgan A. *Labour Law.* Cambridge: Cambridge University Press, 2001, pp. 189–196; Gaymer J. *The employment relationship*, 2001, pp. 60–70.

20 Aubert-Monpeyssen Th. *Subordination juridique et relation de travail.* Paris: CNRS, 1988, pp. 7–51.

21 Couturier G. *op. cit.*

22 Richardi R. Der Arbeitsvertrag im Zivilrechtssystem. *Zeitschrift für Arbeitsrecht*, 1988, p. 252.

of performance. In this context, a new interpretation of the problem of *'Selbstbestimmung versus Fremdbestimmung'* arise[23]. As a contract of employment is a so-called incomplete contract, elements that are not part of the contract must be specified. Performance is made for the employer, in most cases with his assets, etc.; consequently, it is the employer's right to specify the requirements for performance, and this creates subordination placing this employer in an actual or apparent, or in fact a real ruling position. The so-called '*Gestaltungsrecht*' or 'managerial prerogative' is a specific element of labour law, its existence is not disputed, yet its limits should be determined due to its contractual foundation.

1.3 What is the substance of the long-term character of an employment relationship?

The contract of employment could be interpreted as a manifestation of the long-term contract. Nevertheless, it is to be highlighted that basically the essence of employee protection does not depend on the fixed or indefinite term of the employment relationship. Freedland's standpoint is that employment relationship is a long-term legal relationship because the contract of employment has multiple time levels, irrespective of whether it was established for an indefinite or fixed period. This, at the same time, determines the mutuality of rights and obligations. The first tier of the contract of employment is a kind of base tier – which is part of every contract concluded with the purpose of performing work, and it relates to the present. This means that one of the parties is obliged to perform certain work, while the other party is obliged to pay compensation for this work. It is apparent that this is not only part of a contract of employment, but also of business contracts, assignments, brokership, etc. However, Freedland emphasizes that the contract of employment has an inherent promise for continued work and continued provision of work. Eventually, this mutual promise provides the stability of the employment relationship, which can be, in certain cases, crucial to the employer as well, but it is obviously the fundamental, vital interest of the employee[24].

What are the consequences of a long-term employment relationship in general? The essence of the problem is whether, in such circumstances, it is possible at all – or rather more importantly: whether it is necessary at all – to define contractual content in a precise and detailed way. The idea of

---

23 Söllner A. *Arbeitsrecht*. Stuttgart: Kohlhammer, 1969, p. 11.

24 Freedland M., *op. cit.*, pp. 19–21.

the incomplete contract primarily aims to avoid expenses unforeseeable at the time of performance. Periodic review is an immanent feature of such contracts. This is when the parties must reconsider mutual benefits deriving from the legal relationship[25]. Thus, long-term incomplete contracts need periodic review (re-negotiation) also, because this ensures the safe sustainability of this type of legal relationship and, at the same time, the security of the parties' status[26]. Despite the fact that the instrument of the incomplete contract has been subject to a lot of criticism by the economic sphere, many experts have pointed out that contracts of such content were extremely well designed[27]. Regarding the labour law aspects of incomplete contracts, it has been highlighted that there is an increasing number of professions or work types where advance predictability – as a requirement – is simply not feasible. Such unpredictability, along with pre-design particularly based on it, has had, and may still have diverse consequences even today. 'Pre-design' may easily turn into employer 'overpower' which exists in severe and lighter versions.

However, there are other known forms of pre-designing the content of legal relationships. Wank calls an employment relationship *'Äquivalenzverhältnis'*, where the alteration of certain (individual) elements is outside the employer's unilateral decision power[28]. At the same time, the title of his study – *'Change based on agreement'* – reflects well the wide scale of solutions. The essence of these solutions is the parties' prior agreement on the 'unilateral' modification of the terms and content of the employment relationship. It is expressed perfectly in the title of Mentzel's study '*Voran konsentierter Änderungsverträge*'[29].

The above raise the following questions: could contract of employment or employment relationship as long-term contract or long-term relationship be interpreted as a so-called relational contract/relational relationship?[30] If the answer is yes, it is necessary to analyse what solutions can be taken

[25] Tirole J., *op. cit.*, pp. 741–81.

[26] Bernheim D., Whinston M. D. Incomplete contracts and strategic ambiguity. *The American Economic Review*, 1999, p. 902.

[27] *Ibidem.*

[28] Wank R., *op.cit.*, pp. 40–41.

[29] Mentzel T. *Die Änderung von Arbeitsbedingungen kraft Direktionsrecht oder im Wege voran konsentierter Änderungsverträge.* Hamburg: Verlag Dr. Kovać, 2003.

[30] On the relational contract see: Macneil I. R. Values in contract: internal and external. *Northwestern University Law Review*, Vol. 78 (2), 1983, pp. 340–18; Hviid M. *Long-term contracts and relational contracts*, pp. 46–72. Retrieved April 17, 2016 from encyclo.findlaw.com/4200book.

into account in respect of altering the content of the legal relationship in a way that sustains the legal relationship even if the content is changed? Further in this context: are public law intervention or the application of private law principles and rules to be pursued? As the problem of long-term contract–relational contract has arrived in labour law application from the fields of private law and economic law, it is well justified to start with examining the correlations between labour law and private law.

2. Labour law on the border of private and public law

2.1 Analysis of self-evident statements

Why is it important to clarify the relationship between civil law and labour law? The answer lies in the fact that labour law is the law protecting the employee, as a counterbalance to the employee's subordination. However, it makes a difference how the legislator wants to provide this protection and with what tools. Because if labour law is not considered to fall under the branch of private law, the predominance of public law restrictions will prevail. It can be observed that during an economic crisis the use of public law instruments does not provide effective security.

At first sight, the applicability of civil law principles seems unquestionable in practice. The development of a connection between private and labour law is instructive in western European countries. There are lots of unambiguous statements regarding connection and inherence of labour law and civil law, but the real difficulty of this connection lies in the details. Regarding German law, Richardi has drafted the relationship of labour law and civil law as follows: *'Nicht die Geltung zivilrechtlicher Grundsätze, sondern im Gegenteil ihre Nichtgeltung muss begründet werden'*[31]. This idea is reflected in the draft by Henssler-Preis[32]. Section 1 states: *'Das Arbeitsverhältnis wird durch Vertrag begründet. Soweit dieses Gesetz nichts anderes bestimmt, gelten die Bestimmungen des Bürgerlichen Gesetzbuches'*[33].

---

[31] Richardi R., Wlotzke O. (eds.) *Münchener Handbuch zum Arbeitsrecht*. Vol. I, München: Beck C.H., 2000, Rndr. 27.

[32] See Diskussionsentwurf eines Arbeitsvertragsgesetzes (ArbVG) 2. Fassung – Stand: August 2006. Bertelsmann Stiftung; Henssler M., Preis U. *Entwurf eines Arbeitsvertragsgesetzes*. München: Beck C.H., 2015.

[33] In a historical sense see: Potthoff H. *Probleme des Arbeitsrechts*. Jena: E. Diederichs, 1912; Sinzheimer H. *Grundzüge des Arbeitsrechts*. Jena: Fischer, 1927, pp. 7-9; Sinzheimer H. Über Grundgedanken und die Möglichkeit eines Einheitsarbeitsrechts

According to the approach and argumentation of Bydlinsky, Austrian law is remarkable in this context. He underlines that generally the independence of labour law does not exist. It is not possible to reveal the principles and necessity of legal techniques of the connection between civil and labour law based on a 'common starting point'[34]. The main question was whether labour law could be positioned in the legal system as an independent branch. The answer is obvious at first sight, since labour law has a specific subject which is not present in other systems: this is dependent work *(abhängige Arbeit).* However, he formulated his doubts in this respect. Bydlinsky highlights certain points where labour law is connected to traditional civil law and public law. In his view, the independence of labour law is rather relative. It would be impossible to elaborate and regulate dogmatically entirely independent contract, representation, performance or assignment, etc. doctrine for labour law.

The connection between civil and private law, with special regard to the independence of labour law referred to before, has not been subject to similar discussions elsewhere. In French labour law, aspirations for the independence of labour law played a major role in forming the principles of freedom of contract and freedom of work[35]. The Code Civil did not help to determine the identity of labour law within civil law. Regulation of the Code Civil had a significant role in the pursuit of the independence of labour law. The Code Civil could not go beyond the legalization of the so-called 'rent theory'[36]. Regarding the independence of French labour law, there is a remarkable argument by Mazeaud. In his opinion, labour law often seems to be an independent branch within the system of law. However, he points out that it is neither possible to ignore the effect of other disciplines, nor the historical, sociological and cultural traditions. Civil law embraces the principles and general rules on contracts and

in Deutschland. In: Sinzheimer H. *Arbeitsrecht und Rechtssoziologie*, Frankfurt a. M: Europa Verlag, 1976, p. 47.

34 Bydlinski F. *Arbeitsrechtskodifikation und allgemeines Zivilrecht.* Wien – New York: Springer, 1969, p. 11.

35 Camerlynck G. H., Lyon-Caen G., Pélissier J. *Droit du travail.* Paris: Dalloz. 1986, pp. 11–12; Pélissier J., Supiot A., Jaeammaud A. *Droit du travail.* Paris: Dalloz, 2004, pp. 9–11; Mazeaud A. *Droit du travail.* Paris: Montchrestien, 2008, pp. 23–24; Bossu B., Dumont F., Verkindt P-Y. *Droit du travail.* Paris: Montchrestien, 2011, pp. 4–8.

36 *'Le contrat de louage de service'.* See Camerlynck G-H. *Contract de travail.* Paris: Dalloz, 1968, pp. 4, 42; Brun A., Galland H. *Droit du travail.* Paris: Sirey, 1958, p. 66.

relationships (obligations). The independence of labour law can only be judged from this starting point[37].

In the evaluation of the legal nature of labour law, in English law the starting point is the contract as such[38]. It needs to be emphasized that the general principles of contract law are 'invoked and applied' to the contract of employment or contract of service[39]. Freedom of contract means that the terms and conditions of the contract can be established freely. This freedom or this principle is rooted, and has evolved, in common law. The modern concept of contract of employment – and also that of labour law – dates back to the repeal of the Master and Servant Act (1870)[40]. Prior to this, employment relationship was analysed on the basis of the 'general theory' of contract[41]. However, this approach was far from homogeneous. The various definitions of contract of employment and the nuanced differentiations between them took into account economic and social interests[42]. Despite the fact that the Master and Servant Act contained a number of criminal elements, the contract of employment had already appeared in it[43]. Coming back to the contractual basis, it is true that labour law is part of contract law. Nevertheless, the connection between labour law and traditional civil law is questionable at the level of applicability of the rules of civil law. Attention is drawn to this fact in the criticism of the sole contractual model. As referred to above, freedom of contract or this principle is rooted and has evolved in common law. One of the most important points made by critical reasoning is that the contract of employment treated the parties as equal in the labour market. But the 'employer's bargaining power enables the employer to impose its own terms on a take-it-or-leave-it basis'[44]. So, the acts eventually did have a determinant role in the approximation of the contract of employment to 'social practice'; however, the contractual determination of labour law, in its entirety, has never been questioned.

---

37 Mazeaud A. *Droit du travail*. Paris: Montchrestien, 2008, p. 19.

38 Peel E. *The Law of Contract*. London: Sweet & Maxwell, 2011, p. 3.

39 Collins H., Ewing K. D., McColgan A., *op. cit.*, p. 94.

40 Deakin S., Morris G. S., *op. cit.*, p. 25.

41 Gaymer J., *op. cit.*, p. 5.

42 Kahn-Freud O. Blackstone's Neglected Child: 'The Contract of Employment'. *Law Quarterly Review*, 1977, pp. 508–523.

43 See *Emmens v Edgerton* (1853) 13 C.B. 495. Deakin noted that this case had reflected the substance of contractual model which is based 'on reciprocity and mutuality of obligation'. Deakin S., Morris G. S., *op. cit.*, p. 27.

44 Collins H., Ewing K. D., McColgan A., *op. cit.*, p. 98.

2.2 Labour law as employee protection law; tools, opportunities and solutions

Labour law's being tied to an objective can be clearly defined through its protective character. This protection unambiguously aims to stabilize the legal status of the employee. The question remains however; how is it possible to integrate into private law the process through which private labour law becomes increasingly affiliated with public law? The subordination of the employer also means that he can alter the contents of the employment relationship unilaterally. In the lack of protection tools this right or power can be abused. The measures that can be applied to ensure the so-called legal status protection of the employee are therefore important.

Obviously, non-contractual public law intervention is justified in the case of vulnerable employee groups[45]. In other cases, public law prohibition jeopardizes the sustainability of the employment relationship. To avoid this, solutions should be sought that enable the sustainment of the employment relationship, and thereby maintain the security of the employee's legal status. In such a case, those private law solutions which have proved to be effective for certain types of private law contracts should be analysed. To do this, it is necessary however, to re-think the purpose and contents of the contract of employment and the employment relationship.

3. What does the dogmatic basis of new flexicurity means?

3.1 Long-term contracts as relational contracts

Contracts can be grouped into two general categories: short-term and long-term contracts[46]. Many term the former as 'discrete transactions'[47]. In Macneil's evaluation, such contracts are characterized by two general features: they are short and limited in scope[48]. The following are – non-

---

[45] See the abundant literature on the prohibition of dismissal of pregnant women.

[46] Hviid M., *op. cit.*, pp. 46–47; Macneil I. R. The many futures of contracts. *Southern California Law Review*, 1973–1974, pp. 691-816; Macneil I. R. Essays on the nature of contract. *North Carolina Central Law Journal*, 1978-1979, pp. 159–200.

[47] Macneil I. R. The many futures of contracts. *Southern California Law Review*, 1973–1974, p. 693.

[48] *Ibidem*, p. 720.

exclusively – the features of these exchange-type contracts. The transactional type generally involves fewer parties and is monetizable in terms of its contents; from an economic perspective, it is an exchange contract. The time elapsing between contract conclusion and performance is short; contract performance generally does not require continuity. The content of the agreements is clear; it is designed and worded for the present. The actual content of the contract is complete; its design is also complex. The substance of the contract is the act of the exchange itself; its temporal dimension is 'presentation of the future'[49]. Consequently, the parties are fully bound to the plan, i.e. to the contents of the contracts concluded.

In contrast, a so-called 'relational contract' is not simply an exchange contract. Further to the economic effects of the contract, there are other factors, not of economic but basically of social nature. A large part of these contracts cannot be, or is difficult to monetize. Relational contracts are long-term, and deriving from their substance they do not terminate when one or two obligations are met. Macneil highlights that individuals enter into such relations gradually, in some cases with their birth, and the contract ends with their death. The substance of relational contracts is continuous planning. While transactional contracts have the character of 'presentation of the future', in case of relational contracts this is 'futurizing of the present'[50].

However, the question is whether every long-term contract is also a relational contract? Baird's standpoint is that the dilemma of long-term contracts is the 'need to fix responsibilities at the outset' and the 'need to readjust them over time' permeates the long-term contractual relationship. The first one means loyalty to the contractual obligation, while the second refers to the flexible adjustment of the contract to the circumstances that have changed or will change in the future[51]. Hviid emphasizes that this 'tension' is observed both in cases of long-term and

49 In Macneil's theory the term 'presentation' plays an important role in the classification of contracts. 'Presentation is only a manner in which a person perceives the future's effect on the present; but it depends upon events outside the individual psyche, events viewed as determining the future. Presentation is thus recognition that the course of the future is bound by present events, and that by those events the future has for many purposes been brought effectively into the present.' Macneil I. R. Restatement (second) of contracts and presentation. *Virginia Law Review,* 1974, p. 589.

50 Macneil I. R. The many futures of contracts. *Southern California Law Review*, 1973–1974, pp. 738–740.

51 Baird D. G. Self-interest and cooperation in long-term contracts. *The Journal of Legal Studies*, 1990, p. 586.

relational contracts[52]. According to this view, there would be two contract types, 'although closely related, neither is a subset of the other'[53]. Göetz and Scott emphasize that relational contracts 'encompass most generic agency relationships, including distributorships, franchises, joint ventures, and employment contracts'[54]. At the same time, the authors draw attention to the fact that the concepts of simple long-term contract and relational contract are often intermixed. Their standpoint is that classic contingent contracts and relational contracts are to be distinguished[55].

Despite the categorical assertions by Göetz and Scott, the picture is more sophisticated in respect of contract of employment. Without doubt, the contract of employment can be deemed an incomplete contract, in that the parties are often unable to define each and every condition in the contract of employment. An important observation regarding contract of employment is that relational contracts require a lot more creative control mechanism than long-term contracts in general. At the same time, the study by Göetz and Scott reveals a key difference between 'traditional' relational contracts and the contract of employment. In a legal relationship based on a relational contract, in the vast majority of cases, the parties are interested in maintaining the legal relationship and do their best to avoid termination. Generally, this does not apply for employment relationship, and the employee-protective systems of termination are also different in every country[56]. The standpoint of the authors is that the parties are presumably able to seize future risks at the time of concluding contracts to be performed in the future; however, during subsequent performance, circumstances may arise that materially change the costs and profits set at the start. These are the cases when tension arises between the maintenance and unilateral termination of the legal relationship. This is particularly true in respect of the labour law relationship.

---

52 Hviid M., *op. cit.*, p.46.

53 *Ibidem.*

54 Goetz C. J., Scott R. E. Principles of relational contract. *Virginia Law Review*, 1981, p. 1091.

55 Similarly Hviid M., *op. cit.*, p. 46.

56 In respect German labour law, see Hoyningen-Huene G. *Kündigungsschutzgesetz.* München: Beck C. H., 1992; Preis U. *Prinzipien des Kündigungsrechts bei Arbeitsverhältnissen.* München: Beck C. H., 1993; Jüttner J. *Der Vorrang der Änderungskündigung vor der Beendigungskündigung.* Baden-Baden: Nomos, 2011; Wallner F. X. *Die Änderungskündigung,* München: Beck C.H., 2005; Schröder S. *Das Verhältnis von Direktionsrecht und Änderungskündigung,* Frankfurt a. M.: Peter Lang, 2011. In French labour law, termination by the employer must be preceded by certain procedural actions. See Pélissier J., Supiot A., Jeammaud A., *op. cit.*, pp. 765-769.

Bird clearly states that 'employment is a relational contract'[57]. His next sentence nevertheless reveals that his categorization is multi-layered. In particular, he notes that 'Employment relations immediately transcend wage-for-services exchanges and develop into complex whole person relationships based upon trust, commitment, and shared solidarity'. Bird distinguishes the norms applicable to employment from the employment contract. He claims that nearly two-thirds of employees work under conditions outside the contract of employment, and in practice the norms prevail. Further, it is important that all conditions that remain non-contractual – such as corporate culture, office policies, future planning, and the complex social matrix of organizational life – are exclusively ruled by these norms[58]. Making a comparison between the relational contract and the contract of employment for similarities, he emphasizes that there are several conditions that might not be realized through written contracts, but through personal relations, on a non-contractual basis. As a common feature, he mentions that performance is not just a 'spot deal' in either cases; the parties plan for the future, with anticipation to unexpected future circumstances, and they alter their relationship accordingly. He argues that every criterion is in place to regard the contract of employment a *relational contract*. It is a fact however, that due to the existing subordination in the employment relationship, and despite numerous protective regulations to the employer's power, in a given situation termination of the employment relationship may seem a more convenient solution[59].

In the English literature, this connection was addressed by Brodi[60]. He points out that the employment relationship has multiple forms, and more than one of these – such as certain atypical forms of employment – allow the employer to bypass basic employee protection rights. Concerning the traditional contract of employment, there is no doubt that 'the implied term of mutual trust and confidence is much more wide ranking but, in all probability, would not extend to requiring an alteration of the parties' obligations in the light of radically changed circumstances'[61]. Apparently, Brody refers here to unilateral alteration, in which case the

57 Bird R.C. Employment as relational contract. *U. Pa. Journal of Labour and Employment Law*, Vol. 8 (1), 2005. p. 215.

58 *Ibidem*, pp. 150–152.

59 *Ibidem*, p. 216.

60 Brodie D. How relational is the employment contract? *Industrial Law Journal*, 2011, Vol. 40, pp. 232–253.

61 *Ibidem*, p. 236.

employee is not obliged to consent. It is important further on, that the duty of trust and confidence not be used to render the original content of the contract meaningless[62].

Undoubtedly Macneil's criteria are unambiguous when used within his own system. Also, it is observed that the evaluation of the content of the contract of employment has changed: it is now somewhat closer to the values defined by Macneil[63]. However, in respect of the contract of employment, the adaptation of these criteria is questionable despite the fact that Macneil has extended his theory to both commercial agreements and a (traditional) type of employment relationship. With regard to employment relationship, there are at least two key attributes to mention: the inequality of bargaining power, and the personal nature of employment relations. Brody asks the following question: 'Does recourse to Macneil explain why these attributes have taken on such significance?'[64]. He points out that the commercial agreement and the contract of employment stand in two different environments. The employee, in his own environment, is not in a competitive position; he is not able to switch easily to another contractual – that is, his contracting opportunities are limited to the minimum. Brody reaffirms that 'a contract of employment is typically of a longer term and more personal in nature than most contracts, and involves greater mutual dependence and trust, with greater opportunity for harm or abuse'[65]. Nevertheless, there is the question of whether the compensation system applicable for breach of contract by the employer would be recognized in other relational contracts as well. His final conclusion is that the attributes of this legal relationship determine the direction in which the legal nature of the contract of employment evolves[66].

62 See Fish v. Dresdner Bank [2009] IRLR 1035.

63 See in this context: State of South Australia v McDonald [2009] SASC 219. The following argument can be found in this decision: 'The development of the implied term can be seen as consistent with the contemporary view of the employment relationship as involving elements of common interest and partnership, rather than of conflict and subordination'.

64 Brodie D., *op. cit.*, p. 241.

65 With reference to the Wallace v United Grain Growers (1997) 152 DLR (4th) 1, 46 case. See Brodie D. *op. cit.*, pp. 247–248.

66 *Ibidem*, p. 248.

3.2 Possibilities, methods and limits of altering the content of the employment relationship

The dispute over the approach to the contract of employment as a relational contract has significance from the aspect of content of the employment relationship. An attribute of the relational contract is prevention of the collapse of the contract; the continuous verification; and, if necessary, the re-negotiation of conditions. Based on the above, it is shown that an employment relationship has numerous attributes that are present in a relational contract. However, subordination is the quintessence of the employment relationship, which means asymmetry of power not only at the time of contract conclusion but also during contract performance.

Comparative analyses confirm that the ability to alter the content of an employment relationship during its performance has become increasingly important. The first question is: what is the legal basis for altering the content of an employment relationship? The obvious legal basis is the amendment of the contract of employment. The more detailed the content of the contract of employment, the stronger the altering power of the contract, because the employer has less opportunity to make unilateral or contract-based quasi-unilateral alteration to the content of the employment relationship. It can happen that there is no possibility in the contract of employment to authorize the collective agreement or the employer to alter the content of the employment relationship when certain changes occur in the economic environment. In such cases, the only other option is to amend the contract of employment; however, this may lead to questionable results – especially in cases when a large number of employees are involved. If the employee or a group of employees are not willing to agree to the amendment, the only solution is to terminate the employment relationship. My standpoint is that this state is reflected in Hungarian labour law, leaving virtually no room for any other solution.

The contract is decisive in altering the content of employment relationship, even if its content is not regulated in detail. This is because the stability of the employment relationship, and consequently the protection of the employee's legal status are fundamental aspects. In this context, altering the content of the employment relationship due to reasons of the economy is of utmost importance. Let me emphasize that it is not the content of the contract of employment, but that of the employment relationship what we are talking about. The content of the employment relationship is not determined by the will of the parties to the contract of employment only, but also by factors relatively outside their control, such as the collective agreement, or the employer's unilateral alteration power based on contractual entitlement.

In regard to the contract as a legal base, it can either be a contract of employment or a collective agreement. The definition of the level of entitlement, as well as its expansion or limitation, depends on a number of factors. One of these may be legislation itself through entitlements or prohibitions; in an implicit way, the regulation by law on the obligatory content of the contract of employment can also be decisive. A collective agreement, whether it exists or not, may not authorize the alteration of the content of the employment relationship.

According to the points previously mentioned, a distinction should be made between the alteration of the content of employment relationship and the amendment of the contract of employment. Generally, we can state that the contract needs to be amended whenever an event occurs which leads to changes in the essential content elements of the employment relationship[67]. In French labour law, the institution serving the alteration of the employment relationship is the *clauses de mobilité*[68]. The distinction between the content of the contract of employment and that of the employment relationship can also be observed in English labour law.

The content of employment relationship is fundamentally determined by two factors: the express terms laid down in the contract of employment and the implied terms traditionally attached to it. The elements determining the content of the employment relationship are not included in the contract of employment, but generally in the collective agreement. Naturally, the terms of the contract of employment are mutually binding on the parties; but the 'vital part of the contract', or more precisely the dynamics of the employment relationship, are not provided for in this contract. Accordingly, the English employment relationship is viewed as an incomplete contract[69], for a number of reasons. An incomplete contract provides abundant room for the employer to exercise certain 'privileges'. A number of experts support the principle of managerial prerogative from the perspective of the employer, with the argument that every long-term investment comes with risks. These

[67] For example, the period of employment relationship is such an element.

[68] About clauses mobilité in French law, see Antonmattey P-H. *Les clauses du contrat du travail.* Rueil-Malmaison: Liaisons, 2009; Pélissier J., Supiot A., Jeammaud A. *op. cit.*, pp. 466–468.

[69] Pankhurst A. *Work effort under the incomplete contract of employment.* Cambridge: New Hall, 1988, pp. 5–8.

investments are implemented through specific legal transactions, such as contract of employment and its legal effect: the employment relationship. Should the content of a legal transaction implementing a longer-term investment not cover all details, therefore, deriving from privileges based on property/ownership, the investor has unilateral altering right; the effectiveness of the business is guaranteed from the start[70].

The problem of altering working conditions *(Gestaltungsrecht)* is a focal area of German labour jurisprudence[71]. In this context, it is also necessary to distinguish the specifications of the employee's performance and the options of unilateral alteration of or modifications to working conditions. In regard to the former, the perception of German labour law concerning the employer's right to discretion is identical to the concept applied in other labour law systems. The possibility of alteration outside the amendment to the contract of employment is properly reflected by the expression *Fremdbestimmung* – external determination. The content of the employment relationship is not fully 'alien-determined', as its basis is also an entitlement by contract. However, the question is whether such entitlement could be deduced from the structure of the German contract of employment. The employer's unilateral right to alteration cannot be deduced unambiguously from the *Bürgerliches Gesetzbuch.* Birk concludes from all this that the employer's altering and concretizing power became accepted on the basis of unwritten law and judicature – as well as by law history experience[72]. Also in German law, the altering power of the employer is associated with the long-term character of the employment relationship and, consequently, with the uncertainty of contractual promises *(Umbestimmtheit)*[73]. But the question is whether

70 Hart O., Moore J. *Incomplete contracts and ownership: Some new thoughts*, 2007, p. 1. Retrieved April 5, 2016 from https://www.aeaweb.org/annual.../0105_1015_1702.

71 Bötticher E. *Gestaltungsrecht und Unterwerfung im Privatrecht.* Berlin: Walter de Gruyter & Co. 1964; Preis U. *Grundfragen der Vertragsgestaltung im Arbeitsrecht.* Neuwied: Luchterhand, 1993, pp. 37–50, 51–85; Böttner W. *Das Direktionsrecht des Arbeitgebers.* Marburg: Elwer, 1971; Böker A. *Das Weisungsrecht des Arbeitgebers.* Frankfurt am Main: Athäneum, 1971; Birk R. *Die arbeitsrechtliche Leitungsmacht.* Köln: Carl Heymanns, 1973, pp. 23–79; more recently: Mentzel T. *Die Änderung von Arbeitsbedingungen kraft Direktionsrecht oder im Wege voran konsentierter Änderungsverträge.* Hamburg: Verlag Dr. Kovać, 2003; Birk R. *Aktuelle Probleme arbeitsrechtlicher Leitungsmacht.* In: Leser H.G. (eds.) Arbeitsrecht und Zivilrecht in Entwicklung. Festschrift für Hyung-Bae Kim. Berlin: Duncker & Humblot, 1995, pp. 25–25.

72 Birk R. *Die arbeitsrechtliche Leitungsmacht.* Köln: Carl Heymanns, 1973, pp. 58–77.

73 Mentzel T. *Die Änderung von Arbeitsbedingungen kraft Direktionsrecht oder im Wege voran konsentierter Änderungsverträg.* Hamburg: Verlag Dr. Kovać, 2003, pp. 3–4.

concretization through the employer's general right to conduct *(allgemeines Weisungsrecht)* could serve as a base for the employer's so-called extended right to discretion *(erweitertes Weisungsrecht)*. The majority position in German literature assumes that the employer's general right to conduct could be extended through individual contracts. This would be allowed by a clause called *Versetzungsklausel (Versetzungsvorbehalt)* permitting the employer to alter the nature of the employee's activity, as well as the place of work. This would help avoid frequent amendments to the contract of employment in all cases when changes in circumstances require significant modification in the performance, and these changes only become evident after conclusion of the contract. The subject of this – ultimately agreement-based – right to conduct reaches beyond the concretization of the employee's obligation to contract performance, as it would also allow alteration outside the contract, not specified in advance[74].

However, allowing unilateral modifications in cases of unforeseen future events comes with serious risks in respect of employees already in a subordinate position in the employment relationship itself. An essential purpose of labour law regulation is safeguarding the employee's legal status, referred to as status protection. There are three possible options to eliminate, or at least reduce the risks.

The first one is the effective and detailed control of the content of the contract which authorizes unilateral altering of the employment relationship[75]. This control has multiple levels. The first level is the contract of employment, while the second is the collective agreement. To utilize this option, the content of the contract of employment must be flexible and convertible. In other words: it should be made possible to define the fundamental elements of the employment relationship not only in the contract of employment, but also in the collective agreement. With regard to the control of the contract of employment, specific regulations for individual contract types might be helpful[76]. In respect of the control of a collective agreement, it is underlined that the legal nature

---

74 *Ibidem*, pp. 91–92.

75 See as a comparison König D. *Die Inhaltskontrolle von Arbeitsverträgen in Deutschland, England und Frankreich*. Freiburg: Rombach, 2010; and further Watson L. Employees and the Unfair Contract Terms Act. *Industrial Law Journal*, Vol. 4. 1995, pp. 323–336; Freedland M. *The personal employment contract*. Oxford: Oxford University Press, 2003, pp. 190–192.

76 See Section 315 in the *Bürgerliches Gesetzbuch* about the equitable assessment of measures by the employer. Birk R., *op. cit.*, pp. 58–77.

of this agreement is a contract. Accordingly, general contract validity criteria are to be observed.

The second one is the regulation of termination of employment, particularly in respect of dismissal for economic reason[77]. This includes collective redundancy as well as the dismissal of one employee only. Various solutions have evolved in EU Member States, and accordingly there is no uniform level of protection either. Termination of the employment relationship may only be considered as an *ultima ratio* option. In this respect, the aforementioned institution of *Änderungskündigung* is noteworthy in German law; in French law, *l'obligation de reclassement* means an obligation to negotiate prior to termination, indicating the legislator's attempt to establish preventive measures. Naturally, it is possible to agree on a temporary moratorium on dismissal if the employer alters the content of the employment relationship with less favourable terms for the employee. A typical instrument for such agreement is the collective agreement.

The third option is the general influence by collective labour law. In this context it is highlighted that the two parts of labour law – individual and collective – are in a correlative connection with each other[78]. A most important part of collective labour law is the collective agreement. It is assumed that during the negotiations there is a parity of power between parties. By collective autonomy, it is possible to equalize the subordination of individual employees. This, however, requires powerful employee representations. Along with the balance of power provided by the agreement, other employee representations empowered with some extent of authority – such as a works council – may also have a significant role. As the authority of such organizations is not contract-based, appropriate legislative intervention is necessary.

77 It is necessary to refer in this respect to the strict substantive and procedural regulations on the termination of employment relationship in French labour law. See for more details on this procedure: Pélissier J., Supiot A., Jeammaud A., *op. cit.*, pp. 515–524; Hoyningen-Huene G. *Kündigungsschutzgesetz* München: Beck C.H., 1992; Preis U. *Prinzipien des Kündigungsrechts bei Arbeitsverhältnissen*. München: Beck C.H., 1993; Collins H., Ewing K. D., McColgan A., *op. cit.*, pp. 765-799, on unfair dismissal especially: pp. 800–854.

78 *Migschs* claims that individual labour law is a characteristic example for the insufficiency of the regulating function, in itself, of (individual) private autonomy in manifesting the social environment subject to the regulation; there was an attempt to overcome this obvious incapability by utilising the tools of collective norms. This historic experiment was unquestionably successful. Migchs E. *Die absolut geschützte Rechtsstellung des Arbeitnehmers*. München – Salzburg: Wilhelm Fink Verlag, 1972, pp. 12–13.

4. Conclusion with regard to Hungarian regulation

4.1 Connection between civil and labour law in Hungarian law

The determination of a connection between civil and labour law is the decisive prerequisite for the above-analysed approach to the flexibility of employment and protection of the employee's legal status. In Hungary, the relevant regulation is unclear. At first sight, the applicability of civil law principles seems unquestionable in practice. In 1992, a fortunate coincidence was the simultaneous preparation of the new labour code and the new civil code. The first phase of the technical preparation of the new Labour Code was characterized by the strengthening of the relationship between the Civil Code and the Labour Code. But as the work progressed work, this approach was gradually pushed into the background. This is reflected in, among other things, the fact that the LC does not allow the general application of the provisions of the Civil Code, only specific regulations[79]. The selection is unreasonable and random.

As a result, the regulation of the contract of employment breaks away from civil law's provisions on contract, and has a life of its own. This is reflected in the fact that the legislator defines the mandatory elements of the contract of employment. At the same time, it means that the essential elements of the contract of employment may not be converted; agreement on such elements may not be made in the collective agreement only.

Another substantial problem emanates from the regulation of the Labour Code. The second sentence under Section 19 Subsection (1) of the Labour Code reads: 'Any condition that would alter the employment relationship to the disadvantage of workers <...> may not be applied'. According to this rule: 'Unless otherwise provided for by law, the employment contract may derogate from the provisions of Part Two and from employment regulations to the benefit of the employee. Such derogations shall be adjudged by comparative assessment of related regulations'[80]. As a result, the interpretation of the phrase 'more favourable terms for the employee' is far from simple. This problem is in close correlation with the alteration possibilities of a long-term legal

[79] See Section 32 in the Labour Code.

[80] In this context, see the rejection of the so-called Rosinentheorie. See Detlev B. *Günstigkeitsprinzip im Arbeitsrecht*. Berlin: Duncker & Humblot, 1994, pp. 169–171.

relationship, with the simultaneous creation of flexibility, and protection of the employee's legal status.

4.2 Control of contracts

Control of the contract of employment and the collective agreement is needed especially in cases when, upon entitlement by contract, one of the parties can alter the content of the legal relationship. A good example for this is found under Section 315 of *Bürgerliches Gesetzbuch*[81]. In Hungarian labour law, the doctrine of validity of the contract of employment is highly unstable, especially in respect of changing terms that affect the employee. As for collective agreements, no validity doctrine has been worked out at all.

4.3 Protection against dismissal for economic reasons

In Hungarian labour law, dismissal based on economic reasons has been quite automatic. It is safe to say that dismissal for economic reasons in EU Member States is generally considered as an ultima ratio option, preceded by appropriate measures. Further, it is an essential fact that dismissal is only viable with adequate reference to fundamental and justified reasons. In Hungarian labour law, especially in judicature, veracity of economic problems is not scrutinized; the employer has no obligation to take preceding measures. In sum: in the case of economic reasons, the employer can terminate the employment relationship without considerable difficulties.

4.4 The role of collective labour law

A function of collective labour law is to establish a balance between parties. In Hungary, trade union influence continuously decreased in the period following the change of regime, and due to certain shortcomings of the regulation, a network of collective agreements has failed to develop. In other words, the collective agreement's role as a source of law has been negligible. The regulation on employee representation bodies – such as

---

81 § BGB 315 (1) „Soll die Leistung durch einen der Vertragschließenden bestimmt werden, so ist im Zweifel anzunehmen, dass die Bestimmung nach billigem Ermessen zu treffen ist." In any case, it is worth considering Birk's remark asserting that the altering and concretizing power of the employer had been fundamentally adopted on the basis of unwritten law and judicature – also as a consequence of legal history experience. See Birk R., *op. cit.*, pp. 58–77.

the works council – is *lex imperfecta*; as a result, these organizations have no material influence on altering the employment relationship.

Finally, it is safe to conclude that the content of the new interpretation, serving flexibility as well as protection of the employee's legal status, is highly complex. On the one hand, the approach described here is an answer to some endeavours that had sought the rejuvenation of labour law, but mainly rendered unsuccessful. On the other hand, the theory of the contract of employment as a relational contract integrates the elements of a certain type of commercial contract into labour law – and this also raises a range of questions. In any event, labour law is likely to set off on a new road, and I strongly believe that the opportunities lying in these developments should by no means be ignored.

The Freedom of Contract in Lithuanian Labour Law

Tomas Bagdanskis*

Abstract

The problems of the freedom of contract in Lithuanian labour law are analysed in this paper. Employment law is always very close to contract law and the challenge is to decide to what extent the parties are free to decide regarding their rights and obligations. In order to achieve balance in regulation, the Labour Code must be adapted to the current market situation from time to time. However, this is not the case in Lithuania. Therefore, rulings of the Supreme Court of the Republic of Lithuania and principles of labour law become very important sources of labour law when evaluating employer and employee behaviour and freedom of contract: are there limits to the will and consent of the parties?

Keywords: freedom of contract, freedom of will, flexibility, labour law.

Introduction

Until the nineteenth century, labour relations were regulated by civil law rules[1]. An employment contract was a kind of civil contract[2]. The concept of legal labour relations became established over the nineteenth and twentieth centuries and from the 1950s labour relations became one of the most important branches of law.[3] Since then freedom of contract as a principle of labour law has been challenging.

---

* Tomas Bagdanskis is Associate Professor of the Faculty of Law Vilnius University, Lithuania. He is the author and co-author of several publications on liability in employment relations, application of legal principles, individual labour disputes and temporary employment.

1 Dambrauskienė G. Civilinių ir darbo sutarčių sąveika [The interaction of civil and employment contracts]. *Jurisprudencija.* No. 28 (20), 2002, p. 7.

2 See Nekrošius I., Nekrošius V., Vėlyvis S. *Romėnų teisė* [Roman Law]. Vilnius: Justitia, 1999, p. 245.

3 Lushnikov A. M., Lushnikov, N. V. *Kurs trudovogo prava* [Labour Law textbook]. Vol. I. Moscow: Statut, 2009, p. 700–714.

An employment contract is an agreement between an employee and an employer. The content of an employment contract consists of conditions upon which the parties have agreed on, which define the parties' rights and obligations. Nowadays the challenge is how to adapt quickly to changes in the labour market[4]. As there are many types of flexibility[5] and it is understood quite differently depending on the country implementing it, it is quite complicated to discuss *flexicurity* as a homogeneous and universal instrument. In that context it is important to discuss freedom of contract in labour law.

The aim of this paper is to describe the present regulation of freedom of contract in labour law. We shall analyse and discuss the existing legal regulation of the employment relationship and its practical application, and suggest possible solutions. The current object of research was chosen because freedom of contract is becoming more and more important for Lithuanian employment relations in practice. We discuss the obstacles encountered by the parties to an employment contract when trying to agree on employment conditions on their own.

1. The problems of evaluating the validity of agreements

The Labour Code of Lithuania (further – 2002 Labour Code) allows to use 'analogy of law' – to use the rules of other branches of law, which regulate similar relations apply (Article 9 (2) of the 2002 Labour Code)[6]. The Lithuanian Civil Code[7] indicates that the provisions of this code shall apply to labour relations to the extent that they are not regulated by special laws[8]. The Labour Code states that 'If the conditions of an employment contract oppose the Labour Code, the law or collective agreement, then the Labour Code, the laws, normative legal acts or conditions of collective agreements have to be applied' (Article 94 (2) of the 2002 Labour Code). Therefore, the question is what does '*oppose*' mean? After passing the Labour Code in 2003, the traditional attitude towards the Labour Code

4 Social dialogue and restructuring in Europe faced with the crisis: consequences and results. *Europe et Société.* 2010, p. 77-78.

5 Reichold H., Krauch S. The impact of new forms of labour on industrial relations and the evolution of labour law in Germany. *Europäische Zeitschrift für Arbeitsrecht,* No. 4, 2008, pp. 487–494.

6 Valstybės žinios (State Gazette). 2002, No. 64-2569.

7 Valstybės žinios (State Gazette). 2000, No. 74-2262.

8 Article 1.3 (3) of the Civil Code of Republic of Lithuania.

from the Courts was not flexible – protection of rules and no freedom to parties consent[9][10]. However, the ruling of the Supreme Court of Lithuania of 13 November 2015 in civil case No. 3K-3-590-378/2015 provides us with the new insight about the principle of freedom of contract[11]. The dispute arose from the following situation: on 31 August 2007, the parties in dispute concluded employment contract. Under this contract the appellant was hired by a public institution – Kaunas district hospital emergency room as a doctor for full-time position. On 16 October 2016, the parties concluded a second employment contract, upon which the parties agreed that the appellant would work 25% of the time. The question arose as to how to treat this working time in the same hospital: additional work, working time increase, overtime? Since the applicant has voluntarily agreed to work more for a fixed fee, and signed a second (additional) contract of employment with the same employer, the duration of working time should be assessed according to Article 144 (5) of the 2002 Labour Code, whose provisions allow working more than one full time position (more than eight hours per day, but no more than twelve hours per day). The agreement on that kind of job can be executed by signing a secondary employment contract (when there are multiple employers), or a contract for additional work (where the employer is the same); also, if there is agreement between the employee and employer on the job for more than one-time charge, it is allowed to deviate from the provisions of Article 144 (1) of the 2002 Labour Code which sets the maximum weekly working time.

The court did not agree that the maximum working time was exceeded, so it must be considered that the parties were working under the second contract of employment and it should not be considered as overtime. According to the fact that the employee and the employer have the right voluntarily, within the limits laid down by the law of maximum working time limits, to agree on working – scale increase, i. e. longer working time, when the parties agree on a salary in the employment contract, such an agreement with the same employer for identical work functions where they are working in excess of normal working hours, but not exceeding mandatory limits, should be treated as an increase in working hours. As a conclusion, the maximum limits provided by labour law were not breached.

---

9 Supreme Court of Lithuania case No. 3K-7-4/2003.

10 Supreme Court of Lithuania case No. 3K-3-74/2006.

11 Supreme Court of Lithuania case No. 3K-3-590-378/2015.

In its ruling of case No. 3K-7-149/2012, the Supreme Court of Lithuania showed a new attitude towards agreement by the parties[12]. The Court stated that due to the constantly changing situation in the labour market, laws could not control all the actions of entities of labour relations. The expanded panel of judges, noted that in Article 4 (4) of the 2002 Labour Code, it is determined that in those cases where this Code or other laws do not directly permit entities of labour law relations to set their own rights and obligations in an agreement, these entities have to abide by the principles of justice, honesty and prudence. It is particularly important that the real and considered will be expressed in an employment contract. The agreement between the parties might be expressed in writing, for example, when an employee agrees to compensation for their annual vacation together with their salary (or different time); or the agreement might be expressed by actions, for example, if an employee submits an application regarding their vacation when there is only one day left till the beginning of their vacation and the employer agrees. Actions of the parties which reveal their concurrent will which depart from Article 176 (2) of the 2002 Labour Code contain the rules and establish an individual payment order. It expresses the will of the employee to waive the right to demand that the basis of annual leave should be extended, and for an extended period of time, the employee would be paid as for annual leave. The opposite interpretation of those provisions might cause a denial of principles which are consolidated in Article 4 and might not be compatible with the obligations of the parties to act in good faith and to not abuse their right under Article 35 of the Code. As a conclusion, the there is no violation of labour law rules if was a clear will of parties to depart from rules which are consolidated in the law.

2. The gaps of legal regulation that need to be filled by the principles of freedom of the contract

Those looking for flexible ways of working often realise that the employment relationship cannot give them the flexibility they need. They then choose other legal ways of flexible activities. As regards atypical forms of activities in Lithuania, we can mention two groups of self-employed individuals: 1) acting under business certificates[13] or

12 Supreme Court of Lithuania case No. 3K-7-149/2012.

13 A way of personal activity allowing to pay fixed sum of yearly income tax.

2) registered at revenue (tax) office as persons doing individual activity[14]. There is uncertainty still concerning the legal background of the relationship between parties performing duties of babysitters, artists etc. The Government has not been able to provide such people with clear legal definitions for their activities. It is difficult to find borders between atypical employment, self-employment and the employment relationship. However, this is not exclusively a Lithuanian problem, because the issue of false self-employment is widely discussed elsewhere.

Those working in atypical forms of employment are in a rather favourable situation regarding organizing their working time, health and safety and sometimes pay levels also (as compared to the income they would receive for the same job in typical employment under an indefinite full-time employment contract). There are no special control mechanisms to ensure that these rights are not being breached.

There is no freedom of will to choose the status of freelancer and work by civil contract in Lithuania, if the relations have any elements of an employment relationship, such us subordination or regular remuneration. Freelance workers choose to work independently, despite a lower level of social protection, because it offers them more income and more freedom to control their own activity. Freelance workers usually work from their own home or office space, but in certain cases they can also be on-site. As a general rule clients have the right to control or supervise only the result of the work done by an independent contractor, but not the process or methods used to accomplish it.

We can see that the defensive function of labour law is eliminated by avoiding and bypassing the employment relationship. The Labour Code tries to protect people excessively but with no success because people are slowly escaping from its area of regulation. We are in no doubt that Lithuanian labour law should be revised and clear rules of activities defined in order to comply with the realities and needs of the labour market.

The other example of how to fill the gaps in labour law rules is the ruling of the Supreme Court in case No. 3K-3-595-219/2015[15]. Employment relations regulated by the Labour Code do not regulate non-competition agreements. The non-compete agreement by its very nature and essence is regarded as a civil legal contract, despite the fact that it consists of an employment contract and its parties are incorporated in the employment

---

[14] If performing an individual activity individuals pay 15% income tax.

[15] Supreme Court of Lithuania case No. 3K-3-595-219/2015.

contract as extras. The rules governing the legality of transactions and contracts of the Civil Code is applicable when determining about a non-compete agreement. It is important to mention that before the 2002 Labour Code, non-competition agreements, according to Supreme Court of Lithuania practice, were treated as objects of labour law (Law on Employment Contract[16])[17]. As a conclusion, those agreements are not prohibited for the parties to the contract of employment.

3. Avoiding guarantees for employees by their consent

In practice, we face situations in the 2002 Labour Code where we have gaps in the law: no special rules for special situations. Let us consider for example, the zero hours contract. Here the relations could be treated in two ways: if there is no rule, it is forbidden; the second option is that if the parties agree it is allowed. In these circumstances the Lithuanian courts have decided to trust the parties: allow them to go to minimum working time and to increase it, if the parties agree.

Another case is related to Article 158 (2) of the 2002 Labour Code, which states that the period for rest and food shall be used by an employee at their own discretion. This means the employer cannot demand that the employee work during this time. On the other hand, the employer's and employee's right to agree on performing some work functions during the break could not be denied if it is necessary (Article 35 (1), Article 158 (5) of the 2002 Labour Code, ruling of Supreme Court of the Republic of Lithuania)[18].

Conclusion – do not oppose, do not impair, do not directly prohibit, if it is necessary or the parties agree and judicial claims are not raised.

4. Reflection of freedom of contract in collective agreements

The collective agreement of a company – a written agreement between the employer and employees regarding working conditions, payment for work and other social and economic conditions. All types of companies, institutions and organizations might have a collective agreement (Article 59

[16] *Valstybės žinios* (State Gazette). 1991, No. 36-973.
[17] Supreme Court of Lithuania case No. 3K-3-65/2005.
[18] Supreme Court of Lithuania case No. 3K-3-117/2012.

of the 2002 Labour Code). A collective agreement is an agreement, drawn up and signed by representatives of employees and the employer, which consists of organizational, informational, obligatory and normative conditions (Articles 61(1) – 61 (2) of the 2002 Labour Code). According to the of the 2002 Labour Code, collective agreements must respect the so-called *in favorem* principle, which prohibits collective agreements from including conditions which worsen the employee's position compared with that which is established by the laws in force. The principle *in favorem* is consolidated in the Labour Code of the Republic of Lithuania. The form of such principle is revealed by the wording 'deviations are not allowed, unless they are provided for by collective agreements'[19]. The ruling of the Supreme Court of Lithuania No. 3K-3-150/2009 proves the existence of such a situation. According to the evidence in the case the defendant complied with the conditions of the collective agreement, including Article 5.8 of this agreement, which lays down the rules that for the total payroll, with the consent of the employee, he shall be paid a premium for recycled hours which during the day is paid at 100% of the daily rate and at night – at least half the hourly wage rate (salary). The fact that the surcharge for the excess working time specified in the collective agreement has been paid is not disputed. This surcharge was not in dispute until the receipt of a letter on 26 January 2007 from the Klaipėda department of the State Labour Inspectorate in which it was mentioned that working time in the timesheets of employees of Vessel Traffic Service was identified as actual working hours (which included both daily working time and overtime) and the employer paid 100% for this time, i.e. for overtime and for daily working time, workers were only paid the their usual hourly rate instead of the one and half times of the hourly wage as as determined in Article 193 of the 2002 Labour Code. In the letter from the State Labour Inspectorate these conditions of the contract were estimated as being contrary to the law and worsened the position of employees, hence it was suggested that changes to these conditions be initiated. The 100% surcharge for overtime indicated in paragraph 5.8 of the collective agreement was found inconsistent with Article 193 which sets that in such case one and a half times the amount of the employee's salary shall be paid. However, this contradiction itself in a collective agreement does not mean that the position of employees is worse.

---

19 For example, Article 109 of the Labour Code: "It shall be prohibited to concl wording 'unless this is provided for by collective agreements' under a fixed-term employment contract if the work is of a permanent nature, unless this is provided for by laws or collective agreements".

All of the provisions of the collective agreement have to be considered as stated in the 2002 Labour Code and other regulatory legislation:

> *In this case, it is not enough to evaluate only one condition from the collective agreement. because, it might be concluded that collective agreement makes employees' position worse, only after careful evaluation of all the conditions of an agreement, i.e. weighting if the particular conditions which makes position of employees' better, compensate other conditions, which according to the employees', make their position worse.*

In addition, it is important to assess the fact that negotiations on the collective agreement involve both the employer and employee representatives and without their mutual consent provisions of a collective agreement as well as conditions for individual contracts therein could not be adopted. In addition, Article 4 (4) of the 2002 Labour Code, which prohibits worsening the situation of workers in the collective agreement specifies, that when this Code and other laws do not directly prohibit the entities of labour relations to establish mutual rights and obligations, these entities must follow justice, reasonableness and integrity. As a conclusion, the balance of rights and obligations is provided in a collective agreement.

How can we explain such deviations from strict Labour Code rules? The answer could lie in the case-law of the Supreme Court of Republic of Lithuania[20]: The application of norms of labour law does not exclusively mean application of worker-friendly rules of law only. It should be taken into account that one legal entity's account cannot be denied by another entity's interests and must be aimed at the reasonable and fair balance of interests.

Conclusions

Analysis of legal regulation and practical application of freedom of contract in Lithuania Labour Law allows us to state that Lithuanian labour law still lacks freedom of will for the parties to an employment contract. The Labour Code 2002 is not flexible enough in terms of concluding variable employment contracts because the parties cannot freely agree on it. In fact, the regulation consists of many formal rules, and these are not flexible enough in today's labour market. Against this background, the case-law of the Supreme Court of Lithuania has played the reformist role – it developed crucial provisions which allowed parties to the contract of employment engage in individual arrangements more freely.

---

[20] Supreme Court of Lithuania case No. 3K-3-312/2014.

Non-competition Agreements

Lithuanian Experience

Beata MARTIŠIENĖ*

Abstract

This article discuses non-competition agreements in Lithuania: the current situation and problematic aspects, judicial practice and proposed new legal regulation are discussed. The new Lithuanian Labour Code was passed on 21 June 2016 and it declares new legal rules for non-competition agreements. The author of this article gives commentaries on these legal rules and comes to the conclusion that the new Lithuanian Labour Code is considered to be very liberal in general, however in the sphere of non-competition agreements, it could be more oriented towards future challenges.

Key words: non-competition agreements, contract of employment, compensation.

Introduction

Every reform of labour law in Lithuania was aimed at modernizing labour relations. However, after 25 years of reforms, Lithuanian Labour Law is still considered to be rigid and outdated. There may be several reasons for this. Firstly, labour relations themselves are in crisis all over the world. They are changing rapidly, getting new looks, new models and the transformation process is not over yet. Secondly, the mentality of Lithuanian employees and employers is not that modern at all. Thirdly, the so called 'new methods' and 'new rules', implemented so far were not modern. In addition, it is important to mention that labour law is being discussed world wide. So, the Lithuanian situation during the reform of Labour Law is not an exception.

Lithuanian labour law reform faces many challenges: internal problematic issues (is it possible to change the regime radically and to do

---

* Beata Martišienė is a lecturer at Faculty of Law Vilnius University, Lithuania. She is also a judge at the district court. Her particular sphere of interest is in the relations between civil and labour law.

it effectively? The current 2002 Labour Code is very rigid while the new 2016 Labour Code is considered as very liberal. Unlike the previous law, the new Labour Code contains rules on agreements on non-competition. The main goal of this paper is to analyse the Lithuanian experience on regulation and application of rules on non-competition agreements.

1. Historical background

Non-competition agreements in Lithuania are typical examples of antagonism between Lithuanian legal theory and practice. First of all, Lithuanian labour law scientists[1] claim that non-competition agreements should be regulated by labour law rules. There are several reasons to support this attitude. Firstly, a relationship is being developed between an employer and an employee. Secondly, the essence of the agreement is to regulate the performance of work. Actually, non-competition agreements usually involve restrictions on engagement or activity in business as well. This aspect extends beyond the boundaries of labour law. Finally, non-competition agreements are personal obligations which have direct impact on an employee's duties and rights. Despite these reasons, Lithuanian judicial practice decided that non-competition agreements are regulated by the Civil Code and therefore they should be treated as civil agreements (Lithuanian Supreme Court Cases *D. B. v. Kemira GrowHow of* 2003[2]; *'Docpartner' v. L. V.* of 2007[3]; *A. G. v. Aon*

---

1 Davulis T. Dar kartą apie nekonkuravimo susitarimus Lietuvos darbo teisėje [Once again about non-competition agreements under Lithuanian labour law], *Juristas*, No. 4, 2006; Krasauskas R. Nekonkuravimo susitarimai darbo teisėje: ar darbuotojas ir darbdavys yra lygiaverčiai konkurentai? [Non-competition Agreements in labour law: are employee and employer equal?] *Jurisprudencija*, No. 8 (110), 2008; Martišienė B. *Darbo santykių reguliavimo civiliniai teisiniai aspektai* [Civil law aspects in employment relationships]. Vilnius: Vilnius university, 2012.

2 The case: An employee worked for his employer as a manager. The parties entered into a non-competition agreement on 8 March 1999. The initiative to enter a non-competition agreement came from the employer. The employee brought a claim against the court that non-competition agreement was against the interests of an employee and therefore illegal and prohibited by the Lithuanian Labour Code. The Lithuanian Supreme Court indicated that such an agreement is possible under civil law. Therefore it is legal under certain conditions. However, in this case the Supreme Court admitted that the non-competition agreement, excluding the compensation for non-competition, is illegal.

3 The case: An employee worked for his employer as an archivist. The parties to the employment contract decided to make an amendment to the employment contract and to conclude a non-competition agreement. The employer brought a claim to

Lietuva of 2008[4]; *Miesto energija v. J. A. K.* of 2012[5]; *R. S. v. ETB Legal* of 2012[6] etc.). This approach was strongly criticised by Lithuanian scientists[7].

Secondly, Lithuanian labour law scientists claim that the Lithuanian Labour Code prohibits these type of agreements[8]. Article 97 (1) of the Lithuanian Labour Code of 2002 declares that restrictions on admittance to work may be imposed only by laws. As the Labour Code does not allow this kind of restriction, it is prohibited and parties cannot conclude these types of contracts. The Lithuanian Supreme Court (hereinafter SCL) has supported the opposite attitude. The Court has upheld the position that the Lithuanian Labour Code does not regulate non-competition agreements (there are no direct rules and Article 97 is not dedicated to regulating competition agreements, too). The Court has allowed these non-competition agreements according to Civil Law rules – if it is not prohibited in the Civil Code, it is allowed. The Lithuanian Civil Code

---

the court claiming that the employee had broken the contract and started working for a competitor as an archivist. The Lithuanian Supreme Court has decided that a non-competition agreement incorporated in an employment agreement may be seen as a valid civil legal agreement establishing the parties to civil rights and obligations. The employer asked that the employee be obliged to terminate the employment relationship with the new employer but the Supreme Court of Lithuania denied this request because the duration of the non-competition period was already over.

4 The case: An employee worked for his employer as an insurance events administrator. The parties concluded a non-competition agreement which ensured that the employee would receive compensation after the termination of the employment contract. The employment contract was terminated and the order of dismissal set that the non-competition contract was also over. The employee brought a claim against his ex-employer requesting that the employer be obliged to pay the compensation. The Lithuanian Supreme Court decided that the agreement on non-competition was concluded in favour of the employer. So the employer may decline and refuse the non-competition agreement without the consent of the employee. So the non-competition agreement was terminated legally and therefore the compensation should not be paid.

5 The case: An employee worked as a director and concluded a non-competition agreement on the day his employment contract was terminated. The compensation for an employee for non-competition obligation was paid The Lithuanian Supreme Court held that this type of compensation is a legal one and the non-competition agreement was valid.

6 The case: the parties concluded a non-competition agreement which was compensated. The peculiarity is that the compensation was part of a share sale-purchase agreement. Lithuanian Supreme Court held that this type of compensation is a legal one and the non-competition agreement was valid.

7 Davulis T., *op. cit.*; Krasauskas R., *op. cit.*; Martišienė B., *op. cit.*

8 *Ibidem.*

does not prohibit non-competition agreements. On the contrary, Article 2.164 of the Lithuanian Civil Code is dedicated to regulating non-competition agreements between a commercial agent and a principal[9]. According to the latest and currently valid position of the SCL, these rules were applied by analogy to non-competition agreements between an employee and an employer (Lithuanian Supreme Court Case *Docpartner v. L. V. of* 2007; *A. G. v. Aon Lietuva of* 2008; *Miesto energija v. J. A. K. of* 2012; *R. S. v. ETB Legal of* 2012; etc.).

It must be mentioned that on 26 May 2003 a bill on non-competition agreements was proposed to Lithuanian Parliament. Article 11 of this bill suggested that the Lithuanian Labour Code be complemented with an article on non-competition agreements. However the proposed rules[10] were not accepted by the Parliament for political reasons.

So historically, it seems as if the Lithuanian legislator has tried to prevent parties from entering into the non-competition agreements. However, their need came from practice – the necessity to protect intellectual property is as important as the need to protect material property. The author upholds the position that these types of agreements are necessary, and should be allowed, but they should be regulated by labour law rules. The main reasoning for the need for labour law rules is that current regulation of non-competition agreements does not correspond to the need to protect employees (which is at the heart of labour law), therefore changes in this sphere are vital.

---

9 According to the Article 2.152 (1) of the Lithuanian Civil Code a commercial agent shall be an independent person whose basic business activity is to act as intermediary for a principal in conclusion of contracts or conclusion of contracts in his or principal's name and at the latter's expense as well as in his interests.

10 **"Article 107^{1}. Non-competition agreements**

1. An employer and an employee to be can agree that an employee shall not compete with the employer after the termination of employment contract. This restriction can be set only in the area an employee was engaged with at work and for the period not longer than two years.
2. An employer must pay an agreed monthly compensation for his ex-employee which must be no less than 40 percent of his monthly salary. This amount must be not less than minimum wage. An employer may terminate the payment of the agreed compensation if he decides to cancel the restrictions.
3. A non-competition agreement is terminated if an employment contract was terminated on the grounds provided in Article 128 of this Code.
4. An employee who violates a non-competition agreement, must compensate the losses for his employer."

2. Current situation and challenges

2.1 The concept of non-competition agreements

Labour law scientists give different definitions for non-competition agreements. T.Davulis defines non-competition agreements as agreements between an employee and an employer where an employee undertakes not to compete with the employer after the termination of the employment contract: not to work for another employer who is a competitor of his ex-employer and/or not to establish or participate in a competing business[11]. The same concept is upheld by R.Krasauskas[12].

The author has a wider concept of non-competition agreements: non-competition agreements may be entered into at any stage of labour relations and restrictions may be applied not only after termination of the employment contract but also during the employment relationship. The necessity of a wider concept is based on two main arguments. Firstly, according to Article 114 of the 2002 Labour Code an employee may take a secondary job with another employer if legal acts do not so prohibit. The restrictions of legal acts on taking a secondary job are not within the scope of this article so they will not be discussed in more detail here. Therefore, according to the rule just mentioned, an employee may have more than one valid employment contract at the same time. Not necessarily, but the employers may be competitors. So, there is a legal interest for an employer to not only protect his intangible assets after the termination of an employment relationship with an employee, but also during the relationship. Secondly, some lawyers claim that an employee is bound to his employer with a duty of loyalty. And this duty requires that an employee does not work for a competitor or does not establish or participate in a competing business. The author disagrees with this attitude. The Lithuanian Labour Code does explicitly name the duty of loyalty for an employee: there is no article which mentions this loyalty of an employee to his employer. However, Lithuanian judicial practice has formulated this duty in legal cases. For example, the SCL has held (Lithuanian Supreme Court Case *P. G. v. S. K. S. of* 2008) that an employment contract requires an employee to be loyal to his employer, to work honestly, fairly and preserve the property of the employer. In addition, an employee must not carry out illegal actions that would harm the interests of the employer. This position was upheld not only once, but it is a consistent rule set by the SCL (Lithuanian Supreme Court

11 Davulis T, *op. cit.*

12 Krasauskas R., *op. cit.*

Case *N. D. v. Puntukas of* 2012). But it must be mentioned that this duty was not formulated in the context of non-competition cases, but in other cases (liability, performance of job duties, etc.). So, the content of duty of loyalty (as it was named by the Supreme Court of Lithuania) is not wide enough to embrace restrictions on working for a competitor or to establish or participate in a competing business. On the contrary – this duty of loyalty has its own separate meaning in Lithuanian Labour Law which can be described as a certain level of care for the performance of job duties. For these reasons the author maintains that non-competition agreements may be applicable for the period after the termination of employment agreements and during a valid existing employment agreement.

There are several factors affecting the regulation of non-competition agreements that should be discussed in more detail. Firstly, an employee is the weaker party in the employment contract, so legal rules regulating non-competition agreements should have the effect of proper protection for an employee who enters a non-competition agreement. Secondly, Lithuanian peculiarities of legal regulation for non-competition agreements (a fact that it is regulated by civil law rules and those rules were formulated by judicial practice, not by the legislator) mean that the rules applied to non-competition agreements do not protect employees as they should. These cases will be discussed in more detail below.

2.2 Forms of compensation

According to the SCL, a non-competition agreement is invalid if there is no just and fair compensation for the duties accepted by an employee (Lithuanian Supreme Court case *R. S. v. ETB Legal of* 2012). This position of the Supreme Court is very accurate and important, because Lithuanian employers have often challenged this idea. The reasons were various: the will of the employee (if he voluntarily accepted the duty without compensation, it is up to him to take up this commitment) (Lithuanian Supreme Court case *JG reklamos dovanos v. D. S. & UAB Verslo inkorporacijos centras*[13], 2013; *Marilita v. A. B. (A. B.) & R. Č.* of 2013[14])

[13] The case: An employee worked for his employer as a sales manager. A non-competition agreement and an agreement on confidentiality were concluded. The term of non-competition was two years after the termination of employment agreement. The Supreme Court of Lithuania decided that the nature of the job must be evaluated in order to decide whether a non-competition agreement was valid. Furthermore, the Supreme Court has decided that 9% of the average monthly salary (87 euros per month) is obviously too small a percentage for compensation and in absolute expression of its size.

[14] The case: An employee worked for his employer as head of the provisioning department. A non-competition agreement was concluded for not competing for the

the freedom of contract, etc. The Supreme Court of Lithuania was firm in its ruling that the salary is not and cannot be treated as compensation for a non-competition agreement: agreement on compensation for non-competition obligations must be clearly expressed in the definition of its size and purposes and separated from other agreed payments for other purposes between an employer and an employee (Lithuanian Supreme Court case *Marilita v. A. B. (A. B.) & R. Č. of 2013*). So, the requirement of compensation was correctly identified by the judiciary and successfully upheld in numerous cases.

The Supreme Court has also faced problems on the concept of non-competition agreements. An employer has entered a non-competition agreement with his employee and the period of this obligation was dual: during the employment relationship and after the termination. The SCL has decided that it is possible per se to conclude these types of agreements. Furthermore, the Court has decided that compensation must be paid not only after the termination of the employment agreement but also during it (Lithuanian Supreme Court case *A. V. v. 'Robert Bosch'*, 2016[15]). The reasoning was that the obligation not to compete must be compensated. If the obligation is valid during the employment relationship, compensation must be paid too.

However, there were several problematic rules, set by the Supreme Court. First of all, the Court agreed that compensation for a non-competition agreement can be paid during the existing employment relationship. The author considers that if the obligation not to compete is set for the period after the termination of the employment contract, the compensation cannot be paid during the employment relationship. The period of non-competition and the period of payments must coincide. The reasons for this position are the same as those which justify

---

period of labour relations and two years after termination of the employment contract. The territory for non-competition was all of the European Union. The Supreme Court of Lithuania said that compensation for the non-competition agreement should be fair and just. That means it must correspond to the extent of the restraints. Even the compensation which was paid during labour relations must be clearly distinguished from other kinds of payments.

15 The case: An employee brought a claim against his employer for illegal termination of the employment contract. One of the reasons for termination was the supposed breach of the non-competition agreement, so the courts had to decide on its validity. The dispute was whether it is necessary to compensate for non-competition agreements if the retrains forbid to work or participate in a competing business during the employment relations. SCL decided that compensation must be paid both: during the employment relations and after, if the time of non-competition is during the employment relations and after the termination of the employment contract.

the requirement to pay a salary every month. It would be useful for an employee – he would receive a monthly income during the period of restrictions. Furthermore, it would help to avoid erroneous assessment of the actual amount of salary the employee receives. However, the Supreme Court has decided that it is legal to pay compensation for an employee for non-competition agreements during the employment relationship (Lithuanian Supreme Court case *JG reklamos dovanos v. D. S. & UAB Verslo inkorporacijos centras of* 2013; *Kemitek v. P. Z.* of 2015[16]). Moreover, it seems that the Supreme Court has approved that it is possible to pay the compensation for the non-competition agreements as one-time payments (Lithuanian Supreme Court case *Miesto energija v. J. A. K. of* 2012; *R. S. v. ETB Legal of* 2012). For example, compensation may be included in the price of the shares during the purchase contract (Lithuanian Supreme Court case *R. S. v. ETB Legal of* 2012). The author criticizes these legal rules and suggests employees should be given more protection: the regulation of concrete and strict rules on the payment of compensation is necessary and vital.

2.3 The amount of compensation

In addition, the SCL has analysed many non-competition agreements and their validity from the angle of the amount of the compensation. As already mentioned, the Court has decided that the compensation must be just and fair (Lithuanian Supreme Court case *R. S. v. 'ETB Legal' of* 2012). The definition of this 'just and fair compensation' is challenged very often by Lithuanian employers. SCL has decided that 9% of the average monthly salary (87 EUR per month) is obviously too low compensation (Lithuanian Supreme Court case *JG reklamos dovanos v. D. S. & UAB Verslo inkorporacijos centras'* of 2013). The Court mentioned minimum monthly wage – it was considered that the amount of compensation was less than

16 The case: An employee worked for his employer as a manager-technologist. A non-competition agreement was concluded for non-competition for two years after the termination of the employment agreement. The compensation was paid during the employment relations together with the salary every month. It was clearly noted in every payment receipt that 15% of the salary was compensation for non-competition agreement. Compensation after termination of the employment contract was not paid. An employee worked for his employer for almost seven years and received LTL 40,057.03 (EUR 11,601.32) as compensation for two years of non-competition. SCL decided that this manner of compensation is legal. Moreover, it acknowledged that 15% of monthly salary might be enough. SCL has decided to return the case to the lower court for analysis, so the final decision (whether it is enough or not) is not taken by the Supreme Court.

the minimum monthly wage. So, in this case the SCL has successfully identified the criteria and evaluation of the compensation paid by an employer to his ex-employee for non-competition agreements. However, two years later the Court decided that 15% of the average monthly salary (EUR 109.48 per month) might be just and fair compensation for a non-competition agreement (SCL case *Kemitek v. P. Z.* of 2015). The author criticizes this evaluation. First of all, it does not correspond in any way to the minimum monthly – the criteria the Court itself has formulated before. It is a useful criteria and, in the opinion of the author, there can be no discussion on whether the compensation may be less than this amount. The discussion might start with how much bigger the compensation might be because the jobs for which the non-competition agreements are dedicated are usually highly qualified ones. Therefore, the reward may not be the minimum wage. Secondly, the obligation not to compete is a strict one: it deprives an employee of a job for which he is highly skilled. So the loss is not only for the employee himself (not being able to work for some time in a particular job), but also for the state – the employee loses his skills during that break, and productivity and efficiency is being lost. Finally, an ex-employee needs an income on which to live during the period of the existing non-competition agreement. So, these types of obligations should not be cheap. The interests of employees and the state must be guaranteed.

To sum up, the SCL has faced many challenges while formulating legal rules, applicable for the compensation of non-competition agreements. In the opinion of the author, some rules were very progressive and positive (for example, firm rule on the necessity for compensation), other rules were criticized (for example, the amount of compensation). So the need for regulation in the sphere of non-competition agreements is considerable. It is crucial to return these types of contracts to the sphere of labour law regulation. Then, it is vital to set the rules having in mind that the employee is the weaker party to the contract. At the same time it is important to have in mind the idea of non-competition agreements – to weigh up their use and possible dangers. In the opinion of the author, the decision is of great importance and it must be taken not by the judiciary in ad hoc cases, but by the legislator pursuing social objectives of employees' protection.

3. New Lithuanian Labour Code of 2016

Since the Ministry of Social Security and Labour assigned a group of scholars to prepare the new codification of labour legislation and the draft Labour Code was published on 15 March 2015, there has been heated debate in public and among the social partners. The Lithuanian Parliament passed the new Labour Code on 21 June 2016. It should come into force on 1 January 2017. The new Labour Code will have a major impact on the regulation of non-competition agreements in Lithuania.

First of all, the discussion on the nature of non-competition agreements should end. The new Lithuanian Labour Code 2016 does regulate these agreements. Article 38 of the 2016 Labour Code declares:

'1. Parties to the employment contract may agree that an employee shall not compete (shall not work under employment contract or shall not perform or participate in individual commercial or industrial activity) with his employer after the termination of the employment contract, if this activity directly competes with the employer's activity. This agreement is valid for no longer than two years after the termination of employment contract.

2. Non-competition agreements can be concluded only with employees, who have special knowledge or abilities, which can be used for the purposes of competing businesses and cause damage to the employer.

3. Non-competition agreements must include working or professional activity which is prohibited for an employee, the amount of the compensation, the territory of restrictions and the duration of the restrictions. An employee must be paid compensation during the period of restrictions. The compensation must be not less than 40% of the average salary (at the time of the termination of the employment contract) of the employee. The compensation cannot be paid while the employee is still working for the employer.

4. In case of breach of the non-competition agreement an employee must quit his working or professional activity which is in competition with an employer's, return the compensation he received and compensate the damages of the employer. Preliminary agreements on penalties, exceeding compensation for three months, are void.

5. An employee has the right to terminate his non-competition agreement unilaterally if an employer is late with his payment of non-competition compensation or any part thereof'[17].

The 2016 Labour Code 2016 is dedicated to liberalizing the regulation of labour relations. It is expected that flexible and non-bureaucratic labour relations will be created. These new labour relations

[17] This translation is not an official one.

should lead to creation of new jobs, convert emigration of employees to exportation of goods and services, decrease unemployment, increase youth employment, discourage illegal work, and modernize the labour market. The new Labour Code was criticized as being very sympathetic towards employers and unsympathetic to employees. In the case of non-competition agreements, the situation is different. The new Labour Code doesn't mean less regulation, but more regulation in favour of the employee. First of all, according to the new Labour Code, all labour law rules are being applied. So the idea of 'civil agreement' is being eliminated by the legislator. That is very positive in the new Labour Code. Secondly, the legislator has decided that non-competition agreements might be concluded only with special categories of employees – those who have special knowledge or abilities, which can be used for the purposes of competing businesses and cause damage to an employer. Other types of employees cannot enter a non-competition agreement. The author agrees with this restriction. The winners in this restriction are not only the employees (their protection from abusive use of non-competition agreement is being restricted), but society as well – a non-competition agreement prevents former employees from practicing a job function they are good and skilled at. So this human potential is being lost for some time. It is important to mention that the SCL has upheld this position so far in its previous practice (Lithuanian Supreme Court case *A. V. v. Robert Bosch* of 2016).

Moreover, the 2016 Labour Code has set some important rules for the compensation for non-competition agreements. The time of payment of compensation is now expressly stated in the law. The legislator decided that compensation cannot be paid while an employee is still working for the employer. The author agrees with this rule. First of all, the idea of the compensation is to ensure that an employee receives a certain reward (fair and just), which is his income for living. He may receive this revenue from performing a job. As he is restricted from performing certain jobs, a person may receive less or no revenue at all. So, his only income will be the compensation for the non-competition agreement. As this money serves more or less the same function as the salary paid during the employment relationship, it is reasonable to have a rule to pay it every month. Secondly, the requirement to pay compensation after the employment relationship has ended serves as a guarantee to avoid bogus compensations. If it were possible to pay the compensation for non-competition agreements during the employment relationship, the danger for the employee to receive part of his salary as compensation existed. The 2016 Labour Code prevents these situations and thus solves the existing problems that were discussed above.

In addition, the new 2016 Labour Code has set the basis for the compensation of non-competition agreements. As mentioned before, Lithuanian practice was very moderate when setting the minimum for compensation an employee should get. The Lithuanian legislator was more reasonable. A non-competition agreement sets many restrictions for an employee – he cannot work or be active in the same business on his own for the time period agreed, so he does not receive any revenue from his work. Therefore, he must be rewarded for that with a reasonable and fair compensation. As well as this, it is the author's opinion that employers should be encouraged to use non-competition agreements wisely, too. They should be used only if the need for protection of intellectual property really does exist, not for other reasons.

Finally, the new Labour Code has specified the consequences of breach of a non-competition agreement. They are: the termination of infringement of non-competition agreement, the return of the compensation received and the compensation of damages of an employer. Although the application of these rules will have some peculiarities and the courts will have to apply them with care, this enumeration and clarity is very useful especially in light of current case law.

So, there are many examples of where the new Lithuanian Labour Code can set more liberal rules for labour relations than there used to be. However, non-competition agreements are not one of them. On the contrary – the new Labour Code solves many of the current problems, and this is very important for the protection of employees in practicing non-competition agreements. In this respect the new Labour Code is very welcome and it will ensure the rights of employees more efficiently.

4. Challenges for the new Labour Code

Despite the above-mentioned positive aspects of the new Labour Code, there are also some downsides. First of all, the situation of non-competition during labour relations is solved differently from the current situation. The concept of non-competition agreements given in the new Labour Code is a narrow one. So, Lithuanian employees and employers, according to the new Code, might agree not to compete only after the termination of employment agreements. So the question is whether non-competition agreements are prohibited during the employment relationship or are they allowed but may not be compensated as they are not considered to be non-competition agreements according to the new Labour Code? The author takes the position that non-competition agreements should be allowed during labour relations and after the termination of labour relations, they must also be compensated in both instances – during labour relations and after the termination. The difficulties of separating salary from compensation for non-competition agreements during labour relations should not stand in the way of allowing them and rewarding for the obligations taken by the employee.

Secondly, even if the new Lithuanian Labour Code enters into force, challenges for the concept of non-competition agreements will still exist. Lithuanian judicial practice has not answered so far the question of whether it is legal to prohibit an employee from working elsewhere. That does not necessarily mean working only for a competitor. One of the recent cases in SCL (Lithuanian Supreme Court case *A. V. v. Robert Bosch* of 2016) was very interesting in this regard. The non-competition agreement in dispute stated that an employee must not work for or participate in any other business. The phrase 'any competing business' was not used. So, the question is whether an employer may legally prohibit his employees from working elsewhere, not necessarily for a competitor. The Court left this question open – the non-competition agreement in question was declared invalid for other reasons (absence of compensation). So, legal regulation so far in Lithuania is unclear. S.Deakin claims that non-competition agreements should be allowed only if the employer proves the necessity to protect his interests[18]. So, there are restrictions on allowing non-competition agreements. However, the new Labour Code is unclear, too. It seems as if the new Code does not allow prohibiting work or participating in another business – part two of Article 38 of the new Labour Code defines the addressee of this legal rule and mentions that the protection is against competing businesses. The author upholds this position – it is important to protect the immaterial property of the ex-employer but it is also important to ensure protection for the employee. The interest of an employer must not prevail over the interests of employees. Any restriction on competition might be a loss for society.

There are also many challenges for Lithuanian non-competition agreements related to the virtual environment. Duarte Abrunhosa

---

[18] Deakin S., Morris G. S. *Labour Law*. Third edition. Oxford: Oxford University Press, 2001.

e Sousa[19] gives an example of a case resolved by Danish Courts. After the termination of their employment relationship two employees were intending to work for a competitor of the former employer. However, since they had to respect a non-competition agreement for one year, the new employment contract was postponed. During this agreement period, the employees decided to update their LinkedIn profiles with the designation of the new employer. However, LinkedIn does not have any function to allow sharing a future employer so, for all the network's users, both employees were already working for the new company. In this case Western High Court ruled that despite everything, in the activity sector where the employees worked, personal relations where not considered important and the agreement did not rule out the use of the social network. Therefore, both former employees do not have to not pay any damages. So far Lithuanian judicial practice has not faced these types of challenges. However, they are coming to Lithuania, too. Social networks and rights/obligations of employees in this area have been in a grey zone, so far. It must be mentioned that the new 2016 Labour Code is more dedicated to solving current existing problems for non-competition agreements, but not intended to solve future challenges such as the one mentioned in the Danish case law. The new Labour Code is very reserved towards virtual challenges, so the author thinks that the decisions will be left for judicial practice. In this regard the situation remains the same – the Lithuanian legislator is vague, the court will have to deal with the upcoming problems and maybe after a while the legislator will accept this practice and pass a law. This behaviour is very characteristic of Lithuanian labour law.

To sum up, the 2016 Labour Code in the sphere of non-competition agreements solves many of the current existing problems. However, there are several aspects where the decision taken may be criticized as being very conservative and oriented to solving current rather than future challenges. So, while the new 2016 Labour Code is considered to be very modern, the author suggests that there are cases, where the Code proposed should be more modern.

---

19 Abrunhosa e Sousa D. (2016). Employment non-competition clauses – impacts of social network. 2016. Retrieved August 13, 2016 from http://www.tf.vu.lt/dokumentai/PhdNET/PhDConference-VU-Papers-Edition2016Vilnius.pdf.

Conclusions

The historical background of the regulation of non-competition agreements shows that the legislator must be very precise in setting the rules. The rules, which have weak justification, strong motives to do the opposite, are not being followed. Moreover, the effect might be the exact opposite to the goals pursued. In case of non-competition agreements, the goal was to protect employees from harsh restrictions. However, the effect was to displace labour relations with civil ones and the protection, which could have been given to an employee, was lost.

Non-competition agreements set serious restrictions for the employee. Lithuanian practice so far shows that they must be regulated by Labour Law rules. Minimum protection should be provided for the employee in order not to misuse this instrument (use it for unjustifiable reasons, use it in an abusive manner, etc.).

The Lithuanian legislator upholds his practice to wait before regulating non-competition agreements. The rules are being formulated by Lithuanian Courts and practiced for a while. Only then does the Lithuanian legislator accept or reject the rules for non-competition agreements. This practice has led to many violations of employee rights so far and may lead to many more. The faster reaction of the legislator would be appreciated.

The new Lithuanian Labour Code 2016 is considered to be very liberal and favourable towards employers in many areas. In case of non-competition agreements, the situation is different – it enforces many legal rules which ensure better protection for employees in the sphere of non-competition agreements.

Business Transfer in the Context of Labour Law Reform

Eglė TAMOŠIŪNAITĖ*

Abstract

The paper seeks to overview how the regulation of business transfer might change in the newly adopted Labour Code and what should still be considered for improvement. The analysis is made from the perspective of identifying the object of a business transfer and legal forms of the transfer. The author holds the view that there was some linguistic misinterpretation while implementing Directive 2001/23/EC, which meant that under the former Labour Code (but which is still being used as of the time of writing the article) and under the newly adopted Labour Code both an activity (business or in Lithuanian 'verslas') and an organizational unit (undertaking or in Lithuanian 'įmonė'), which pursues such business activity, can be distinct objects of a transfer. Despite the significance of the notion of 'economic entity' under Directive 2001/23/EC, neither the former Labour Code, nor the new Labour Code uses this term and the article will also look at this anomaly. Accordingly, neither of them provide a requirement that the transferred economic entity retain its identity, though such test is obligatory under Directive 2001/23/EC. Lastly, the legal forms by which a certain business transfer can take place and which are named in the new Labour code are discussed. These legal forms – a transaction and a legal act – fully conform to the scope and the interpretation of Directive 2001/23/EC. However, the fact that the new Labour Code finds the reorganization of an employer and business transfer as separate grounds for applying guarantees for continuity of employment is confusing. There is still need for a more comprehensive explanation that business transfer can take place by way of transaction or due to a legal act in the course of an undertaking's reorganization or restructuring. Therefore these situations of an undertaking's reorganization or restructuring are an integral part of the business transfer notion.

Keywords: business, transfer, Directive 2001/23/EC, reform.

* Egle Tamošiūnaitė is practicing lawyer and PhD student at Facvulty of Law Vilnius University, Lithuania.

Introduction

Lithuania has been long and eagerly looking forward to a comprehensive labour law reform, which finally seems very close to implementation. The main axis of this reform is the new Labour Code, which has been recently adopted by the Parliament and which is about to substantially change the previous labour relationship regulation as of 1 January 2017. The main focus of the new Labour Code is the introduction of new legal forms of labour organization, balancing of employers' rights and obligations in order to revitalize the labour market, attract and encourage investors, and stimulate the creation of new jobs. Among the many changes, the changes to the business transfer regulation have a small but notable stake. Since the new Labour Code is currently at the very centre of public debates, this paper seeks to overview how the regulation of business transfer will change, why these changes are important ant what should still be improved.

Prior to analysing the national business transfer regulation, it should be mentioned that such regulation derived from the Council Directive 2001/23/EC of 12 March 2001 on the approximation of the laws of the Member States relating to the safeguarding of employees' rights in the event of transfers of undertakings, businesses or parts of undertakings or businesses[2] (hereinafter – Directive 2001/23/EC). As per Clause 1 Article 1 of the Directive 2001/23/EC, it applies to any transfer of an undertaking, business, or part of an undertaking or business to another employer as a result of a legal transfer or merger. Directive 2001/23/EC also provides that there is a transfer within the meaning of the Directive where there is a transfer of an economic entity which retains its identity, meaning an organised grouping of resources which has the objective of pursuing an economic activity, whether or not that activity is central or ancillary.

Such wording of the Directive 2001/23/EC allows summarizing that:

1) the object of transfer is an undertaking, business or part of an undertaking or business;
2) the object can be transferred by a legal transfer or merger.

---

2 *Official Journal*, L 82, p. 16.

Accordingly, the analysis shall be made from the perspective of identifying the object of the transfer and the legal forms of the transfer, which, in the author's opinion, are the most problematic.

1. The object of transfer

Article 138 (1) of the Lithuanian Labour Code of 2002[3] provides that changes of the owner of an enterprise, establishment or organization, subordination, founder or a name thereof, as well as any merger or division by the formation of a new enterprise, establishment or organization, division by acquisition, or merger by acquisition, the transfer of business or a part thereof may not constitute a legitimate reason to terminate the employment relationship. It should be noted, that this exact rule existed long before Lithuania became a member of the European Union, except for the words 'transfer of business or a part thereof', which were included as a result of the implementation of Directive 2001/23/EC after Lithuania's accession.

Such mechanical inclusion of the words 'business transfer or a part thereof' in Article 138 of the 2002 Labour Code resulted in several questions of a theoretical nature. Firstly, whether the legislator considered business or a part thereof as an object transfer distinct from the notions of an enterprise, establishment or organization, which remained also mentioned in Article 138 of the 2002 Labour Code. Also, why is the transfer of an undertaking or a part thereof not mentioned if the legislator intended to literally follow the wording of Directive 2001/23/EC. Accordingly, the former wording allowed discussing that either the legislator deemed that the previous wording of Article 138 of the Labour Code, which was silent regarding business transfer, included the cases of business transfer or a part thereof, or took the position that business transfer or a part thereof also covers cases of transfer of an undertaking or a part thereof. In both cases, using a formalistic approach, it is not consistent with the wording of paragraph A Clause 1 Article 1 of Directive 2001/23/EC, according to which an undertaking, part of an undertaking, business and part of a business are identified as different objects of transfer.

A similar rule to that established in Article 138 (1) of the 2002 Labour Code is established in the new Labour Code, however the rule's

---

[3] *Valstybės žinios* (State Gazette), 2002, No. 64-2569.

wording has changed. Following Article 51 (1) of the 2016 Labour Code, the changes in participants of the employer, its subordination or name, employer's division or merger by acquisition, employer's merger or division by the formation of a new enterprise, establishment or organization, or restructuring does not change the employment conditions of the employer's employees and may not be a legal reason to terminate the employment. In addition, as per Article 51 (2)of the new Labour Code, if due to a transaction or legal act, or several transactions or legal acts the business or a part thereof is transferred from one employer (transferor) to another (transferee), the latter also automatically takes over the employment relationships attributable to that business or a part thereof.

If Article 51 (1) of the 2016 Labour Code is compared to Article 138 (1) of the 2002 Labour Code, it can be noticed that business transfer or a part thereof is no longer mentioned in the new Labour Code as an illegal ground for employment termination. However, the case of business transfer or a part thereof is discussed separately in Article 51 (2). So both in the former Labour Code and in the new Labour Code the legislator chooses to see the situation of a business transfer and, for example, the situation of the merger of undertakings as two distinct cases. Although in both of these cases the legislator provides for the guarantee of employment continuity, it is still unclear what the ground for such distinction is.

The author considers there are a couple of reasons that determine the wording of Article 51 of the 2016 Labour Code. On the one hand, it is possible that the legislator chose to keep mentioning the cases of division or merger by acquisition and merger or division by the formation of a new enterprise, establishment or organization, due to the fact that a similar clause has existed in the Lithuanian Labour Code for a long time. Accordingly, there is a significant amount of related case law, which elaborated an understanding of the scope of this provision and therefore the elimination of such wording could cause some confusion. On the other hand, it must be admitted that the object of a business transfer is unclear. It should be noted that Directive 2001/23/EC itself does not make any clear difference between the transfer of an undertaking, its part and transfer of a business or a part thereof. In other words, the wording of Directive 2001/23/EC implies that a transfer of each of them has its own distinct differences. However, the existence of such difference is not obvious since the Directive does not contain definitions for 'undertaking', 'business', 'part of undertaking', 'part of business'. In addition, those differences have never been explained in detail by the Court of Justice of European Union.

Furthermore, the author finds that both Article 138 of the 2002 Labour Code and Article 51 of the 2016 Labour Code use the term 'business transfer' as a general term referring both to the transfer of an undertaking and the transfer of a business. However, such choice is not completely accurate and this is revealed while investigating the terminology used in Directive 77/187/EC[4], a predecessor of Directive 2001/23/EC.

Directive 77/187/EEC was released in the Danish, Dutch, English, French, German and Italian languages first, later it was translated to other languages. The French version of Clause 1 Article 1 of Directive 77/187/EEC states – *La présente directive est applicable aux transferts d'entreprises, d'établissements ou de paragraphies d'établissements à un autre chef d'entreprise, résultant d'une cession conventionnelle ou d'une fusion.* Whereas, the English version states – This Directive shall apply to the transfer of an undertaking, business or part of a business to another employer as a result of a legal transfer or merger. Accordingly, it can be seen, that in French version of Directive 77/187/EEC the object of transfer is defined by words '*enterprise*' and '*établissement*', which in the Lithuanian version of 2001/23/EC are translated as '*įmonė*' and '*verslas*'.

In the French language, the notion of '*entreprise*' can have various definitions. Some sources define '*entreprise*' using the word '*établissement*' by arguing that '*entreprise*' is an industrial or commercial 'établissement'[5]. Others argue that '*entreprise*' is an organization that produces goods or provides services while being independent from other organizations and may consist of multiple 'établissements'. Also it is noted that the definition of '*établissement*' is an integral part of '*l'entreprise*' but it is common to separate them in the context of labour law.

Whereas the notion of '*établissement*' is defined in multiple sources as tools, machinery and equipment necessary for that industry while claiming that it is the smallest set of legal units that composes an organizational unit that manufactures or provides service and which owns a certain degree of autonomy, especially regarding the resource distribution[6].

---

4 Council Directive 77/187/EEC of 14 February 1977 on the approximation of the laws of the Member States relating to the safeguarding of employees' rights in the event of transfers of undertakings, businesses or parts of businesses. *Official Journal,* L 61, p. 26.

5 Cornu G. *Vocabulaire juridique*. Presses Universitaires de France: Paris, 1987, p. 312.

6 Retrieved May 10, 2016 from http://www.insee.fr/fr/methodes/default.asp?page=definitions/entreprise.htm.

While other sources state that '*établissement*' is a geographically defined manufacturing unit that is dependent on '*l'entreprise*'. Yet other sources claim that '*établissement*' manufactures goods or provides services that might be a factory, bakery, clothing store, hotel chain etc[7]. It should be noted that French legislation[8] also defines '*l'entreprise*' as containing several '*établissement*' the activities of which may differ.

All these cases of usage of the terms '*entreprise*' and '*établissement*' show that, despite some diversity of definitions, the main interpretation of '*établissement*' is as an integral, smaller part of '*entreprise*'. It should be noted that such liaison of meanings is uncharacteristic for Lithuanian notions of '*įmonė*' or '*verslas*', since, according to the Modern Lithuanian Dictionary[9], '*įmonė*' refers to a production, sales unit, whereas 'verslas' means occupation, work, and production.

In comparing the French version of Directive 77/187/EEC to the German or English versions it is clear that the French equivalent of '*enterprise*' in German is '*Unternehmen*', in English – 'undertaking', while the French '*établissement*' is defined by the German '*Betrieben*' and English 'business' notions. The main Lithuanian definition for the term '*Unternehmen*' in German dictionaries[10] is '*įmonė*', while the term '*Betrieb*' is defined as a local organizational-technical unit[11], others define it as a factory or enterprise[12].

To compare, Article 1161 of the UK Companies Act of 2006 describes 'undertaking' as a body corporate or partnership, or an unincorporated association carrying on a trade or business, with or without a view to profit. Meanwhile, the term 'business' both in spoken and legal English has multiple definitions, although acknowledged dictionaries[13] along with other connotations mention a definition that refers to a commercial or industrial division, store or factory.

---

7 Retrieved May 10, 2016 from https://www.sirene.fr/sirene/public/static/definitions.

8 Retrieved May 10, 2016 from https://www.legifrance.gouv.fr/affichTexte.do;jsessionid=C89D11C3579F0F9E70B945BF817AA8FC.tpdila20v_1?cidTexte=JORFTEXT000000369490&dateTexte=20160225.

9 Retrieved May 10, 2016 from http://dz.lki.lt/.

10 Mačienė V. *Lietuvių-vokiečių, vokiečių – lietuvių kalbų žodynas* [Litahuanian-German, German-Lithuanian Dictionary]. Vilnius: Žodynas, 2000, p. 505.

11 Gabler Wirtschafts Lexikon, 1988, p. 710.

12 Mačienė V., *op. cit.*, p. 333.

13 Neufeldt V., Guralnik D.B. (1988). *Webster's New World Dictionary of American English*. Simon & Schuster, 1988, p. 189.

Although it is not the author's intention to go into a thorough study of semantics and differences between definitions in various Member States, the descriptions mentioned above allow to state that the definitions used in Clause 1 Article 1 of Directive 77/187/EEC refer to the transfer of an enterprise, its divisions and subdivisions. In other words, in the author's opinion, Directive 77/187/EEC intends to define as its object of transfer – organizational structures of various degrees, starting with the largest – the enterprise to the smallest – subdivision. Therefore, the usage of the Lithuanian term 'verslas' to define the French word '*établissement*' or the English '*undertaking*' (as was done in the official Lithuanian version of Directive 2001/23/EC) is flawed, since it results in stating that both an activity (i.e. business or '*verslas*') and an organizational unit (i.e. undertaking or '*įmonė*'), which pursues this business activity, can be distinct objects of transfer.

However, while the author criticises the choice of the notion '*verslas*' for describing the object of transfer under Directive 2001/23/EC and accordingly in Article 51 of the 2016 Labour Code, it has to be acknowledged that due to the widely spread usage of the term 'verslo perdavimas' it is purposeful to explain the conditional nature of the term 'verslas' in the context of Directive 2001/23/EC instead of replacing it.

As regards the object of the transfer, it also must be kept in mind that Paragraph B Clause 1 Article 1 of Directive 2001/23/EC states that transfer in the context of the Directive is a transfer of an economic entity which retains its identity, meaning an organized grouping of resources which has the objective of pursuing an economic activity, whether or not that activity is central or ancillary. This clause reveals that the legislator intended to look for what is common to all transfers of an undertaking, part of an undertaking, business or part of a business instead of naming their differences, and such common denominator is an economic entity. Since the requirement to identify the economic entity which retains its identity is the essential condition defining the scope of Directive 2001/23/EC, the author finds that the notions of 'undertaking', 'part of an undertaking', 'business', 'part of a business' became only supplementary and to have only an illustrative purpose.

The fact that economic entity has become a universal reference to a transfer object is well illustrated when paraphrasing Paragraph A Clause 1 Article 1 of Directive 2001/23/EC that the Directive applies to any transfer of an economic entity, which retains its identity, to another employer as a result of a legal transfer or merger. Despite the significance of this notion 'economic entity' for identification of the transfer, neither the 2002 Labour Code, nor the 2016 Labour Code uses this term. Accordingly, neither of them provide for a requirement to establish that the transferred economic entity retain its identity, although such test is obligatory under Directive 2001/23/EC.

To summarize, the current wording of the new Labour Code has potential for changes in several aspects. Firstly, the naming of business transfer or a part thereof as a ground to apply certain employment guarantees, however, leaving aside the transfer of an undertaking or a part thereof is confusing since it is not in line with the wording of Directive 2001/23/EC. Even if the 2016 Labour Code uses the term 'business transfer' as the one which also embodies situations of transfer of an undertaking or a part thereof, it is still confusing why merger or division of undertakings remain mentioned next to business transfer, since the latter includes all of these situations. Finally, the confusion regarding the object of a transfer could be at least partially solved if the notion of an economic entity was introduced. Since the wording of the 2016 Labour Code remains silent on 'economic entity' and a requirement to establish its identity, execution of Article 51 of the 2016 Labour Code will be impossible without a thorough knowledge of the text of Directive 2001/23/EC.

2. Legal Forms of Business Transfer

Paragraph A Clause 1 Article 1 of Directive 2001/23/EC defines that business transfer can result from a legal transfer or a merger. To compare, Article 138 of the former Lithuanian Labour Code did not name these means of transfer and stated solely that the legal ground of a transfer does not influence the scope of guarantees as they are applicable in case of business transfer. An analogous statement can be found in Clause 3 Article 51 of the new Labour Code. However, in Clause 2 of the same article the legislator additionally states that business or a part thereof can be transferred from one employer to another under a transaction, legal act, several transactions or legal acts. In order to evaluate, how such wording of the former Labour Code and the new Labour Code correspond to the wording of Directive 2001/23/EC, the notions of 'legal transfer' and 'merger' must be analysed. The definition of these notions was developed in the case law of the Court of Justice of European Union (hereinafter – Court of Justice or CJEU), since the directive itself does not provide for them.

The first preliminary ruling of the Court of Justice regarding the definition of a 'legal transfer' was introduced in the *Abels*[14] case. After a linguistic analysis of Article 1 of Directive 77/11817/EEC, the Court of Justice noticed that translations of the Directive into different languages of the Member States do not exactly correspond. In the court's opinion, due to such differences in semantic meaning, the scope of the Directive could have been misinterpreted. The Court of Justice expressed its opinion that the scope of the Directive cannot be decided only by a textual interpretation of the Directive 77/187/EEC[15], which was a predecessor of Directive 2001/23/EC. While establishing the scope of the Directive, it must be analysed systematically while bearing in mind its place and aims in the legal system of the European Community.

In this case the Court of Justice refused the General Advocate's suggestion to interpret Directive 77/187/EEC more narrowly by establishing that only relationships of a contractual nature fall within the scope of the Directive. The Court of Justice admitted that a consensual nature is characteristic to business transfer, however, the transfer itself can take place not only because of a contract.

In 1992[16] the Court of Justice broadened the interpretation of 'legal transfer' by declaring that this notion also embodies situations when a subject of public authority decides to terminate a subsidy to a private legal entity, due to which the activities of such a legal entity are also terminated, however, it transfers this subsidy to another legal undertaking, which pursues the same objectives. Since in some countries subsidies are given by a unilateral decision, in others, contracts are made, the Court of Justice clarified that the legal form of business transfer has no impact on the application of Directive 77/187/EEC.

In 1996, another preliminary ruling[17] of the Court of Justice followed, in which the court stated that direct contractual relationship between the

---

14 CJEU case C-135/83.

15 Directive 77/187/EEC of 14 February 1977 on the approximation of the laws of the Member States relating to the safeguarding of employees' rights in the event of transfers of undertakings, businesses or parts of businesses. *Official Journal*, L 61, p. 26.

16 CJEU case C-29/91.

17 CJEU cases C-171/94 and C-172/94.

transferor and the transferee is not obligatory. In 2007[18] the Court of Justice elaborated that the notion of legal transfer includes both a written and an oral agreement between the transferor and the transferee or even a tacit agreement. To sum up, the Court of Justice's position that 'legal transfer' must be understood broadly, without linking it solely to the transfer of ownership, specific content or form requirements, allowed the concept of a legal transfer to embody different legal forms of business transfer.

Probably one of the most common legal forms of a legal transfer is a transaction. In the case law, the Court of Justice has mostly dealt with lease transactions. The cases of *Daddy's Dance Hall*[19] and *Ny Mølle Kro*[20] are the best known. Significant are also cases of outsourcing, such were the cases under the claims submitted by *Anne Watson Rask*[21], *Christel Schmidt*[22], and *Carlito Alber*[23].

Another possible, though less common, legal form of a legal transfer is an administrative act. This can be illustrated by the preliminary ruling in the *Scattolon*[24], in which in Italian public schools the maintenance of auxiliary services, such as cleaning, and administrative support used to be ensured by employees of local authorities or certain services were bought from private undertakings.

However, in 1999 a law was adopted which provided that such employees of local authorities were to become civil servants of another institution of public authority. The Court of Justice found that this situation fell into the business transfer definition under Directive 77/187/EEC. It should be noted that Lithuanian case law also provides for corresponding situations, for example, it was recognized that business transfer took place due to orders of the head of a municipality or a decision of the council of a municipality.

There is also single case in the case law of the Court of Justice in which the court held that a transfer can take place on the basis of a court decision. Such is the case of *Berg and Busschers*[25], in which the Court of

18 CJEU case C-458/05.
19 CJEU case C-324/86.
20 CJEU case C-287/86.
21 CJEU case C-2209/91.
22 CJEU case C-392/92.
23 CJEU case C-340/01.
24 CJEU case C-108/10.
25 CJEU case C-145/87.

Justice stated that business transfer can take place not only on the basis of a contract but also on the basis of a judgment terminating the contract. The Court of Justice elaborated that if the transferor and the transferee enter into a contract resulting in a transfer of business, but such contract is terminated by a court's decision, the fact that the business is returned to the initial business manager on grounds of a court decision, does not limit the applicability of Directive 77/187/EEC. The same applies to those cases in which the contract is terminated unilaterally.

To summarize the foregoing, legal transfer can take place in three legal forms – a transaction, an administrative act and a judgment. Since Clause 2 Article 51 of the new Labour Code provides that transfer of a business or a part thereof can result from a transaction, a legal act or several transactions or legal acts, and the notion of 'legal act' in legal theory embodies both an administrative act and a decision of a court, it must be acknowledged that such regulation is fully in conformity with the case law of the Court of Justice. Though the said article of the new Labour Code is silent on the term 'legal transfer', in the author's opinion, the legislator wisely chose to name the forms of legal transfer instead, which makes the article more comprehensive, since otherwise it would be hard to understand the scope of 'legal transfer' without analysing the aforementioned case law of the Court of Justice.

On the other hand, following Directive 2001/23/EC, legal transfer is only one of the methods of business transfer next to merger. Like most of the other terms, 'merger' is not defined in Directive 2001/23/EC. However, the Third Directive[26] and in the Sixth Directive[27] state that each of the merging companies and companies involved in the merger shall be regulated in accordance with Directive 77/187/EEC. Therefore, this suggests that the term 'merger' should be interpreted in conformity with the Third and Sixth Directives[28].

---

26 Third Council Directive 78/855/EEC of 9 October 1978 based on Article 54 (3) (g) of the Treaty concerning mergers of public limited liability companies. *Official Journal*, L 295, p. 36.

27 Sixth Council Directive 82/891/EEC of 17 December 1982 based on Article 54 (3) (g) of the Treaty, concerning the division of public limited liability companies. *OJ* L 378, 31 December 1982, p. 47–54.

28 Blanpain R. *European Labour Law*. Hague: Kluwer Law International, 2006, p. 632.

The Third Directive defines merger by acquisition[29] and merger by the formation of a new company[30]. The Sixth Directive provides for a definition of a division by acquisition[31]. If the view that the term 'merger' should be interpreted in conformity with the Third and Sixth Directives is accepted, then it can be noticed that definitions provided in the aforementioned directives correspond to ways of legal entity reorganization, established in Article 2.97 of the Civil Code of the Republic of Lithuania[32].

Accordingly, it follows that the notion of merger under Directive 2001/23/EC refers to the case of a business transfer resulting from reorganization of a legal entity. As already mentioned, under Clause 1 Article 138 of the former Labour Code, the situation of business transfer and situations of reorganization of a legal entity were named as separate grounds to apply certain guarantees re the continuity of an employment relationship. Therefore, such wording of the said clause provided an image that the notion of business transfer did not embody the situations of reorganization of a legal entity. Since such an approach would be contrary to the existing case law of the Court of Justice, this leads to the conclusion that naming the reorganization situations is superfluous.

---

29 Article 3 clause 1. For the purposes of this Directive, 'merger by acquisition' shall mean the operation whereby one or more companies are wound up without going into liquidation and transfer to another all their assets and liabilities in exchange for the issue to the shareholders of the company or companies being acquired of shares in the acquiring company and a cash payment, if any, not exceeding 10% of the nominal value of the shares so issued or, where they have no nominal value, of their accounting par value.

30 Article 4 clause 1. For the purposes of this Directive, 'merger by the formation of a new company' shall mean the operation whereby several companies are wound up without going into liquidation and transfer to a company that they set up all their assets and liabilities in exchange for the issue to their shareholders of shares in the new company and a cash payment, if any, not exceeding 10% of the nominal value of the shares so issued or, where they have no nominal value, of their accounting par value.

31 Article 2 clause 1. For the purposes of this Directive, 'division by acquisition' shall mean the operation whereby, after being wound up without going into liquidation, a company transfers to more than one company all its assets and liabilities in exchange for the allocation to the shareholders of the company being divided of shares in the companies receiving contributions as a result of the division (hereinafter referred to as "recipient companies") and possibly a cash payment not exceeding 10% of the nominal value of the shares allocated or, where they have no nominal value, of their accounting par value.

32 *Valstybės žinios* (State Gazette), 2000, No. 74-2262.

Such a separate naming of reorganization next to business transfer is not only incorrect, but is also misleading. For example, Clause 2 Article 138 of the 2002 Labour Code declared that in the case of business transfer, the employment relationship continues under the same conditions. However, the latter clause was silent as regards the same regulation being also applicable in the reorganization of a legal entity. Therefore, such wording left space for a grammatical interpretation that reorganization cannot be a legitimate reason for employment termination, but the conditions of an employment relationship can be unilaterally changed. It must be noted that the same problems have been left in the wording of Article 51 of the 2016 Labour Code, since the division between the concept of business transfer and the cases of legal entity reorganization remained.

Similarly, such division results in certain interpretation problems. For example, following Clauses 2 and 3 of the said article, the business transferee acquires the business transferor's – as the employer's – rights and obligations existing at the time of transfer. If these rights and obligations are established by collective agreements, they are to be applied two years after the business transfer, unless the collective agreement expires or a new collective agreement is being introduced. It is also established that a change in employment conditions due to business transfer is prohibited and the business transferor and the transferee may agree on compensation for the takeover of the transferor's rights and obligations.

All of the abovementioned guarantees are explicitly tied only to the business transfer case. Since the reorganization of the employer and related restriction to terminate the employment is described in Article 51 separately, this allows interpretation that the abovementioned guarantees are not obligatory in the case of an employer's reorganization. The author believes that these theoretical problems could be avoided if the legislator made a clear statement on the relationship between the concept of business transfer and the cases of legal entity reorganization. In other words it would be advisable to explain that reorganization of a legal entity is just one possible precondition for a business transfer.

To summarize, the analysis shows that in comparison to the 2002 Labour Code 2002, the new Labour Code has finally named the legal forms by which a certain business transfer can take place. These legal forms – a transaction and a legal act – fully conform to the scope and the interpretation of Directive 2001/23/EC. However, the fact that the new 2016 Labour Code finds reorganization of an employer and business transfer as separate grounds to apply guarantees of employment continuity is confusing. There is still a need for a more comprehensive explanation that a business transfer can take place by way of a transaction or due to a legal act, as well as in the course of an undertaking's reorganization or restructuring. Therefore these situations of an undertaking's reorganization or restructuring are an integral part of the business transfer notion.

Conclusion

The new Labour Code of 2016, if compared to the Labour Code of 2002, is about to regulate the notion o business transfer more broadly. Among such changes, the new Labour Code finally names the legal forms by which business transfer can take place. However, the current wording of Article 51 of the 2016 Labour Code has potential for changes in several aspects. Firstly, there is a need for reasoning why the new Labour Code names only business transfer or a part thereof without mentioning the transfer of an undertaking or a part thereof, since the latter are named as objects of transfer under Directive 2001/23/EC. The abovementioned problem could be solved if the notion of an economic entity, which retains its identity, was introduced. Since the wording of the draft Labour code remains silent on what is meant by 'economic entity' and a requirement to establish its identity, Article 51 of the 2016 Labour Coded does not provide for a full understanding of business transfer as it is established under Directive 2001/23/EC. Lastly, Article 51 of the 2016 Labour Code is confusing due to the fact that it finds reorganization of an employer and business transfer to be separate grounds to apply guarantees of employment continuity. It is advisable to establish a clearer link between the notion of business transfer and the cases of an undertaking's reorganization or restructuring, which are integral parts of the business transfer notion.

Arbitration Agreements in Individual Labour Law

Arnas PALIUKĖNAS*

Abstract

International legislation does not prohibit the resolution of individual labour disputes in arbitration. Lithuanian legal regulation allows individual labour disputes to be resolved by arbitration only if it is agreed upon in the event of a dispute. This article analyses whether it is possible to broaden the legal regulation on arbitration by establishing an advance arbitration clause in collective agreements. It can be concluded that in order to get certain mutual concessions in negotiations between employers and employees, it is feasible to set such a clause regarding individual labour disputes. It must be emphasized that such a possibility should not be considered as making the position of an employee less favourable. In all cases, all the conditions of a collective agreement shall be assessed.

Key words: arbitration, individual labour dispute, collective agreement.

Introduction

It is self-evident that labour disputes between employers and employees are inevitable. Labour dispute resolution by courts causes a lot of problems, and creates social conflicts between the employer and employee, which in turn might become a reason for future disagreements. Therefore, issues related to individual labour disputes are common in arbitration procedures of foreign countries, where parties try to resolve their disputes through independent arbitrators. In these countries, in line with the main goal of arbitration – to bring the positions of the parties closer together by encouraging them to avoid demands that are too categorical – the decision issued by the arbitrators often helps to restore social peace between the parties. Lithuanian law does not provide for the resolution of individual labour disputes by arbitration.

* Arnas Paliukėnas is practicing lawyer and lecturer at the Faculty of Law Vilnius University, Lithuania. His research interests are related to sports law and labour law.

Today, increasing globalization and changing economic conditions influence new developments in labour law. Also, the introduction of new methods and forms in labour dispute resolution show an increasing need for the parties to labour relations to have a right to agree on working conditions, inter alia on individual dispute settlement in collective agreements. Therefore, this article focuses on the possibility of setting an arbitration clause in relation to individual labour disputes in collective agreements. Furthermore, legal preconditions to establish such a mechanism in the Lithuanian legal system are assessed bearing in mind the doctrine of international law and other countries law in this field.

1. Labour disputes arbitration

Labour disputes, as one of the institutes of labour law, never lose their relevance and have been the object of theoretical research at international and national level for several decades. At the same time labour law is always in the spotlight of legislative process in a number of countries, and often in the international community. So far there is no consensus on the doctrine, legal regulation and case law on individual labour dispute resolution by arbitration.

Existing legislation in Lithuania provides the possibility to settle an individual labour dispute through commercial arbitration. Article 12 paragraph 2 of the Law on Commercial Arbitration states that disputes arising from employment and consumer contracts cannot be submitted to arbitration unless the arbitration agreement was concluded after the dispute arose. Thus, current legislation allows the resolution of individual labour disputes by arbitration only if it is agreed upon in the event of a dispute, and to agree in advance on the arbitration clause is prohibited. The question is whether such regulation is justified, and how this issue is regulated by international legislation.

Poudret and Besson note that the prohibition to arbitrate labour disputes is based on the weaker position of one of the parties[1]. This leads us to question how the employee's legal situation is assessed in Lithuania. The Supreme Court of Lithuania (SCL) in its decision of 12 April 2011 in civil case No. 3K-3-176/2011 clearly stated that the 2002 Labour Code of the Republic of Lithuania makes no provision on the basis of which the

---

1 Poudret J.F., Besson S., Berti S., Ponti A. *Comparative Law of International Arbitration.* Sweet & Maxwell, 2007, p. 313.

employee should be considered as the weaker party, therefore the equality principle of employment parties is dominating (2002 Labour Code Article 2 (1) point 4, 15, 16). The only employee-friendly exception in legal regulation is that in cases where there are contradictions between the provisions of labour regulatory acts, the provision which is more beneficial to the employee shall be applied (Article 11 (2) of the 2002 Labour Code).

The general principle which connects non-arbitrating categories of disputes in different legal systems is the importance of the public interest. This importance requires that, inter alia, the interests of non-case parties must be properly evaluated by the application of public law. Therefore, dispute arbitration can be restricted on the grounds that settlement of disputes in arbitration may violate imperative norms of national law, which are set forth to protect the public interest. The state has the right to require that certain categories of disputes shall remain exclusively within the jurisdiction of national courts. This obligation is recognized by the New York Convention, in which Paragraph V, part 2 lays down that recognition and enforcement of an arbitral award may be refused if the subject matter of the difference is not capable of settlement by arbitration under the law of that country of the recognition or enforcement of the award would be contrary to the public policy of that country. As previously mentioned, labour disputes may be heard by arbitration in Lithuania, but only if this has been agreed in the event of a dispute. In general, such recognition proves that labour dispute resolution through arbitration does not prejudice the public interest.

In addition, it shall be held that labour dispute settlement in arbitration would be beneficial for both parties of an individual labour dispute. Individual labour dispute resolution by courts causes a lot of inconvenience, and also leads to social conflicts between parties. The court by issuing its decision resolves a legal dispute, but often at least one of the parties is not satisfied with its decision, and this provides opportunities for further conflicts in the future. This problem could be solved by application of an arbitration procedure where arbitrators resolve the dispute by encouraging social partnership. By appointing a representative of the employer and employee to arbitration, this institution has both the employer's and the employee's trust, and the third arbitrator (designated arbitrators by the consensus of the employer and the employee) ensures the impartiality of the arbitration. In addition, the arbitration award can be adopted very quickly, while taking into account the fact that the arbitration award becomes effective immediately and may be appealed only to the Court of Appeal; the dispute resolution time can be reduced to three months. Therefore, the possibility of the social partners to resolve disputes in arbitration tribunal, in which structure /formation they are directly involved, basically serves for both expeditious and fair dispute resolution, and social peace. The prohibition stipulated in the current legal regulation of Lithuania is not supported by any public interest and makes it impossible for social partners to resolve disputes in a socially friendly manner, without state intervention.

In addition, the possibility to arbitrate this category of dispute certainly does not lead to the assumption that the employer's or employee's rights will be abused, because arbitration is only possible with agreement between the employer and the employee, as the Lithuanian Law on Commercial Arbitration[2] prohibits the appointment of an arbitrator by only one of the parties. Hence, it can be considered that the limitation of resolution of pre-arranged individual labour disputes in arbitration, is not really based on solid arguments. Moreover, settlement of a dispute by arbitration can be agreed in the event of a dispute, so it can be recognized that, in principle, labour disputes can be solved by arbitration.

Newmark and Monaghan advocate that individual labour disputes are particularly suitable for arbitration, because in most cases the labour dispute is based on individual issues which are easier to resolve in arbitration than in court. Arbitration provides many flexible instruments that can be used to resolve individual issues and to achieve a result that is satisfactory to both sides. For most people work is one of the key elements of their daily lives. It provides both their income and opportunities for self-expression. If employee interests are not assessed in the employment relationship, this can cause severe negative emotions. Arbitration provides an individual and structurally well-defined opportunity to share these emotions, and after that it is easier to resolve legal issues[3].

2. International labour disputes resolution regulation and foreign countries practice

International legislation does not prohibit the resolution of individual labour disputes in arbitration. For example, the United Nations Committee on Economic, Social and Cultural Rights by the interpretation of Article 6

---

2 *Valstybės žinios* (State Gazette), 2012, No. 39-961.

3 Newmark C., Monaghan A. *Mediators on Mediation: Leading Mediator Perspectives on the Practice of Commercial Mediation*. 2005, p. 184.

of the International Covenant on Economic, Social and Cultural Rights states that each person or group of persons whose right to work has been violated must be provided with effective legal or other type of measures to ensure that their rights are protected on the national level[4]. Hence, the covenant does not directly create a specific dispute settlement mechanism, but only indicates that if a person's right to work has been violated, such person should be able to use an effective dispute resolution mechanism created by national law.

D. Petrylaitė states, that the Recommendation concerning the Examination of Grievances of the International Labour Organization (ILO)[5] indicates the employee's right to use a competitive legal system when a dispute arises, i.e. independent mediation, arbitration, and, of course, independent legal aid in the protection of their violated rights[6]. Thus, the ILO states that it is permitted to solve individual labour disputes in arbitration.

When analysing labour dispute settlements, it is appropriate to mention the Recommendation concerning Labour Inspection No. 81 of the ILO. Article 8 of this Recommendation sets forth that functions of labour inspectors should not include conciliation or arbitration functions for resolution of labour disputes that arise. The same provision is also repeated in the Recommendation concerning Labour Inspection in Agriculture No. 133 (in agriculture field)[7] in Article 3 paragraph 1. The ILO maintains that labour inspectors are supervisors, advisors and institutions, whose primary mission is to provide guidance for improving working conditions and productivity. It is important to ensure that labour inspectors are not assigned tasks, which by their nature can be seen as incompatible with their main function – execution of legal provisions. In one of the first ILO recommendations regarding individual labour dispute resolution, rudiments were indirectly formed – the fact that

---

4 Committee on Economic, Social and Cultural Rights, General Comment 18, Article 6: the equal right of men and women to the enjoyment of all economic, social and cultural rights (Thirty-fifth session, 2006), U.N. Doc. E/C.12/GC/18 (2006). Retrieved 1 March 2016 from https://www1.umn.edu/humanrts/gencomm/escgencom18.html.

5 ILO Recommendation 130 (1967).

6 Petrylaitė D. Vientiso darbo ginčo instituto perspektyvos Lietuvos darbo teisėje [The perspectives of the uniform institute of labour disputes in Lithuanian labour law]. *Jurisprudencija*, No. 8 (110), 2008, p. 54.

7 ILO Recommendation No. 133 (1969).

individual labour disputes must be solved by an independent body[8] and it does not matter whether this is a court or tribunal.

Article 24 (2) of the European Social Charter (revised) stipulates that the parties undertake to ensure that a worker who considers that his employment has been terminated without a valid reason shall have the right to appeal to an impartial body. Thus, the Charter does not provide the particular kind of authority – a court or an arbitral tribunal – which should solve individual labour disputes. The only requirement is that the right conditions should be created for resolution of the dispute and that it should be solved by an impartial authority. Hence, it is assumed that such an institution can be both a court and an arbitral tribunal.

Analysis of the law of other countries, despite the fact that legal regulation various from country to country, proves that in nearly all legal systems it is appropriate to resolve disputes firstly in an extrajudicial way. Also, international law promotes the creation of third party extrajudicial conciliation methods, which could assist the parties to settle a dispute without formal court proceedings.

For example, the Belgian labour courts system was created in 1970. This system adopted the whole competence of the pre-trial labour disputes commission. Two levels of labour courts function in Belgium, i.e. labour tribunals (*Arbeidshof*) and labour courts (*Arbeidsrechtbank*). Labour tribunals operate in five districts of Belgium and they are the courts of first instance, which settle disputes, arising from individual labour agreements.

The adoption of the new law in 2005, created an opportunity to use the new forms of individual labour dispute settlement[9]. This law has introduced two mechanisms: a conciliation procedure in court and mediation through a third party. Before resolving the dispute in court, the judge must invite the parties to resolve a dispute through mediation or conciliation, and if both parties accept this proposal, the dispute cannot be settled in court. However, it should be noted that these methods

---

8 Petrylaitė D., Petrylaitė V., Blažienė I. Darbo ginčų instituto reguliavimo tarptautiniai teisiniai standartai ir jų įgyvendinimas nacionalinėje teisėje [International legal standards of labour disputes institute and their implementation at national level]. *Teisė*, No. 88, 2013, p. 100.

9 Belgium: Individual disputes at the workplace – alternative disputes resolution. Retrieved March 15, 2016 from www.eurofound.europa.eu/observatories/eurwork/comparative-information/national-contributions/belgium/belgium-individual-disputes-at-the-workplace-alternative-disputes-resolution.

are not very widely used, especially since they can only be operated on voluntary basis. The primary obligation to try to resolve a conflict by mediation can be set in individual contracts of employment.

In Denmark, conciliation and arbitration is very important in dealing with labour disputes. Both of these techniques are reflected in legislation and collective agreements. Both arbitration and conciliation procedures are mandatory[10]. In the United States (with the exception of a few categories of employees) [11], Great Britain, the Netherlands and Sweden, their legislation also allows agreeing about individual labour dispute resolution both in advance and in the event of a dispute[12]. Switzerland's courts have exclusive jurisdiction in labour relations disputes, with the exception of international arbitration cases, when labour legal relations related to monetary issues are solved. In France and Belgium, it is permitted to agree to solve disputes of employment legal relations in arbitration only after a dispute arises[13]. In Greece, disputes arising from employment relations which are associated with subordination, or for any other reasons related to performance of employment functions, implementation of the employment contract or its termination, the violation of employee's rights and others disputes arising between the employee and employer are resolved in courts by simplified and expedited order. The court in the initial stage of proceedings tries to offer the parties a way to reach a peaceful compromise, but if the parties do not use such action it does not cause any legal effects[14]. In Germany, individual labour disputes are resolved in a specialized court, so they are not resolved by arbitration[15]. Settlement of individual labour disputes in arbitration is prohibited in Italy, unless the arbitration clause is established in the collective agreement[16].

---

10 Petrylaitė D., Petrylaitė V., Blažienė I., *op. cit.*, p. 101.

11 Moffitt M. L., Kordone R. C. *The Handbook of Dispute Resolution.* John Wiley and Sons, 2005, pp. 321–322.

12 Poudret J.F., Besson S., Berti S., Ponti A., *op. cit.*, p. 313.

13 Moffitt M. L., Kordone R. C., *op. cit.*, pp. 321–322.

14 Greece: Individual disputes at the workplace – alternative disputes resolution. Retrieved March 9, 2016 from http://www.eurofound.europa.eu/observatories/eurwork/comparative-information/national-contributions/greece/greece-individual-disputes-at-the-workplace-alternative-disputes-resol ution.

15 Reimann M., Zekoll J. Ebke W. *Introduction to German Law.* Kluwer Law International, 2005, p. 303.

16 Rubino-Sammartano M. *International Arbitration Law and Practice.* Kluwer Law International, 2001, p. 174.

It can be concluded that the practices of other countries are different, but in many countries intensive reforms are being implemented with the aim of ensuring, as far as possible, that this kind of conflict ends peacefully, allowing the parties to reach an agreement based on mutual compromise before going to court. International organizations and the institutions of the European Union actively promote social peace values and alternative dispute resolution approaches which could ensure them[17].

3. The possibility to establish an arbitration clause in collective agreements

In the absence of the limitation of individual labour disputes to be settled by arbitration enshrined in international law and according to the very different practices of other countries, the question arises of whether the Italian model, where an arbitration clause could be agreed in collective agreements, could serve as an example for Lithuania. It should be noted that the current Lithuanian legal regulation, with the aim of determining imperatively the majority of labour relations in the LC as well as the lack of institutions protecting employees' interests which causes the lack of collective agreements, forces social partners to solve their labour issues separately rather than together by applying to the Government or the Seimas in order to reinforce their provisions by a statute or by a sub-statutory act. This pattern could be considered as complicated, inflexible and an imperfect way of solving labour issues. Complicated – the state is forced to solve the issues of social partners which they should solve themselves. Inflexible – the interests of those who apply to the state, do not necessarily coincide with the interests of all employees and is defective as such practices reduces the possibility of local social dialogue[18].

Even in the 1990s, scientists[19] criticized the increasingly expanded, very detailed regulation of labour relations by law. When evaluating the growing number of ILO standards, they argued that unbalanced labour

---

17 Simaitis. R. Teisminis sutaikymas [Judicial conciliation]. *Teisė*, No. 52, 2004.

18 Usonis J., Bagdanskis T. Dispozityvumo įgyvendinimas Lietuvos darbo teisėje [Implementation of dispositive method in Lithuanian labour law]. *Socialinių mokslų studijos*, No. 3(2), 2011, p. 579.

19 Cordova, E. Some Reflections on the Overproduction of International Labor Standards. *Comparative Labor Law Journal.* 1992-1993, Vol. 14, p. 138; Morris G., Fredman, S. Is There a Public/Private Labour Law Divide. *Comparative Labor Law Journal*, 1992-1993, Vol. 14, p. 115.

law regulation by the state can destroy the social–economic order in which these standards have been developed and successfully operated. It could be said that Usonis and Bagdanskis (2011) are correct in saying that the too broad and detailed Lithuanian regulation unbalances the environment, where an effective social dialogue may take place. As a result of the too detailed regulation of labour relations by mandatory provisions of the Labour Code, some employers or even entire economic sectors can seek to 'bypass' such regulation. In this case, in practice such mandatory provisions can be followed only when a labour dispute has arisen (usually at the employee's dismissal). Therefore, this situation creates assumptions offering to remove some mandatory national rules established in the Labour Code, making the conditions to agree about them in individual employment or collective agreements. It is assumed that by reducing the extensive mandatory rules in the Labour Code and by extending dispositive regulation possibilities, negotiations by parties to labour relations on working conditions would be fostered.

According to Article 59 of the 2002 Labour Code, a collective agreement of an enterprise is a written covenant between the employer and the staff of the enterprise about the work, remuneration for work and other social and economic conditions. A collective agreement is mandatory to both parties and its normative part is recognized as the law source. Such requirements are formed by the Recommendation concerning Collective Agreements No. 91 of the ILO[20].

The legislator, by establishing the institute of collective agreement in legal acts, provided an opportunity for participants to regulate at least some labour relations autonomously. This autonomous/independent legislation by collective agreements has more advantages than an individual contract of employment, as negotiations between the parties on the signing of the collective agreement create conditions at least in part to align the legal position of both the employee and the employer.

In this way, the collective agreement protects the employee from the dictation of the employer's conditions and ensures self-regulation of labour relations. It also brings more flexibility as it allows to adapt the rules of law, and set out standards in a realistic way, and ensures social peace between the employee and the employer. In the normative part of the collective agreement, the provisions that are included cannot be in a conflict with laws and other higher power standard acts. During the negotiation of

---

20 ILO Recommendation No. 91 (1951).

the provisions of collective agreements, an employer's financial resources, and financial capacity must be taken into account, in order to maintain a reasonable balance between the interests of the parties.

It is assumed that in order to obtain certain mutual concessions in negotiations between employers and employees, there should be a provision in the collective agreement that individual labour disputes shall be settled by arbitration. The LC does not prohibit the resolution of individual labour disputes by arbitration, although it does not establish a direct access. The provisions of the above-mentioned Law on Commercial Arbitration provide the possibility for individual labour dispute resolution by arbitration, but allows the parties to agree only in the event of a dispute.

Of course, the establishment of the provision that individual labour disputes shall be settled by arbitration in the collective agreement could be an opportunity to contest the legality of such a provision, according to the established regulation of the Law on Commercial Arbitration. However, as already mentioned, such regulation is not supported by any public interest and prevents the possibility for social partners to resolve disputes in a socially friendly manner, without state intervention. This problem can be solved in two alternative ways: by amending Article 12 paragraph 2 of the Law on Commercial Arbitration, or by adopting a new law on individual labour dispute arbitration. Obviously, the first solution is easier, particularly because the Law on Commercial Arbitration regulates arbitration procedures in detail, and this currently does not cause any problems in their application or in the settlement of labour disputes.

It should be noted that this is consistent with the interest of employees and their representatives; for instance, in 2003, the Lithuanian trade union confederation suggested that employers federations set up a joint operating agreement with the aim of achieving that individual disputes should be settled by arbitration, if this was agreed upon in advance.

It is believed that the proposal to include the provision that an individual labour dispute can be solved by an arbitration award if it was agreed in advance in a collective agreement, may lead to doubts that the provisions of such a collective agreement could weaken the employee's position. However, such doubts are entirely unjustified, because the resolution of the dispute by arbitration, as already mentioned, really does not impair the employee's position; it just allows a good relationship to be maintained with the employer, and a compromise that satisfies both parties to be reached.

Moreover, even assuming that a condition of a separate collective agreement could make the position of an employee less favourable compared with that established in the Labour Code, in this case it is important to remember the principle of the exchange, which is necessary for the negotiations, for example, for a company's collective agreement. The essence of this principle is that one party by obtaining something in negotiation, makes concessions to the other party by refusing something. The SCL in its 2009 order clearly stated the position; it is considered that a collective agreement makes the position of the employee less favourable compared to norms established in the 2002 Labour Code and other laws. The SCL has indicated that one condition of the collective agreement which makes an employee's situation less favourable does not automatically mean that the whole collective agreement (when all working conditions and social guarantees are set), determines a worse situation of employees in comparison with the situation, which is enshrined in the Labour Code and other legal regulations. In deciding, whether a collective agreement makes the position of the employee less favourable, it is not sufficient to evaluate just one of the employee's working conditions in a collective agreement since the finding that a collective agreement makes the position of the employee less favourable can only be done after assessing all of the conditions of the agreement, by analysing how some of the employees' conditions compensates other conditions, which according to employees makes their position less favourable. It is also important to remember that in the negotiations on the collective agreement both employer and employee representatives are involved, because without them mutual consent could not be achieved and the collective agreement with individual conditions therein could not be conducted. In addition, Article 4 (4) of the 2002 Labour Code, which prohibits making the position of employees less favourable in a collective agreement, also lays down that the Labour Code and other laws do not directly prohibit the subjects of legal relations pertaining to labour to establish, of their own accord and by way of an agreement, mutual rights and obligations, the above subjects shall be guided by the principles of justice, reasonableness and good faith[21].

Hence, it can be considered that by establishing the provision that individual labour disputes shall be settled by arbitration and by agreeing on certain conditions of improvement for employees in the collective agreement, the collective agreement would be in force, although its

21 Lithuanian Supreme Court case No. 3K-3-150/2009.

provisions would not formally match the regulation of the Law on Commercial Arbitration. According to this fact, it is advisable to change the relevant provisions of this law by leaving the regulation of labour relations in labour laws and collective agreements.

It should be noted that Article 3 (8) of the new 2016 Labour Code sets the provision that employer and labour council agreements, local regulations, resolutions of the government and provisions of other state institutions cannot make the position of the employees less favourable compared to this Code and laws, with the exception of the following legislation allowed exceptions. If the employer and the labour council agreement, local regulations of the government or other acts of public authorities are contrary to this Code or law norms, the norms of this Code and laws are applicable. Article 180 (3) of the 2016 Labour Code provides that trade unions, in cases set in this Code, and other laws collectively represents their members – employees and persons, working on the basis set in the Law on Employment.

Trade unions also protect their members and represent them in individual labour relations. Collective bargaining, conclusion of collective agreements, and the initiation of collective labour disputes over interests are the exclusive rights of trade unions. According to the fact that the above-mentioned provisions of the 2016 Labour Code do not lead to larger discussion, it can be concluded that both the social partners, and the legislator recognize that the employer and the labour council agreements cannot make the position of employees less favourable and that collective agreements can be concluded only by trade unions. Therefore, the linguistic interpretation of this provision reveals that it is not prohibited to agree on such provisions, although, at first glance it may seem as making the position of employees less favourable. It is clear that trade unions could agree in a collective agreement to establish dispute settlement by arbitration in the collective agreement. All this would ensure flexible labour relations, and increase the possibility for trade unions to negotiate better conditions for the employees they represent through collective bargaining.

Conclusion

Lithuanian legislation allows individual labour disputes to be solved in arbitration only with agreement in the event of labour disputes and prohibits agreement on a arbitral clause in advance. Such a prohibition is not supported by the provisions of international law or well-established legal arguments. International law stipulates that individual labour disputes may be settled in court or in an arbitral tribunal, ensuring that disputes would be resolved by an independent body and the rights of employees ensured. Where it is believed that resolution of a labour dispute by arbitration could violate the public interest or does not guarantee the interest of an employee, as the weaker party, the legislator should be consistent and should prohibit the resolution of such disputes in arbitration in all cases. Since this absolute prohibition is not set, it can be stated that the prohibition of a preliminary agreement is also unreasonable.

In order to achieve certain mutual concessions in employee negotiations with the employer, the collective agreement can include a provision that individual labour disputes shall be settled by arbitration. Such a collective agreement should not be considered as making the position of employees less favourable. In all cases, all of the conditions of the collective agreement should be assessed. The 2002 Labour Code does not prohibit the resolution of individual labour disputes by arbitration, although it does not establish a direct access. In this case we face the prohibition of the Law on Commercial Arbitration to agree in advance on the arbitration clause. As this prohibition is not supported by any public interest and prevents the possibility for social partners to resolve disputes in a socially friendly manner, without the state's intervention, it should be recommended that Article 12 paragraph 2 of the Law on Commercial Arbitration be amended by eliminating such prohibition.

Labour Rights Defence

The Experience of the Baltic States

Gintautas Bužinskas*

Abstract

At different times Lithuania, Latvia and Estonia reformed the mechanism of labour disputes resolution. The most recent reform has been introduced in Lithuania, where a national labour disputes model, regardless of clear differences, was linked to the Estonian one. However, despite common historical, political and cultural features of these countries, with several commonalities they have chosen different ways to resolve labour disputes. This paper focuses on the regulation of labour disputes resolution in the Baltic States, with particular focus on the resolution of Lithuanian labour disputes.

Key words: labour dispute resolution, pre-trial institutions, labour disputes commissions, Baltic States.

Introduction

On 1 January 2013 a new mechanism for the resolution of individual labour disputes in pre-trial stage entered into force in Lithuania. This was a very exceptional event in the short history of the 2002 Labour Code: the structure of Chapter XIX of the Code, the procedure for the settlement of individual labour disputes, the composition Labour Disputes Commissions have changed. As a result, the attitude of society towards the defence of labour relations, in general, has changed, which is persuasively illustrated by the numbers.

It is well known that the national model has been designed with close reference to the Estonian one. Therefore, the first reviewers of the new order have called it 'the Estonian' model. The author of this article strongly objects to this for the following reasons: first of all, the Labour

* Gintautas Bužinskas is Professor of Law in Utena Colledge of Applied Sciences and Mykolas Romeris University, Lithuania. He is the author and co-author of several books on labour law. He specialises in labour law disputes.

Disputes Commission of the Republic of Lithuania has remained as the main obligatory pre-trial body (Article 287(1) of the 2002 Labour Code), whereas, the Individual Labour Dispute Resolution law of the Republic of Estonia allows the parties to a dispute to choose the body for individual labour dispute resolution – a labour disputes commission or a court, however, there is an imperative norm set prohibiting the parties to an individual labour dispute to apply both to a labour disputes commission or a court to resolve an individual labour dispute. Actually, Article 5(2) of the Labour Dispute Law of the Republic of Latvia establishes the freedom of agreement between the parties 'the employer and the representative of employees may agree regarding the establishment of a labour disputes commission in the undertaking for the settlement of individual disputes regarding rights in relation to which an agreement between the employee and the employer has not been reached in negotiations; the employer and the representatives of employees may also agree regarding other procedures according to which individual disputes regarding rights shall be settled in the undertaking'. Secondly, the Individual Labour Dispute Resolution law entered into force on 1 January 1996 and it is not quite clear what Lithuania has been doing for seventeen years – 'incubating' corresponding social-economic circumstances and waiting until the 'Estonian' experiment suffers a fiasco? Both, the first and the second circumstances undoubtedly reveal the peculiarities of our national legislation, therefore, all the circumstances should be evaluated in a very responsible way.

The first conclusion relevant to all the Baltic States may be drawn here: the reform of the entire labour law system and a part of that system – the institute of labour disputes – has been going and is still going following different scenarios and tempos, in addition, they differ in their starting points: 1996 in Estonia, 2003 in Latvia and 2013 in Lithuania.

Secondly, despite the common past, similar national legislation practice, geopolitical issues and many other common issues, a unified 'Baltic' model for labour rights defence has not been created. Here are some close examples. Let us take for instance a 'Scandinavian' version: a labour court that resolves collective labour disputes, a number of labour judges resembling trilateral cooperation, individual disputes resolved in common courts and aiming at reconciling the parties before the formal hearing of the dispute, a special order for publicizing the court decision, etc.

However, the Baltic region has remained united regarding one very important aspect – the pre-trial institution for individual labour dispute resolution. In this respect, we are truly unique in the European

Union. We have made very significant reforming steps: labour disputes commissions have been established under territorial divisions of the State Labour Inspectorate on the basis of trilateral agreement. However, labour dispute commissions are no longer said to be in the 'pockets' of the employers. The distance that directly and figuratively appeared between the parties of an employment contract and commissions has raised their prestige and trust in society. This is clearly seen by statistics in Estonia and Lithuania; for instance, the number of claims addressed to the State Labour Inspectorate has decreased from 8,933 to 4,159 in Lithuania, whereas the dynamics of the number of applications received is showing a steady but insignificant increase (there were 5,302 applications in 2013, 5,323 in 2014, 5,358 in 2015). The number of employers' applications is increasing significantly – 207 applications were received in 2015 which is 34% more than in 2014, and 56% more than 2013.

In its 2002 edition of the law, Latvia has left labour disputes commissions to be in force as an 'opportunity' – the principle of their formation. However, the Law on Labour Dispute established the division of labour disputes into individual disputes regarding rights, collective disputes regarding rights, and collective disputes regarding interests. In its law Latvia has established negotiations and discussions as early prevention of labour disputes (Estonia has established the same measures). This is a desirable aspiration for Lithuania since Article 293 (2) of the 2002 Labour Code indicates that the procedure has been started and agreement reached. Latvia has followed the example of Estonia and allows the parties to the dispute to choose between the institutions for the dispute resolution, including even the court of arbitration. One must not forget that there are specific labour courts in Latvia. Why is so much said about Latvia and its model of labour rights' defence? It is done to avoid the temptation to evaluate the situation from just one perspective because today it is the missing link in the design of a visionary model.

It would not be ethical to miss certain critics regarding our national legislation. Regretfully, pre-trial and judiciary practices are being harmonized too slowly, after having provided the opportunity for an employer to apply to the labour disputes commission and a court, the provisions of Chapter XX of the 2002 Labour Code are not tune in with today's actuality, and only 12% of matters resolved by labour disputes commissions end in an agreement. From the perspective, neither positive law nor doctrine provides a definition of labour rights defence, the defence of rights is blended with the implementation of rights, in textbooks, the defence is related to – at best – self-defence, trade unions, etc. However, these are temporary drawbacks to development and evolution, and in the future, cooperation among the professionals of the Baltic States will lay the grounds, for instance, for the law of labour procedure.

Discussion

An individual labour dispute in the Republic of Estonia may be resolved by a labour disputes committee or a court as is foreseen by the provisions of the Code of Civil Procedure of the Republic of Estonia[1] applied to the solution of civil matters. In accordance with the code, individual labour disputes are cases arising from a private law relationship, since the code defines that 'civil matters are disputes arising from civil law or labour law relationship'; it serves as the basis for the execution of justice in civil matters and the jurisdiction of the court to identify that the purpose of civil procedure is to guarantee the following:

- the adjudication of civil matters shall be executed justly, within a reasonable period of time and at the minimum possible cost;
- the parties have equal rights and opportunities in substantiating their claims, and to refute or contest the submissions of the opposing party;
- the parties may choose the facts submitted in order to substantiate the claim;
- the court shall take all possible measures to settle a matter or a part thereof by a compromise or in another manner by agreement of the parties if this is possible in the opinion of the court;
- as a rule, the civil procedure is public.

The settlement of matters is based on case law. Case law shall not be treated as the source of law of the Estonian legal system; however, there is a widespread practice when the decisions of the Supreme Court are acknowledged as recommendations for the lower courts. However, the law on individual labour dispute resolution should be treated as the main source in Estonia[2]. Following Article 2 of the respective law, an individual labour dispute is a disagreement between one or more employees and

---

1 Code of Civil Procedure of the Republic of Estonia. Retrieved June 1, 2016 from https://www.riigiteataja.ee/en/eli/513122013001/consolide.

2 It should be noted that this law entered into force in 1996 in Estonia.

the employer which arises from individual labour dispute resolution law, application of administrative legal acts or the rules set by the employer to regulate labour relations, or from a collective agreement or from the execution of a labour contract, and where the parties do not come to a mutual agreement. This law provides an opportunity to resolve the arisen disagreement amicably, with the participation of a mediator from either of the parties. Where the parties do not agree amicably, they decide where to apply: a labour disputes commission or a court. A labour disputes commission is not a mandatory pre-trial institution for the resolution of an individual labour dispute, but a recommended one.

In Estonia, as in Lithuania, a labour disputes commission is established under a territorial division of the labour inspectorate. Article 10(1) of the law indicates that a labour disputes commission is an independent individual labour dispute resolution body which operates pursuant to international agreements, administrative acts and other rules[3]. It is important to stress that recourse to a labour disputes commission is exempt from state fees for the parties since all the expenses are covered by the local labour inspectorate from the State budget. Concurrent filing of an application with a labour disputes commission and with a court is prohibited by the Individual Labour Resolution Act of the Republic of Estonia. In a case where the parties to the dispute do not agree with the decision of a labour disputes commission, they may file a statement of claim with a district or a county court within one month from the day the true copy of the decision of the labour disputes commission was received. In accordance with Article 64(1) of the Code of Civil Procedure of the Republic of Estonia, 'the court may extent a term set hereby on the basis of a reasoned petition or at its own initiative if good reason exists thereof'. However, the law does not define what reasons shall be treated as good ones, therefore it allows inferring that a court resolves this issue at its own discretion. In the case where a term is extended more than once, the consent of the opposing party is required. In addition, Article 64(2) foresees an opportunity to shorten the term by agreement of the parties, however, the agreement concerning shortening of a term is submitted to the court in writing. Article 6 of the Individual Labour Dispute Resolution Act of the Republic of Estonia sets the period for filing a claim:

---

3 Individual Labour Dispute Resolution Act of the Republic of Estonia. Retrieved June 8, 2016 from https://www.riigiteataja.ee/en/eli/504112013010/consolide.

- concerning the recognition of rights or protection of violated rights arising from an employment relationship in order to take recourse to a labour disputes commission or a court is four months starting from the day an employee or the employer learned or might have learned about the violation of the rights;
- to challenge the cancellation of an employment contract is thirty days as of the receipt of a notice of cancellation;
- for payment of wages is three years.

The following individual labour disputes are heard directly by courts:
- regarding the terms of an employment contract;
- regarding redundancy;
- regarding unpaid wage or unlawful deduction from wage;
- regarding the cancellation of disciplinary penalties.

An essential practice to be followed is that the Individual Labour Disputes Resolution Act of the Republic of Estonia provides the parties to the dispute with the right to decide the manner how their labour dispute shall be resolved:

- by filing a claim to a labour disputes commission and this way be exempt from state fees;
- by filing a claim directly to court and undergo the operation of law that regulates the duty to divide all the expenses between the parties.

It is very important to note, that the law defines the cases when an employee (who is always to be treated as the weaker party of the dispute) is released from the state fee:

- hearing of a matter regarding unpaid wages, termination of the employment contract, changing the wording of the termination of the employment contract;
- hearing of a matter concerning certification of years of pensionable service;
- hearing of an action or appeal for compensation for damage caused by bodily injury, another health disorder or the death of an employee.

In the Republic of Latvia labour law is regulated by separate laws. There is no common labour law codification in Latvia. Labour law in

Latvia is regulated by the following: Labour Law[4], Labour Dispute Law[5], Labour Protection Law[6], Strike Law[7], etc. The defence of labour rights is regulated by the Labour Dispute Law. The law was adopted in Latvia in 2002. The main purpose of this is law is to ensure the fair and rapid settlement of labour disputes.

Article 2(1) of the Labour Dispute Law of the Republic of Latvia defines what a labour dispute is. A labour dispute shall be any differences of opinions arising from employment legal relations or related to employment legal relations between an employee, employees (a group of employees) or representatives of employees and an employer, employers (a group of employers), an organization of employers or an association of such organizations, or the administrative authority of the sector. Article 2(2) of the respective law clearly distinguishes between the types of labour disputes: depending on the object of a dispute and persons involved. Labour disputes shall be divided into individual disputes regarding rights, collective disputes regarding rights and collective disputes regarding interests. In accordance with Article 4 of the respective law, individual labour disputes are defined as such differences of opinion between an employee or employees (a group of employees) and an employer that arise by concluding, altering, terminating or fulfilling an employment contract, as well as by applying or interpreting the provisions of regulatory enactments, the provisions of a collective labour contract or working procedure regulations. In accordance with Article 9 of the Labour Dispute Law of the Republic of Latvia, a collective dispute regarding rights shall be such differences of opinions between employees (a group of employees) or representatives of employees and an employer, employers (a group of employers), an organization of employers or an association of such organizations, or an administrative authority of the sector that arise in concluding, altering, terminating or fulfilling an employment contract, as well as in applying or interpreting provisions of regulatory enactments, provisions of a collective labour contract or working procedure regulations.

---

[4] Labour Law of the Republic of Latvia. Retrieved May 15, 2016 from http://likumi.lv/doc.php?id=26019.

[5] Labour Dispute Law of the Republic of Latvia. Retrieved May 15, 2016 from http://likumi.lv/doc.php?id=67361.

[6] Labour Protection Law of the Republic of Latvia. Retrieved May 15, 2016 from http://likumi.lv/doc.php?id=26020.

[7] Strike Law of the Republic of Latvia. Retrieved May 15, 2016 from http://likumi.lv/doc.php?id=48074.

Article 5 of the Labour Dispute Law of the Republic of Latvia foresees the opportunity to settle individual labour disputes as far as possible in negotiations. When an agreement of the parties has not been reached in negotiations, they may apply to a labour disputes commission. Article 6 of the respective law regulates the establishment of the labour disputes commission and its operation. The labour disputes commission is established in the undertaking; in addition, its establishment may be regulated by a collective labour contract as well. The employer and the representatives of the employees shall conclude a written agreement regarding the establishment of the labour disputes commission in the undertaking in which the numerical composition of the labour disputes commission, the procedures for election, the competence of its members, the procedures and time periods for the settlement of individual disputes regarding rights, as well as other issues related to operation shall be agreed on and confirmed. All the costs related to the establishment and operation of the labour disputes commission shall be covered by the employer unless otherwise provided for in the agreement.

Article 6(2) of the Labour Dispute Law of the Republic of Latvia establishes the order for the formation of the labour disputes commission. The labour disputes commission shall consist of an equal number of the representatives of employees and employer, as well as of a chairperson of the labour disputes commission elected by its members. Matters shall be examined by the labour disputes commission consisting of not less than three members including the chairperson, and in any matter the number of members of the labour disputes commission shall be an odd number. Part 3 of Article 6 of the respective law defines when a member of the labour disputes commission is not entitled to participate in the examination of a matter. This is when he or she is personally, directly or indirectly, interested in the outcome of the particular matter, or if other circumstances exist which cause doubt as to his or her impartiality.

Article 6(4) of the Labour Dispute Law of the Republic of Latvia indicates that the members of the labour disputes commission performing their duties shall be independent. Interference in the work of the labour disputes commission, as well as influencing of members of the labour disputes commission is permitted. Further on, in part 5 of the same article, it said that the labour disputes commission shall examine the matter within a time of ten days from the day when the submission of the party of an individual dispute regarding rights has been submitted to the labour disputes commission. The parties are notified regarding the time and place for examination of the matter not later than three days before the commencement of examination of the matter. Non-appearance of the parties in a meeting of the labour disputes commission shall not be an impediment to the examination of the matter and taking of the decision.

In accordance with Article 6(6) of the Labour Dispute Law of the Republic of Latvia, the labour disputes commission shall take decisions by a simple majority. None of the members is entitled to abstain from voting. The decision of the labour disputes commission shall include the following: the name and composition of the labour disputes commission, the time when and the location where the decision was adopted, the participants in the matter, the subject of the dispute, the explanations and evidence submitted by the participants of the matter, the reasons for the decision, the adjudication of the labour disputes commission, and the rights of participants in the matter to apply to the court. Part 8 of the same article indicates that the decision shall come into force within a time period of ten days of the day when participants in the matter have received a true copy of the decision, if during such time period none of the parties has brought an action in court. Part 9 highlights that the decision in force taken by the labour disputes commission shall be mandatory to the parties and executed voluntarily within a time period of 10 days if another execution period has not been determined in the decision of the labour disputes commission. Further on in the article, part 10 suggests the actions of the parties when the decision of the labour disputes commission is not executed voluntarily. The interested party is entitled to apply to the court according to the location of the employer with an application regarding the issue of a writ of execution for compulsory execution of the decision of the labour disputes commission.

Article 7 of the Labour Dispute Law of the Republic of Latvia lists the cases when individual labour disputes regarding rights are to be settled in court:

1. any party to an individual dispute regarding rights has the right to apply to the court if the individual dispute regarding rights has not been settled in negotiations between an employee and an employer or any of the parties is not satisfied with the decision of the labour disputes commission;
2. the fact that parties have not tried to settle an individual dispute regarding rights in mutual negotiations may not serve as a basis for refusal to accept an application and examination of the matter on its merits;

It also indicates which individual disputes regarding rights shall be settled directly in court and not applying to the labour dispute commission:

1. regarding the declaration of an employer's notice of termination invalid, as well as the reinstatement of the employee to the previous employment;
2. following an application from the employer if the employee trade union does not agree to the notice of termination of the employment contract concluded with a member of the employee trade union;
3. regarding the recovery of work remuneration not paid in a timely manner;
4. following an application from an employee or employer if the undertaking does not have a labour disputes commission;
5. upon an application of an employee or employer if a third person requests to terminate the employment contract.

If there is a basis for a collective dispute regarding rights, the party shall submit a submission in writing to the other party in which its requirements shall be specified. The other party which has received a submission shall examine it immediately and shall within a time period of three days following receipt of the submission provide its reply in writing. If the reply to the submission is negative or is not provided, a collective dispute regarding rights shall be settled in accordance with the procedures prescribed by Article 11 of the Labour Dispute Law in the conciliation commission. Parties to the collective dispute regarding interests shall establish a conciliation commission not later than within a time period of three days by authorising an equal number of representatives. In the matter of a collective dispute, the parties shall write a report regarding the differences of opinions and submit it to the conciliation commission not later than within a time period of three days. The conciliation commission shall examine the referred-to report and take a decision within a time period of seven days following receipt of the report. The meetings of the conciliation commission shall be recorded. If parties to a collective dispute so agree, the conciliation commission may settle the collective dispute and also take a decision following the expiry of the mentioned time period. The conciliation commission shall take a decision by agreement of the commission members. The decision shall be binding on both parties of the collective dispute. Article 12 of the respective law establishes that any party to a collective dispute has the right to apply to the court within a time period of one month if the collective dispute regarding rights is not settled in the conciliation commission; and if a conciliation commission is not established or the settlement of the collective dispute is not commenced in a conciliation commission. If parties so agree in writing, a collective dispute regarding rights may be transferred to an arbitration court for settlement.

Collective disputes regarding interests may also be settled in the conciliation commission. The decision of the conciliation commission shall be binding on both parties to the dispute.

1 January 2013 a new order for individual labour dispute settlement entered into force in Lithuania. What are the essential changes? First of all, the formation of labour disputes commissions has changed, a territory-based formation principle shall be applied, when labour disputes commissions shall be formed based on territory and established under operating territorial divisions of the State Labour Inspectorate. This is the first essential novelty. Another novelty which is very significant in the author's opinion is that both an employee and an employer may apply with a claim to a labour disputes commission. This is a rather revolutionary provision that has been needlessly waited for: Lithuania is one of the last countries of all the Baltic States reforming the institution of individual labour disputes.

Another significant novelty of the new 2016 Labour Code is that labour disputes commissions are formed as constantly operating pre-trial bodies. It is very acceptable that the formation of a labour disputes commission will follow the principle of social partnership which means that only one member – the chairperson of the labour disputes commission, a civil servant of the State Labour Inspectorate who possesses higher university degree in law – will be appointed by the Chief State Labour Inspector of the Republic of Lithuania, and the rest of the members of the labour disputes commission will be appointed respectfully by the trade unions operating in the respective divisional territory of the State Labour Inspectorate, and authorised administrative bodies of employers' organizations. The final lists of the representatives of employees and employers shall be drafted by the Trilateral Board secretariat. The members of the labour disputes commission shall be approved and replaced by the Chief State Labour Inspector of the State Labour Inspectorate of the Republic of Lithuania.

Therefore, the new mechanism has helped to demarcate the status of the labour disputes commission and the issues settled by it. The author of the article may witness it based on his personal experience since he has been appointed as a representative of employers' associated structures to Vilnius Labour Disputes Commission II. In the author's opinion, the bigger the demarcation is, the better are the opportunities to draw an impartial and just decision which was lacking under the old procedure, when the commissions were based on the operational principle which meant that both the members of the labour disputes commissions and the parties to the dispute were the members of the same organization.

Conclusions

The reform of the entire labour law system and a part of that system – the institute of labour disputes – has been going and is still going following different scenarios and tempos, in addition, they differ in their starting points: 1996 in Estonia, 2003 in Latvia and 2013 in Lithuania. Despite the common past, similar national legislation practice, geopolitical issues and many other common issues, a unified 'Baltic' model for labour rights defence has not been created. Here are some close examples. Let us take for instance a 'Scandinavian' version: a labour court that resolves collective labour disputes, a number of labour judges resembling trilateral cooperation, individual disputes resolved in common courts and aiming at reconciling the parties before the formal hearing of the dispute, a special order for publicising the court decision, etc.

The Baltic region has remained united regarding one very important aspect – the pre-trial institution for individual labour dispute resolution. We have made very significant reforming steps: labour disputes commissions (committees) have been established under territorial divisions of the State Labour Inspectorate on the basis of trilateral agreement, however, labour disputes commissions are independent tripartite bodies. The distance that directly and figuratively appeared between the parties of an employment contract and commissions (committees) has raised their prestige and trust in society.

In its 2002 edition of the law, Latvia has left labour disputes commissions to be in force as an 'opportunity' – the principle of their formation. However, in terms of the labour law reform it has introduced some very significant novelties: established the division of labour disputes into individual disputes regarding rights, collective disputes regarding rights, and collective disputes regarding interests. In its law, Latvia has established negotiations and discussions as early prevention of labour disputes (Estonia has established the same measures). This is a desirable aspiration for Lithuania since Article 293(2) of the 2002 Labour Code indicates the procedure that has been started and agreement reached. Latvia has followed the example of Estonia and allows the parties to the dispute to choose between the institutions for the dispute resolution, including even the court of arbitration.

Although late, the reform of the institution of labour disputes resulted in some significant outcomes. The number of claims addressed to the State Labour Inspectorate has been consistently decreasing from 8,933 to 4,159 in Lithuania in the last three years, whereas the dynamics of the number of applications received to resolve the dispute in the labour disputes commission shows a steady but insignificant increase (there were 5,302 applications in 2013, 5323 in 2014, 5,358 in 2015). The number of employers' applications is increasing significantly – 207 applications were received in 2015 which is 34% more than in 2014, and 56% more than 2013. However, there are still many issues to be solved in Lithuania. We do not know why Lithuania only started implementing its national labour rights defence model on 1 January 2013. Regretfully, pre-trial and judiciary practices are being harmonized too slowly, after having provided the opportunity for an employer to apply to the labour dispute commission and a court, the provisions of the 2002 Labour Code are not tune in with today's actuality, and only 12% of cases resolved by labour disputes commissions end in an agreement. From the theoretical perspective, neither positive law nor doctrine provides a definition of labour rights' defence.

Part Four

Social Security and Labour Market Policies

The Recent Reform of the Social Security System in Italy

Silvia SPATTINI*

Abstract

The recent reform of the Social Security system in Italy occurred with a reforms' strategy – concerning a broad range of fields and topics – launched in 2014 by the government in office in order to deal with the persisting effects of the economic crisis which started in 2008. The so-called Jobs Act, inspired by the EU principles of flexicurity, introduced more flexibility in the Italian legal system by reducing restrictions of the employment protection legislation (regulations concerning hiring and firing). At the same time, in order to balance the increased flexibility with a higher level of security, on one hand the government approved two Legislative Decrees concerning reform of the unemployment benefit system and short-time working arrangements. These pieces of legislation extended the field of application of the unemployment benefits and compensations linked to short-time work arrangements and introduced new support measures. On the other hand, the Legislative Decrees concerning public employment services and active labour market policies aimed at increasing employment security. The reorganization of the social safety nets had the goal of striving for greater equity of the system through the rationalization and universalization of the benefits. The implemented reforms and the innovations introduced went undoubtedly in that direction, even if it is not possible to say that the goal of universalizing social security benefits has been fully realized. But, together with measures aiming at income security, we need to implement effectively the reform of public employment services and active labour market policies in order to ensure employment security.

Keywords: social security system reform; STWA; unemployment benefit; Italian Jobs Act.

---

* Silvia Spattini is ADAPT Senior research fellow and expert on labour law at the Centre for International and Comparative Studies of Marco Biagi Department of Economics, University of Modena and Reggio Emilia, Italy. She is a member of the direction for the ADAPT Labour Studies e-Book Series (ADAPT University Press) and the ADAPT Book Series (ADAPT University Press), member of the editorial board for the review Diritto delle Relazioni Industriali (Giuffrè Ed.) and member of the Scientific Board for the review *E-Journal of International and Comparative Labour Studies*. Her research interests mainly concern labour market regulation, public and private employment services, job matching, active labour market policies, social security system and unemployment insurance system, agency work, high apprenticeship, also in a comparative perspective.

1. The economic background

The recent reform of the Social Security system in Italy occurred with a reforms strategy launched in 2014 by the Government in office in order to deal with the persisting effects of the 2008 economic crisis, which strongly affected Italy and the consequences of which are still evident. Looking at the figures (Table 1) and at the trend of employment and unemployment rates, the impact of the economic crisis on the situation of the Italian labour market, compared with EU labour market performances, is evident. Between 2007 and 2013, Italian GDP fell by 8.9 percentage points, while EU GDP decreased by 0.8 percentage points. This huge fall of the Italian GDP caused a reduction of labour demand (Massarelli, 2009) and, accordingly, a decrease in employment and an increase in unemployment. In fact, the total employment rate fell by 3 percentage points from 58.6% to 55.5%, while the EU employment rate grew by about 2 percentage points. In the same period, the Italian unemployment rate almost doubled from 6.1% to 12.1%, whereas the EU unemployment rate increased by 3.7 percentage points from 7.2% to 10.9%. Young people were particularly hit by the lack of job opportunities: the youth unemployment rate reached 40%, 16.3 percentage points higher than the EU youth unemployment rate (23.7%).

This is the economic context in which Italian labour market reforms took place.

Table 1. Selected Indicators of Italian Labour Market

	2007	2008	2009	2010	2011	2012	2013
GDP Italy	**1.7**	**-1.2**	**-5.5**	**1.7**	**0.4**	**-2.4**	**-1.9**
GDP EU	3.2	0.4	-4.5	2.0	1.6	-0.4	0.1
Employment rate Italy	**58.6**	**58.6**	**57.4**	**56.8**	**56.8**	**56.6**	**55.5**
Employment rate EU	70.3	70.7	70.8	71.0	71.1	71.7	72.0
Unemployment rate Italy	**6.1**	**6.7**	**7.7**	**8.4**	**8.4**	**10.7**	**12.1**
Unemployment rate EU	7.2	7.0	9.0	9.6	9.7	10.5	10.9
Youth Unempl. rate Italy	**20.4**	**21.2**	**25.3**	**27.9**	**29.2**	**35.3**	**40.0**
Youth Unempl. rate EU	15.9	15.9	20.3	21.4	21.7	23.3	23.7

Source: Eurostat, 2014.

2. The Italian Reform Strategy

From 2008, in order to tackle the economic downturn and minimize its social consequences, European countries adopted anti-crisis measures to maintain employment levels, these included short-time work and temporary lay-off arrangements (Mandl and Salvatore, 2009; Hurley, Mandl, Storrie, and Ward, 2009). In Italy too, anti-crisis measures were adopted, even if a well-developed system of short-time work and temporary lay-off support schemes already existed (the so-called wage guarantee fund – *cassa integrazione guadagni*). Since this system was and still is not universal, in order to extend the coverage of social protection provisions to the categories of employees excluded from the wage guarantee fund (in particular because of the economic sector of the employer), the anti-crisis legislation introduced in 2008–2009 approved derogations from the existing law. More recently, in 2012, the so-called '*Legge Fornero*' (Law no. 92/2012) introduced a first reduction of the restriction of employment protection legislation and reformed the unemployment benefit system and the short-time working schemes. Starting from 2014, however, the new Government (led by Prime Minister Renzi) launched a reform strategy concerning a broad range of fields and topics, developing: the Constitutional and Electoral Reform, the Public Administration Reform, the School Reform, the Fiscal Reform, the Justice Reform and the Labour Market Reform.

3. The Italian Jobs Act

The Jobs Act introduced in the Italian legal system a new Labour Market Reform, completing, in some way, the reform started with the '*Legge Fornero*'. The Jobs Act is not actually just an act but consists of a number of pieces of legislation. In fact, the first piece of legislation (Law Decree No. 34/2014) was approved in 2014, and introduced more flexible rules for fixed-term contracts. At the end of the same year, the enabling law no. 183/2014 was passed, through which the Government was delegated by the Parliament to: reorganize social safety nets; improve public employment services and active labour market policies; reduce red tape and simplify administrative procedures and requirements concerning employment relationships; revise the types of job contracts and reduce restrictions of the employment protection legislation; support maternity and work-life balance.

Moreover, at the end of 2014, with the aim of supporting job creation, high economic incentives to open-ended employment contracts were introduced through the Budget Law for 2015 by setting social contributions to zero for three years. This was a very effective measure in increasing new open-ended employment contracts, but as was conceived, the effect was short term.

During 2015, the guidelines defined in the enabling law no. 183/2014 were implemented by several Legislative Decrees. The Italian Jobs Act is inspired by the EU principles of flexicurity[1], whose purpose is to address simultaneously the flexibility of labour markets, work organization and labour relations, and security – employment security and income security[2]. More flexibility was introduced in the Italian legal system by reducing restrictions of the employment protection legislation (regulations concerning hiring and firing).

In order to balance the increased flexibility with a higher level of security, on one hand the Government approved two Legislative Decrees concerning the reform of the unemployment benefit system and short-time working arrangements. These pieces of legislation extended the field of application of the unemployment benefits and compensations linked to short-time work arrangements and introduced new support measures. On the other hand, the Legislative Decrees concerning public employment services and active labour market policies aimed at increasing employment security.

4. The social security system reform

Within the reform strategy and especially the Jobs Act, legislative interventions have reorganized the system of social safety nets: Legislative Decree No. 22/2015 revised the unemployment benefit system, while Legislative Decree No. 148/2015 reformed short-time working arrangements.

---

1 With reference to the concept of flexicurity, see Wilthagen T., Tros F. The concept of "flexicurity": a new approach to regulating employment and labour markets. *Transfer*, No. 10 (2), 2004. *Varieties of flexicurity: reflections on key elements of flexibility and security. Background paper*, Dublin, 4-8. With reference to the EU principles of flexicurity, see European Commission, *Towards Common Principles of Flexicurity: More and better jobs through flexibility and security*, COM (2007) 359 final, 27 June 2007.

2 According to the principles of *flexicurity*, the aim is to ensure employment security instead of *job security* see Spattini S. The Reform of Social Protection Systems and Flexicurity from a European Perspective. In: W. Bromwich, O. Rymkevich, S. Spattini (eds), *The Modernization of Labour Law and Industrial Relations in a Comparative Perspective*. Alphen aan den Rijn: Kluwer Law International, 2009.

4.1 The unemployment benefit system

With the purpose of a more equal and universal unemployment benefit system, a new unemployment benefit (called *Nuova Assicurazione Sociale per l'Impiego*, NASpI) has replaced two former different benefits, whose accessibility depended on different qualifying periods and contributions paid. According to the previous legislation, unemployed people with at least two years of social insurance seniority and one year of social security contributions during the two years before unemployment could have access to the 'main' unemployment benefit, otherwise they had access to a 'reduced' unemployment benefit.

In order to unify the two previous unemployment benefits in just one type of allowance, the insurance contribution requirements have been reduced and are now less restrictive than before.To be more specific – the time frame within which the requirements must be satisfied is longer. In fact, the new legislation foresees that all unemployed with at least 13 weeks of contributions during the four years before the unemployment period and with 30 working days in the last 12 months before the unemployment spell have the right to access the new unemployment benefit (NASpI).

4.1.1 The field of application

The new unemployment benefit applies to all employees, including apprentices, members of cooperatives and show-business employees. The aim of the reform was to universalize the benefit. Actually, it cannot be defined as universal, since it applies only to employees and not to the self-employed or to people who have never been in employment. However, as mentioned, since the contribution requirements to obtain the benefit are much less restrictive than before, the number of eligible recipients has widened. Therefore, even in the case of discontinuous career paths, with a limited number of working days in the last year before the event of unemployment and contribution weeks in the previous four years, unemployed people can have access to the new unemployment benefit, whereas they would be excluded under the previous regulation.

The main conditions for accessing the unemployment benefit are to be involuntarily unemployed, capable of working, registered as unemployed with the public employment services, actively seeking new employment and available for new work, not benefiting from any other pension treatment.

4.1.2 The duration

The novelty of the new regulation concerning unemployment benefit is the definition of the duration of the allowance. While in the past, the duration of the benefit was fixed (12 months and 18 months for unemployed and at least 55-years old), it is now calculated on the basis of social contributions paid, namely the duration is equal to half the number of weekly contributions paid during the last four years before the start of the unemployment period. Moreover, in principle, the duration of the benefit has been extended. Indeed, the maximum duration of the new income support measure is 24 months. The unemployment benefit has to be claimed within 68 days from the beginning of the unemployment period and the waiting period is set at eight days.

4.1.3 The rate of the benefit

The rate of the benefit amounts to 75% of the monthly reference earning (namely the average monthly gross income earned in the last four years before the unemployment) within a monthly ceiling of EUR 1,195. For monthly reference earning over EUR 1,195, the benefit is increased by 25% of the worker's actual monthly pay exceeding the said ceiling. The maximum payable amount is equal to EUR 1,300 (gross) per month. As of the first day of the fourth month (91st day) of receipt of the benefit, the amount is reduced by 3% for each subsequent month.

4.2 The social assistance scheme

The Jobs Act introduced (with effect from 1 May 2015) in the Italian social security system means-tested unemployment assistance, which did not exist before. This subsidy extends the income protection to unemployed workers who have exhausted their right to unemployment benefit and who are still unemployed and in need, that is they have a so-called 'economic index' lower or equal to EUR 5,000. The access priority to the subsidy is foreseen for members of a household in which there is at least one minor or people aged 55 years and over. Actually, the social assistance subsidy is for few people because of the fact that the criteria are very selective, since the allocated economic resources are very limited. The rate of the social assistance subsidy amounts to 75% of the last unemployment benefit sum, with a maximum amount of EUR 448,07 per month. The duration is six months.

4.3 Allowance for quasi-subordinate

Another novelty of the Jobs Act is the introduction of a monthly allowance for workers with a so-called *'continuous and coordinated collaboration'* contract, that is quasi-subordinate or economically dependent workers. Actually, the guideline of the enabling law no. 183/2014 foresaw the extension of the employees' unemployment benefit to quasi-subordinate workers, but at the end the adopted legal solution was a specific allowance for this category of workers (called DIS-COLL). The main conditions for access to this allowance are to be involuntarily unemployed, capable of working, registered as unemployed with the public employment services, actively seeking new employment and available for new work, not benefiting from any other pension treatment. The qualifying period is three months of contributions in the period of reference (between 1 January of the year before the year of unemployment and the beginning of the unemployment spell), along with one month of contributions during the year of the start of the unemployment itself. The allowance has to be claimed within 68 days from the beginning of the unemployment period. The waiting period is fixed at eight days and the allowance is granted for the number of months corresponding to half the number of monthly contributions paid in the same period of reference. The maximum duration is six months. The rate of the allowance is calculated in the same way as the unemployment benefit, but the earnings reference is the monthly average income calculated in the period of reference (between 1 January of the year before the year of unemployment and the beginning of the unemployment spell). So, the rate of the allowance amounts to 75% of the monthly reference earning with a monthly ceiling of EUR 1,195. For monthly reference earning over EUR 1,195, the benefit is increased by 25% of the worker's actual monthly pay exceeding the said ceiling. The maximum payable amount is equal to EUR 1,300 (gross) per month. As of the first day of the fourth month (91st day) of receipt of the benefit, the amount is reduced by 3% for each subsequent month.

4.4 Short time working arrangements: the wage guarantee fund

The second half of the reform of the social security system concerns short-time working arrangements. This system consists of two different channels: on one hand the wage guarantee fund and on the other hand the solidarity funds.The wage guarantee fund is a public fund, working like insu rance, aimed at protecting workers' income in case of suspension of work or reduction of working hours. The fund is financed by social security contributions paid both by the employers and the employees and compensates employees for reduction in their wage in case of short-time work or temporary lay-off. Actually, there are two types of fund: ordinary and extraordinary.

The Jobs Act (specifically Legislative Decree No. 148/2015) has reviewed the regulation on this institution. First of all, it has rationalized the regulation itself, organizing it in one act rather than in different pieces of legislation.

4.4.1 The field of application and conditions

The field of application has been extended and now, together with employees, includes apprentices as well. But, in order to access the compensation, the workers need a work seniority of at least 90 days in the manufacturing unit. With reference to the 'objective' field of application, the wage guarantee fund operates in the industry/manufacturing sector. In particular, the extraordinary wage guarantee fund concerns industrial enterprises with more than 15 employees. With the passage of time, the field of application of the extraordinary wage guarantee fund was extended for example to commercial enterprises with more than 50 employees.

The reasons justifying compensation for suspension of work or reduction of working hours have been re-defined by Legislative decree No. 148/2015. The reasons are:

- suspension of productive activity due to unexpected and unavoidable circumstances which cannot be ascribed either to the employer or to the employees, or due to temporary market situations (lack of orders)
- suspension of productive activity resulting from the restructuring, reorganization of the activity, as well as in cases of severe financial difficulties for the undertaking, bankruptcy or liquidation.

4.4.2 The duration and the rate of the benefit

The duration of the compensation within this system varies in relation to the reason for the suspension or reduction of productive activity. The compensation to employees within the ordinary wage guarantee fund is up to 13 weeks, while the compensation relevant to the extraordinary wage guarantee fund is 12 months in case of financial difficulties for the undertaking and up to 24 months, with reference to restructuring. In a five-year period, the maximum duration of all compensations is 24 months. An important and significant novelty concerns the amount of compensated hours in case of short-time work rather than temporary lay-off. Unlike the previous regulation, the reform introduced a maximum number of hours that can be compensated, in order to encourage short-time work (reduction of working hours) rather than temporary lay-off (suspension of work). The rate of the benefit is 80% of the total remuneration for non-worked hours with a maximum amount defined each year (for 2016 the maximum amount is EUR 1,167.91 gross.

4.4.3 Financing: the social contributions

As mentioned, the wage guarantee funds are financed by social security contributions. With reference to the ordinary wage guarantee fund, the ordinary social security contributions are fully paid by employers falling within the field of application. The reform has slightly reduced the rate of these social contributions from 1.90% of the total gross remuneration paid to employees to 1.70% for companies of up to 50 employees and from 2.20% to 2.00% for companies with more than 50 employees.

As regards the extraordinary wage guarantee fund, the ordinary social security contributions have remained unchanged compared to the past legislation: 0.60% of total gross remuneration payable by employers falling within the field of application and 0.30% payable by employees.

At the same time, in order to develop a co-payment mechanism by employers and promote a responsible use of the schemes, the reform has increased additional social security contributions paid by employers in case of use of compensations for short-time work or temporary lay-off with reference to both ordinary and extraordinary wage guarantee funds. The rates: 9% of the total remuneration for non-worked hours in case of wage compensations up to 52 weeks in a five-year period; 12% in case of wage compensations between 53 weeks and up to 104 weeks in a five-year period; 15% in case of wage compensations over 104 weeks over a five-year period.

4.5 Short time working arrangements: solidarity funds

The system of solidarity funds has been introduced in the Italian legal system by the '*Legge Fornero*'. The Jobs Act has re-regulated these funds.

Since the system of wage guarantee funds does not apply to all employers (in some cases only to the manufacturing/industrial sector and in some others only to employers with more than 15 employees), the solidarity funds have been introduced in order to ensure wage compensation in case of short-time work or temporary lay-off to employees working in companies or for employers excluded from the field of application of wage guarantee funds.

Actually, the system foresees bilateral funds and a public fund. The bilateral funds are instituted by collective agreements for a specific sector and managed by social partners that signed the relevant agreement, while the public fund is established by the state and managed by the National Institute of Social Insurance. The public fund covers employees working in sectors where social partners did not create bilateral funds.

4.5.1 The field of application and conditions

In general, as mentioned, the field of application involves employers excluded from the scope of wage guarantee funds. To be more specific – the reform has widened the scope of solidarity funds. Within the previous legislation, solidarity funds were applicable to employers with more than 15 employees, while the regulation defined by the reform defines that solidarity funds now include employers with more than five employees. Within the system of solidarity funds, the reasons justifying wage compensation for suspension of work or reduction of working hours are the same as defined for compensations within the wage guarantee funds system.

4.5.2 The duration and the rate of the benefit

Like the wage compensation granted by wage guarantee funds, benefits paid by solidarity funds amount to the 80% of the total remuneration for non-worked hours. The duration of the compensations varies a lot depending on the kind of solidarity fund. The duration of the wage compensation granted by bilateral funds is defined by collective agreements between at least 13 weeks and a period no longer than the spell foreseen for benefits within wage guarantee funds. Within the public fund, for employers with more than 15 employees, the wage compensation can last a maximum period of 26 weeks in a two-year period. For employers with more than five employees, in order to avoid redundancies, the public fund can grant a benefit of 12 months.

4.5.3 The financing of the solidarity funds

Within the system of solidarity funds as well, employers have to pay an ordinary contribution in order to finance the funds and an additional contribution in case of use of compensations for short-time work or temporary lay-off. Particularly, as regards bilateral funds, contributions are defined by a ministerial decree establishing each bilateral fund. Ordinary contributions consist of two-thirds paid by the employer and one third by employees. Additional contributions are paid by employers in the event of the use of compensations and are calculated in proportion to the remuneration for non-worked hours, based on a rate of not less than 1.5%.

Concluding remarks

The reorganization of social safety nets had the goal of striving for greater equity of the system through the rationalization and universalization of the benefits. The implemented reforms and the innovations introduced went undoubtedly in that direction, even if it is not possible to say that the goal of universalizing social security benefits has been fully realized. But, along with measures aiming at income security, what we also need is to implement effectively the reform of public employment services and active labour market policies in order to actually ensure employment security.

The Analyses of the Legal Measures Taken to Combat Unemployment (to Boost Employability) among Older People According to the Last Amendments of the Polish Law on Employment Promotion and Labour Market Institutions

Tatiana Wrocławska*

Abstract

The study investigates the influence of Polish legal statutory regulations in the area of combating unemployment among older people and the legal instruments that strengthen the efforts taken to foster their employability. The author presents some considerations related to the significance of legal instruments provided in Polish legal regulations, by analysing their adherence to the changing social and economic conditions.**

Keywords: combating unemployment, fostering employability, older unemployed, ageing workforce, pre-retirement benefit, intervention works.

Introduction

The legal statutory regulation of 20 April 2004 on Employment Promotion and Labour Market Institutions[1] was amended on 12 May 2014[2]. A profound amendment was made to the provisions of this Act, including the support forms addressed to people referred to as 50 plus. The aims

---

* Tatiana Wrocławska is a researcher and academic teacher at the Faculty of Law and Administration, University of Lodz, Poland. She specializes in employment law (labour law). This paper is an attempt to provide certain conclusions that will be used in the final monograph, entailing scientific research results concerning the model of legal instruments taken to combat unemployment among older people.

** Contribution financed by the National Center of Science (Poland) DEC-2013/09/B/HS5/04137. Scientific research project: 'Model of legal instruments taken to combat unemployment among older people – legal analysis'.

1 *Journal of Laws* [Dz.U.] of 2014, item 598, named for the purposes of this contribution as Law on Promotion.

2 Consolidated text in *Journal of Laws* [Dz.U.] of 2008, No. 69, item 415, with amendments.

of the changes implemented are to increase the influence of the labour market policy on the boost to employment, to ease the consequences of structural incompatibility, especially in relation to the qualifications and competences of the unemployed, and to restore the skills of the unemployed in entering the labour market permanently. It also aims at the improvement of the efficiency of the labour market (due to better cooperation with employers) of the activities of employment offices, including their client-care standards and the employment rate achieved thanks to the introduction of new forms of work organization and to the cooperation between employment offices and non-public institutions. The solutions applied are meant to increase the flexibility of the activities of employment offices through the better tailoring of their activities to the needs of a specific unemployed person and a specific employer, by improving the efficiency of the activities of employment offices (increasing the role of social partners in the process of Labour Fund management), by improving the quality of services provided to the unemployed according to their needs (profiling the aid granted to the unemployed), by using new tools supporting the creation of new jobs and the return to taking on the unemployed, including those who return to the labour market, as well as by shortening the average unemployment time of people over 50 years of age through support granted to employers taking on such people (Justification to Draft from 18 November 2013).

Pursuant to Article 49 of the Act, the unemployed aged 50 and over (as well as the long-term unemployed, the unemployed granted social aid, the unemployed with at least one child under six or at least one disabled child under 18) are referred to as the unemployed in a particularly difficult situation in the labour market. As a consequence, under the Act in question they are granted priority in being assigned to participate in special programmes. In the glossary of the Act, the term unemployed person over 50 years of age refers to an unemployed person who was at least 50 on the day when the services or labour market instruments were applied to them (Article 2). Therefore, the term elderly person, meaning someone who requires preferential treatment because of their age, refers to people who cross the above age threshold. It is worth mentioning, however, that this applies only to those who reach the age indicated on the date of the adoption of support measures.

Before the amendment to the Act was made in 2014, special labour market instruments had been addressed to people who were in a particularly difficult situation in the labour market. Thus, the methods of counteracting unemployment had been classified by taking into account the group to whom it was addressed. Therefore, some instruments had been of a universal character and some had been of a special character addressed to specific groups.

The amendments to Article 49 of the Act apply to the derogation from the general principle that the labour market instruments such as intervention works, public works, traineeships, refunds of social benefit premiums, or vocational preparation of adults, are addressed only to the unemployed who are in a particularly difficult situation in the labour market, who are mentioned in Article 49. As a result of the above-mentioned meaningful amendment, the legislator introduced the flexible application of instruments to particular unemployed people, taking into consideration the results of profiling, in order to optimize their choice, making it suitable to the needs of a particular person, not only groups of unemployed who are in a particularly difficult situation in the labour market. As a consequence of this, instruments for people in a particularly difficult situation in the labour market, were the novelties introduced[3].

Despite the great number of positive aspects of the changes and the implementation of new instruments and legal measures to counteract unemployment, it is hard not to notice that there are no separate and numerous legal instruments directed at people who are over 50 years of age. Therefore, the direction taken by the legislator may raise doubts not only with regards to the derogation of this group from the preferential treatment, but also with respect to accuracy of supportive measures. The following remarks are related to both aspects mentioned above.

1. Doubts caused by the definition of an unemployed person, taking into account the legal instrument addressed to older people

The definition of an unemployed person plays an important role because of the subjective scope of the addressees of support measures. The question of correctness, flexibility and narrowing of the defining elements constitute a separate issue. The definition included in the Polish Act is extremely detailed and as a result of subsequent amendments it has become more and more complex. The cross-references, which are inserted (Article 2 (2) set forth conditions in a-m), cause many problems in the

---

[3] *Ibidem*, p. 47.

construction of the definition of an unemployed person. Undoubtedly, however, due to the involvement of public measures, only some groups of people considered by the legislator to qualify for support in certain socio-economic circumstances may become the targets of the support measures.

In short, an unemployed person within the meaning of the Employment Promotion Act is understood as a person fulfilling a lot of additional requirements. Those which are the most important for the legal analysis at issue include: lack of employment and lack of another kind of paid engagement, employment capability and readiness to work full-time as it is in a particular profession, service or another kind of paid engagement, turning eighteen and not reaching retirement age within the meaning of the provision of law of 17 December 1998[4], not acquiring the rights to a retirement pension or pension due to inability to work, not earning an income stipulated in the Act.

First of all, the negative criteria deserve attention. The first of these is related to not reaching retirement age. According to the law of 11 May 2012 on amending the law on pension benefits[5] the requirement concerning not reaching the age of 60 by women and 65 by men was deleted from the definition of an unemployed person. The above change was caused by amendments to the retirement law, connected with the gradual increase of retirement age for women and men to the same level of 67 years, as well as the opportunity to retire partially before reaching this age (Wrocławska 2014, 2015a, 2015b). Shifting the age limit also means a mobile limit which the Act under discussion links to enjoying the status of an unemployed person. The plan of changes related to lowering the retirement age forecast by the ruling team may lead to prompt systemic changes and, consequently, to the influence on the definition under discussion.

It must be highlighted that the above premise, which is a constituent of the definition of an unemployed person, is not connected with the acquisition of the right to a retirement pension, but it is linked to not reaching the retirement age. Not reaching the retirement age as a premise, conditioning the acquisition or retention of the status of an unemployed person within the meaning of the Act, may raise justified doubts (Hajn, 2009; Sanetra, 1997; Wagner, 2001). It must be noted that the statutory catalogue of situations in which one loses their status of an unemployed

---

4 Law on pension benefits and disability pension benefits from the Social Security Fund. *Journal of Laws* [Dz.U.] of 2013, item 1440 with amend.

5 *Journal of Laws* [Dz.U.] of 2012, item 637.

person, strictly linked to the premises of considering a person to be unemployed (because it refers to them), has a closed character under the Act and the occurrence of a cause stipulated in the Act obliges an administrative organ to issue a decision about the deprivation of status, and therefore such a decision does not have a discretionary character (Skoczyński, 2005, pp. 23–4)[6].

Here another issue which may raise doubts is the fragmentary application of the provisions of the Retirement Act, which also mentions the lower retirement age. Above all, objections may be raised by the fact that under this Act it is of no importance whether a person fulfils the conditions for obtaining retirement benefits. Not acquiring the right to a retirement pension, as mentioned before, constitutes, however, a separate premise defining an unemployed person.

The critique of the direction selected by the legislator was presented by Professor Z. Góral in his commentary to the law on Employment Promotion (Góral, 2011). The remarks lose none of their immediacy and become much more pertinent in view of the changes to the policy of active ageing and the considerable effort of all the countries of the European Union, including Poland, to keep elderly people longer in the labour market. The author notes that one of the hypothetical reasons why age is indicated as a circumstance excluding the status of an unemployed person is the fact that it is treated as being tantamount to a loss of employment capability in its psychophysical sense, forgetting that the ability to work has already been taken into account as one of the positive premises of being unemployed.

That is why the above-mentioned positive premise of the definition, which is the retention of the ability to work, requires a few words of commentary here. In accordance with the definition of an unemployed person, it is about the requirement of employment capability and readiness (jointly) to work full-time as it is in a particular profession, service or another kind of paid engagement. It must be observed that there is a differentiation between employment and another kind of paid engagement. The term another kind of paid engagement within the meaning of the Act in question refers to performing work or services under civil law contracts, inclusive of contract of agency, mandate contract, contract of specific work or work during the period of membership in agricultural production cooperatives, farmers' cooperative associations

[6] See judgement of Supreme Administrative Court in Warsaw from 12 September 2012, I OSK 859/13, LEX No. 1664419.

or agricultural services cooperatives. Nevertheless, the requirement of employment capability and readiness to work full-time was reserved for employment within the meaning of the provisions of the Act understood as performance of work in an employment relationship, a service relationship or a home-based work contract. The binding provision can be therefore construed as one combining the requirement of employment capability and the readiness to work full-time with an employment relationship and thus not excluding taking on employment on another basis of its performance regardless of the time of employment (whether it is full- or part-time). Here it must be added that the disabled are an exception to the requirement of employment capability and readiness to work full-time. They may achieve the status of an unemployed person if they are able and ready to take on at least half-time employment within an employment relationship (within the meaning presented above). This makes one pose the question whether the above mentioned solution should not also be applied to unemployed people who are over 50 years of age as they fall into the group of the addressees of special programmes.

The premise discussed, which defines the term of an unemployed person, should be combined with the psychophysical capabilities to perform work, even full-time when employment relationship is at issue. However, one wonders why the identification of the category of people who are over 50 years of age and specifying them as one of the groups that are in a particularly difficult situation in the labour market and who are owed priority to be assigned to take part in special programmes did not result in the derogation from the requirement of employment capability and readiness to work full-time. It seems that flexible forms of employment applied in relation to people who exceed a certain age, and who have, in fact, an appropriate wealth of professional experience might contribute to their faster return to the labour market. Within the existing legal framework, however, elderly people who have the status of a disabled person pursuant to the Act will have greater chances.

Thus, the point is to individualize the approach for each person with the status of an unemployed person or applying for this status. In the light of the remarks presented, it is hard to agree with the opinion that the psychophysical capability to work might be determined by the upper age limit[7]. Nevertheless, one might have the impression that reaching

---

7 The analyses are related to the definition of unemployed. In the case of some professions or types of work the age threshold is justified by ability to work. These situations are exceptional and couldn't be generalized.

retirement age was treated by the legislator as always tantamount to the loss of employment capability. Actually, there are no legal obstacles for a person who has reached retirement age or who even receives a retirement pension from performing gainful work. Retirement age within the meaning of insurance law constitutes an additional incentive to undertake employment because of the lack of limits to obtaining retirement benefit. Under Polish law, in such a situation incomes earned remain without the influence on the benefit received (then, unlike with the earnings of people at pre-retirement age, their benefit will not be suspended or limited).

The acquisition of the right to receive a retirement pension (just like the acquisition of the right to a pension due to inability to work, training benefit or social benefit) constitutes an additional circumstance excluding the opportunity to receive or maintain the status of an unemployed person. This right must be granted with the applicable decision of the Social Insurance Institution[8]. It is not important then whether the benefit is really received. This is a separate negative premise stipulated in the definition of an unemployed person. Much as the exclusion of people from the group of the unemployed with a source of income is socially justified, it highlights additionally, however, the negative overtone of determining the retirement age as a circumstance leading to the loss of status of an unemployed person. On the other hand, it is rightly observed that the acquisition of the right to a retirement pension, confirmed by the appropriate decision of an authorized body, is not identical with the receipt of the benefit by the person entitled (Góral, 2011).

Taking the above remarks into account, one finds convincing the opinion that in the definition of an unemployed person the determination of retirement age in relation to people who despite reaching retirement age are able to work may be considered to be a matter of discrimination based on age[9]. Among the remarks presented above, there are no legal arguments which would confirm the reasonableness of the premise of retirement age, which, as it should be especially highlighted, is not always connected with the acquisition of the right to an additional source of income in the form of a retirement pension.

The justification for the binding regulation should be sought in another area. What turns out to be *prima facie* convincing within the sphere discussed are the arguments of a social nature, which refer to

---

[8] Special attention should be paid to judgement of Administrative Court in Łódź from 22 October 2008 (III SA/Łd 219/08, LEX No. 477198).

[9] *Ibidem.*

the emphasis on offering aid (due to the scarcity of financial means) to those who do not have additional security in the form of a retirement pension. Support measures, as well as subsidies and funding, target the unemployed, and alternatively employers taking on the unemployed. They fail, however, when we take into consideration the fact that reaching retirement age does not always mean acquiring a retirement pension. In addition, one should consider the fact that among the unemployed there is a differentiation between those who have the right to receive a benefit and those who do not have such an entitlement. Thus, acknowledging the need to safeguard aid for people who despite reaching retirement age are interested in finding appropriate employment with the help of employment services, the potential differentiation of the status of the unemployed with regard to age might be seen as a different stipulation of the right to benefit, which would exclude people who have acquired the right to benefit when they reach the retirement age.

It is also worth emphasizing that the legislator combines the premise of not acquiring the right to a retirement pension and other benefits mentioned (pension due to inability to work, training benefit, social benefit and survivor's pension) with receiving benefit in the amount exceeding half of the minimum remuneration. Taking into account the amount of the minimum benefit, which is PLN 1,850 in 2016, the limit for someone qualifying as falling under the definition of an unemployed person is half the amount of the above-mentioned benefit. In the ruling of 24 September 2013 of the Provincial Administrative Court in Lublin[10] it was stressed that granting the status of an unemployed person is excluded if the applicant has acquired the right to a retirement pension or a pension due to inability to work whose crucial feature is the lowest amount stipulated under the provisions. In turn, in the further part of the provision there is the requirement that, after termination of employment or another kind of paid engagement, or after ceasing to conduct non-agricultural business activities, a person will not receive the indicated benefit. This may lead to the conclusion that the benefit may be in such cases granted by an appropriate decision of an authorized body, but a person willing to register as an unemployed person cannot just receive it. In the light of the position of the Administrative Court[11], the term 'receiving' benefit should be construed in its broad sense. The

[10] III SA/Lu 340/13.

[11] Judgment of Supreme Administrative Court in Warsaw from 19 of October 2011, I OSK 900/11, LEX No. 1149455.

decision of the Administrative Court was similar in its previous ruling[12]. To sum up, the legislator excluded not only people who actually receive a specified income but also people who have a secure source of livelihood of a specified minimum amount regardless of whether they use this source or not.

Point 2ca added to Article 2 of the Act by means of the amendment in 2014 stipulates that an unemployed person may be a person who has not acquired the right to a retirement pension or to a pension due to inability to work, granted by a foreign retirement and disability pension body at least in the amount of the lowest retirement pension or pension due to inability to work, stipulated under the law of 11 May 2012. The amount of benefit qualifying or disqualifying someone from the group of unemployed persons was established at the level of the lowest national retirement pension.

Finishing the analysis of the issues discussed, one should also pay attention to the definition of a person seeking employment laid down in Article 2 (2) (22) of the Employment Promotion Act. In the light of the mentioned provision, this is a person referred to in Article 1 (or a foreigner – a family member of a Polish citizen), seeking employment or another kind of paid engagement or another support form set forth under the Act, registered in the *poviat* [district] employment office. Persons who have reached retirement age may rely on the aid stipulated in the Act as long as they register in the appropriate employment office as seeking employment. However, the scope of such aid, guaranteed to people seeking employment by the Act is different, that is to say, narrower than that provided for the unemployed. One must add that the opportunity to register as a person seeking employment does not depend on remaining unemployed.

2. Legal instruments addressed directly to older unemployed

As has already been mentioned, before the amendment of 2014 people over 50 years of age had also been included in the group of people in a particularly difficult situation in the labour market, for whom the opportunity of applying special services and instruments in the labour

[12] Judgment of Administrative Court in Gliwice from 16 October 2009, IV SA/Gl 197/09, LEX No. 574075.

market, stipulated at that time in Article 50-61 (a) of the Act, was provided. Also, earlier age, determined by the limit of 45 years, had been treated as a circumstance justifying the granting of special entitlements in the labour market. They had been binding starting from 1 February 2009[13]. This solution had provided instruments supporting unemployed persons, as well as instruments directed at people who were employed but at risk of loss of employment (Włodarczyk, M., and Paluskiewicz, M., 2011, p. 35). As remarked in the introduction to this analysis, the legal solutions currently applied to the indicated groups have become much scarcer. The solutions which target elderly people at a certain age, namely unemployed people over 50 years of age, will be presented below.

2.1 Right to receive the pre-retirement benefit

After six months from the day of registration in the district employment office the unemployed who are over 50 years of age may apply for the grant of the right to pre-retirement benefit if they fulfil the conditions for the acquisition of such benefit stipulated in separate provisions. The above conditions are provided in the Pre-retirement Benefits Act of 30 April 2004[14]. They include the general conditions related to being registered as an unemployed person for a specified minimum period of time, as well as specific conditions related to the manner of termination of the employment relationship, years of service, and the age of a person. It is worth highlighting that the benefit received remains without influence on the amount of retirement pension that will be received in the future. However, pre-retirement benefit may be lowered or suspended depending on the income received from employment, among others. The fact that one receives it has significance also with regard to the refund, which results from assigning a person over 50 years of age to intervention works.

2.2 Referral to the intervention works

The amendment of 2014 broadened the group of the unemployed to whom this instrument of the labour market may be applied, as a result of which all unemployed, regardless of whether they are in the risk group or not, may take advantage of intervention works. In this respect, the qualification for the specific profile of aid is crucial, as

[13] Article 43 of Law on Promotion amended by law from 19 of December 2008 r., *Journal of Laws* [Dz.U.] of 2009, No. 6, item 33.

[14] *Journal of Laws* [Dz.U.] from 2013, item 170, consolidated text with amendments.

only the unemployed qualified for profile II of aid may take advantage of intervention works. This leads to the exclusion of the unemployed qualifying for profiles I and III.

Because of the introduction of the new approach to the individualization of forms of support addressed to the unemployed through the profiling of aid, the catalogue of district self-government tasks in connection with the labour market policy was broadened. What is important is that when establishing the profile of aid, the employment office takes into consideration two variables: the distance of the unemployed person from the labour market and the person's readiness to return to the labour market[15]. As for the distance of an unemployed person from the labour market, what is considered are factors which make it difficult for the unemployed to enter or return to the labour market, including, among others, age, sex, work experience, accessibility of modern forms of communication with the employment office and employers.

It is rightly observed that most of the above factors are reflected in the catalogue of people who are in a particularly difficult situation in the labour market stipulated by the legislator in Article 49 of the Employment Promotion Act. Until the amendment of 2014, being stipulated in this catalogue determined the scope of differentiation of entitlements applicable to particular categories of the unemployed. The catalogue of activities which were possible in relation to them was quite broad. The introduction of profiling of the unemployed to a great extent reduces the significance of the statutory catalogue of people who are in a particularly difficult situation in the labour market. As has been mentioned before, they are only entitled to have priority in being assigned to participate in special programmes used by employment offices when establishing the profile of support (Staszewska, 2016). In the provision of the Act which stipulates the conditions in which the authority to deprive an unemployed person of the status of an unemployed person is vested in the district governor a reservation was introduced. Pursuant to this stipulation, the lack of an unemployed person's consent to establishing the profile of support results in the loss of such status. The obligation to establish the profile of support for each unemployed person immediately after their registration, as well as to prepare an individual action plan adjusted to the profile of support, was introduced.

---

15 Retrieved June 15, 2016 from http://wsge.edu.pl/index.php/aktualne-wydanie-joms/rok-2015-2-25-2015.

The district employment office, providing the support laid down in the Act, prepares an individual action plan adjusted to the profile of support. An individual action plan may also be prepared for someone who is seeking employment. An individual action plan is prepared by the counsel of the client with the participation of the unemployed person or the person seeking employment. The preparation of an individual action plan takes place not later than 60 days from the establishment of the profile of support. It may be modified to suit the changing situation of an unemployed person or a person seeking employment.

Three profiles of support for the unemployed were stipulated. Support profile I applies to the active unemployed for whom basic support will comprise job placement, and in justified cases, employment consultancy or specified forms of support such as training sessions, paying the costs of exams, financing the cost of travelling, granting non-refundable funds for starting a business activity, an activation benefit, a loan for starting a business activity. Support profile II refers to the unemployed who require support and whom the employment office will apply labour market services and instruments, activation measures ordered by the employment office and other forms of support with the exclusion of the Activation and Integration Programme. Support profile III applies to the unemployed who are distant from the labour market, who for various reasons are at a risk of social exclusion and who because of their own choice are not interested in taking up employment or refuse to take up legal employment. Towards such a group, the employment office will be able to apply such forms of support as the Activation and Integration Programme, activation measures ordered by the employment office, special programmes, assigning the unemployed person to employment supported at the employer's or to taking up employment for a social cooperative set up by legal persons, as well as employment consultancy in justified cases.

Returning to the issue of sending elderly people to intervention works, it must be stressed that the amendment to Article 61 (a) of the Employment Promotion Act allowed for the possibility to assign the unemployed to intervention works for entrepreneurs who are not employers within the meaning of the Act and who do not take on employees in compliance with the principles provided for employers[16].

---

[16] *Ibidem.*

The rules for assigning people who are over 50 differ from those provided for the other unemployed. The district governor may assign the unemployed over 50 to perform work related to intervention works for a period of 24 months and refund the costs of remuneration and social insurance premiums incurred by an employer. Moreover, assigning the above people and the refund of the above costs may extend to a period of four years if it includes costs incurred for every second month of employment. The amount of the refund depends on the legal situation of the unemployed person over 50. If the unemployed who are sent to intervention works meet the conditions essential to acquire pre-retirement benefits, the refund is granted in the amount of 80% of the minimum remuneration for work and social insurance premiums on the refunded remuneration. However, if they do not meet the conditions essential to acquire pre-retirement benefits, the refund is granted in the amount of 50% of the minimum remuneration for work and social insurance premiums on the refunded remuneration. The other conditions are the same as in the case of the other unemployed. Thus, pursuant to the agreement concluded, an employer is obliged to retain the assigned unemployed person in employment for a period during which the remuneration for work and social insurance premiums on the refunded remuneration are refunded and for a period of six months following the termination of such refund. Non-fulfilment of the condition stipulated in section 3 or breach of other terms of the contract concluded results in the obligation to return the support received together with statutory interest on the total amount of the support received from the day of receiving the first refund within thirty days from the receipt of the district governor's request for payment. Intervention works for people who are over 50 cannot be organized in district and *voivodship* [provincial] employment offices.

2.3 Refunding of remuneration of unemployed aged 50 plus

In the justification to the draft of the Act it was indicated that the introduction of a new form of activation for the unemployed who are over 50 years of age in the form of a refund of their remuneration enables this group of people to remain in the labour market[17]. The activity taken up should alleviate the negative tendencies of low activity and employment rates of people who are 50 and 60 plus.

[17] For further see justification to draft of law from 18 November 2013, *op. cit.*, p. 111.

Pursuant to the contract concluded, a district governor may grant to an employer or entrepreneur a refund of remuneration of the person assigned who has turned 50. The duration of the period of refund is subject to the age of the person assigned. It must be emphasized that the refund is granted in compliance with the conditions of permissibility of *de minimis* support.

One is entitled to a refund of remuneration for a period of 12 months in the case of employing an unemployed person who has turned 50 and has not yet turned 60, and for a period of 24 months in the case of employing an unemployed person who has turned 60. The maximum refund amount is half of the amount of the minimum monthly remuneration applicable on the day of entering into the contract for each employee taken on. Likewise, as in the above mentioned cases of granting support to employers taking on the people assigned, there is a requirement of retaining employment for a specified period after the refund ceases. An employer or entrepreneur is obliged to further employ an unemployed person assigned after the period of remuneration refund expires, which is six months or twelve months respectively, depending on the duration of the period for which the refund was granted.

Non-fulfilment of the conditions for retaining employment for the period indicated above, as well as during the period during which one receives a refund, results in the obligation to return all the financial resource received together with statutory interest on the total amount of the financial resources received from the date of first payment of the refund of cost paid for remuneration within 30 days of the date of delivery of the district governor's request for payment. However, if the employment of an unemployed person assigned to work is retained for the period for which the of cost paid for remuneration was granted and for at least half of the mandatory period of retaining employment, an employer or entrepreneur is obliged to return 50% of the total amount. The term non-fulfilment of conditions for retaining employment does not refer to situations in which the contract is terminated by the person assigned to perform work themselves, the contract is terminated for disciplinary reasons, or the employment contract of a person assigned to perform work expires. In such a case, the district governor assigns another unemployed person for the vacancy. If there is no appropriate person for the position, an employer or entrepreneur does not return the refund of cost paid for remuneration granted for the period of employment of the person assigned to perform work.

3. Selected legal instruments addressed to the unemployed in specific situations in the labour market

3.1 Special Programmes

In the introduction to this analysis it was mentioned that, in accordance with the definition of an unemployed person over 50 under Article 50 of the Act, such people are qualified as belonging to the group of persons in a particularly difficult situation in the labour market. As a particular risk group they are entitled to have priority in being directed to participate in special programmes. It is worth highlighting that under Article 49 (a) additional people are entitled to participate in special programmes. This includes not only people who are referred to in the definition of an unemployed person, but also those stipulated in Article 43 of the Act, namely those who seek employment if they were selected by the district governor taking into consideration the analyses and prognoses concerning the local labour market. Pursuant to the provisions, additional special programmes may be applied to such people.

Special programmes are provided for in chapter 13 (a) of the Employment Promotion Act. Under Article 66 (a) of the Act the aim of a special programme is the professional activation of people to whom this Act refers. A special programme may lead to the activation of an indicated group of employees, especially through the adaptation of one's professional qualifications or obtaining new professional qualifications, as well as through the support of work places which are at risk of liquidation or which already exist. According to the glossary of the Act, whenever special programmes are mentioned, it refers to a set of activities aiming at the adaptation of one's professional qualifications or obtaining new professional qualifications, as well as through the support of work places which are at risk of liquidation or which already exist or are being created. Special programmes are implemented following the opinion of a district employment council and they are financed from the resources of the Labour Fund, allocated on the basis of an algorithm, and granted for financing the tasks in the district. They may also be subsidized by means of other resources.

3.2 Employment of referred unemployed

The district governor may enter into a contract with an employment agency to make an unemployed person assigned to perform work, who is in a particularly difficult situation in the labour market, take up appropriate employment or another kind of paid engagement under civil law contracts for a period of at least six months. The contract should set forth, among others, the sum of granted resources in the amount not higher than 150% of the average remuneration applicable on the day of contract conclusion for one unemployed person assigned. If an agency does not fulfil the condition of making the unemployed person take up employment or paid work, the resources transferred to the agency are to be returned in the amount which is proportional to the period during which the condition mentioned above was not fulfilled. If an employment contract concluded with the assigned unemployed person is terminated for reasons attributable to a specific person, or a civil law contract is terminated by an assigned unemployed person before the period of six months expires, the agency is not obliged to return the financial resources received. During the period when an unemployed person participated in the activities performed by an employment agency, the district employment office does not address to such unemployed person other forms of support specified in the Act.

3.3 Programme of Activation and Integration (PAI)

In order to improve the labour market situation of the unemployed who take advantage of the social welfare benefits and whose profile of support was identified by the employment office as showing a big distance from the labour market or lack of readiness to take up work, there is a possibility to include such people in the Activation and Integration Programme (PAI).

This solution is optional and its application is conditioned by the financial opportunities of a *commune* (municipality). It is a special programme which involves close cooperation between employment offices and social welfare institutions. In the justification to the draft of the Act it was pointed out that the underlying reason for its introduction was to minimize the number of cases in which the benefits are received for a long time without the person being professionally activated. The fact that most clients of employment offices are also clients of social welfare institutions was not without significance here[18].

A district employment office may on its own or in cooperation with a social welfare institution initiate activities aimed at the professional activation and social integration of the unemployed, undertaken within

[18] Justification to draft of law, *op. cit.*, p. 5 and 62.

the framework of the PAI under Article 62(a). The unemployed who meet additional conditions are assigned to participate in the programme, so it does not suffice to turn 50. This refers to those with support profile III, who take advantage of social welfare benefits, especially performing a social contract, who are referred to in the provisions on social welfare. Activities aiming at professional activation of the unemployed are implemented by a district employment office as socially useful work referred to in Article73(a), whereas activities aiming at the social integration of the unemployed and whose role is to shape active attitudes in social and professional lives may be implemented through group job counselling, training workshops, and support groups of at least ten hours a week. Activities within the scope of social integration may be implemented by a social welfare institution or entities which undertake activities stipulated in their statute aimed at professional and social integration and reintegration of people at risk of social exclusion or counteracting addictions and social pathologies in compliance with the provisions on public benefit activity and voluntary service.

The implementation of PAI takes two months. After its termination, a district employment office may take the decision to reassign an unemployed person to participate in the Programme (however, for a period not longer than six months jointly) or, in agreement with a social welfare institution, assign an unemployed person to supported employment in compliance with the rules stipulated in the provisions on social employment, or to take on work in a social cooperative. Another option is to establish a profile of support again, and if there is a change in the profile, to adapt the individual action plan and present the unemployed person with the offer of support set forth in the Act.

During the period when the unemployed participates in PAI, the district employment office does not assign an unemployed person to other forms of support laid down in the Act. However, under Article 33 of the Act in question, the refusal to participate in activities within the framework of PAI without a justified reason results in the deprivation of the status of an unemployed person for a period of 120, 180 or 270 days depending on the number of refusals.

4. The other supports taken to combat unemployment among groups at risk in the labour market

Due to the limited scope of this analysis there must be only a brief mention of some other instruments and programmes introduced under the amendment of 2014 which may be of particular significance to groups of older unemployed people. What is meant here are, among others, programmes which involve increasing local government participation in counteracting unemployment: regional programmes and ordering activation actions.

The regional plan of actions in favour of employment stipulates priority groups of the unemployed and people who are in need of support. Additionally, the priority which was accepted for implementation within the framework of the regional programme must be compliant with the priorities in the area of the labour market of the country stipulated in the National Action Plan. The priorities related to increasing adaptability in the labour market were stipulated in the National Action Plan for Employment for the years 2015–2017. The main directional activities include supporting the mobility and employability of employees in the labour market. The point is to support people who fall into groups which are not favoured in the labour market, including, among others, people who are 50 plus and the disabled (Paluszkiewicz, 2016, pp. 721).

Moreover, a new chapter, 13c, was introduced in order to increase the efficiency of active policies of the labour market, as well as of the support granted to employment offices in order to improve the situation of the unemployed. In this chapter there is a solution which makes it possible for such people to access various activation activities provided by external entities referred to in the Act as activation activities implementers. The long-term unemployed, inclusive of the unemployed whose support profile will be established as showing a big distance from the labour market or lack of readiness to take up work, profile II or II (including the unemployed who are beneficiaries of PAI) will be assigned to an activation activities implementer. The mechanism of ordering introduced is also referred to as outsourcing of activation activities or 'contracting of labour market services.'

The amendment of 2014 also resulted in the replacement of previous solutions within the scope of human resources development. On the basis of these provisions the National Training Fund was created. In the justification to the draft of the Act it was indicated that the above change resulted from the need to pursue the aims of the Europe 2020 strategy, to increase competitiveness and to counteract the social exclusion of people with qualifications which are low or not adapted to the needs of the labour market. The new solutions will allow investment in human capital to be better supported[19]. Only a small number of firms took advantage of the previous solutions, which involved a refund from the Labour Fund resources of a part of the costs incurred on employees' training sessions granted to employers who created a company training fund. Thus, the fund is a useful tool for the improvement of professional qualifications, making it possible for employees to adapt to the changes occurring in the economy as well as to the directions of activities which result from the strategy of an enterprise. It plays a vital role in motivating employees to further develop professionally and, what is important, in motivating employers who may also take advantage of financial support if they undertake training themselves. Therefore, as far as employers are concerned, it facilitates the obtaining of financial resources for training their staff. In the justification to the draft of the Act it was assumed that the above solutions would bring about a positive influence on the labour market and that microenterprises and employees at the age of 45 and over would enjoy particularly significant advantages thanks to these solutions[20].

Subsequent new solutions introduced by means of the latest amendment, which may be applied regardless of age but which may be particularly applicable to older people, are instruments in the form of a grant for telework, activation benefits, as well as the vocational preparation of adults and loans for starting a business activity.

Concluding remarks

The definitions of an unemployed person, consisting of many references and specific terms, among others referring to retirement age, may raise justified doubts, as it seems that the main condition excluding someone from the group of people entitled to special support measures should be their income achieved and not their age.

The Act, apart from setting forth basic labour market services (such as job placement, vocational counselling and trainings), specified labour

---

19 *Ibidem*, p. 26-27.

20 *Ibidem*, p. 121.

market instruments applied to the unemployed (and supporting the above services). Some of them are also applied to people seeking work. It refers, however, to a narrower subjective category linked to a great extent to a greater risk of long-term employment. It deserves to be emphasized that there is a broader selection of support instruments for those who were assigned by a district employment office.

The fundamental aid measures were directed at people fulfilling the conditions for being categorized as unemployed within the meaning of the Act. Distinguishing the category of the unemployed over 50 years of age is also worth highlighting. Programmes and legal instruments supporting the employment of the unemployed over 50 are scarce. However, special solutions that are laid down in the Act are conditioned on the fulfilment of additional conditions (related to the profiling of support for the unemployed and categorization to a specific profile), which is often connected with long-term unemployment, the assessment of the situation in the local labour market, difficulties in returning to the labour market, care of a dependant or taking advantage of social welfare benefits, etc. It must also be highlighted that some kinds of support were addressed to people seeking employment, sometimes providing them with the same entitlements as those enjoyed by the unemployed. Nonetheless, the subjective group of entitled people was subjected to additional restrictions.

The refund granted for the employment of people who are over 50, namely people who are in the pre-retirement age, is one of the most important instruments whose role is to foster both an increase in employment and people remaining in the labour market. The justification of the activities undertaken for the real employment of people who are over 50 is to be found in the research whose results at the stage of preparing the draft of the Act showed that 34% of the surveyed people at the age of 45 and over recognized the need to create incentives for employers to take on people who are over 45 in the form of raising qualifications, whereas 39% indicated lowering employment costs (refunding remuneration) as the factor encouraging employment[21].

Despite the change in the approach of the legislator in the area of legal measures to counteract unemployment among elderly people, the introduction of new solutions, which activate the unemployed and are applicable in most cases regardless of age, must be assessed in a positive way. One should recognize a great chance in the programmes addressed

21 *Ibidem*, p. 113.

to people in a particularly difficult situation in the labour market, based on the assessment of their individual situation and not on age criteria. Therefore, addressing support to the unemployed through profiling, related to the monitoring of the process of seeking employment and sanctions for non-fulfilment of the requirements specified in individual action plans, must be considered to be effective activation activities (Report from 18 May 2016).

Bibliography

Góral Z. (2011). Komentarz do artykułu 2 ustawy o promocji zatrudnienia i instytucjach rynku pracy [Comment to the article 2 of Law on Employment Promotion and Institutions of Labour Market]. In: Góral Z. (ed.) *Law on Employment Promotion and Institutions of Labour Market. Practical Commentary,* Lex No. 97780, legal status for 2011.02.01.

Góral Z. (2016a). Komentarz do artykułu 2 ustawy o promocji zatrudnienia i instytucjach rynku pracy [Comment to the article 2 of Law on Employment Promotion and Institutions of Labour Market], pp. 42-101. In: Góral Z. (ed.). *Law on Employment Promotion and Institutions of Labour Market. Practical Commentary.* Warsaw: Wolters Kluwer.

Komentarz do artykułu 33 ustawy o promocji zatrudnienia i instytucjach rynku pracy [Comment to the article 2 of Law on Employment Promotion and Institutions of Labour Market], pp. 303-343. In: Góral Z. (ed.) *Law on Employment Promotion and Institutions of Labour Market. Practical Commentary.* Warsaw: Wolters Kluwer.

Hajn Z. (2009). Dopuszczalność wypowiedzenia stosunku pracy ze względu na osiągnięcie wieku emerytalnego lub nabycie prawa do emerytury [Possibility to termintle employment contract according to retirement age or entitlement to a retirement pension]. In: Góral Z. (ed.), *Anniversary Book for Prof. H. Lewandowski*, pp. 277-291. Warszawa: Oficyna a Wolters Kluwer.

Paluszkiewicz M. (2016). Komentarz do artykułu 66 c ustawy o promocji zatrudnienia i instytucjach rynku pracy [Comment to the article 66 c of Law on Employment Promotion and Institutions of Labour Market], pp. 718–725. In: Góral Z. (ed.), *Law on Employment Promotion and Institutions of Labour Market. Practical Commentary.* Warsaw: Wolters Kluwer.

Sanetra W. (1997). Wiek emerytalny jako przyczyna rozwiązania stosunku pracy [The retirement age as a clause of employment termination]. *Journal Praca i Zabezpieczenie Społeczne,* No. 6, 1997, pp. 21–26.

Skoczyński J. (2005). 'Wiek emerytalny pracownika jako uzasadnienie wypowiedzenia umowy o pracę' [Retirement age as reason for termination of the employment contract]. *Journal Praca i Zabezpieczenie Społeczne*, No. 4, 2005, pp. 23-24.

Staszewska E. (2016). Komentarz do artykułu 51 ustawy o promocji zatrudnienia i instytucjach rynku pracy [Comment on Article 51 of the Law on Employment Promotion and Institutions of Labour Market], pp. 523-547. In: Góral Z. (ed.), *Law on Employment Promotion and Institutions of Labour Market. Commentary.* Warsaw: Wolters Kluwer.

Wagner B. (2001). Wiek emerytalny jako zdarzenie prawa pracy [Retirement age as the event of labour law]. *Journal Praca i Zabezpieczenie Społeczne*, No. 3, 2001, pp. 20–27.

Włodarczyk M., Paluskiewicz M. (2011). Legal forms of equalisation of opportunities in the Polish labour market for people aged 50+/45+, pp. 35-47. In: Urbaniak B., Wiktorowicz J. (eds.), *An Analytical Report on Programmes for People 50 + Implemented in Poland between 2004 and 2009*, Łódź: Max Druk Krzysztof Cempura. 2011. Retrieved 15 June 2016 from <http://zielonalinia.gov.pl/upload/50plus/Raport_eng.pdf>.

Wrocławska T. (2016). Komentarz do rozdaiału 13 c ustawy o promocji zatrudnienia i instytucjach rynku pracy [Commentary to the do chapter 13 c of Law on Employment Promotion and Institutions of Labour Market], pp. 726–745. In: Góral Z. (ed.) *Law on Employment Promotion and Institutions of Labour Market. Practical Commentary.* Warsaw: Wolters Kluwer.

Wrocławska, T. (2015a). Permanence (stability) of an employment relationship of older employees – analysis of changes. In: Florczak I., Góral Z. (eds.) *Developments in Labour Law from a Comparative Perspective*, Łódź: Wydawnictwo Uniwersytetu Łódzkiego, 2015, pp. 99–118.

Wrocławska T. (2015b). Idea międzypokoleniowego podziału pracy jako kryterium obowiązkowego przejścia na emeryturę w świetle stanowiska Trybunału Sprawiedliwości UE' [Idea of workforces replacement as the criterion for mandatory retirement in the light of judgments of European Court of Justice]. In: Bińczycka-Majewska T., Włodarczyk M. (eds.), *Współczesne problem prawa emerytalnego*, Warszawa: Lex a Wolters Kluwer business, 2015, pp. 109–133.

Wrocławska, T. (2014). Rozwiązanie stosunku pracy w związku z osiągnięciem przez pracownika wieku emerytalnego [Employment termination when employees reach retirement age]. In Frey R. (ed.), *Świadczenie pracy jako przedmiot zobowiązania umownego, cz.II.* Kelce: Panzet. 2014, pp. 223–239.

Reform of the Labour and Social Security Law in Latvia with Regard to the Rights of Employees in Connection with Parental leave

Kristīne Dupate*

Abstract

The article reflects the rights of employees in connection with the use of rights to childcare from the perspective of both social security and labour law. It describes numerous reforms in social security law regarding the entitlement conditions and amount of benefits related to childcare leave, and the reasons behind them during the last 10 years. The article provides an analysis of the connection between and interaction of the legal regulation concerning the right to childcare leave under social security and labour law. Finally, the article provides analysis on the effectiveness of legal regulation and its reforms from the perspective of their impact on the demographic situation and well-being of families regarding social rights in the long term.

Keywords: childcare leave, social rights, labour rights, reforms, impact, effectiveness

Introduction

The title of this article includes a very broad set of rights and problems. This might include legal regulation in labour and social security law relating to pregnancy, maternity, paternity and parenting. However due to the limited space, the scope of this article is limited to the rights connected with childcare leave, i.e. the rights to childcare leave and the effects on other rights in connection with the use of the right to childcare leave.

Europe has been experiencing a demographic crisis for a long time. This is mainly due to changing attitudes in society not only with regard to the family in general, but also in connection with the welfare

* Kristıne Dupate is Associate Professor at the Faculty of Law of University of Latvia. She is a member (national expert) of the Network of Legal Experts for the EU Commission in the fields of gender equality, labour law and the free movement of workers. She has participated in various research projects in international and EU institutions as a national expert. Prof. Dupate is the author of numerous publications on gender equality, non-discrimination and labour law.

considerations of individuals. Welfare considerations are the prospects of parents in the labour market, i.e. non-discrimination, work-life balance, social protection during the childcare period and the effects of childcare from the perspective of their life-long social security rights. Therefore the rights in connection with having children are topical, first of all, for the purposes of increasing the birth-rate.

The main aim of this article is to analyse whether the reforms undertaken during the last 10 years in Latvia with regard to childcare leave and allowance have been effective, i.e. if they have stimulated an increase in the birth rate, while at the same time protecting parents, especially the interests of mothers and the family from the life-long perspective.

The first part will describe the history of the development of the right to childcare allowance under social security law and the current state of affairs. The second part provides the rights to childcare and related rights under the Labour Law. The third part will elaborate on harmony (disharmony) between rights under Social Security laws and Labour Law with regard to childcare. The fourth part finally analyses if the current legal regulation helps to attain major goals such as an increase in the birth rate and the protection of the interest and well-being of children, parents and family in the long run.

1. Social security law reforms and the current state of protection of working parents in connection with childcare under Social Security Law

The Social Security Law with regard to childcare leave allowance has been under constant reform since 2005 and it does not seem to be over yet. In Latvia, special attention has been paid to the short-term rights, i.e. the amount of childcare allowance paid until a child reaches 12, 18 or in some cases 24 months of age, and the conditions under which parents are entitled to it. Taking into account the low level of income in general in Latvia, the right to an allowance during childcare leave is the primary precondition for the use of such a right.

Until 1 January 2005 the amount of the childcare leave allowance was a symbolic amount. It was awarded under the state social allowances system which provides for flat-rate allowances payable from the state budget[1]. At that time the amount was EUR 39 for the parents of a child

[1] Law on State Social Allowances (*Valsts sociālo pabalstu likums*), *Official Gazette* No. 168, 19 November 2002.

up to the age of 18 months and EUR 30 for a child from the age of 18 up to 24 months. Parents who were employed, but who were on childcare leave, or who were in part-time employment during the respective period were entitled to the allowance[2].

On 1 January 2005 a new regulation entered into force providing for the right to a substantially higher childcare allowance. In particular, it provided that the amount of the allowance until a child reaches 12 months of age depends on the salary of a parent, i.e. the allowance constituted 70% of the salary (or insurance contribution salary), with, however, a ceiling of EUR 515 and a lower limit of EUR 73[3]. However, only parents who were employed and who were on childcare leave during this period were entitled to the allowance[4]. The respective legal regulation precluding parents who continued working from any right to childcare allowance was contested before the Constitutional Court. The Constitutional Court found that a system which requires a parent to stop working during childcare leave may, firstly, negatively affect the prospects of the parent in the labour market, because in many professions interruption in professional activities may lead to the loss of a post (e.g. the case of one of the claimants who was an assistant professor at a university and the date for re-election to the post was approaching). Secondly, although the new system is aimed at fully replacing the income lost from employment[5] the Court established that for parents who earn low salaries (taking into account the statistics on the average amount of a childcare allowance for 2005 which was only EUR 105) it is impossible to provide a family with sufficient financial means, especially if there are other children in the

[2] Regulation of the Cabinet of Ministers of 1 July 2003 No. 349 'Regulations on the amount of childcare allowance, its review and procedure of award and pay-out' (*Noteikumi par bērna kopšanas pabalsta apmēru, tā pārskatīšanas kārtību un pabalsta piešķiršanas un izmaksas kārtību*), *Official Gazette* No. 100, 4 July 2003, not effective since 1 January 2005.

[3] The Regulation of the Cabinet of Ministers of 7 December 2004 No. 1003 'The procedure under which awards and pays-out of childcare allowance and supplement payment to the childcare allowance on account of the birth of twins or more children born in one delivery' (*Kārtība, kādā piešķir un izmaksā bērna kopšanas pabalstu un piemaksu pie bērna kopšanas pabalsta par dvīņiem vai vairākiem vienās dzemdībās dzimušiem bērniem*), *Official Gazette* No. 198, 14 December 2004, entered into force 1 January 2005.

[4] Amendments to the Law on State Social Allowances (*Grozījumi Valsts sociālo pabalstu likumā*), *Official Gazette* No. 198, 11 November 2004, entered into force on 1 January 2005.

[5] The amount of childcare allowance – 70% of salary corresponds to net salary (after payment of taxes).

family apart from the new-born, or it is a single-parent family. Thus, the chosen means for the attainment of the legitimate aims – protection of the rights of a child by providing full care by a parent restrict the rights of the parents and the interests of the whole family in the long-term, in addition, such aims may attained by less restrictive means, for example, by allowing part-time employment during childcare leave[6]. Consequently, the Constitutional Court declared that the total restriction on working during childcare leave was contrary to Article 110[7] of the Constitution[8] and announced that the unconstitutional legal regulation would lose its force as from 1 March 2006.

Following this judgment the Parliament adopted a new regulation which entered into force on 8 March 2006. This regulation allowed parents who remain in active employment to work and receive childcare allowance, however they receive only 50% of the allowance they would receive if they were on childcare leave[9].

On 2 November 2006 the Constitutional Court reviewed the next constitutional claim contesting the restriction on partners in active employment, namely, that they are entitled to only 50% of the allowance. This time the Court found that right to receive 50% of childcare allowance for working parents is not contrary to Article 110 of the Constitution, but it is contrary to the principle of equal treatment provided by Article 91 of the Constitution. The Court based its decision on the factual situation, in particular, the Court stressed that the average amount of the full childcare allowance is still exceptionally low (EUR 90 or LVL 68.5), thus the present system is appropriate for full families with high incomes and absolutely inappropriate for families with low incomes and single parent families. Therefore the Court concluded that restriction on the amount for working parents is a means which is not appropriate for the attainment of the legitimate aims – protection of the social and economic well-being of the family and children and such restriction is contrary to Article 91 of the Constitution. The decision led

6 The decision of the Constitutional Court of Latvia of 4 November 2005 in case No. 2005-09-01.

7 'The State shall protect and support marriage – a union between a man and a woman, the family, the rights of parents and rights of the child. The State shall provide special support to disabled children, children left without parental care or who have suffered from violence'.

8 *Latvijas Republikas Satversme*, *Official Gazette* No. 43, 1 July 1993.

9 Amendments to the Law on State Social Allowances (*Grozījumi Valsts sociālo pabalstu likumā*), *Official Gazette* No. 38, 7 March 2006, entered into force 8 March 2006.

to amendments to the Law on State Social Allowances which, although with a delay, removed the restriction and in substance provided the right to childcare allowance equal to the net pay irrespective of whether a parent was in active employment, part-time employment in combination with childcare leave or was entirely on childcare leave[10].

Furthermore, on 11 December 2006 the Constitutional Court delivered its next decision regarding the system of childcare allowances. In the particular case the claimants contested the ceiling on childcare allowance, namely, that the maximum amount of the allowance may not exceed EUR 515 (LVL 392). The Court ruled that such restriction is compatible with the Constitution[11]. The Court reached this conclusion mainly on the basis of the fact that the childcare allowance, although to a certain extent attached to the level of the previous earnings of a parent, nevertheless was awarded under the state social allowances system payable by the state budget and not under the social insurance system based on the contributions of employees. However, a problem was highlighted – normally the state social allowance system is a flat-rate system, thus mixing it with the social insurance system, which is contribution based, may give rise to complex legal consequences.

The latter decision was a clear signal that the system had to be changed. The new approach was adopted in 2007 and came into force from 1 January 2008. The new system introduced a new social insurance case – childcare and the right to a parent allowance under the statutory social insurance system[12]. In other words, employed parents were entitled to a parent allowance during childcare leave in the event of the birth of a child. This to a certain extent reinforced the traditional approach in the social security system – the allowances whose amounts vary and whose amount is linked to the earnings from employment are provided under the statutory social insurance system which is contribution based. In substance, however, the right to the allowance remained the same – the parent allowance was awarded irrespective of whether a parent remained in active employment or was on childcare leave, also the amount remained

---

10 Amendments to the Law on State Social Allowances (*Grozījumi Valsts sociālo pabalstu likumā*), *Official Gazette* No. 164, 11 October 2007, entered into force 25 October 2007.

11 Decision of 11 December 2006 of the Constitutional Court of Latvia in case No. 2006-10-03.

12 Law on Maternity and Sickness Insurance (*likums "Par maternitātes un slimības apdrošināšanu*), *Official Gazette* No. 182, 23 November 2008, respective amendments to OG.No. 190, 27 November 2007, entered into force as from 1 January 2008.

the same – 70% of the salary (social insurance contribution salary) equal to the net salary. Consequently, the parents of a child up to the age of 1, who are in active full time employment were in substance entitled to double income – salary and the full parental allowance.

This remained the case until the economic crisis which occurred in Latvia in 2008. Because of the crisis several important amendments took place over the following periods.

First, in June 2009 the Parliament among various budgetary cut measures adopted amendments precluding the right to parent allowance for those remaining in active employment[13]. The legality of such amendments was contested not only before the Constitutional Court but also before the European Court of Human Rights (hereinafter ECtHR).

The parents contested the compliance of the restrictions with general, principles of law, namely Article 91 – equal treatment and Article 1 – legal certainty. The court found that there was no breach of the principle of equal treatment because parents of small children in active employment are not in a comparable situation with parents on parental leave[14]. In the former case the state has an obligation to provide support for the family, while in the latter case the state has an obligation to replace the income lost from employment. Furthermore, the restriction complies with the principle of legal certainty. This is because the provision of social security rights is dependent on the resources available, and in the sphere of provision of social security rights there is considerable political dimension where the legislator enjoys a wide margin of discretion. In addition, one may not expect from the legislator the same actions in the field of economic, social and cultural rights as can be expected in the field of civil and political rights. Even though the principle of legal certainty implies an obligation to provide a transitional period, nevertheless, in a situation where the necessity to protect the essential interests of society and legal certainty collide, the former must be given priority. Taking into account the fact that the restriction has the legitimate aim – sustainability of the social security budget, and thus protection of the welfare of the

---

[13] Amendments to the Law on Maternity and Sickness Insurance (*likums 'Par maternitātes un slimības apdrošināšanu)*', *Official Gazette* No. 100, 30 June 2009, entered into force as from 1 July 2009.; the Law on Pay-out of the State Pensions and State Allowances for the Period from 2009 till 2012. (*likums 'Par valsts pensiju un valsts pabalstu izmaksu laika periodā' no 2009.gada līdz 2012.gadam)*, *Official Gazette* No. 100, 30 June 2009.

[14] Decision in case No. 2009-44-01, 15 March 2010.

whole of society, and that families, even after the restriction entered into force, retained the support from the state in the form of social allowances, the restriction corresponds to Articles 1, 91 and 110 of the Constitution.

But this was not the end of the saga on restriction of the amount of parental allowances and compliance with the principle of legal certainty. The restriction was contested before the ECtHR on the breach of Articles 6, 8, 14 of the ECHR and Article 1 of Protocol 1. The application lodged by 23 applicants in the case *Šulcs v. Latvia and 22 other cases*[15] was found by the ECtHR to be inadmissible. The ECtHR in its decision relied to a great extent on the arguments provided in decision No.2009-44-01 of the Constitutional Court. It also ruled that the restriction was compatible with Article 1 of Protocol 1 of the ECHR because '*the overall financial situation in the respondent State had an adverse effect on the parental benefit scheme which, if it had remained unchanged, would have endangered the sustainability of the overall social budget*'[16]. In addition it found that the the applicants were not deprived of the right to parental allowance in its essence because they were given the choice either to continue working and receive 50% of the allowance or to take parental leave and receive 100% of the parental allowance, thus the principle of proportionality has also been observed. Consequently, even the ECtHR accepted the cuts itself and the way it was done in the circumstances of economic crisis.

Further, since the Constitutional Court found the cut to the old-age and long-term service pensions, as well as the restriction for those pension recipients in active employment to be unconstitutional[17], the state had to search for other solutions on how to cut expenses of the social insurance budget.

The Parliament envisaged other kinds of restrictions of the social security rights which concerned almost all other social security risks[18]. They envisaged, in particular, that persons in the case of maternity,

---

15 Application No. 42923/10. Retrieved 19 May 2014 from http://hudoc.echr.coe.int/sites/eng/Pages/search.aspx#{%22docname%22:[%22%C5%A0ulcs%22],%22documentcollectionid2%22:[%22GRANDCHAMBER%22,%22CHAMBER%22,%22DECISIONS%22],%22itemid%22:[%22001-108352%22]}.

16 Paragraph 29.

17 Decisions in cases No. 2009-43-01, 21 December 2009; No. 2009-76-01, 21 April 2010; No. 2009-86-01, 21 April 2010, No. 2009-88-01, 15 April 2010.

18 The amendments to the Law on Pay-out of the State Pensions and State Allowances for the Period from 2009 till 2012 (*Grozījumi likumā "Par valsts pensiju un valsts pabalstu izmaksu laika periodā no 2009.gada līdz 2012.gadam"). Official Gazette No.200, 21 December 2009.*

paternity, parenting, accidents at work and illness are entitled to a daily social insurance allowance not exceeding EUR 16.37. Where the statutory social insurance salary exceeds the defined amount, persons were granted an allowance of 50% of the sum EUR 16.37[19].

The said restrictions were effective till 31 December 2014[20]. On 1 October 2014 the basic system was changed again. Parents who are insured under the statutory social insurance system and who are on full-time parental leave will be entitled to a parental allowance in an amount equal to 60% of their average salary (statutory social insurance contribution salary) until the child reaches the age of 12 months. If a parent were to opt to receive the parental allowance until the child reaches the age of 18 months the amount of the allowance will be 43.75% of their average salary. If a parent were to decide to stay in full-time or part-time employment during the period that the child is younger than 18 months, he/she will be entitled to 30% of the parental allowance (30% of the full allowance (60% of the salary))[21]. In addition, one of the parents will be entitled to another type of allowance – a flat-rate state social allowance – childcare allowance until the child reaches the age of 18 months of EUR 171 per month. The latter allowance will also be provided to parents who are not employed[22].

This system is still in force, however, there is widely held belief that it is not sustainable.

---

19 By amendments to the Law on Pay-out of the State Pensions and State Allowances for the Period from 2009 till 2014 (*Grozījumi likumā "Par valsts pensiju un valsts pabalstu izmaksu laika periodā no 2009.gada līdz 2014.gadam", Official Gazette* No. 192, 6 December 2012, the daily maximum amount of allowance was increased respectively from EUR 16.37 daily to EUR 32.75.

20 Law on Pay-out of the State Pensions and State Allowances for the Period from 2009 till 2014 (*likums "Par valsts pensiju un valsts pabalstu izmaksu laika periodā no 2009. gada līdz 2012.gadam), Official Gazette* No. 100, 30 June 2009; as amendment until 1 January 2014, *Official Gazette* No. 194, 4 October 2013.

21 Article 10^6 of the Law on Maternity and Sickness Insurance (*likums 'Par maternitātes un slimības apdrošināšanu'*). Amendments OG No.228, 22 November 2013; entered into force on 1 October 2014. Example, if a parent's gross salary were EUR 1,000, then the amount of parental allowance would be EUR 600 or 60% of the social insurance contribution salary. This applies to employed parents who are on full-time parental leave. If however a parent decided to stay in active employment he/she would be entitled to 30% of the parental allowance, i.e. 30% of EUR 600 (or normal parental allowance, which would constitute EUR 180.

22 Amendments to the Law on State Social Allowances (*grozījumi Valsts sociālo pabalstu likumā*), *Official Gazette* No. 228, 22 November 2013, entered into force on 1 October 2014.

2. Labour Rights

The rights in connection with childcare under employment law is provided by the Labour Law[23].

A worker has the right to take parental leave (in one period, or split into various periods of time) until the child reaches the age of eight years. The right to parental leave is individual and may be taken by either parent irrespective of whether the other parent is working or is on parental leave too[24]. The period spent on childcare leave has to be included in the term of service for the purposes of seniority[25]. Further, Article 134(1) stipulates the obligation for employers to provide part-time employment if this is requested by the parent of a child under the age of 14 years; however, there is no legal regulation on how and under what conditions a parent may claim back full-time employment.

Article 156(4) of the Labour Law stipulates that parents are entitled to the same job and same working conditions they had before taking parental once they return to work. If this is not possible they must be given work of similar or equal value. In addition, Article 149(6) provides that after all types of leave (including parental leave) an employee must be provided with the same working conditions and improvements of employment conditions as if he/she had not been on leave but had remained in active employment. However, these two norms might lead to contradiction, because the one requires provision of working conditions similar to those before the parental leave, while the other requires provision of all improvements in working conditions which have taken place in the absence of the employee. In this context there is uncertainty regarding whether the term 'working conditions' under Article 149(6) also includes pay[26], i.e. whether a person returning from parental leave is entitled to an immediate salary increase if the salaries in the business have been raised in general during his/her absence on parental leave.

The Labour Law has no explicit provision stipulating that less favourable treatment on the grounds of the use of the right to parental leave constitutes discrimination. However, since the absolute majority of the persons taking parental leave are women, indirect discrimination

---

23 *Darba likums, Official Gazette* No. 105, 6 July 2001, in force from 1 June 2002.

24 Article 156 of the Labour Law.

25 Article 156(3) of the Labour Law.

26 Telephone interview with the Director of the Employment Relationship and Health and Safety Protection Department of the Ministry of Welfare (31 March 2016).

may occur. It follows that the protection granted under the Labour Law is good, however, in certain aspects it is incomplete, because some of the provisions might be applied in an inconsistent manner and some lack clarity.

3. The interrelation between social security and employment rights with regard to childcare

As previously explained, under the Labour Law, a worker has the right to take parental leave (in one period, or split into various periods of time) until the child reaches the age of eight years and this is an individual right which may be used by both parents[27]. However, in reality the childcare leave is usually used by one parent only until the child reaches the age of 12 or 18 months, and not until the child attains the age of eight years. This is because salaries are so low in Latvia that in principle parental leave is not possible without the entitlement to parental allowance. Consequently, usually workers have no resources to build up any savings to cover interruptions in employment (income). Parental leave allowance (in the amount of the salary) under the statutory social insurance system is provided only until the child is 18 months old and only to one of the parents at the same time. Consequently, labour law rights with regard to childcare leave are more formal than practical. They are used only as far as adequate rights are provided by the social security law.

In addition, the main legal problem which Latvian legal regulation has now is the lack of recognition of part-time childcare leave under the Labour Law while such right is granted under the Social Security Law since 1 October 2014.

For example, although Article 134(1) of the Labour Law obliges an employer to provide part-time employment for the parent of a child under the age of 14 years, it does not identify a situation such as part-time childcare leave. Consequently, the Labour Law does not regulate if and how an employee after the end of part-time parental leave may return to full-time employment. Furthermore, Article 156(4) of the Labour Law requires the provision of the same work after parental leave and not less favourable working conditions as before the leave, and if this is not possible the provision of work of similar or equal value. On the other hand, such provision has so far only been applied in the case

27 Article 156 of the Labour Law.

of full-time childcare leave and since the Labour Law does not expressly recognize part-time parental leave it may be questionable whether such provision is applicable in the latter case. Consequently, it is questionable whether the Labour Law provides adequate protection for parents who use the opportunity now granted under social security law to work part-time and receive parental allowance. Such situation might be contrary to the requirements of Directive 2010/18/EU requiring the provision of the same work and working conditions after childcare leave and does not distinguish between full-time and part-time leave.

Second, there might be problems with regard to the rights related to the childcare leave. For example, a worker has accumulated his/her right to paid annual leave during full-time employment, but wants to use this right while on part-time employment on account of part-time childcare leave. According to Article 75 of the Labour Law the pay during annual leave has to be calculated on the basis of the previous six months' salary. So, this might lead to a situation where an employee has accumulated paid annual leave rights while earning a full-time salary but has used it during part-time employment and receives only the part-time salary during annual leave. Such a situation according to the CJEU is contrary to Directive 2010/18/EU[28].

It follows that the lack of harmonization of the rights related to childcare leave under the Labour Law and Social Security Law may lead to the breach of rights.

4. The social impact or attainment of the aims of the social security reforms with regard to childcare

There are several aims of the social security reforms with regard to childcare. The first aim is the protection of the interests of a child and family as provided by Article 110 of the Constitution[29]. By introducing the childcare and parental allowance, parents are provided the opportunity to take childcare leave, because of the financial support of the state and can take care of their child until the age of 12 or 18 months. In addition, if parents of small children are supported by the state then it leads to an increase in the birth rate. However, taking into account

28 CJEU case C-486/08.

29 See, for example, the decision of 4 November 2005 of the Constitutional Court of Latvia in case No. 2005-09-01.

the reality – in order to attain such aims the financial support must be adequate in relation to the needs of the family and there must be the possibility to combine childcare with professional activities. The latter is especially important with regard to the long-term interests of the whole family, namely, employment of the parents and their professional growth providing financial means for the family in the future. In addition, the combination of childcare with professional activities is becoming more and more real when we consider the rapid development of flexible forms of employment, for example, working from home via internet.

Therefore the question is, have the various reforms of the social security rights of parents with regard to the childcare attained such aims?

The statistics show that an increase of birth rate coincides with periods where, firstly, the amount of the childcare allowance reflects the average pay of the parents and, secondly where childcare allowance is also granted to parents who remain in active employment[30]. However, some scholars argue that an increase in the birth rate coincides with overall economic growth and consequent increase of welfare.

Notwithstanding this, there are nevertheless negative effects of the system. First, there is a negative impact on long-term family interests if parents remain in full employment and receive a full or partial parental allowance. Such a system was in force from March 2008 until May 2010 and is currently in force since 1 October 2014. In particular, the statistics shows that under such conditions there is a significant increase in the number of father-recipients of parental allowance. During periods when the parental allowance was only available to those parents who were on full-time childcare leave the proportion of father-recipients of parent allowance is stable – around 7%. As soon as there is a possibility to remain in employment and receive parental allowance, the proportion of father-recipients increased significantly – for example, in 2008 there was 35.5% of fathers receiving a parental allowance. The rate of fathers even continued to increase in 2009 irrespective of the fact that in the middle of that year the right of actively employed parents to parental allowance was cut to 50%. Between 2012 and 2014 the proportion of fathers – recipients of parent allowance returned to 'normal', i.e. 7%, because

30 Central Statistical Office of Latvia. Retrieved May 6, 2016 from http://data.csb.gov.lv/pxweb/lv/Sociala/Sociala__ikgad__iedz__dzimst/ID0010.px/?rxid=cdcb978c-22b0-416a-aacc-aa650d3e2ce0. 2003 – 21 151; 2004 – 20 551; 2005 – 21 879; 2006 – 22 871; 2007 – 23 958; 2008 – 24 397; 2009 – 22 044; 2010 – 19 781; 2011 – 18 825; 2012 – 19 897; 2013 – 20 596; 2014 – 21 746.

parental allowance was provided only to those parents on full childcare leave. However starting from 2015 the rate has increased considerably – there were 18.9% of fathers receiving a parental allowance in 2015[31]. This is due to the reforms enforced from 1 October 2014 providing the right to partial parental allowance for parents in active employment. Such statistics prove, first of all, that fathers are not child carers, but only recipients of parental allowance. The childcare is still provided by mothers; the family decides that the father has to be the recipient of the parental allowance, because his pay is usually higher, thus, he is entitled to a higher amount of parental allowance. The positive effect is that the family is provided with the most effective financial means in the short-term, namely up to age of 12 (or 18) months However, there are more negative effects in the long-term. First, the state provides social insurance contributions for a parent who is on childcare leave and receives parental allowance[32]. Since many mothers are not recipients of the parental allowance they are not socially insured during childcare leave, and this leads to loss of protection in case of unemployment at the end of the period of childcare leave and contributions to their old-age pension. Secondly, mothers who take an extended period of childcare leave due to sequential births lose their professional skills, term of seniority and thus their prospects in the labour market in general.

Such statistics show that the system is not used by the parents as intended, namely, to provide a much higher degree of flexibility, because it grants thc right to state support in the form of social allowances to parents who decide not to interrupt their career[33] and thus grants morc equal opportunities in the labour market especially for women who are still the main child carers.

Second, the deficiency of the current and previous reforms is that in substance the parents do not take childcare leave simultaneously although the Labour Law provides such an opportunity. This is because only one parent is entitled to the social allowance. Such a system does not encourage the sharing of childcare responsibilities between the parents. Thus, it still reinforces the role of the mother as the main child carer. Furthermore, if both parents remain in active full-time employment, in

---

31 Data provided by the Ministry of Welfare, 6 May 2016.

32 The Law on State Social Insurance (*likums "Par valsts sociālo apdrošināšanu"*), *Official Gazette*, No. 274/276, 21 October 1997.

33 Telephone interview with senior expert of Department of Social Policy Planning and Development Ministry of Welfare, 23 April 2015.

principle they spend the parental allowance awarded to one of them on paying someone else to mind their child. In addition, choosing this fails to attain one of the aims – provision of childcare by the parents. Further, if one of the parents remains in part-time employment, the welfare of the family decreases. If one parent works only part-time, he/she receives a lower salary and partial parental allowance which might be almost the same as a full salary. However, the family has extra expenses – for childcare services which are necessary while a parent is at his/her part-time employment.

It follows that the current system fails to promote the long-term interests of the children and parents and family altogether and needs to be reformed again.

Conclusions

The social security law with regard to childcare leave allowance since 2005 has been under constant reforms and it seems that they are not over yet. Such reforms were important, because taking into account the low level of income in general in Latvia, the right to an allowance during childcare leave is the primary precondition for the use of such a right.

Many of the reforms have been contested before the Constitutional Court of the Republic of Latvia leading to new amendments and new reforms, mainly regarding the right of parents who remain in active full-time employment to the childcare allowance. The rights and entitlements under the social security system during childcare leave were affected by the economic crisis starting from 1 July 2009 until 31 December 2014. During that period only parents on full-time childcare leave were entitled to the childcare allowance. The last reform which entered into force on 1 October 2014 re-introduced the right to remain in active employment and to receive a partial childcare allowance.

The protection of employees during childcare leave and matters related to it are extensive, and are provided for in the Labour Law; at the same time due to uncertainty with regard to the interrelation between some norms, the rights might be applied in an inconsistent manner.

Although the legislator on 1 October 2014 introduced the right to use childcare leave on a part-time basis, this right however, was only introduced with regard to entitlement to the childcare allowance under the Social Security Law, while the Labour Law does not 'recognize' part-time childcare leave. The lack of harmonization of the rights related to childcare leave under the Labour Law and Social Security Law may lead to breach of rights.

The statistics show that the increase in birth rate coincides with the periods where, firstly, the amount of childcare allowance reflects the average pay of the parents, and, secondly, where the childcare allowance was granted also to parents who remain in active employment. However, some scholars argue that an increase in the birth rate coincides with overall economic growth and consequent increase of welfare.

Although the right to childcare allowance for parents remaining in active employment should lead to retention of the parents in the labour market and protection of their and their family's interests in the long-term perspective, nevertheless in practice such right is used in different ways. Namely, the childcare allowance is claimed by fathers who remain in full-time employment while the real full-time carers are the mothers. Therefore, the current system fails to attain it aim, because full-time child-carer mothers risks losing their place in the labour market and they lose entitlements during childcare under the statutory social insurance system. The reforms taken so far fail to address the possibility of shared simultaneous childcare – a system ensuring that both parents remain in the labour market and do not lose their social insurance protection. Taking into account statistics demonstrating the use of the right to part-time childcare leave in a way not envisaged by the legislator, i.e., not attaining the legitimate aims, it is most likely that another reform is due in Latvia.

The Legal Framework of Unemployment Benefits in Russia

Olga CHESALINA*

Abstract

The article is dedicated to the question as to what legal factors contribute to the low unemployment rate in Russia and what explains the difference in figures between persons registered as unemployed and the unemployment rate according to ILO criteria. The author examines the influence of different legal factors on the unemployment rate. The legal factors considered refer to the employment protection level; part-time work; state policy on the labour market and unemployment benefits. The author explores the question as to whether the functions are fulfilled with regard to unemployment benefits. Further, the author scrutinizes the constitutional guarantees (protection) with a view to unemployment.

Keywords: unemployment, unemployment benefits, labour market, subsistence minimum, constitutional guarantees

Introduction

Despite the financial and economic crisis (in 2015 the Russian economy contracted by almost 4%, real incomes declined by about 10%[1] due to inflation, and the average inflation rate was 12.91% as compared with 2014)[2]. The unemployment rate in the Russian Federation (henceforth RF) has been relatively low in comparison with southern European countries that were hit by the crisis. In February 2016, approximately 1.1 million persons were registered as unemployed; by comparison, 901,600 persons were registered as unemployed in 2013. In February 2016, there were 900,000 persons registered as unemployed and with entitlements to

---

* Olga Chesalina is PhD in Law (Minsk), LL.M. (LMU, Munich), Senior Researcher at the Max Planck Institute for Social Law and Social Policy

1 Rubelverfall und Rezession – Russlands Wirtschaft Schrumpft. *Euronews.* Retrieved May 23, 2016 from http://de.euronews.com/2016/01/25/rubelverfall-und-rezession-russlands-wirtschaft-schrumpft/.

2 Таблица инфляции [Inflation Table]. Retrieved May 23, 2016 from http://xn----ctbjnaatncev9av3a8f8b.xn--p1ai/таблица_инфляции.aspx.

unemployment allowance[3]. The number of unemployment allowance recipients has not significantly increased as compared with the 2012–2014 period, and in comparison with 2011–2010 has even experienced a clear drop. For instance, statistical data on unemployment allowance recipients within the Central Federal District of the Russian Federation show the following development from 2015 back to 2010: November 2015 – 143,800 persons, November 2014 – 106,900 persons, November 2013 – 115,700 persons, November 2012 – 143,100 persons, November 2011 – 193,800 persons, November 2010 – 215,300 persons, November 2009 – 317,500 persons[4].

At the same time, however, the unemployment rate according to ILO criteria is more than 4.3 times higher than the number of registered unemployment allowance recipients and stands at 4.6 million persons (6%) (as per March 2016)[5]. In 2014 the unemployment rate according to ILO criteria was 4.5%. However, by comparison with southern European countries, this is still a rather low rate of unemployment (Greece – 24%, Portugal – 12.3%, Spain – 20.4%, figures as per February 2016[6]).

Comparably low in comparison to other crisis countries, the unemployment rate cannot be explained without including economic factors in the equation. At this stage, an attempt shall be made at determining the legal factors which, firstly, contribute to this low unemployment rate and, secondly, explain the difference in numbers between persons registered as unemployed and the actual number of unemployed persons according to ILO criteria.

From a legal point of view, the following reasons are considered as contributing to a low unemployment rate:

---

[3] Занятость и безработица в марте 2016 года [Employment and Unemployment in March 2016]. *Federal Service for State Statistics of the RF.* Retrieved May 23, 2016 from www.gks.ru/wps/wcm/connect/rosstat_main/rosstat/ru/statistics/wages/labour_force/#.

[4] Трудовые ресурсы [Labour Force]. *Federal Service for State Statistics of the RF.* Retrieved May 23, 2016 from http://cbsd.gks.ru/.

[5] Уровень безработицы в России составил 6% [The Unemployment Rate in Russia Amounted to 6%] Retrieved May 23, 2016 from www.job.ru/seeker/career/news/48845-uroven-bezrabotitsy-v-rossii-sostavil-6.html.

[6] Unemployment Statistics. Eurostat. Retrieved May 23, 2016 from http://ec.europa.eu/eurostat/statistics-explained/index.php/File: Unemployment_rates, seasonally_adjusted,_February_2016.png.

1) with a view to employees, labour legislation provides for a high protection of existing labour relationships.;
2) part-time employment;
3) public labour market policies and promotion of employment, particularly regarding intermittent public works;
4) low level of unemployment allowance.

1. Labour legislation

According to Kovács, Lyutov and Mitrus (2015, p. 425) 'Russian legislation protects employees from the very fact of dismissal'. Statistical OECD data for the 2008-2013 period demonstrate that Russian labour legislation stipulates a high level of protection of the status quo for employees with regard to the dismissal of individuals (Employment Protection Index (henceforth EPI) – 2.86[7]). This value is comparable to the EPI of Germany (2.53) and significantly higher than the average EPI among OECD countries (2.04)[8]. However, concerning collective dismissals in particular, Russian legislation is less strict (EPI 1.50). This index is considerably lower than the average index among OECD countries (2.90)[9].

With regard to individual dismissals, however, the Russian EPI remained constant during the 2008-2013 period (and labour legislation was not amended in this field). Yet it must be noted that the unemployment rate changed significantly during this period[10] (for instance, in line with ILO criteria it amounted to 8.4% in the crisis year of 2009[11]).

There is strong evidence, however, that the low number of individual dismissals is not only due to employee-friendly labour legislation, but also due to other relevant factors. Statistical data have shown – and economic studies have confirmed this – that in times of crisis a decline

7 In version 1 (1985-2013) the EPI was even at 3,06.

8 Strictness of Employment Protection – Individual Dismissals (Regular Contracts). *OECD*. Retrieved 23 May 2016 from https://stats.oecd.org/Index.aspx?DataSetCode=EPL_R.

9 *Ibidem*.

10 Various studies elaborate on the question whether there is a connection between the level of protection of the status quo in line with the labour legislation and the unemployment rate. Various opinions prevail, see Howe J., Sánchez E., Stewart A. Job loss. In: Finkin M., Mundlak G. (eds.) *Comparative labour law*. Cheltenham, UK/Northampton, MA: Edward Elgar Publishing, 2015, p. 291.

11 Тенденции на рынке труда [Trends in the Labour Market]. *Federal Service for State Statistics of the RF*. Retrieved 23 March 2016 from www.gks.ru/bgd/regl/b12_04/IssWWW.exe/Stg/d03/2-rin-trud.htm.

in employment in Russia is not effected by an increase in dismissals, but by a slowdown on recruitment. In 2013, the number of newly hired persons was at 10,114,500, while in 2014 this number included a mere 9,763,800 persons. Similarly, fewer employees were made redundant in 2014 than in 2013: 10,205,200 persons in 2014 as compared to 10,328,300 persons in 2013[12]. This may, on the one hand, be the effect of the high level of legal protection of the status quo of employees. On the other hand, this development can also be interpreted in line with Deakin, Malmberg and Sarkar (2014, p. 18), who considered that 'employment protection laws could have mutually offsetting effects on unemployment, limiting hiring but also making dismissals more costly'. A study of Капелюшников and Ощепков [Kapeliushnikov and Oshchepkov] (2014, p. 86) illustrates that a decision of this sort on the part of the company can be explained in terms of the higher expenditure incurred for dismissals, which might be further increased due to informal pressure exerted on companies by the regional authorities[13].

While no direct connection has been established between the protection of the status quo and the level of unemployment in Russia, the strict protection against individual dismissals does, in fact, influence the rate of hiring and firing.

2. Part-time work

In the third quarter of 2015, there were 127,100 persons working part-time at the instigation of the employer for economic, technical or structural reasons. By comparison, in the third quarter of 2014, there were only 81,200 part-time workers[14] (in the course of 2015, part-time work due to such circumstances rose to 40% as compared to the beginning of the year)[15]. Persons affected by this have not been included

12 Трудовые ресурсы [Labour Force]. *Federal Service for State Statistics of the RF.* Retrieved May 23, 2016 from http://www.gks.ru/wps/wcm/connect/rosstat_main/rosstat/ru/statistics/wages/labour_force/#.

13 See also Dokuchaev D. Russia's Unemployment Rate Resilient to Economic Crisis. *Russia Direct,* 22 October 2015. Retrieved May 23, 2016 from http://www.russia-direct.org/analysis/russia's-unemployment-rate-surprisingly-resilient-economic-sanctions.

14 Трудовые ресурсы [Labour Force)]. *Federal Service for State Statistics of the RF.* Retrieved May 23, 2016 from http://www.gks.ru/wps/wcm/connect/rosstat_main/rosstat/ru/statistics/wages/labour_force/#.

15 Unemployment in Russia Rises 15 Percent. *The Moscow Times*, 22 October 2015. Retrieved 14, June 2016 from http://www.themoscowtimes.com/business/article/unemployment-in-russia-rises-15-percent/540117.html.

in the general statistics on unemployment. On 2 March 2016, Federal Law No. 36 on Ratification of the Part-Time Work Convention (C 175) was adopted. Pursuant to this convention, full-time employees who are affected by partial unemployment – i.e. by a collective and temporary reduction of their standard working hours for economic, technical or structural reasons – are not regarded as part-time employees (Article 1 d). In Russian legislation, there is no provision for partial unemployment, and this is also why – in accordance with the Ratification of the Part-Time Work Convention (C 175) – persons affected by it are not included in the statistics on unemployment[16]. In spite of this circumstance, statistical data on unemployment are not considered substantially 'manipulated'. In relation to 4.4 million unemployed persons, 127,100 persons working part-time for economic, technical or structural reasons have no significant impact on the level of unemployment.

3. Labour market policy and public promotion of employment / intermittent public works

One of the new directions in Russian labour market policy has, since 2008, been the provision of means from the federal budget to the constituent territories of the Russian Federation for the implementation of various measures of employment promotion and of protection against unemployment, including the financing of public works for employees whose jobs are at risk and for workers who are still in employment but are looking for a new job. The legal basis for this has recently been provided in terms of Decree No. 35 issued by the Government of the RF on 22 January 2015 ('On Additional Measures in the Sphere of Employment Designed to Reduce Tension on the Labour Market').

This applies in cases where work or production has been cut, or where working hours have been reduced by the employer for operational reasons, or where a termination of employment for reasons of downsizing has been notified.

---

[16] These statistical data do not take into consideration the informal economy. Experts estimate that the informal economy of 2009/10 represented a quarter to a third of overall employment, see: Karabchuk T. *Analyse: Arbeitslosigkeit in Russland: Entwicklungen nach der Krise von 2008*. Bundeszentrale für politische Bildung, 6 December 2012. Retrieved 23 March 2016 from http://www.bpb.de/internationales/europa/russland/137892/analyse-arbeitslosigkeit-in-russland.

'Intermittent public works' are defined as works of social importance which, for instance, may be significant for the development of the city infrastructure, and which are organised on a contractual basis with the employment offices. Factually, these works consist of the same jobs that were priory – and that continue to be – offered to unemployed persons as 'works of social importance'.

On principle, 'works of social importance' are intended to motivate the long-term unemployed to pick up work. 'Intermittent public works' cannot fulfil this objective as they are designed for persons still working. In cases where an employee was dismissed on grounds of downsizing, 'intermittent public works' would not qualify as suitable for the former, as a 'suitable' job should be related to the person's former job, education and qualifications, and take into account the person's work experience and previous salary.

'Intermittent public works' are organised by the employment offices, who in their turn conclude contracts with the employers on the execution of intermittent public works by employees. Legislation provides for a per capita reimbursement of costs to the employer for each contracted employee equal to the subsistence minimum for adults (of RUB 9,662 on average), plus social insurance contributions. In this context, the employer must deploy the respective employee for the performance of 'works of social importance', but not for services that are connected to the main activity of the employer or that are solely in the interest of the employer. All employers are actively involved in the execution of 'intermittent public works'. No provision is made for reimbursement for the latter. This is not in the interest of all employers and contradicts the functions of labour law. As a consequence, it may be that employers in practice violate contracts concluded with the employment office by deploying their employees for activities that are to be carried out in the interest of the company[17]. This, however, is punishable according to Article 159.2 part 4 of the Criminal Code of the RF, particularly if public funds are received.

As per 1 November 2015, 65,600 persons have carried out intermittent public works. The funds made available from the federal budget for this purpose amounted to RUB 3.9 billion. By comparison, approximately RUB 40 billion were deployed in 2015 to finance the unemployment

17 Appeal of the Supreme Court of the Chuvash Republic on 21 August 2013 in case No. 33-3016/2013.

allowance[18]. Compared with the scope of funds available for unemployment allowance, the scope of funds available for subsidies is much smaller. The scope of the financing measure and the number of employers involved indicate that this measure cannot play a decisive role in terms of protection against unemployment.

Subsidies related to 'intermittent public works' are intended to reduce tensions within the labour markets of the constituent territories of the Russian Federation. Further, measures of this sort help avoid more unemployment and a further aggravation of the difficult budgetary situation concerning labour market funds[19]. On the one hand, this form of publicly funded employment lowers the unemployment rate and is, in this context, of particular importance in regions where there is only one predominant industry that can offer employment. On the other hand, publicly funded employment all too often merely hides non-productive labour.

4. Unemployment allowance

The benefits level for unemployed persons as amended in the latest version of Federal Law No. 1032-1 of 09 March 2016 'On Employment of Population in the Russian Federation' has – by comparison with the 2003 version – been significantly reduced. Up to 2005, unemployment allowance was paid in terms of income replacement, and the amount (at least during the first four months) was based on the involved person's average salary during the three months prior to receipt of the allowance, respectively amounting to 75%, 60% or 45% of the average salary. For this purpose, provision was made for an indexation of the unemployment allowance to previous earnings.

As per 1 January 2005, minimum and maximum ceilings for the unemployment allowance were introduced. At the time, the minimum amount was at RUB 750 per month, the maximum amount was RUB 2,880 per month. The last time the minimum and maximum ceilings for the unemployment allowance were raised was in 2009 (RUB 850

---

18 Минтруд предлагает увеличить максимальный размер пособия по безработице [Labour Ministry Proposes to Increase the Maximum Amount of Unemployment Allowance]. *Russian news agency*, 30 September 2015. Retrieved May 23, 2016 from http://tass.ru/obschestvo/2304814.

19 О мониторинге социально-экономического положения в моногородах [On Monitoring the Socio-Economic Situation in Single-industry Towns]. *Government of the Russian Federation*, 21 September 2014. Retrieved May 23, 2016 from http://goverment.ru/orders/14958.

and RUB 4900 respectively). Furthermore, as per 1 January 2005, cuts were effected with a view to the reimbursement of expenses previously provided for in the case of voluntary relocation for the purpose of taking up work elsewhere, as well as to other monetary benefits for unemployed persons and to the indexation of the unemployment allowance.

While no benefit cuts were effected in connection with the financial and economic crisis, the strong inflationary devaluation of the unemployment allowance (the sum of RUB 850 in 2009 was the equivalent of approx. EUR 19, and in 2016 of approx. EUR 10; the sum of RUB 4,900 in 2009 was the equivalent of approx. EUR 109, and in 2016 of approx. EUR 59) was factually tantamount to a benefit cut.

Unemployment allowance offers no protection against poverty. In principle, every recipient of unemployment allowance can potentially draw social assistance (families and citizens in need are entitled to social assistance if they have, through no fault of their own, a per capita income below the subsistence minimum; Article 7 of Federal Law No. 178 of 17 July 1999 'On State Social Assistance').

Russian legislation indirectly provides for the obligation to participate in works of public importance: refusal to participate results in a suspension of unemployment allowance payments for three months. The same applies after refusal of two suitable job offers. Considering the level of benefits provision during unemployment, these sanctions are disproportionate.

Unemployment allowance should fulfil two functions: that of replacing income and that of motivating the unemployed to search for work. Today, the amount of the unemployment allowance is too low to replace the income or to at least offer protection against poverty. The low amount also forces the unemployed to actively seek work; however, 71% of unemployed persons search for work without the involvement of the employment office[20]. This leads to the circumstance that unemployment allowance plays nearly no role for the unemployed and that, for this reason, many do not even bother registering with the employment offices[21]. It can be agreed with *Капелюшников* and *Ощепков* [Kapeliushnikov and Oshchepkov] (2014, p. 79), therefore, that the number of registered unemployed persons not only depends on the objective situation on the labour market, but also, and particularly so, on the financial appeal of the

20 Количество безработных в России выросло на 5,5% [The Number of Unemployed Persons in Russia Grew by 5.5%], *Vesti Finance*, 17 November 2015. Retrieved May 23, 2016 from http://www.vestifinance.ru/articles/64488.

21 See also Karabchuk T., *op. cit.*

unemployment allowance and on the way the administrative procedure governing unemployment allowance is handled. The fact, too, that the number of unemployed persons according to ILO criteria is 4.3 times higher than that of actually registered unemployment allowance recipients indicates that the unemployment allowance neither fulfils the function of income replacement (or even covers the vital needs of an unemployed person), nor provides incentives for the unemployed to seek work.

The problem has also been acknowledged by the Ministry of Labour of the RF. The explanatory statement of the programme on 'Active Employment Policy and Social Assistance of the Unemployed' emphasizes that the unemployment allowance – due to its low amount – no longer fulfils its specific, primary income replacement function and thus does not guarantee a minimum subsistence level; this in turn allegedly keeps the unemployed from actively concentrating on their search for work. In 2014, the Ministry of Labour had intended to increase the unemployment allowance while shortening the duration of receipt. This plan, however, has still not materialized. In Decree No. 1382 issued by the Government of the RF on 17 December 2014, the minimum and maximum ceilings for unemployment allowance were not adjusted either for the year 2015 or the 2016/2017 planning period. This omission was justified by the argument that the number of job offers listed with the employment offices was twice as high as the number of persons registered as unemployed[22]. The issue of 'suitable work' was not addressed in this context.

It is questionable whether minimum standards for benefits assessment in the case of unemployment can be derived from the Constitution of the RF, and how the judicature of the Constitutional Court of the RF develops in this field in the future.

5. Constitutional protection against unemployment

The Constitution of the RF contains two articles with provisions concerning unemployment. In these articles, two different – but in terms of content overlapping – aspects of unemployment are regulated[23]. On

[22] Минимальный и максимальный размеры пособия по безработице на 2015 год не изменятся [The Minimum and Maximum Amount of Unemployment Allowance for 2015 Will Not Change (own translation)]. *System Garant*, 19 December 2014. Retrieved May 23, 2016 from http://www.garant.ru/news/590066/#ixzz3y3qI2DWe.

[23] The Constitutional Court bases its decisions in cases related to social protection in the event of unemployment on Article 37 Part 1 and 3 of the Constitution (right

the one hand, protection against unemployment is a constituent part of the right to work (Article 37 part 3 of the Constitution). Protection against unemployment in the broader sense of the word also comprises the social services and benefits for unemployed persons[24]. According to the opinion of Russian constitutional expert S. Avakian (2016, p. 971), the right to protection against unemployment should be understood to mean that the state guarantees the citizen free assistance with the search for suitable work and employment through the employment offices. On the other hand, the right to social security stipulated in Article 39 Part 1 of the Constitution also implies a right to social security in the event of unemployment. Article 39 Part 1 of the Constitution contains a non-exhaustive list of cases in which social security is guaranteed (age, illness, invalidity, loss of breadwinner, raising of children). The case of 'unemployment' is not explicitly mentioned in Article 39 Part 1 of the Constitution; it is included in the 'other cases established by law' in which social security is guaranteed in line with this provision. Several other, more recent, eastern European constitutions do not mention the social risk of 'unemployment' either[25].

In Russian constitutional theory, differentiation is made between immediately applicable constitutional provisions and those that are to be specifically defined in the legislation. The latter include the socio-economic rights (particularly in cases where the constitutional norm refers to a law)[26]. The right to protection against unemployment has been

---

to work, protection against unemployment), as well as on Article 39 Part 1 of the Constitution (right to social security). Notably, the aspect of, employment promotion and employment services' including the regulation of rights and obligations of unemployed persons and the provision of social guarantees to the unemployed is considered to be part of labour law. The relevant chapters can be found in all labour law textbooks. However, textbooks on social security law only deal with unemployment allowance in terms of social benefits for the unemployed.

24 Lasarev L.V. (ed.) *Комментарий к Конституции Российской Федерации* [Commentary to the Constitution of the Russian Federation]. Moscow: Eksmo, 2009, p. 364.

25 Nußberger A. Die Verfassungsrechtliche Dimension der Neugestaltung des Arbeits- und Sozialrechts in den mittel- und osteuropäischen Staaten [The Constitutional Dimension of the Restructuring of the Labour and Social Legislation in the Central and Eastern Europe States, Eastern Europe Law]. *Osteuropa Recht*, 2004, p. 231.

26 Гаджиев Г. Непосредственное применение судами конституционных норм [Direct Application of Constitutional Provisions by the Courts], Российская юстиция, No. 12, 1995, p. 24; Конюхова И. Комментарий к ст.18 Конституции' [Commentary on Article 18 of the Constitution]. In: Dmitriev J. (ed.) *Scientific-practical Commentary on the Constitution of the Russian Federation*, Moscow, 2007,

specifically defined in the Labour Code of the RF and the Federal Law of the RF 'On Employment'. It is debatable whether one might directly invoke rights that are to be specifically defined[27].

It is contentious whether the guarantee of a social minimum standard can be derived from Article 39 of the Constitution of the RF in connection with the welfare state principle[28]. Some voices from the scientific community merely see Article 39 Part 1 of the Constitution of the RF as a programmatic principle[29]. According to prevalent opinion, Article 39 Part 1 obliges the State to guarantee material security once the contingency of a social risk arises, but does not specify the exact scope and level of social services or benefits[30]. The Constitutional Court urges the legislator to provide for some kind of social protection system for social risk contingencies (i.e. requires end-to-end social protection in combination with a certain scope of discretion on the part of the legislator). One could call it a social right with elements of social progression[31]. Accordingly, the Constitutional Court of the RF in its Decision No. 20-P of 16 December 1997 regarded the limitation of state-supported benefits to 30 days in the case of temporary incapacity for work of an unemployed person as unconstitutional on grounds of violation of Article 39 Part 1 of the Constitution of the RF, arguing that upon expiry of the stated 30 days no social protection system of any kind was made available (Pt. 5 of the Decision).

---

p. 42; Berger A. *Die Bindung der Bürger an die Grundrechte* [The Commitment of the Citizens to the Fundamental Rights]. Berlin, 2014, p. 77.

27 Berger A *op. cit.*, p. 77.

28 Гусева Т. (2008). Конституционные принципы социального обеспечения: понятие, содержание, значение [The Constitutional Principles of Social Security: Term, Content, Meaning]. Черные дыры в российском законодательстве, No. 1, 2008, p. 65.

29 Лейбо Ю, Толстопятенко Г., Экштайн А. Права и свободы человека и гражданина. Научно-практический комментарий к главе *2* Конституции Российской Федерации [Rights and Obligations of Man and Citizen. Scientific and Practical Commentary on Chapter Two of the Constitution of the Russian Federation], Moscow, 1999.

30 Lasarev L.V. (ed.), *op. cit.*, p. 376.

31 Arnold R. Allgemeine Prinzipien des verfassungsrechtlichen Grundrechtsschutzes in Mittel-, Ost- und Südosteuropa [General Principles of the Constitutional Protection of Fundamental Rights in Central, Eastern and Southeastern Europe]. In: *Handbuch der Grundrechte in Deutschland und Europa*, Bd.IX (Grundrechte in Ostmittel- und Osteuropa), 2016, p. 1032, Fn.119.

Article 39 Part 1 of the Constitution does not stipulate any minimum standards of social security. The qualitative minimum standards for the level of social protection to be guaranteed can be derived only from the few decisions of the Constitutional Court.

In an older decision (Decision of the Constitutional Court of the RF No. 153-O of 26 October 1999) the Constitutional Court interpreted Article 39 Part 2 of the Constitution to mean that the legislator should, when determining the old age pension level, consider the fact that old age pension was the sole source of livelihood for retirees; further, that the legislator should endeavour to gradually increase the level of social protection for pensioners whose pensions were below the subsistence minimum (Pt. 2, Paras. 2 and 3). At the same time, the Constitutional Court emphasized that a review of the legally stipulated old age pension through the Constitutional Court would mean an assessment of the functionality and of the economic merit of the legislator's decision. Thus, no constitutional mandate had been imposed on the legislator.

This only happened in line with Decision No. 17-O of 15 February 2005 made by the Constitutional Court of the RF, through which the latter imposed a constitutional mandate on the legislator in the field of pension legislation, requiring that old age pension, in combination with further social benefits or services (irrespective of type), was to guarantee a person's minimum subsistence level. The Constitutional Court based its substantiation of the benefits level on the guaranty of human dignity (Article 21 Part 1 of the Constitution/Pts. 2-4 of the Decision). Yet, constitutional law derives the right to social benefits and services at minimum subsistence level not from the guarantee of human dignity, but from the welfare state principle (Article 7 Part 1) and from the right to social security (Article 39 Part 1 and 2). Even though the Constitutional Court in this decision concludes on matters solely related to pension provision, these conclusions could, in line with Article 39 Part 1 and 2 of the Constitution, also be transferred to other fields of social security, such as social protection in the event of unemployment; however, the Constitutional Court has not commented on this as yet.

Many decisions made by the Constitutional Court are based on the broad scope of discretion of the legislator in the field of 'unemployment'. Not only pension claims (conditions for eligibility) and the specific circle of persons selected for entitlement, but also the amount of the unemployment allowance may be stipulated by the legislator in line with the material and financial capacities of the State[32].

As regards the constitutional guidelines for the determination of the unemployment allowance level, the Constitutional Court based its Decision No. 550-O-O of 12 April 2011 on the functions of unemployment allowance and the legal nature of the latter:

1) The unemployment allowance is to ensure the livelihood of unemployed persons for an appropriate period of time that is deemed necessary to find suitable employment.
2) On the other hand, the unemployment allowance should be calculated so as to motivate unemployed persons to actively seek employment and keep them from refusing job offers for no reason.
3) Due to the legal nature of the unemployment allowance in its function as a support benefit financed from state funds (i.e. not an insurance benefit financed from contributions), the legislator has wide discretion in determining the respective amount. Accordingly, the Constitutional Court does not solve the question as to what would have to be considered if the unemployment allowance was an insurance benefit[33].

Possibly, the Constitutional Court sees the difference between old age pension and unemployment allowance (which grants the legislator more discretion) not only with regard to the type of financing (benefits financed through contributions versus benefits funded from the state budget), but also with regard to the expectation that unemployment allowance recipients are persons capable of work, who can earn their livelihood through gainful activity (as opposed to pensioners, who are dependent on their pensions as their only means of subsistence[34]). For

[32] Decision of the Constitutional Court of the of the Russian Federation No. 550-O-O of 12.04.2011; Wieser B. Kommentar zum Artikel 37 der Verfassung [Commentary on Article 37 of the Constitution]. In: Wieser B. (ed.) *Handbuch der russischen Verfassung*, Wien: Verlag Österreich, 2014, p. 365 (Rn. 23).

[33] Decision of the Constitutional Court of the Russian Federation of 12.04.2011 No. 550-O-O; Decision of the Constitutional Court of the Russian Federation of 02.11.2011 No. 1625-O-O.

[34] The Constitutional Court emphasizes that the implementation of the constitutional obligation to create guarantees of social protection requires consideration of the particular situation of certain groups of persons (children, persons with disability, persons in need, etc.) for whom state support represents an indispensable means of livelihood. See Decision of the Constitutional Court of of the Russian Federation 10 October 2002, No. 258-O.

the assessment of the amount of the unemployment allowance, however, factors influencing the individual situation[35] of the unemployed person, e.g. underage children, family status etc. are not taken into account.

Even though, pursuant to Article 21 of the Constitution, the State is obliged to protect human dignity in every aspect, the decisions of the Constitutional Court regarding the issue of unemployment allowance do not make clear that it is not only the minimum, but also the maximum ceiling of the unemployment allowance (RUB 4,900) that is below the minimum wage (RUB 6,204) and more than twice below the subsistence minimum (RUB 9,452), which makes the prospect of a dignified life doubtful.

No decision of the Constitutional Court regarding the amount of unemployment allowance mentions the Decision of the Constitutional Court of 15 February 2005 related to the minimum protection level in old age pensions. In its Decision of 2 November 2011 the Constitutional Court concluded on nearly the same result as in its Decision of 15 February 2005, namely that unemployment allowance in combination with further social benefits (e.g. social assistance, additional support benefits) could, at least, guarantee the minimum subsistence level (Point 2.4). This however, levels the difference between an insurance benefit and a support benefit from the state budget.

One difference is the fact that the female single pensioner with disability referred to in the Decision of 15 February 2005 of the Constitutional Court was entitled to social benefits of another sort. By contrast, the granting of social assistance benefits to unemployed persons (in addition to granting them unemployment allowance) is at the discretion of the relevant authority. Additional entitlement to such extra social assistance is granted to unemployed persons after proof is furnished that they are in need or, respectively, if they have concluded a 'social contract' that stipulates particular obligations on the part of the unemployed person.

This shows that unemployment allowance no longer fulfils the function of income replacement. Unemployment allowance alone

---

35 An exception is only provided for underage unemployed persons who are ‚orphans or children not under the care of a parent'. In the first six months of initial registration with the employment office they are entitled to an unemployment allowance amounting to the average salary common to the region (Article 9 point. 5 of Federal Law No. 159 of 21 December 1996 'On Additional Guarantees Respecting Social Protection of Children-Orphans and Abandoned Children') – this regulation concerns only a smaller group of minors between the age of 14 (mostly 16) and 18 years.

(without further possible social benefits) can neither protect against the risk of unemployment nor against poverty[36].

The benefits level in the event of unemployment does not comply with the international obligations of the Russian Federation (Article 12 Para. 1 European Social Charter). The European Committee of Social Rights held the opinion that the minimum amount of the unemployment allowance was quite obviously inappropriately low, and that the Russian ruling on it contravened the principles of the European Social Charter (Article 12)[37].

Conclusion

The low unemployment rate is also due to legal factors. However, these factors are not so much related to part-time employment or to certain measures effected in state labour market policies. The strong protection of the status quo of the employee in labour legislation has only little effect on the level of unemployment and, if anything, merely slows down the rate of hirings and firings. From a legal perspective it is, first and foremost, the low level of social support benefits for unemployed persons that has an impact on the low rate of unemployment. The very low level of unemployment allowance and the disproportionate sanctions imposed on unemployed persons who do not fulfil their obligations have resulted in more than 70% of the unemployed seeking work without the assistance of the employment office. This explains the difference in numbers between persons registered as unemployed and the number of unemployed persons according to ILO criteria. No qualitative minimum standards for the level of social protection to be guaranteed can be derived from the Constitution of the RF itself or from the decisions ruled by the Constitutional Court. The legally stipulated minimum subsistence level can, in certain cases, be guaranteed only if other social benefits are granted in addition to the unemployment allowance. This practice contravenes the international obligations of the RF derived from the European Social Charter.

---

36 Сторожук Д. (2009). Пособие по безработице как основная форма материальной поддержки безработных граждан [Unemployment Allowance as the Most Important Support Benefit for the Unemployed]. Вестник Омского унивеситета. Серия 'Право'. No. 2 (19), 2009, pp. 111- 121 (119).

37 Conclusions 2013 (Russian Federation). Articles 3, 11, 12 and 14 of the Revised Charter. *European Committee of Social Rights*, p. 31. Retrieved May 23, 2016 from http:/www.coe.int.

Unemployment Benefits System in Lithuania

Problems of the Regulation and New Reforms

Audrius Bitinas*

Abstract

The aim of this article is to analyse the regulation of the Lithuanian unemployment benefits system, constitutional jurisprudence, problems and the latest draft legislation. The article will also consider the problems of the Lithuanian unemployment benefits system in the context of an ageing society, the social insurance budget deficit and the trend towards a longer working life: today unemployment benefits are paid for a short-time period and there is no unemployment benefits regression. The implementation of the draft legislation (longer period of unemployment benefits with benefits regression, the introduction of active labour market measures, the cancellation of early-retirement pensions, higher unemployment benefits limit) could create better conditions for unemployed persons to return to the labour market and to ensure higher pensions benefits in the future. In this article, the jurisprudence of the Lithuanian Constitutional Court and draft legislation is analysed in the light of the new Lithuanian social model concept. The outcomes of this article may be used as the methodical literature for studying the unemployment benefits system and reforms in Lithuania.

Keywords: unemployment benefits, reform, European Union, Lithuania, social model.

Introduction

The concept of unemployment emerged in parallel with the industrial revolution in the nineteenth century in Europe. At this time, unemployment protection was raised as a private initiative to protect individuals from poverty, later – special unemployment insurance funds were created. The

---

* Audrius Bitinas is an associate professor of the Faculty of Law Vilnius University, Lithuania. He has extensive management and scientific research experience in the field of social insurance and labour (as the Chairman of the State Social Insurance Fund Council and as the Vice-minister of Social Security and Labour) and in the field of European Union social, labour and commercial law (as an advocate, professor and European Union expert).

first state social unemployment insurance schemes were introduced in the early twentieth century and subsidies for private unemployment insurance funds were also introduced. Under the Lord Beveridge initiative, the basic state unemployment insurance system appeared in the United Kingdom in 1911. Mandatory unemployment social insurance was introduced in Germany in 1927. After the proclamation of independence in 1918, Lithuania had to create a new social insurance system, primarily focused on the prevention of occupational accidents and healthcare, sickness and pension insurance. Social security pensions and health insurance were created in interwar Lithuania, but the universal unemployment insurance system was not introduced before the Second World War. The main reason was the lack of labour relations regulation, high unemployment and flexibility in the area of dismissal. Despite the introduction of severance payments and public works (in 1933), a modern unemployment social insurance system was not created in Lithuania.

In recent decades the Member States (MS) of the European Union have started to reform their state social insurance systems (including unemployment benefits system) in order to reduce the social budget deficits because of ageing populations; they have introduced active labour market measures and implemented more effective social insurance management. According to projections, ageing and the need for additional finances in the European Union will intensify: despite the modest recovery of the total fertility rate (from 1.52 births per woman in 2008 to 1.64 by 2060) and the growth of life expectancy at birth (this will increase from 76 years in 2008 to 84.5 in 2060 for men and from 82,1 in 2008 to 89 in 2060 for women), the number of old persons (aged over 80 years) will increase significantly (from 22 million in 2008 to 61 million in 2060. In addition, the ratio of people aged 65 or above related to the working age population (15-64 years) is projected to increase significantly – from 25.4% in 2008 to 53.5% in 2060[1].

Today we can underline the main challenges in Europe: more personal choice and quality improvements in services and benefits; the impact of globalization (free movement of persons, goods, services and capital across national borders); ageing and economic, fiscal and social fallout during the economic crisis[2]. Social insurance reforms should be oriented

---

1 *The 2009 Ageing report: economic and budgetary projections for the EU-27 member states (2008-2060).* European Commission. Retrieved April 14, 2016 from http://ec.europa.eu/economy_finance/publications/publication14992_en.pdf.

2 *Dynamic social security for Europe: choice and responsibility. Developments and trends.* Geneva: International social security association, 2010.

to the rise in a person's individual responsibility; to provide opportunities for complementary entitlements; to work longer and increase access to supplementary savings schemes[3]. As a result of the reforms, we see that social security benefits have decreased and the requirements for benefits have become stricter: a longer work record is required; social security benefits are more targeted; private savings systems have been developed; austerity policies have been introduced and incentives to work longer are today the main aim of national and European strategies. The European Commission supports and complements the Member States' policies in the field of employment and social protection and the Europe 2020 Strategy for smart, sustainable and inclusive growth sets targets to lift at least 20 million people out of poverty (and social exclusion) and to increase employment of the population aged 20-64 to 75%[4].

Despite the European Union's recommendations for the MS, reforms to unemployment benefits are still ongoing because of changing economic, political and social phenomena, impact of the economic crisis and the development of labour relations. Today, the concept of unemployment social insurance reform should be complex and implemented in the labour law and other branches of social insurance. The focus of the reform of the unemployment system should allow people to work longer, apply new active labour market measures, create flexible labour relations and provide better access to supplementary insurance schemes. In addition, reform in the unemployment field should be carried out in conformity with the constitutional principles: rule under the state of law, justice, protection of legitimate expectations and social solidarity.

1. Regulation of the Lithuanian unemployment insurance system

1.1 Organisation of the national unemployment insurance system

The social insurance system in Lithuania comprises six social insurance types: pensions, maternity, health and sickness insurance, unemployment insurance, accidents at work and occupational diseases. Social insurance is based on the reference salary and qualification periods. Expenses for

3 *Green paper: towards adequate, sustainable and safe European pension systems.* European Commission, COM(2010) 365 final.

4 *Europe 2020: a strategy for smart, sustainable and inclusive growth.* European Commission, COM(2010) 2020 final.

social benefits by branch (percentage of total benefits) are as follows: unemployment benefit – 2.72%, sickness/healthcare benefit – 27.34%, disability benefit – 9.72%, old-age pensions – 43.68%, survivors' benefit – 3.07%, family/children benefit – 8.75%, housing benefit – 0.02%, social exclusion benefit – 4.70%[5]. The main principles for organizing the financing and management of the unemployment system are set in the Law on State Social Insurance, in the Law on Indicators of the Budget of the State Social Insurance fund of 2016 and in the Law on Structure of the State Social Insurance Fund budget.

The modern unemployment insurance system introduced in 2004 (Law on Unemployment Social Insurance) regulates that the amount of unemployment social insurance benefit depends on the work record. Unemployment insurance benefit is paid to persons who are dismissed from work or from the office of civil servant through no fault of the employee or the civil servant; due to circumstances beyond the control of an employee or civil servant; due to the bankruptcy of an employer or if the person is registered as a jobseeker at the local labour exchange.

The Law on Unemployment Social Insurance stipulates that in order to be eligible for unemployment insurance benefit, a person (prior to registration at a local labour exchange) should have an unemployment insurance record of at least 18 months during the last 36 months (general rule). The Law on Unemployment Social Insurance establishes the concept of unemployment social insurance, the categories of persons covered by unemployment insurance, the entitlement to unemployment social insurance benefits, the conditions for granting the benefits, the calculation and payment of benefits, the funding and management system.

The national unemployment insurance system is based on the social insurance principle and it is mandatory, there is no possibility for voluntary state social unemployment insurance. Self-employed persons are not insured by the state unemployment system (except for those persons who receive income from sports activities, performing activities or who receive incomes as authors of written works).

The national unemployment insurance system is financed from the state social insurance fund (this fund is separate from the state budget). The national unemployment benefit system can be characterized by three criteria: insurance period is required; benefit amount is linked to the previous salary and there are ceilings to the benefits. There are no

5 Retrieved April 14, 2016 from http://www.ec.europa.eu/eurostat.

special unemployment social assistance benefits, however, there is general support for deprived persons.

The Lithuanian Labour Exchange is responsible for the administration of unemployment benefits and the State Social Insurance Fund Board is responsible for paying the unemployment benefits.

The aim of the unemployment social insurance system is indicated in Article 2 of the Law on Unemployment Social Insurance: unemployment social insurance should compensate persons for their loss of income due to unemployment. According to Article 2 of the Law on Support for Employment, an unemployed person is a person of working age, who is not learning according to a general education programme, or who is not learning in a formal training programme, or who is not studying in a higher education institution in a full-time programme and is registered in the local labour exchange.

1.2 Interconnections between the unemployment social insurance and other social security risks or social assistance schemes

The Law on Unemployment Social Insurance indicates that *maternity benefits* or maternity (paternity) benefits, which are granted after a person's registration in the labour exchange, can be partially accumulated with unemployment insurance benefits. The payment of the unemployment insurance benefit shall be extended on the basis of sick leave or maternity leave.

Persons covered by the state social insurance, the social assistance scheme or who are receiving state pensions (with the exception of survivor's, orphan's and loss of breadwinner's pensions), periodic compensations for lost *capacity to work* (due to occupational accidents and occupational diseases), are entitled to receive benefits from the unemployment insurance funds, if the part of the unemployment insurance benefit exceeds the sum of the pensions or compensations received. The payment of unemployment insurance benefit to unemployed persons who during the period of payment of unemployment insurance benefit are temporarily not capable of working due to a disease or a trauma shall be extended for the number of calendar days the person was sick, but for not more than 30 calendar days. The payment of unemployment insurance benefit to women who during the period of payment of the unemployment insurance benefit are temporarily not able to work due to pregnancy and childbirth shall be extended for the period corresponding to the period of payment of the maternity benefit during maternity leave.

The main principles of the social assistance in cash are set in the Law on Cash Social Assistance for Poor Residents. The *social assistance* in-cash scheme starts, when the unemployed benefits are exhausted (social assistance benefits are means-tested and the monthly income per person is less than EUR 102). The monthly social assistance in-cash benefit level is 100% of the difference between the state supported income per person per month and the actual income of a family (persons living together) or single resident, 80% – for the second family member and 70% – for the third and subsequent members. Social allowance is reduced as follows: 20% reduction – if social benefit is paid for 12–24 months; 30% reduction – for 24–36 months; 40% reduction – for 36–48 months; 50% reduction – for 48–60 months.

The Law on Cash Social Assistance for low-income families (single residents) provides:

a) supplementary social benefit: 50% of the average social benefit (that a person has received in the last 12 months before taking up employment) may be granted to a person who becomes employed if the person is paid a wage that is not lower than one minimum monthly wage and not higher than two minimum monthly wages; was registered at the local labour exchange for a minimum of 12 months prior to the employment; has received social benefit at least once during the last three months; and has children.
b) unemployed person registered with the labour exchange receive the following additional social guarantees: compensation for heating; compensation for hot and cold water; benefits for children; free meals at school and financial support at the start of the academic year; social allowance. Social benefit and compensations are means-tested and they are paid to families (or single persons) under the condition that family members work or do not work. If a person takes a low paid job the social benefit is not cancelled immediately.

According to the Law on Early Social Insurance Pensions, the *early-retirement pension* cannot be granted, if the person is in receipt of unemployment benefit. The period during which unemployment benefits were paid to a person, under the provisions of the Law on Support of the Unemployed (in force before 1 January 2005), shall be included in the state social pension insurance record. The same rules apply for incapacity to work pensions.

Regarding the *sickness in-cash benefits and health insurance*, an unemployed person can also receive sickness in-cash benefits. If an unemployed person is in receipt of sickness in cash benefits, the unemployment benefits are not suspended. Unemployed persons are covered by health insurance and receive benefits in-kind (if they have registered at the local labour exchange). The terms are the same for *the invalid pension*. If a work incapacity pension (or invalid pension) is granted, part of the unemployment benefit can be paid (the part which exceeds the sum of the invalid pension).

1.3 Financial arrangements

The unemployment benefits are financed from the social insurance contributions (paid by employers): the contribution rate is 1.1% of the basic salary (the Seimas (Lithuanian parliament) adopts the contribution rate every year). There are no special unemployment social assistance schemes in Lithuania. The unemployment insurance benefit is calculated as the sum of the fixed and variable parts. The fixed part of the unemployment insurance benefit is equal to the amount of state supported income valid in the month of payment. The variable part is calculated according to a person's work record.

The replacement ratio of the unemployment benefits is regressive, but rather high (even above 60%) in the case of small wages (close to minimal). This is capped at 40% of the average national wage.

State subsidies cover the deficit of the social insurance fund (by providing loans to the social insurance fund). Lithuania joined the Eurozone in 2015 and must comply with requirements set out in the Treaty on the Functioning of the European Union (protocol No. 12 'On the excessive deficit procedure'). This Treaty indicates, that MS shall avoid excessive government deficits, firstly, 3% for the ratio of planned or actual government deficit to gross domestic product at market prices and, secondly, 60% for the ratio of government debt to gross domestic product at market prices.

1.4 Qualification periods and calculation principles

The Law on the Unemployment Social Insurance indicates that the minimum period of insurance is 18 months within the three years preceding unemployment. However, there are exceptions: because of an insufficient social insurance record; due to important reasons (if a person was dismissed on the initiative of the employer, etc.); for persons with mandatory military service or alternative military service. The unemployment insurance benefit shall be paid on the eighth day following registration at the local labour exchange.

The duration of the payment of unemployment insurance benefit depends on the length of the work record: less than 25 years – six months; from 25 to 30 years – seven months; from 30 to 35 years – eight months; 35 years and over – nine months.

The monthly unemployment insurance benefit comprises a fixed and a variable component. The fixed component is equal to the state supported income of EUR 102 (in 2015). The variable component is calculated by taking the amount of person's monthly wage during the previous 36 months before the registration at a local office of labour exchange (the variable component of the unemployment insurance benefit corresponds to 40% of this amount). The unemployment benefit cannot exceed 70% of the insured income amount of the current year (approved by the government). The size of the unemployment insurance benefit cannot be less than the State Supported Income (EUR 102 in 2015) and the maximum unemployment benefit in 2015 is EUR 303.80.

We could conclude that the national legislation provides detailed norms regarding payment of benefits, modalities, assimilated periods, exemptions for specific categories or situations, maintenance of rights regarding temporary interruptions of unemployment. However, the unemployment benefits comprised only 2.72% of the total social insurance budget[6] and the level of the unemployment benefits in Lithuania is only 0.4% of GDP (average of EU-28 is 1.6% of GDP)[7]. Another problem is the black economy: low unemployment benefits create incentives to work illegally: black market in Lithuania is about 28% of GDP[8]. Unemployed persons are vulnerable to poverty and the social assistance system covers the additional part of unemployed income. The European Union's Council states that Lithuania should take action in 2015 and 2016 to improve the coverage and adequacy of unemployment benefits and cash social assistance and improve the employability of those looking for work: over 30% of Lithuania's population is at risk of poverty

---

6 Retrieved April 14, 2016 from http://www.ec.europa.eu/eurostat.

7 *Unemployment statistics*. Retrieved June 1, 2016 from http://ec.europa.eu/eurostat/statistics-explained/index.php/Unemployment_statis.

8 *The shadow economy in Europe*, 2013. Retrieved April 14, 2016 from http://www.atkearney.com.

or social exclusion and active labour market measures and other services for supporting beneficiaries are still, however, limited[9].

2. Constitutional jurisprudence

In the jurisprudence of the Lithuanian Constitutional Court, the principles of solidarity, social justice, systematic coherence and construction of the unemployment system are analysed. Application of these principles is important in light of the reform of the unemployment social insurance system

Article 52 of the Constitution of the Republic of Lithuania) indicates that the state shall guarantee its citizens the right to receive old age and disability pensions as well as social assistance in the event of unemployment, sickness, widowhood, loss of the breadwinner, and in other cases provided by the law. In the jurisprudence of the Lithuanian Constitutional Court, the provisions of Article 52 of the Constitution were analysed. In the ruling of 12 March 1997, the Constitutional Court indicated that the state should implement the social guarantees to citizens (the right to receive old age and disability pensions, as well as social assistance in the event of unemployment etc.). These provisions express the social character of the state and recognise the right to social protection. This principle has the status of a constitutional value[10]. The Constitutional Court has held that Article 52 of the Constitution expresses the social orientation (social character) of the state with respect to social protection. The social security measures express the idea of social solidarity and help a person to protect himself from possible social risks[11]. In the rulings of 12 March 1997, 25 November 2002 and 3 December 2003, the Lithuanian Constitutional Court explained the importance of the construction of the unemployment social insurance system: the Court noted that the provisions of Article 52 guarantee the right of citizens to social protection and, at the same time, oblige the state to establish adequate measures for the implementation of social protection[12]. The state should create a system of social protection which

---

9 Council of the EU recommendation No. 2015/C 272/18 of 14 July 2015 on the 2015 Council of the European Union. National Reform Programme of Lithuania and delivering a Council opinion on the 2015 Stability Programme of Lithuania. *Official Journal*, C 272, p. 70.

10 Constitutional Court of the Republic of Lithuania case No. 5/96.

11 Constitutional Court of the Republic of Lithuania cases No. 35/04-37/04-72/06.

12 Constitutional Court of the Republic of Lithuania case No. 5/96, cases No. 47/2001-08/2003-20/2003-32/2003-38/2003.

maintains conditions for living that are in line with human dignity, and, if necessary, provide a person with the necessary social security[13].

In its decision of 7 February 2013 the Lithuanian Constitutional Court indicated that persons who receive a state social insurance disability (lost capacity to work) pension shall be paid only that part of the unemployment insurance payment which exceeds the pension received from the unemployment insurance funds[14]. The Court noted, that the constitutional principle of social solidarity also implies that the legislator, while taking account of, inter alia, the purpose of social assistance in the event of unemployment and the financial possibilities of the state and society, may establish such legal regulation whereby, with regard to persons who receive different forms of financial social assistance from the state and which is capable of ensuring conditions for living in line with human dignity, social protection should be provided in a form other than financial assistance in the event of unemployment.

The legislator, taking account of these factors and respectively regulating the said relations, has broad discretion to choose and consolidate by law the types of social protection, as well as the amounts of financial assistance, in the event of unemployment. Sub-statutory legal acts (government resolutions) may establish only the procedure for the implementation of the laws regulating the relations of social security and social assistance; a sub-statutory legal regulation of the said relations may comprise the establishment of relevant procedures, as well as such legal regulation where, based on laws, the need to provide more details about and particularise in sub-statutory legal acts a certain legal regulation established by law is objectively caused by the necessity in the law-making process to draw upon special knowledge or special (professional) competence of a certain area. However, any sub-statutory legal regulation of the relations specified in Article 52 of the Constitution may not establish any conditions for the appearance of the right of an individual to social assistance, nor may it limit the extent of that right[15].

---

13 Constitutional Court of the Republic of Lithuania cases No. 46/2010-47/2010-48/2010-49/2010-51/2010-52/2010-70/2010-77/2010-82/2010-83/2010-84/2010-85/2010-86/2010-87/2010-94/2010-100/2010-101/2010-109/2010-114/2010-123/2010-124/2010-128/2010-129/2010-133/2010-134/2010-142/2010-143/2010-1/2011-2/2011-5/2011-8/2011-16/2011-21/2011-23/2011-25/2011-29/2011-32/2011-37/2011-39/2011.

14 Constitutional Court of the Republic of Lithuania case No. 42/2009.

15 Constitutional Court of the Republic of Lithuania case No. 9/02, case No. 26/06, case No. 08/2008-23/2009, case No. 21/2009-32/2009.

Regarding the implementation of the constitutional principles, such as the state under the rule of law, justice and social solidarity, the Lithuanian Constitutional Court in the decision of 3 December 2003 indicated that the constitutional principle of a state under the rule of law must be taken into account, the content whereof is to be construed inseparably from the striving for an open, just and harmonious civil society which is declared in the Preamble to the Constitution and is to be revealed while assessing all the values entrenched in, and protected and defended by the Constitution, and while taking account of the content of various other constitutional principles, such as justice and social solidarity[16]. The social solidarity principle is consolidated in the Constitution and implies that the burden of fulfilment of certain obligations should also be distributed among members of society to a certain extent, however, such distribution should be constitutionally reasoned, it cannot be disproportionate, it cannot deny the social orientation of the state and the obligations to the state, which arise from the Constitution[17].

According to the jurisprudence of the Lithuanian Constitutional Court, the *legitimate interests and legitimate expectations of a person* may not be violated, since persons who have acquired certain rights according to the law, have the right to reasonably expect that these rights will be maintained and implemented for the established time period[18].

However, the Government cannot create the preconditions for all members of society to take care of their own welfare independently rather than rely solely on state social security. If, due to certain reasons, a person loses their job and cannot take care of their welfare, the duty arises for the state to establish the legal regulation under which social assistance would be ensured for such persons in the event of unemployment; the legislature may choose and consolidate in laws a certain model of the provision of the said support, inter alia, various forms thereof; however, it is not permitted to establish any legal regulation that would create

---

16 Constitutional Court of the Republic of Lithuania case No. 47/2001-08/2003-20/2003-32/2003-38/2003).

17 Constitutional Court of the Republic of Lithuania cases No. 46/2010-47/2010-48/2010-49/2010-51/2010-52/2010-70/2010-77/2010-82/2010-83/2010-84/2010-85/2010-86/2010-87/2010-94/2010-100/2010-101/2010-109/2010-114/2010-123/2010-124/2010-128/2010-129/2010-133/2010-134/2010-142/2010-143/2010-1/2011-2/2011-5/2011-8/2011-16/2011-21/2011-23/2011-25/2011-29/2011-32/2011-37/2011-39/2011; cases No. 39/2009-40/2009-46/2009-48/2009-51/2009-10/2010-23/2010-137/2010-7/2011-38/2011.

18 Constitutional Court of the Republic of Lithuania case No. 26/06.

preconditions for the emergence of a situation where persons who, due to certain reasons, have lost their job, would not receive adequate social assistance; In addition, the duty arises for the legislature to regulate the legal relations of social assistance in such a way that preconditions would be created for all members of society to take care of their own welfare independently rather than rely solely on state social security[19].

We could conclude that under the Lithuanian Constitution, the legislation should establish legal regulation such that a person who, due to certain reasons, has lost their job, would receive adequate social protection. The legal regulation should also establish sufficient measures for the implementation of the right to social protection in the event of unemployment and the principles of social solidarity, justice and the state under the rule of law should be applied.

3. Unemployment benefits' reform in the context of the new social model of Lithuania

The new unemployment benefits system reforms are influenced by the recommendations of the European Union and the deterioration of the social–economic indicators. Lithuania is facing a substantial fall in its working-age population, driven by demographics, migration and poor performance of the healthcare system[20]. Structural unemployment remains high, suggesting skills mismatches, in particular for the low-skilled. A comprehensive review of the labour law, with the involvement of social partners, is needed to find ways of alleviating the administrative burden on employers[21].

The EU Council recommendation of 14 July 2015 'On the 2015 National Reform Programme of Lithuania and delivering a Council opinion on the 2015 Stability Programme of Lithuania' of 2015 indicates, that Lithuania should take action in 2015 and 2016 to improve

---

[19] Constitutional Court of the Republic of Lithuania case No. 09/06-30/06-01/07-30/08.

[20] Council of the EU recommendation No. 2015/C 272/18 of 14 July 2015 on the 2015 Council of the European Union. National Reform Programme of Lithuania and delivering a Council opinion on the 2015 Stability Programme of Lithuania. *Official Journal,* C 272, p. 70.

[21] Council of the EU recommendation No. 2014/C 247/13 of 8 July 2015 on the National Reform Programme 2014 of Lithuania and delivering a Council opinion on the Convergence Programme of Lithuania. *Official Journal,* C 247, p. 67.

the coverage and adequacy of unemployment benefits and cash social assistance and improve the employability of those looking for work. Lithuania has introduced financial support measures for the elderly and financial incentives for employing older workers. A comprehensive active ageing strategy is however, still lacking[22]. There were similar recommendation for 2014–2015: better target active labour market policy measures to the low-skilled and long-term unemployed; improve the coverage and adequacy of unemployment benefits and link them to activation; underpin pension reform with measures that promote the employability of older workers[23].

OECD stressed that older workers need help to preserve and augment their human capital to make them more employable, seniority-based wage structures (which make it expensive to employ older workers) need to be reconsidered, the health of older workers, working conditions (through rehabilitation, training, improvements in occupational health and raising awareness of the work needs of older workers), to prepare older workers for greater job mobility at the end of their careers and working-time arrangements also play an important role in retirement decisions[24].

We could note the importance of the Constitutional Court's jurisprudence in reforming the unemployment system in Lithuania also. The Constitutional Court has noted that the requirements arising from the constitutional principles of a state under the rule of law, equality of rights, justice, proportionality, protection of legitimate expectations, legal certainty, legal security and social solidarity, as well as other constitutional imperatives, must also be heeded when there is an extreme situation in the state (economic crisis etc.) due to which the economic and financial situation in the state is affected[25]. This means, that the constitutional principles should be evaluated in the light of reforms.

---

[22] Council of the EU recommendation No. 2015/C 272/18 of 14 July 2015 on the 2015 Council of the European Union. National Reform Programme of Lithuania and delivering a Council opinion on the 2015 Stability Programme of Lithuania. *Official Journal*, C 272, p. 70.

[23] Council of the EU recommendation No. 2014/C 247/13 of 8 July 2015 on the National Reform Programme 2014 of Lithuania and delivering a Council opinion on the Convergence Programme of Lithuania. *Official Journal*, C 247, p. 67.

[24] *Pensions at a Glance 2011. Retirement–income systems in OECD and G20 countries.* Paris: OECD publishing, 2011.

[25] Constitutional Court of the Republic of Lithuania cases No. 41/2000, 47/2001-08/2003-20/2003-32/2003-38/2003, 7/03-41/03-40/04-46/04-5/05-7/05-17/05, 35/04-37/04-72/06, 38/04-39/04, 06/05-08/05, 09/06-30/06-01/07-30/08, 15/98, 33/03; case No. 39/2009-40/2009-46/2009-48/2009-51/2009-10/2010-23/2010-137/2010-7/2011-38/2011.

The Lithuanian Parliament reached a political consensus and on 24 May 2011 adopted the Guidelines for Pensions and Social Security Reform[26]. The main aim of the reform, as indicated in the Guidelines, is to ensure that in the future persons should receive adequate benefits, the social insurance fund budget should be stable and the social insurance system should better adapt to economic and demographic changes. Several principles indicated in the Guidelines, such as the separation of social insurance and social assistance (this means better correlation between contributions and benefits and make the labour market more flexible) and better management of the social insurance fund to achieve the main goal – to balance the social security budget.

Today, unemployment benefits do not encourage unemployed persons to integrate into the labour market. Fixed maximum unemployment benefit can be paid for nine months and the one criteria of the work record applies. It could be stressed, firstly, that the level of unemployment benefit should be linked to the length of a person's unemployment and not only to the personal working record. Secondly, the unemployment benefit could be reduced proportionately every three months. Article 14 of the Law on Unemployment Social Insurance[27] provides that the unemployment insurance benefit may be extended for unemployed persons until retirement age (no more than five years to the retirement age). This regulation can be attributed to passive labour market policy measures and does not encourage older persons to integrate into the labour market. In addition, persons have additional guarantees five years before the retirement age: early-retirement pension; the employment contract may be terminated only in special circumstances. We could conclude that Article 14 of the Law on Unemployment Social Insurance creates prerequisites for the duplication of benefits (unemployment benefits and early-retirement pension) and encourages persons to remain registered as unemployed. For the long-term unemployed, the social assistance benefit should be paid and active labour market policy measures should be applied (after assessment of the person's financial situation), rather than continued payment of the unemployment benefit. In addition, tax incentives should be applied to the unemployed who have less than

---

[26] Decision No. XI-1410 of the Parliament of the Republic of Lithuania of 24 May 2011 'On the adoption of Guidelines of the state social insurance and pension system reform'. *Valstybės žinios* (State Gazette), 2011, No. 66-3103.

[27] Law No. IX-1904 of 16 December 2003 on Unemployment Social Insurance. *Valstybės žinios* (State Gazette), 2011, No. 4-26.

five years before retirement or the employer's part of the social security contributions should be subsidized. These measures could reduce labour costs and could help the integration of to integrate unemployed persons into the labour market.

Another problem is related to the early-retirement system in Lithuania. In 2004, an early-retirement pension scheme for the long-term unemployed (if there were less than 5 years until the retirement age) was introduced (0.4% reduction for every full month remaining until and after the retirement age). This early-retirement pension scheme should be cancelled: longer activity in the labour market could ensure higher pensions. Instead of the early-retirement pension, social assistance and active labour market measures should be introduced.

The draft regulation on the unemployment benefits system[28] was prepared in the light of the scientific analysis of researches of Vilnius University, Mykolas Romeris University and the Centre of Social Researches, commissioned by the Ministry of Social Security and Labour of the Republic of Lithuania[29]. The establishment of the complex draft legislation in the field of social insurance, labour relations, social assistance and employment could create a single, economically based and balanced social protection and labour system, targeted at increasing employment, improving working relationships and enhancing investment. We could stress several proposals in the field of the unemployment benefits and related employment areas:

1. The draft Law on Unemployment Social Insurance is related to the calculation of the unemployment benefit: the unemployment insurance benefit is calculated as the sum of constant and variable parts. The constant part consists of 30% of the minimum monthly wage. The variable part of the benefit is gradually reduced every three months, seeking to encourage individuals to return to the labour market as soon as possible (from the first to the third month – 50% of the average monthly earnings; from the fourth month to the sixth month – 40%; from the seventh month to the ninth month – 30%).

---

28 Draft Law on Unemployment social insurance. Retrieved 14 April 2016 from https://e-seimas.lrs.lt/portal/legalAct/lt/TAP/e23aef50110511e5b0d3e1beb7dd5516?positionInSearchResults=3&searchModelUUID=a6a005ca-330a-4b7f-bf1f-a4f13968a7a8.

29 *The legal-administrative model of labour relations and state social insurance*. Retrieved 14 April 2016 from http://www.socmodelis.lt/wp-content/uploads/Modelio-ataskaita.pdf.

2. The insurance period requirement for unemployment benefit is 12 months during the last 24 months prior to registration at the local labour exchange (today – 18 months). The period for payment of unemployment benefit is extended to nine months and is no longer related to the work record.
3. It is proposed to set a maximum unemployment insurance benefit limit, which cannot exceed 75% of the average national wage.
4. New active labour market measures are proposed: recruitment under vocational training and apprenticeship contracts, internship, prepaid service vouchers.
5. The draft law on Employment Support indicates that practical internships can be organized for persons, who have appropriate professional qualifications or non-formal competence if they have been unemployed for six months and they can be given a scholarship once per month.

We could conclude, that today the unemployment benefits are paid for a short time period and there is no unemployment benefits regression (benefit decreases over the longer unemployment period). The implementation of the draft legislation (longer period of unemployment benefits with benefits regression, the introduction of active labour market measures, cancellation of the early-retirement pensions, higher unemployment benefits limit) could create better conditions to encourage unemployed persons to return to the labour market and ensure higher pensions.

Conclusions

The fundamental problems of the Lithuanian unemployment benefits system are the low level of benefits and low coverage. The unemployment benefits are paid for a short time period in Lithuania and there is no unemployment benefits regression (benefit decreases the longer one is unemployed): the unemployment benefits system reforms should seek a better balance between incentives to work and unemployment benefits. Future reforms of the unemployment benefits system should be included in the complex reform of social insurance, labour relations, social assistance and employment, targeted at increasing employment, improving working relationships and enhancing investment. The problem of unemployment should be solved through introducing social assistance forms and active labour market measures.

Reforms in the unemployment benefits system should be in conformity with the constitutional principles as well: the state under the rule of law, justice, protection of legitimate expectations and social solidarity. The early-retirement pension scheme should be cancelled: longer activity in the labour market could ensure higher pensions. Article 14 of the actual law on Unemployment Social Insurance (the extension of the unemployment benefit up to retirement age) overlaps with the early-retirement pension: instead of the early-retirement pension, social assistance and active labour market measures should be introduced. Tax incentives should be applied to unemployed person who have less than five years before retirement or the employer's part of the social security contributions should be subsidized.

Cultures juridiques et politiques

Vol. 1 Stephanie Rohlfing-Dijoux (éd)
La Transmission de Terminologie et de Concepts Juridiques dans l'espace Européen. *Allemagne / France / Russie*
2012, ISBN 978-3-0343-1094-9

Vol. 2 Otmar Seul & Tomas Davulis (éds./Hrsg.)
La Solidarité dans l'union Européenne / Solidarität in der Europäischen Union. *Actes de la 5ème Université d'été franco-germano-lituanienne et européenne en sciences juridiques Vilnius, 3-10 juillet 2008 / Tagungsband der 5. Deutsch-Französisch-Litauischen und Europäischen Sommeruniversität in den Rechtswissenschaften, Vilnius 3.-10. Juli 2008*
2012, ISBN 978-3-0343-1122-9

Vol. 3 Ralf Alleweldt, Raphaël Callsen, Jeanne Dupendant (eds.)
Human rights abuses in the contemporary world.
Tri-National Workshop, Tbilisi, September 2011
2012, ISBN 978-3-0343-1147-2

Vol. 4 Stefanie Bouquet
La réglementation européenne relative à la discrimination fondée sur l'âge: conséquences sur le droit du travail français.
Préface du Professeur Joachim Gruber, Université Paris Ouest - Nanterre La Défense
2012, ISBN 978-3-0343-1174-8

Vol. 5 Izabela Kraśnicka & Magdalena Perkowska (éds.)
How to become a layer?
2013, ISBN 978-3-0343-1290-5

Vol. 6 Kerstin Peglow et Géraldine Demme (éds.)
La protection des intérêts privés sur le marché intérieur.
La situation des consommateurs et entrepreneurs.
2015, ISBN 978-3-0343-1615-6

Vol. 7 Sam Lyes
Crimes internationaux et immunité de l'acte de fonction des anciens dirigeants étatiques.
2015, ISBN 978-3-0343-1690-3

Vol. 8 Fabien Bottini, Harold Gaba et Pierre Chabal (dir.)
Le régionalisme et ses limites. Regards croisés franco-kazakhs.
2016, ISBN 978-2-87574-335-0

Vol. 9 Otmar Seul, Kaïs Slama, Kerstin Peglow (Hrsg.)
Kulturvermittlung und Interkulturalität, ein deutschfranzösisch-tunesischer Dialog. Politische, rechtliche und sozio-linguistische Aspekte
2017, ISBN 978-2-8076-0133-8

Vol. 10 Stephanie Rohlfing-Dijoux (ed./dir.)
Developing Intraregional exchanges through the abolition of commercial and tariff barriers. Myth or reality?
L'abolition des barrières commerciales et tarifaires dans la région de l'océan Indien. Mythe ou réalité ?
2017, ISBN 978-2-8076-0126-0

Vol. 11 Sagyngaliy Aidarbayev, Pierre Chabal, Zhuldyz Sairambaeva (dir.)
Mutations de société et réponses du droit.
Perspectives franco-asiatiques comparées.
2017, ISBN 978-2-8076-0187-1

Vol. 12 Tomas Davulis (ed.)
Labour Law Reforms in Eastern and Western Europe.
2017, ISBN 978-2-8076-0416-2

www.peterlang.com